THE ENDS OF PHILOSOPHY

THE ENDS OF PHILOSOPHY

AN ESSAY IN THE SOCIOLOGY OF PHILOSOPHY AND RATIONALITY

HARRY REDNER

Rowman & Allanheld
PUBLISHERS

ROWMAN & ALLANHELD

Published in the United States of America in 1986
by Rowman & Allanheld, Publishers
(A division of Littlefield, Adams & Company)
81 Adams Drive, Totowa, New Jersey 07512

Copyright © 1986 by H. Redner

Library of Congress Cataloging in Publication Data applied for.
ISBN 0-8476-7498-3

Printed and bound in Great Britain

CONTENTS

PREFACE

'After all, am I a philosopher?', asked Nietzsche. And he replied, 'but what does it matter?' Would it be too presumptuous of me to give the same reply to the self-same question? Like Faust, 'I have, alas, studied philosophy'; unlike him, I was never called upon to teach it, though once again I am in very good company. Philosophy is not just for professional philosophers. Indeed, if Wittgenstein is right, it may not be for them at all: 'A philosopher is not a citizen of a thought-community. This is what makes him a philosopher.'

A few words are in order about the origin of this book. I worked on it for over a decade and have had it complete for some time now. Parts of it were already finished more than ten years ago. These parts, the chapters on Nietzsche and on Wittgenstein, were originally to be included in my *In the Beginning was the Deed*, as indeed their titles still indicate, and that book was first submitted for publication in 1977. The other chapters were finished in 1980, and slightly revised in 1982. This is the work as it here appears apart from some extra notes that I included as the book was going to press.

In taking this opportunity to express my gratitude to those who read the work prior to publication, I find myself as usual with embarrassingly few names to acknowledge. Above all my sincerest thanks to Norman Jacobson for his perspicacious advice on revisions, and to John Schaar for his warm response to the final version.

The manuscript was first typed by the indefatigable Joy Smith, now in retirement, and corrected by Cecilia Thorei.

I take this opportunity to acknowledge that this book was published with the assistance of the Monash University Publication Committee.

For Jill

SYNOPSIS

The work divides into a brief Introduction, three Parts which comprise the body of the book and two short appendices. Each of the Parts is composed of two complementary chapters. Part One and Part Two observe the history and course of philosophy as it were from the opposite ends of the telescope. Part One looks at the broad expanse of the philosophical firmament, pinpoints the largest of its stars and maps its leading constellations of thinkers, schools and movements. It is an exercise in what might be called macro-philosophical thinking. Part Two is the converse micro-philosophical analysis. It narrows its focus onto the two brightest luminaries of modern philosophy: Nietzsche and Wittgenstein, and subjects them to close scrutiny. The choice of these as the cynosures of modern philosophy is explained in terms of their role, in Ricoeur's phrase, as the 'Great Destroyers' of metaphysics and ultimately of philosophy itself in its traditional aspects. The two separate chapters in Part Two, the first on Nietzsche and the second on Wittgenstein, complement each other: in them the main themes of philosophy, such as the key principles of metaphysical Reason, the Logos and the Cogito, are subjected first to a Nietzschean destruction, then to a Wittgensteinian one. Analogously the two chapters of Part One are also complementary, the first examining the reduction of metaphysics, as it were externally in terms of the various secessions of science from philosophy; and the second considering the same course of reduction from the inside in terms of the *reductio* or conceptual destruction by argument practised by the main schools of modern philosophy and the leading individual thinkers: Marx, Nietzsche, Heidegger and Wittgenstein. Part Three is the conclusion which emerges from the argument of the other two Parts. It, too, divides up into two complementary chapters, the first setting out new ends or functions of philosophy, the second adumbrating a model for philosophy.

Introduction

The introduction sketches briefly the contemporary situation of philosophy and then goes on to outline the 'logic' of the book. This 'logic' is an attempt at a kind of *reductio-ad-absurdum* whose ultimate aim is a refutation of itself, so in that sense it is a reduction of a *reductio*. Thus the very attempt at showing that philosophy is impossible only succeeds in showing that philosophy does continue. This is a modern variant of the pyrrhic victory of scepticism whose history will be further expounded in Chapter 1. The Introduction also aims to intimate the new subject of the sociology of philosophy which is to take its place beside the sociology of science and the sociology of culture in general. To do so it draws on the work of the great sociologist Max Weber, claiming that his theory of ideal-type concepts is one of the greatest tools of conceptual analysis and language description ever devised. In Chapter 4 it will be argued that it has major advantages over Wittgenstein's language-game conception. In the spirit of Weber, the Introduction concludes by calling philosophers back to their vocation.

Part One — Metaphysics, Science and Reduction: A History

Chapter 1   Metaphysics and the Sciences

This chapter outlines the historical relation between philosophy and science. To begin with, in Aristotle, philosophy and science are not distinguished. Aristotle's *Metaphysics*, expounding a metaphysical conception of rationality, that is, Reason, was supposed to serve as the general foundation of all the separate sciences developed in the ancient world. This close relationship persisted till the Scientific Revolution of the seventeenth century when the first secession of science from philosophy took place. Science or natural philosophy broke away from the scholasticism of metaphysics. But nevertheless, the scientific method of the classical sciences was based on rational norms that might be called Rationalism, in contradistinction to the Reason of metaphysics, and it also required epistemological foundations. Together these still constituted the quasi-metaphysics of Rationalist and Empiricist philosophers. It was only with the second secession of the sciences from philosophy, the nineteenth-century development of the new humanities and social sciences, that even that residual metaphysics began step by step to be abrogated. This produced numerous anti-metaphysical schools of philosophy such as Positivism, and others that sought to define a role for themselves outside science, such as Existentialism.

The third and possibly final secession of the sciences from philosophy began to take place after World War II, when the sciences took a technological direction based on methods of Rationalisation or calculating rationality. This could potentially spell the end of philosophy, which seems to have no function to fulfil within the prevailing intellectual dispensation.

Chapter 2   The End of Metaphysics

This chapter explores the socio-logic of the reduction of metaphysics, the correlative conceptual investigation to the sociological process of secession examined in the previous chapter. It is granted that the main task of science was reduction, typically the reduction of higher entities to lower ones, and it is allowed that scientific reduction is the cultural basis for those taking effect in other intellectual areas, above all in philosophy. Nevertheless reduction in science must not be interpreted along Positivist lines as reductionism, for reasons given in Appendix 2. The opening section of the chapter outlines a history of the concept 'reduction' and shows how this term changes its meaning and function from one scientific age to another. The role of reduction in philosophy during the three scientific secessions is also disclosed, ending with an account of the various modes of Positivism and their role in the history of philosophy. Positivist philosophies are shown to practise an annihilating mode of reduction and this is contrasted to that of the Faustian philosophers, Marx, Nietzsche, Heidegger and Wittgenstein. The chapter continues by giving an account of what the destruction of metaphysics means in each of these thinkers. In each of them there is to be found a distinct and *sui-generis* concept of 'destruction'. The chapter concludes with a critique of Derrida's notion that one cannot do without metaphysics in order to destroy metaphysics. This leads into Part Two on the two 'Great Destroyers', Nietzsche and Wittgenstein.

Part Two — Destroying the Destroyers

Chapter 3   The Genealogy of Reason: An Attack

The aim of this part of the work is to carry through a critique of Nietzsche and Wittgenstein — as it were, a destruction of the destroyers — in accordance with the main line of argument, the *reductio-ad-absurdum*, of the work as a whole. The chapter begins with a critique of Nietzsche's critique of Reason and rationality in general. According to Nietzsche, 'faith in the categories of Reason is the cause of Nihilism' (*Will to Power*, par. 12), and this faith he traces back to the origins of metaphysical philosophy. He subjects the genealogy of Reason to an attack analogous to that which he deploys against the genealogy of morals. This chapter is meant to act as a counter-attack. It shows that in accounting both for the genealogy of morals and of Reason and the degeneration of both into Nihilism, Nietzsche is relying on an implicit eschatological scheme of history. Nietzsche's attempt to go even further back for the origins of Reason, to trace it back to the grammar of primitive language, suffers from the even worse failing of judging the end result by its origins. Analogous faults vitiate his attempt to account for Reason in terms of evolutionary utility. This specific refutation broadens out into a general critique of Nietzsche's key terms, such as will to power, value, perspectivism, the overman and others. Nietzsche's thinking is shown to be at least partly mythological, and from this derive its weaknesses as well as its strengths. The attack on Nietzsche in this chapter must be read in the context of the exposition of the strengths of his thinking undertaken in Chapters 2 and 6.

Chapter 4   *A Philosophical Walpurgisnacht*

This chapter is a critical analysis of Wittgenstein's philosophy. It begins by showing that this philosophy was inescapably lacking in the kind of reflexive self-awareness needed to account adequately for what it was actually doing when it 'dissolved' metaphysical problems by reducing them to the simple, common ground of language. In actual fact any such dissolution is also a destruction and is implicated in the very Nihilism it seeks to overcome. The first section of the chapter outlines some of the main features of Wittgenstein's mode of philosophising, such as his insistence on pure description without interpretation or theory, his contention that concepts can be so described, as if they were objects laid out for view, and that the grammar of concepts and language in general is in no way altered through being described; the second section criticises these assumptions, arguing instead that the description of concepts is an interpretative-hermeneutic task, that any such description of meanings must to some degree alter what it is describing and that theoretical concepts are crucial for this to be accomplished. Wittgenstein's one theoretical 'tool' is the idea of the language-game, and this is subjected to a critical analysis designed to show that the 'language game' is only a simplified application of Weber's theory of ideal-types. The rest of the chapter is mainly concerned with exemplifying the scope and limitations of Wittgenstein's destruction of metaphysics. It concentrates on two arguments derived from Wittgenstein against the metaphysical notions of Logos and Cogito; these take the same logical form of a *reductio-ad-absurdum* as does the book itself. What is at stake in these arguments is the nature and status of Logic or Rationality and Subjectivity or Mind. These issues are presented in terms of the whole of Wittgenstein's opus ranging from the *Tractatus* through to his unpublished writings. The chapter closes by assessing Wittgenstein's remarkable achievements in redefining fundamental concepts such as 'language', 'rational argument' and 'subjective existence'.

Part Three — Philosophy and Rationality

Chapter 5   The Ends of Philosophy

The issue of the end of philosophy first mooted in the Introduction, and relentlessly pursued throughout the long *reductio-ad-absurdum* of the main body of the work, comes to its own end in Part Three. The problem of the end of philosophy has already been raised by all the 'Great Destroyers', above all by Marx, Nietzsche, Heidegger and Wittgenstein, each in his own peculiar way. But the paradox that this reveals, one which this work itself exemplifies, is that precisely by contemplating and facing up to its own end philosophy can continue to be. This paradox is pushed further in the concluding chapters, where a reconsideration of the end of philosophy permits a derivation of new ends for philosophy. For there must be no mistaking the end of this book itself — it is to enable philosophy to find new functions, purposes and goals.

This chapter brings the development of modern philosophy up to date by examining some leading contemporary philosophical heirs of Nietzsche and Wittgenstein, as well as some who have been more influenced by Marx and Heidegger. Special attention is devoted to opposed neo-Nietzschean thinkers of the school of Paris, such as Derrida and Foucault, and opposed neo-Wittgensteinians of the school of Cambridge such as Toulmin and Feyerabend, and to opposed neo-Marxist Weberians of the Frankfurt school, Adorno and Habermas. Certain common themes and relations between these thinkers are pointed up. Following this, the conclusion goes on to consider at length some possible functions or ends of philosophy, and it offers new ways of philosophising which might be of interest to contemporary thinkers and students. Such functions as destructive criticism, translation and mediation, and recollective concrete philosophising are specified and considered at some length, with examples drawn from the works of philosophers and scientists.

Chapter 6   Models for Philosophy

The final chapter of the work considers the role of models in philosophy. After outlining some of the traditional models, such as the dramatic, the geometric and the organic, the chapter goes on to define a new model for philosophy, that of language-analysis. This model had already been employed in the main body of the work, where it was derived from the language philosophies of Marx, Nietzsche, Heidegger and Wittgenstein, and in turn applied to them in a destructive critique. The main source of the model is, of course, psycho-analysis. The language-analysis of philosophies and cultural symbolic systems is a highly speculative undertaking, and it is only in that spirit, aware of the difficulties and problems this entails, that the work engages in it. Nevertheless, it does attempt a language-analysis of Reason and Rationalisation, the initiating and concluding forms of rationality in the philosophical tradition.

Appendix 1   A Model of Rationality

This Appendix brings together and summarises the main strands of argumentation, developed in separate places in the book, concerning rationality in its three ideal-type forms of Reason, Rationalism and Rationalisation. To some extent this is subsidiary to the main case concerning philosophy, so that disagreeing with it need not entail rejecting the overall thesis of the book.

Appendix 2   Reduction and Reductivism

This Appendix pertains mainly to the exposition of reduction in Chapter 2. It considers the nature of reduction in science and seeks to distinguish the necessary and unavoidable role of reduction in science from the interpretation placed upon this in Positivist philosophy. The latter, which can be called reductivism, is a mistaken philosophical construction which can be dispensed with.

INTRODUCTION

I

After a brilliantly provocative critique of traditional and contemporary philosophy in *Philosophy and the Mirror of Nature* Rorty closes with these reassuring words:

> Whichever happens, however, there is no danger of philosophy's 'coming to an end'. Religion did not come to an end in the Enlightenment, nor painting in Impressionism. Even if the period from Plato to Nietzsche is encapsulated and 'distanced' in the way Heidegger suggests, and even if twentieth-century philosophy comes to seem a stage of awkward transitional backing and filling (as sixteenth-century philosophy now seems to us), there will be something called 'philosophy' on the other side of the transition.[1]

Even at a glance these analogies seem implausible and make one doubt precisely that which the author wishes to affirm. If philosophy is only as sound as religion and painting there is less reason to be sanguine about its continuing viability than Rorty suggests. For it is not religion after the Enlightenment, two centuries past, nor painting after Impressionism, a century ago, that must act as the points of comparison, but religion and painting as they are now towards the end of the twentieth century.

We know that after the severe rationalist critiques of the Enlightenment there came, during the nineteenth century, a Romantic revival of religiosity. But that is now long over. All is not well with religion at a time when Nietzsche's atheistic declaration 'God is dead' is echoed by theologians — one calls himself 'a Christian atheistic theologian' — or when the Bishop of Woolwich, drawing on another contemporary philosophy, tries to explain that belief in God need no longer mean what it has always meant; another theologian has sadly acknowledged that 'all important spheres of human life — learning, economy, politics, law, state, culture, education, medicine, social welfare — have been withdrawn from the influence of the churches, of theology and religion, and placed under the direct responsibility and control of man, who has himself thus become "secular"'.[2] Of course the last quoted, Hans Küng, is not saying that religion is at an end, but he is keenly aware of the desperate straits of Christianity in a secularised world, as are most other theologians.

We know, too, that after Impressionism painting did not come to an end for there eventuated the remarkable achievements of the post-Impressionists. But that too was a long time ago. What is left of painting now, after Abstract Expressionism, after Minimalism, after 'op' and 'pop' art, after 'conceptual' art and 'photo-realism'? Many distinguished art critics have already declared an end to painting, as Peter Fuller, an English critic, states: 'in the early 1970s the assertion of "The Death of Painting" had become a commonplace of "progressive" taste'.[3] Another critic, John Berger, writes that 'it is a mistake to think of publicity supplanting the visual art of post-Renaissance Europe; it is the last moribund form of that art'.[4]

Even Rorty's historical analogy between the confused state of philosophy now and that of the Renaissance is highly questionable. The highly technical, professionalised philosophy of today hardly bears comparison with that of the great age of speculative and eclectic thought when all the ancient philosophers were revived and given currency, the age of Erasmus, Pico, Ficino, Montaigne, Bruno and Boehme, and many other such virtuosi. It cannot be simply assumed that, like Renaissance philosophy, present philosophy is a transitional stage to something else that will also be called philosophy.

It is true that philosophy as a profession is not at present in any serious danger; it will go on because, as Rorty puts it, 'the need for teachers who have read the great dead philosophers is quite enough to insure (sic) that there will be philosophy departments as long as there are universities'.[5] But that is not the sense in which we raise the issue of the end of philosophy. Religion, too, will go on as long as there are churches to fill, even if nobody any longer believes in what goes on within them. And painting will continue as long as there are art schools, even though these turn out mere commercial artists. Philosophy as a living discipline with something to offer for contemporary intellectual and spiritual endeavours cannot be safeguarded by institutional provisions alone. Nobody would want to prevent anyone else teaching or studying the history of philosophy, anymore than the history of religion and painting; professional philosophers will continue to earn their living at least as historians of philosophy, no matter what else it is they claim to be doing.[6]

But why must it be assumed that philosophy as an intellectual endeavour cannot come to an end? Why should it be supposed that philosophy is somehow exempt from the numerous problems confronting other endangered dimensions of cultural and intellectual life? Why must its present state be regarded as only a transition to a future state? Perhaps the philosophers to whom Rorty points as the great exemplars of contemporary philosophy have been the very ones bringing it to a close?

'Great systematic philosophers, like great scientists, build for eternity. Great edifying philosophers destroy for the sake of their own generation.'[7] The edifying philosophers Rorty mentions are 'the later Wittgenstein and the later Heidegger (like Kierkegaard and Nietzsche)' — among whom are three of the thinkers with whom we shall be concerned. But if these are the philosophers who 'destroy for the sake of their generation', what is to prevent there ensuing a general destruction of philosophy at a time when 'great systematic philosophers' who 'build for eternity' are no longer produced by this same generation? It might well be that too much edification without construction is just so much destruction. Anyone who speaks in the name of Nietzsche, Heidegger and Wittgenstein cannot flinch from this prospect, for have not these been called 'the great destroyers'?[8]

To raise the question of the end of philosophy is neither to wish nor to further it — especially as it is being raised in the context of a book on philosophy that cannot be so presumptuous as to claim to be the last word on the subject. On the contrary, this book, like Rorty's, is dedicated to ensuring that 'there will be something called "philosophy" on the other side of the transition', or rather to ensuring that the present stage of philosophy is indeed a transition. But it is no longer confident that this must necessarily be so. Philosophy can come to an end. *Philosophia perennis* does not of itself guarantee the perennial endurance of philosophy. At a time when so many of the fundamental values and cultural traditions of Western civilisation are threatened with extinction, philosophy cannot claim to be exempt. Civilisation itself can no longer be taken for granted, and even the life of humankind is uncertain. In such a general condition of historical doubt, philosophy cannot but doubt itself. And indeed, as we shall show, it is precisely by doubting itself and confronting the possibility of its own end that philosophy may avert its end.

Few philosophers, however, are prepared to philosophise on these extreme terms. Most share Rorty's confidence about philosophy's continuing, even perennial, viability. They insist with Rorty that 'there is no danger of philosophy coming to an end'. An outstanding contemporary exception is the philosopher Derrida for whom the end of philosophy is indeed the first question for philosophy. In the first words of his essay, 'Violence and Metaphysics', he states:

> That philosophy died yesterday, since Hegel or Marx, Nietzsche, or Heidegger — and philosophy should still wander toward the meaning of its death — or that it has always lived knowing itself to be dying (as it silently confessed in the shadow of the very discourse which *declared philosophia perennis*) that philosophy died *one day*, *within* history, or that it has always fed on its own agony, on the violent way it opens history by opposing itself to non-philosophy, which is its past and its concern, its death and wellspring . . . — all these are unanswerable questions. . . . Nevertheless, these should be the only questions today capable of founding the community, within the world, of those who are still called philosophers; and called such in remembrance, at very least, of the fact that these questions must be examined unrelentingly, despite the diaspora of institutes and languages, despite the publications and techniques that follow on each other, procreating and accumulating themselves, like capital or poverty. A community of the question . . .[9]

As Derrida makes clear, to pose the question is not necessarily to know the answer. It is not even to know whether the answer can be known, or if known, whether it can be given within philosophy: 'by right of birth, and for one time at least, these are problems put to philosophy as problems philosophy cannot solve'.[10] Whether or not Derrida is right about this point, it remains true that these are questions that can only be given sense within philosophy; that is to say, no matter what other meaning they may be given, they acquire their essential meaning only as philosophical questions. Philosophy has not only the right but the duty to ask such questions of itself. It has also the right to propose some tentative answers concerning itself.

Though the name 'philosophy' has indeed been scattered throughout the 'diaspora of institutes and languages, publications and techniques', this fact has been obscured by the academic process known as 'the professionalisation of philosophy'. Philosophy has finally attained in our time the dignity of the professional discipline: like every science, it now has its conferences, journals, disciplinary associations, channels of promotion and appointment, and the resultant hierarchies of professional competence and authority. Most of these nationally based philosophical organisations are, however, barely on speaking terms with each other. Every induced or incited colloquium between philosophers of different persuasions results in a dialogue of the deaf — all speak but nobody hears — or a debate in sign language like that of Panurge and the Englishman. In philosophy, as in science, specialisms proliferate as each man narrows his competence to a particular corner of the field, from where he can no longer talk to those in the other corners. Scattered to the corners of the world — are philosophers who once aspired to the heights of Being suffering a second Babel? In the absence of a common language to sustain philosophical communication and therefore 'community', the traditional question 'what is philosophy?' must be redefined: is philosophy any longer possible?

If enough philosophers were to raise the question of the end of philosophy then at least a 'community of the question' would arise. Such a community might even constitute a living answer to its own question. Thus despite 'the diaspora of institutes and languages, publications and techniques' there might arise a common concern which would rightfully be called philosophy. And those who shared in this concern might be called philosophers by vocation and not merely by profession.

II

Many philosophers are now instinctively aware, though few openly admit to it, that something is rotten in the state of their discipline. Even those who are still too engrossed in the business of philosophising to look up and review their own activity are slowly being forced by outside pressures to face the question of their own *raison d'être*. That philosophy as a profession continues to be possible is, as we have seen, institutionally guaranteed for the time being, as is the continued being of such antiquated disciplines as dogmatic theology, anatomy or traditional philology, all of which are still being taught for training purposes or on account of faith and sentiment, but with little hope for their intellectual future. Whether philosophy as a real vocation is any longer possible does very much depend on one's belief in its eventual future, that is, on how one faces up to and answers the question of the end of philosophy.

This question follows closely on the heels of another equally decisive one, which by now seems to have been conclusively settled, that of the end of metaphysics. Nearly all thinkers are now agreed that metaphysics has concluded, though it has taken nearly two centuries for this degree of unanimity to be reached. The question of the end of philosophy that confronts us at present is the direct historical consequence of the end of metaphysics. If one were simply to postulate a trend, then it would seem that once metaphysics, the mainstay of philosophy, was finished, philosophy itself must sooner or later end. Philosophical conservatives who follow this trend have even begun to read out accusingly an historical judgement on philosophy: modern philosophy, which destroyed metaphysics, thereby removed its own ground of being, and so must collapse for lack of anything on which to base itself. A kind of poetic justice might be read in this verdict, offering bitter consolation to those who always say 'I told you so'. Philosophical radicals, by contrast, welcome this world-historical judgement confirming the verdict on a condemned mode of thought. Philosophy, some Marxists would contend, must overcome itself by realising itself in Praxis: philosophy, some Positivists would argue, must give way to logic and scientific method; philosophy, some of the new post-Structuralist anti-humanists assert, must deconstruct itself so as to make possible a new episteme. For all of them the question of the end of philosophy has already been prejudged and the only thing remaining at issue is whether to lament or celebrate it.

Though it is true that the end of metaphysics puts the end of philosophy on the historical agenda, it does not follow that the conclusion of the one business also decides the other. Philosophy might yet continue on after metaphysics, even if only with a bad conscience; perhaps 'philosophy, which once seemed obsolete, lives on because the moment to realize it was missed',[11] as Adorno's lapidary epigram has it. (If so, it is a moot point whether this is because of the world's incapacity to realise philosophy as it ought to be, or because of philosophy's continuing capacity to realise the world as it is.) If we assume that philosophy has not come to an end, still its primary 'task would be to inquire whether and how there can still be a philosophy at all'.[12] But since this is surely itself a philosophical question; does it not alone ensure that there can still be a philosophy? We must not grasp too readily at this self-referential, self-validation of philosophy; all it might be granting is the conceptual illusion of an empty formal possibility. Philosophers have long practised the trick of formal self-reference to try to establish something substantial out of sheer doubt, and this instance might be no more than its final despairing self-application. In short, though the question of the end of philosophy is itself, as Derrida maintains, a philosophical question, still it may be the last one of all, the one to which philosophy has no answer.

The question of the end of philosophy is genuinely philosophical because only within philosophy can it be asked in the right way. To ask it properly means to make it meaningful, to define it and give it its proper signification; as a question it only has meaning if it is properly posed or composed — the composition of a question being not altogether unlike musical composition. And here we do strike a peculiar self-referring irony of thought, that only philosophy can compose and make meaningful the question of its own end, only philosophy can properly ask itself whether it is at an end. It is as if philosophy alone can compose itself for its own death. And perhaps that is the last philosophical function of all — to bring itself to an end and dispose of itself, or literally to argue itself to death. Only an out-and-out nihilist would be pleased by the perverse logic of this. But, nihilist or not, the question of the end of philosophy has to be taken to the point of no return if necessary. Philosophical thought cannot hold back at the prospect of its own demise.

It is this peculiar self-referential self-refutation that distinguishes the question of the end of philosophy from the question of the end of anything else. The end of metaphysics is not a question that can be meaningfully put within metaphysics, nor can the end of theology be a theological matter, the end of tragedy is not itself tragic . . . and so on for all the other perfectly valid questions about ending that have often been raised in our time. In the way they are posed they might be asked as either philosophical, or sociological, or historical, or literary questions, or all of these at once. However, the question of the end of philosophy, though it may be asked outside philosophy, can only be given its decisive meaning as a philosophical question. Asked merely historically or culturally, or in any other way that is short of philosophical, the question lacks that essential dimension of its meaning peculiar to itself: its self-referentiality, that inherently self-reflexive aspect of thought. Hence, only through its own self-refutation can philosophy dissolve itself, only through its own self-reduction can it destroy itself. If it were shown merely historically, or sociologically, or from the standpoint of some other mode of criticism extraneous to philosophy, that philosophy cannot be continued — that it has lost its *raison d'être*, that it fulfils no intellectual function, that it is mere ideology, or whatever else might be brought against it — it still would not follow that philosophy has failed in itself. This can only be demonstrated, as it were, from the inside of its own thought. Only philosophy can show what is wrong with itself on a level that is adequate to itself.

The question of the end of philosophy is no longer a new question. Many have already asked it and some have already come to a conclusion about it, though few have managed to raise the question to the level of philosophy itself. Frequently, scientists and logicians conclude that philosophy is finished because they can find no use for philosophical thinking; sometimes historians of culture and ideas or sociologists of knowledge see the writing on the wall for philosophy, believing this to be the judgement of history on an outmoded way of thought; and there are those who think they possess a form of knowledge that surpasses philosophy. Thus Comte thought that sociology would make philosophy obsolete, just as philosophy made theology *passé*. In our own time Norbert Elias holds a similar view that philosophy has been displaced by the sociology of knowledge. Many Marxists believe something similar with regard to dialectical materialism: Althusser, for example, takes dialectical materialism to be the philosophy of the science of historical materialism, and this is the sole form of philosophy he is willing to countenance, one that is tied to Marxist science and engaged in a political intervention in discourse. Foucault wishes to replace philosophy altogether with a new historical discipline which he calls 'the archeology of knowledge'. Some of the Frankfurt school thinkers, such as Horkheimer, were tempted to a similar view even earlier.

This work begins with a view-point that seems not unlike some of these earlier ones — though it will eventually become apparent that it is very different — for at first it poses the question of the end of philosophy in a merely sociological sense. For this purpose it seeks to develop a new sub-discipline which might be called the sociology of philosophy, on the model of the already established discipline of the sociology of science, and which would become a branch of the sociology of knowledge. But the work recognises that this perspective is not fully adequate to the question of the end of philosophy. Merely to show extraneously that philosophy has at present little if any social relevance or intellectual function, especially in regard to the sciences, the most important of our intellectual concerns, is in itself not to demonstrate that philosophy is at an end; though such a sociological argument, if sustained, does lend a strong sense of urgency to this question. As the question must be posed from inside philosophy itself, following the logic of the question this work gradually shifts its focus from the sociology of philosophy to the socio-logic of the history of philosophy, that is, to the dialectic of philosophical development, and in the end it moves to the problematic of the present state of philosophy where the issue of the end of philosophy is dealt with in philosophical terms. But at no point can a firm separation be made between one mode of questioning and another, and this shows that there is no break between the sociology of rational thought, the dialectic of rationality and rational problematic itself in the sphere of philosophy.

Logically considered, one of the ways of constituting or composing the question of the end of philosophy as fully philosophical is to set about arguing for an end of philosophy. This procedure will not only test how far such an argument can be taken; it will also ensure that it is philosophically meaningful in the required way: that it is a self-referring argument relying on philosophical thought for the purposes of demonstrating the impossibility of that thought. This argument must attempt to show philosophically that every mode of philosophising is now futile. It would have to begin by once more affirming the end of metaphysics. But then it would have to go on to show that every anti-metaphysical philosophy is equally at an end and has no further thought-function to perform. It would have to carry through the destruction of metaphysics and also the destruction of the destroyers of metaphysics.

In its most general logical form this kind of argument for the end of philosophy is a *reductio-ad-absurdum*, the standard form for every destructive argument. A *reductio-ad-absurdum* of philosophy such as will be attempted in this work has some well-known historical precedents, perhaps the most famous one being that deployed by the ancient Sceptics. Pyrrho and his school attacked all the other schools, and especially the early metaphysical school of Plato and Aristotle, which they termed dogmatic. This attack took the form of a *reductio-ad-absurdum* of any and every philosophical assertion; including the assertion that there can be no philosophical assertion. It constitutes, therefore, the earliest and perhaps most radical attempt to prove philosophy impossible, incorporating its own self-denial by insisting that it was itself not philosophical. Thus Diogenes Laertius reports:

> The Sceptics . . . were constantly engaged in overthrowing the dogmas of all schools, but enunciated none themselves; and though they would go as far as to bring forward and expound the dogmas of the others, they themselves laid down nothing definitely, not even the laying down of nothing. So much so that they even refuted their laying down of nothing, saying, for instance, 'We determine nothing', since otherwise they would have been betrayed into determining; but we put forward, say they, all the theories for the purpose of indicating our unprecipitate attitude, precisely as we might have done if we had actually assented to them . . . 'Every saying has its corresponding opposite', equally compels suspension of judgement; when facts disagree, but the contradictory statements have exactly the same weight, ignorance of the truth is the necessary consequence. But even this statement has its corresponding antithesis, so that after destroying others it turns round and destroys itself, like a purge which drives the substance out and then in its turn is itself eliminated and destroyed.[13]

The purge that purges itself as well is the exact image of a self-destructive philosophy. The *reductio-ad-absurdum* argument against philosophy completes itself by reducing itself away as well. In its rigour and sophistication Scepticism could have gone no further.

Historically considered, as we shall eventually show, Scepticism was unavailing against the main metaphysical trend, which, despite itself, it helped to further. A merely logical *reductio-ad-absurdum* against philosophy cannot succeed, quite apart from the sociological reasons that Scepticism was shunted aside in the ancient world. Philosophy cannot be refuted on rational sceptical grounds as if it were no more than a dogmatic or false way of reasoning. In our own time some schools, such as the Logical Positivists and Linguistic Positivists, have also attempted a purely rational reduction of philosophy, going as far as to argue that they were not themselves determining any philosophy whatever, as for example in Wittgenstein's *Tractatus*. These critiques were met by other philosophers much in the way that the dogmatic philosophers answered the

Sceptics; they simply retorted that these counter-philosophies were themselves equally given to propounding philosophical assertions.

The *reductio-ad-absurdum* that we shall be attempting in this work is no such rationalistic way of demonstrating the fallacy of philosophy. It is much more a form of transcendental historical argument that seeks to attack the presuppositions necessary for philosophical thought, ostensibly to show that such thought has become historically impossible. It will begin by accepting philosophical premises, derived mainly from the philosophies of Nietzsche and Wittgenstein, from which it can be concluded that metaphysics or the traditional way of philosophising has become historically impossible. In other words, it will show that metaphysics has been historically bereft of meaning — which is not the same as saying that it was meaningless from the start. The argument will then proceed to show the impossibility of the very premises it had initially accepted as a matter of hypothesis, this being largely accomplished by attacking the philosophies of Nietzsche and Wittgenstein. Thus, like the traditional *reductio* it ought to turn full circle and consume itself. But this is where the similarity ends.

The historically transcendental *reductio-ad-absurdum* — which is being attempted in this work in order to make meaningful the question of the end of philosophy — is no logical ploy as encountered even at its most sophisticated in Scepticism, but a new kind of critical self-destruction, or literally a reduction to Nothing. It is an intellectual expression of the historical process of reduction characteristic of modern culture in general.[14] Science in particular, as we shall go on to show, is inherently reductive, not only in itself but also in its effect on other modes of thought such as philosophy. The destruction of forms is characteristic of modern art as well as thought, and both are linked to the nihilistic impetus of modern culture in general. As argued in *In the Beginning was the Deed*, these destructive phenomena of culture are not to be regarded purely negatively, as the traditionalists are wont to do, for some of the greatest achievements of art and thought accomplished by the modern world are owing to them. Some of these achievements have traditional analogues, as we have seen with regard to ancient Scepticism, but never before have they been carried to such a pitch of destructive perfection. The *reductio* has been pushed to the *absurdum* of nothingness whose meaning is an unprecedented destruction of meaning.

III

All this, here referred to only in the greatest generality, will have to be spelled out in detail later. However, there are obvious limits to the thoroughness with which this can be undertaken. Thus, for example, the destruction of metaphysics would in principle have to be studied in all the modern philosophies and examined argument by argument, which is in practice impossible. In a work of restricted scope the choice must always be made either to aim for a broad perspective on philosophical developments, thus possibly erring on the side of generality, or to attend to the detail of argumentation, possibly erring on the side of particularity. In the first half of the work the choice has been for generality; the end of metaphysics has been reviewed from the highest vantage point. In the second half the choice has fallen on two specific thinkers, the two greatest destroyers of metaphysics, Nietzsche and Wittgenstein. Attention will be focused on the detailed texture of their *reductio-ad-absurdum* of metaphysics with the greatest possible specificity. This will in turn permit a close scrutiny of these two key modern philosophers, involving an attempt to subject them to a critical self-reduction by uncovering those implicit principles inherent in them which, if made explicit, would expose the philosophy to its own self-refutation. Thus, the destruction of metaphysics by argument will itself be exposed to a destructive critique. If this can be done in these two key instances, it will provide a salient example of a general critique of modern philosophy. It is true that each such philosophy is its own *causa sui*, born of a critical confrontation with the problems of philosophising at the end of metaphysics, so that each must be subjected to its own specific critique and no general argument can be applied to modern philosophy as a whole; nevertheless, the examination of these two leading philosophies will permit some general conclusions about modern philosophy as such.

Taken together, the first two parts of the work carry through the first two moments of a *reductio-ad-absurdum* of philosophy itself. In the first moment the viability of the kind of modern philosophy that would be necessary to destroy metaphysics is assumed as given, and the basic principles of such philosophy are not questioned further. The two key principles on which most modern philosophies are premised are the principle of activity or the Deed, and the principle of language as the matrix of meaning and the basis of human reality.[15] Taken together these principles necessarily destroy any metaphysic of being and the rational categories into which modes of being are differentiated. In this work only two key categories, or general concepts of metaphysics, are subjected to critical destruction: the Logos, which has been the basic principle of metaphysical Reason since its origin, and the Cogito, the originating principle of philosophy in the modern Rationalistic scientific period. Both of these will be subjected to a *reductio-ad-absurdum* argument based first on the philosophy of Nietzsche and then on that of Wittgenstein. But in the course of that argument, as its second moment, the very same reductive procedure will be turned on these two modern philosophies, and they will be subjected to the same destructive critiques. Nietzsche's philosophy of the will to power and the transvaluation of values will be shown to be eschatological and ultimately metaphysical. Wittgenstein's philosophy of Language will be shown to be incapable of adequately accounting for its own linguistic destruction of metaphysical concepts, and ultimately for itself as a mode of philosophical-critical language. If these counter arguments succeed, they will demonstrate a method of critically destroying every other modern philosophy. This method, if systematically carried through, should in theory leave no possible way of philosophising.

The whole course of the work tends towards this conclusion as it follows the logic of the *reductio* through its two destructive moments. But in the end the dialectical paradox — that in arguing for the end of philosophy we have of course been philosophising — will make itself felt. Like any argument for the end of philosophy that is itself genuinely philosophical — as it must be to make its case — our argument too will necessarily be self-referring and so self-refuting. This is not the first time that philosophy, by questioning its own being, has paradoxically continued to be. The general form of all such arguments is this: philosophy doubts its own being, *ergo*, philosophy is. And it might seem that all such arguments are merely formal and based on the nature of thought itself, for thought *is* merely by thinking on itself, and so is unable to show that it is not. Descartes relied on this formal feature of thought in framing his Cogito to meet a similar contingency of sceptical self-doubt launched against all knowledge by such Renaissance Pyrrhonists as Montaigne, and itself deriving from the ancient Sceptics. Descartes turned doubt against itself and so made it seem that the triumph of Pyrrhic doubt is always of necessity a Pyrrhic victory, provided the doubt is radical enough.

However, in contemporary philosophy doubt is no longer the generalised, abstract scepticism of the philosophers of antiquity and the late Renaissance. Indeed, what philosophy has to contend against now is not simply epistemic doubt but a conceptual reduction that removes the very foundations on which any philosophical thought can rest. Descartes could rely on the self-reflexive nature of thought in order to bring about the self-refutation of sceptical doubt, but this is no longer possible when abstract doubt has become historical reduction. This is where the parallel between Descartes' Cogito and our own self-refuting *reductio-ad-absurdum* breaks down, though formally speaking the strategy is analogous.

Reduction is not doubt but an historical process of conceptual destruction, one which Descartes himself unknowingly inaugurated. It is the basic principle of scientific method that Descartes first propounded as the famous Rule V of his *Rules for the Direction of the Mind*. Since then the major triumphs of science have been successes of reduction, of the ever more thoroughgoing reduction of higher entities to lower ones. And the principle of reduction did not stop with science; it entered philosophy as well as other areas of Western thought. Step by step with the progress of science there arose reductivist philosophies, such as Positivism, which directed themselves against philosophy itself, in the first place seeking to carry through a conceptual reduction of metaphysics. In a sense, then, our own *reductio-ad-absurdum* is the culmination of this philosophic project to reduce philosophy to nothing. But carried through to its logical conclusion, as we intend to show, this trend is self-defeating, for ultimately the reductive impetus reduces itself. Like the purge that also purges itself, spoken of by the ancient Sceptics, the contemporary conceptual destruction of philosophy also in the end destroys itself. As we shall show, the attempt to destroy the concepts of philosophy itself gives rise to a concept of destruction that is indeed philosophical.

IV

By facing up to its end and radically doubting itself philosophy wins for itself the first principle of its own new 'method': that of critical destruction. Out of its own attempted self-destruction philosophy can perfect the principle of critical destruction to a degree never before achieved. Philosophy might thereby establish a critical function within modern culture and society that is peculiarly its own. By subjecting everything else to its principle of doubt it becomes capable of a critical destruction in thought that goes beyond all previous ways of doubting developed from Pyrrho to Descartes. These appear mere quibbles compared with the destructive negation put at our disposal by the great destroyers of modernity, such as Marx, Freud, Weber, Nietzsche and Wittgenstein. Through this critical power of self-reflection we now possess new methods of 'negative dialectics' which leave nothing intact: no foundations, axioms, assumptions, first principles, absolute truths, common sense or conventional acceptations.

This critical destructive function is of essential value for a modern civilisation that unthinkingly annihilates its past and unknowingly becomes entangled and trapped in its own rational and technological systems, caught up in self-imposed forms that constrict its further development. Technological rationality is one such form of constraint which can only be broken, at least in thought, by means of destructive critique. And the same holds true of many other modern cultural and ideological forms as well. Whatever becomes frozen and fixed, and so unchangeable, must be thawed in the fire of destructive thought, which now as always is the 'devil's element' necessary for creation. Of course, thought in itself is impotent, it cannot change reality; for this other powers must be called on. Nevertheless, thought, even as philosophy, can provide insight and instigation that can be made to work socially in unpredictable ways. It is most likely that philosophy will have to continue to confine itself to the university; but it is precisely there that its critical functions need to commence.

As a state-owned and state-directed institution the university proliferates and diversifies, but at the same time it fixes and hardens itself. As the sciences fragment further under the instigation of specialisation, and as each speciality institutionalises itself in a separate department, so gradually the possibilities of anything radically new emerging decrease, and the scientific establishment becomes ossified. Institutional establishments and their prevailing power arrangements impede the entry of new ideas or theories; they fetishise techniques and methods of research and restrict intellectual debate. In such an institutional setting philosophy has a necessary, though highly difficult and dangerous, critical function to perform. It must continually endanger itself so as to provide a critical challenge to the prevailing disciplines. Its tactic must be the opposite to that of conventional philosophy departments, which wall themselves off in their own specialist ghettos so as to remain pure and untroubled by 'worldly' concerns. Philosophy must enter the arena of battle for scientific truth. It must intrude even where it is now not wanted.

The philosopher's critical intervention into the sciences can, of course, only occur on condition that he knows them, not necessarily in the way in which their specialised practitioners do, but sufficiently to perform another of the functions of philosophy apart from critique, that of mediation between sciences that can no longer communicate with each other. And once again this is a dangerous role, for he who is in the middle stands to be buffeted from either side. Nevertheless, there has to be such an intermediary if mediation is to occur at all.

Mediation takes many forms. In the first place mediation is a mode of translation between two languages otherwise incomprehensible to each other. The role of translation has been made mandatory in the tower of Babel of the sciences, each one speaking its own tongue of technical methods and concepts and a professional jargon specifically designed to leave outsiders guessing. And translating here is not simply a matter of making lucid in another language what scientists have garbled in theirs; rather, it is a matter of transferring and interpreting the results of one science in terms of those of another. Thus for example, the work done on the neurological structure of the brain has little direct relation to the work done on mental states and dispositions, partly because the neurologist and psychologist speak such different scientific languages. In some cases this is a problem with immediate practical relevance: how is communication to be brought about between those who treat patients neurologically with electrodes or drugs and those who treat them with a 'talking cure'? The philosopher is not confronted here with a mere abstract problem of how the mind acts on the body (that hoary old chestnut which professional philosophers are still trying to pull out of the fire!) but with an actual problem of how the language of a physiological science translates into that of a mental one. Any abstract mind–body theory is bound to be useless in this kind of an enterprise.

There are other problems of mediation awaiting the philosopher which go beyond translation to the establishing of conceptual connections or inference-paths where none as yet exist. There are many conceptual problems demanding this kind of treatment which professional philosophers are incapable of dealing with because they regard such issues as mere intellectual puzzles. Thus what they take to be the problem of the relation of empirical propositions to evaluative ones, and for which they seek a general philosophical answer, is really not a logical problem requiring a neat solution but a task waiting to be accomplished: a matter of mediating between the humanists who make value judgements and the more factual social and cultural scientists. This task has to be achieved differently in each discipline. It arises in one way in literary studies, where it is a matter of relating the judgements of the critics to the researches of historians and sociologists of literature; it arises in another in political studies, where it is a matter of referring the points of view of those who cultivate a general political outlook to the theories of political scientists; and still otherwise it arises in every factual field where value judgements play a role. There are no generalisable solutions for such problems, valid for all cases and all contexts. The philosopher has no inherent advantages in dealing with them, except perhaps one: that his is a mind cultivated to encounter such problems in a number of fields and that he is practised in the arts of mediation. For not only should he be familiar with mediation in the sciences, but also between diverse areas of social life which are now cut off from each other: between science and art, politics and economy, and also between the private and public dimensions of everyday life.

This extended task of social mediation merges into another function of philosophy, one which departs furthest from university and academic studies: that of recollection. Recollection does not simply mean remembering the past, though this is part of it; more importantly, it is the self-recollective function of making the present aware of itself in relation to its past and to its possible futures. Self-recollection is the modern equivalent of the classical philosophical dictum 'know thyself', but it is addressed to the collective present, not merely to the thinking individual, and so it involves an historical dimension that classical recollection did not require. The present has to recollect itself historically so as to realise its own predicament and re-establish its own self-presence in time. The loss of self-presence in the present is a basic distemper of modern time. The question of time abuts on the even more ominous one of death. Philosophy's fundamental task is to recollect death as it has manifested itself in contemporary consciousness, when the old meanings of death are no longer viable. Humankind is threatened with a new kind of death, now that the human species as a whole is vulnerable, and this changed meaning of death has profoundly altered the significance of mortality for the individual. *In the Beginning was the Deed* took this predicament as its point of departure and developed on its basis a philosophy which was beyond philosophy as traditionally understood, since traditional philosophy took into account only the death of the individual.

To enable such recollection of time and death a new mode of philosophising is called for, one that addresses itself to the present and to things as they are in the present. This function of philosophy was identified some time ago and dubbed 'concrete philosophising' by Walter Benjamin. Adorno takes it as a mode of philosophising that follows on the destruction of metaphysical systems and abstract categorial schemes; he explains it as follows:

> The dismantling of systems, and of the system at large, is not an act of formal epistemology. What the system used to procure for the details can be sought in the details only, without advance assurance of the thought: whether it is there, or what it is. Not until then would the steadily misused word of 'truth as concreteness' come into its own. It compels our thinking to abide with minutiae. We are not to philosophize about concrete things; we are to philosophize, rather, out of these things.[16]

Thus we need to philosophise out of the concrete conditions of life in our time, so that at the very forefront of our attention as objects of philosophising are the specific concrete things that hold primary significance for us all for they threaten the death of mankind or a transformation of the human condition: nuclear weapons, for example, and space probes. The real meaning of these things is not apparent to the specialists; neither the physicists and engineers who build them, nor the politicians and strategic thinkers who plan and dispose of them know what they are really about. To know this calls for a peculiar kind of thinker, one who is only to be called a philosopher for want of a better name, one able to see the relevance of such things for the state and meaning of mankind in general. We need 'eschatological' thinkers, such as Günther Anders, capable of thinking through the 'end of things' without relying on traditional religious comforts; thinkers able to think the unthinkable, not as exercises in either lurid imagining or unimaginative rational strategy but as intellectual tasks of courage and devotion.

And it is not only the Bomb or space travel — both subjects of great 'transcendental' consequence — that require concrete philosophising; there are other objects in our world that demand it as well. All the products of technology that impinge on daily life need to be recollected philosophically. The new media of communication, as well as cybernetics and the medical pharmacopeia are already having a decisive impact on human faculties and capacities: on language, perception, behaviour, knowledge, life and death. They ought to be receiving as much attention from thinkers as did once the opening up of a cosmopolitan environment outside the polis, or the discovery of other civilisations, or the great revolutionary upheavals. By pursuing such concrete recollective thought the philosopher can ensure a relevance of academic studies to society beyond that of rendering professional advice and technical services. Such questions of relevance ought not to be decided simply through the pressure of social problems, or the inroads of politics and publicity; they demand a philosophical re-conception of the point and purpose of the subjects taught in the university. The self-recollection of the university is the task of the philosopher; he has to carry it through concretely without resorting to any abstract Idea of the University.

In general, it must be stressed that if philosophy is to accept the three functions of thought as here outlined, then it must resign itself to abandoning many of the higher and nobler purposes on which it has always prided itself. A philosophy dedicating itself to critical destruction, mediation and recollection must give up the attempt to understand Being, or to define essences, or to specify the good life, or to propound world-views, or to ensure authenticity, or to overcome Nihilism, or to establish the foundations of the sciences, or to draw the limits of reason, or indeed most of the other things philosophers have tried to do. A modest philosophy exercising its three functions together — for they are interconnected and to practise one without the others is impossible — could still, however, achieve much both for intellectual and social life as well as for individual existence.

V

Unfortunately, this is not the way contemporary academic philosophers, on the whole, exercise their function. Within the departmentalised university environment they have surrendered to the prevailing rule of specialisation. They accept the position of philosophy within the total economy of disciplines as one more speciality among others. This is the culmination of a process that had already begun last century. As Adorno puts it:

> The most patent expression of philosophy's historical fate is the way the special sciences compelled it to turn back into a special science. If Kant had, as he put it, 'freed himself from the school concept of philosophy for its world concept', it has now, perforce, regressed to its school concept.[17]

However, there is this difference between the philosopher as specialised expert and every other expert: the philosopher has no specific object or field that is peculiarly his own. He is the expert on nothing — and everything. Every speciality that philosophy has sought to preserve for itself has been taken over by the sciences and expropriated from philosophy. Over the last two centuries philosophy has been gradually displaced from one field to another as it has tried to escape the relentless pursuit of the sciences. After metaphysics had to abandon the claim to the whole of Being, philosophy sought refuge in epistemology and the mind, but that had to be given up to psychology and the scientific methodologies. Philosophy tried to retreat into concepts and ideas, only to have to abandon these to the new cultural sciences. The escape into consciousness was blocked by psychoanalysis, which revealed the secondary nature of the conscious Ego as compared with the unconscious systems that subtend it. For analogous reasons History had to be given up to the sociologists and world-historians, Life to the biologists and cyberneticists and Thought to the logicians and methodologists. Language had seemed a last refuge for philosophers but philology, linguistics and semiology are now making it insecure, and, before long, it, too, may have to be given up. A history of wrecks of modern schools of philosophy since Kant is like a swathe of ruins beaten by the flight of philosophy from the world, crushed under the relentless pursuit of ever newer sciences and humanities.

Philosophers have consoled themselves in their forcible retreat into ever more rarified regions of abstraction by seeing it as a voluntary withdrawal from the turmoils of the world into calmer realms of pure thought. The Existentialists thought they had purified philosophy by removing it from mere existence into the higher being of Existenz which no science could enter. Fundamental ontologists went even further by pushing thought into Being and Nothing which, according to them, was beyond every science as a kind of new metaphysics, but which underlay all of 'what-is' with which the sciences were dealing. The Phenomenologists who followed Husserl 'back to the things themselves' were no more prone to be more concrete, for through their *epoché* of all presuppositions and judgements they removed all specificity from everything and saw things with a purely 'essential vision' which abstracted all but the basic categories. The Logical Positivists transformed all thinking in philosophy into formal logic and methodology with which they then tried to purify the sciences and to unify them into one total system. The Linguistic philosophers seemed to be doing the opposite by locating their thinking in the basic concreteness of common language, but since common language was divorced by them from all so-called 'technical' languages and the historically developed concepts of the sciences, and so deprived of ideas, the ultimate effect was to place philosophy in a court of judgement in which commonsense and basic-usage became the accepted criteria of truth. Even some Marxists as philosophers elevated themselves above the scientific world of empirical knowledge by aspiring to pre-ordained dialectical schemas of historical truth. And as each of these philosophies purified itself so it also separated itself from all the others. Philosophy, which had maintained itself till Kant as a common language of rational discourse, began to break up into these separate 'schools', each with its own increasingly esoteric language; now it is no longer possible for philosophers to communicate in what Derrida has called the 'diaspora of institutes and languages, publications and techniques'.

Sociologically considered, the retreat of philosophy from the scientific world and its withdrawal into its own purified spheres must be seen as a way of preserving itself from having to face the scientific challenge. In their own departmental fastnesses philosophers could busy themselves with matters in which by stipulation no scientist had any competence and for which no philosopher need know any science or have any other specialised knowledge. Indifference to outside knowledge began to typify the professional philosopher. Secure from serious outside challenge, such philosophy has *ipso facto* rendered itself obsolete. The problems and solutions of 'school' philosophy are usually of no concern to anybody else. No scientist, historian or critic waits on the deliverances of philosophy to resolve any one of his difficulties, for that which the philosophers say is likely to be irrelevant to him.

However, this separation of science from philosophy, or in general of knowledge from thought, exacts its toll from both sides. The philosopher falls into inanity and the scientist into ever narrowing technicality. Much of the confused state of the sciences is due to the absence of a guiding philosophy. There is nothing now to exercise the unifying function for the sciences once carried out by metaphysics. It would be futile to wait for a new philosophy to recover the metaphysical function. Yet, the problems arising from the absence of metaphysics are there and have to be met in some way or other. The sciences, whose development brought about the ending of metaphysics and the withdrawal of philosophy into isolation, are themselves succumbing to the problems of their own making. The consequences of their own precipitate expansion are now catching up with them, as they find themselves incapable of coping with difficulties that extend beyond their own specialised reach.

Has philosophy still a function to perform for the sciences in the university? The urgency of this question demonstrates that the question of the end of philosophy is no mere historical curiosity, or simply an administrative matter of what to do with a few near obsolete antiquarians. A philosophy that properly exercises its functions of critical destruction, mediation and concrete philosophising has much to contribute to the sciences and other areas of scholarship. But for it to do so, it is necessary that philosophers find ways of entering into close contact with scientists and scholars. The philosopher who has nothing to say to scientists and scholars may well have nothing to say at all.

It is possible that the philosopher will be able to exercise his function if he can find a way of entering into the kind of cross-disciplinary research that requires the co-operation of different kinds of scientists. This is likely to be increasingly the precondition for original scientific work since highly specialised research makes it difficult for anything new to originate. As Norbert Wiener pointed out some time ago, it is between the disciplines, in 'these boundary regions of science which offer the richest opportunity to the qualified investigator',[18] that new areas can be opened up; and he described the origin of his own new science of cybernetics as having arisen precisely out of such an interaction of men from many disciplines and sciences. But, as Wiener sees it, the precondition for such a team-effort is that these scientists not be complete specialists:

> . . . a proper exploration of these blank spaces on the map of science could only be made by a team of scientists, each a specialist in his own field, but each possessing a thoroughly sound and trained acquaintance with the fields of his neighbours; all in the habit of working together, of knowing one another's intellectual customs, and of recognizing the significance of a colleague's new suggestion before it has taken on a full formal expression.[19]

This requirement made of scientists begins to approximate to the universalising predisposition of philosophy. The philosopher has himself to satisfy at least part of its demand; though he be no expert or even scientist, his knowledge has to be adequate to enable him to work with scientists. Wiener broadens his plan of a collective scientific team into the vision of a new kind of scientific institution:

> We had dreamed for years of an institution of independent scientists, working together in one of these back-woods of science, not as subordinates of some great educative officer, but joined by the desire, indeed by the spiritual necessity to understand the region as a whole, and to lend one another the strength of that understanding.[20]

In such a place the philosopher, too, would be able to find his home.

But who is the philosopher now? It is anybody, no matter from what profession, who carries out knowingly or unknowingly the functions of philosophy; often it is a scientist or scholar totally divorced from official philosophy. Norbert Wiener, once a pupil of Russell, is an example of a scientist who succeeded in raising some of his thought to the level of philosophy. An even more outstanding example is the sociologist Max Weber who was a philosopher *malgré lui*, as Karl Jaspers declared:

> Max Weber developed no philosophical system. It would be impossible to expound his philosophy as a doctrine. He declined to be called a philosopher. But to us he is the true philosopher of the time in which he lived. Because philosophy is not a gradually progressing science, which recognizes a timeless truth, each

philosophy must achieve its reality as a historical existence rooted in the absolute and oriented towards transcendence. Max Weber taught no philosophy: he was a philosopher.[21]

Unfortunately, when it comes to saying something specific about Weber as philosopher, Jaspers concentrates almost exclusively on Weber's pronouncements on academic philosophy and scientific methodology, where Weber is at his thinnest and least interesting. The philosophical lesson to be learnt from Weber is contained in his actual scientific work, where he in fact carries out some of the real functions of philosophy.

Perhaps Weber's greatest and most specifically philosophical accomplishment was his formulation of the conceptual theory of ideal-type concepts. Few philosophers have realised the philosophical importance of this conception. It permits an escape from the dilemma of either having to resort to abstract definitions, as in traditional philosophy, or succumbing to quasi-empirical conceptual analysis, as in most modern philosophy. In this work extensive use will be made of ideal-type specifications in lieu of definitions or analysis of concepts, and by this means it will be possible to study meanings as historical and changing, not fixed once and for all in universal concepts or in language taken as a given. This is why it constitutes one of the great conceptual discoveries in philosophy, and must be placed alongside the original Socratic definition of exact concepts and Aristotle's elaboration of this into an organon and a metaphysics of categories. The ideal-type permits for the first time an exact and systematic definition of objects in social and cultural reality, that is, a definition of complex historical terms; 'a "definition" of such synthetic historical terms according to the scheme of *genus proximum* and *differentia specifica* is naturally nonsense'.[22] Adorno is perhaps the first philosopher to realise that to approach cultural objects through a 'constellation' of such ideal-types, in the way that Weber practises in his science, is to have discovered a completely new mode of description that no longer requires the postulation of inner essences or natures:

How objects can be unlocked by their constellation is to be learned not so much from philosophy, which took no interest in the matter, as from important scientific investigations. The scientific accomplishment often ran ahead of its philosophical comprehension . . .[23]

Even Weber's own philosophical comprehension was not up to his scientific accomplishment and its philosophical implications. Adorno considers thinking in terms of constellations of ideal-types a mode of philosophical thought that goes beyond any available in modern philosophy:

> In Weber's case the constellations take the place of systematics, which one liked to tax him with lacking, and this is what proves his thinking to be a third possibility beyond the alternative of positivism and idealism.[24]

What takes Weber's philosophic thought even further beyond the alternative of Positivism or Idealism is the way in which, utilising his ideal-type theory, he succeeds in dealing with rationality, perhaps the most important issue in Western philosophy. The main metaphysical tradition has interpreted rationality and developed it in accordance with the ideal of universal Reason, the Logos of Greek philosophy and the Ratio of subsequent Latin translations of that philosophy. In different versions, including in its late forms the *raison* of the Enlightenment and the *Vernunft* of German Idealism, the tradition of the unity and universality of Reason has persisted in philosophy ever since, so that even Positivism with its emphasis on logicality has maintained these tenets. Western civilisation has derived its sense of itself from this tradition, considering itself the only one that is rational and seeing its rational discourses, above all its sciences, as the rational standards for all other civilisations. As Weber puts it, 'in Western civilization only, cultural phenomena have appeared, which (as we like to think) lie in a line of development having *universal* significance and value'.[25]

Weber is equivocal about the universality of these phenomena, not committing himself to saying whether their significance is indeed universal or it is only we who like to think so. Weber, in other words, never explicitly spells out a philosophy of rationality. Nevertheless, a comprehensive theory of rationality can be derived from his work. It is an interpretation of rationality that goes counter to the philosophical tradition of Reason. Extrapolating from Weber it can be shown that there is no essential unity of Reason for there are always irreconcilable inner tensions between different forms of rationality, the conflict between Formal and Substantive rationality being one of the key leitmotifs of Weber's historical analysis. It occurs in all dimensions of social life, in economy, law, morality and wherever there is a confrontation of opposed rational standards according to the extremes of form and substantive content. Rationality is thus divided against itself; it does not have the ideal unity of Reason, but assumes different forms which can contradict each other. In the course of this work we shall distinguish many such forms of rationality, among them some which are non-Western, and among the Western ones we shall be separating Reason, Rationalism and Rationalisation.

If, then, rationality assumes different and potentially opposed forms, it follows that the ideal of its universality cannot be maintained in the way the philosophical tradition of Reason expects. There can be no one universal standard of rationality according to which everything can be unequivocally measured or judged. But it does not follow from this that rationality is completely relative and so also completely arbitrary, that everyone can have his own subjective standards, or even that every age, culture, or nation has a different one. Rationality is not a matter of arbitrary choice or of historical decision, it is a socio-cultural form inherent in the meaningful activities and, above all, the discourses of civilisations. We can no more devise a form of rationality at will than we can devise a form of science at will; the forms of science to which we are bound contain inherent standards of rationality.

This also holds for other discourses and modes of action to which the concept of rationality applies. And because a given discourse, such as a science, is not universally one and the same from beginning to end, but assumes a set number of historically specific different forms, it follows that rationality, which is bound to such discourses, in a parallel way has a limited number of forms. Each of these forms is historically formed and consequently historically variable. But it is not historically relative in the sense that each social entity, society, nation or tribe can be said to have a separate one for itself. Nor are these forms subjective in the sense that they can be changed at the behest of any given individual; which is not to deny that some individuals, great philosophers, scientists and artists, have in the course of history partially altered the prevailing form of rationality by transforming the norms of discourse or the procedures of science. It is this social, historical dimension that gives rationality its objectivity and compels those subject to given modes of discourse to conform to its standards on pain of being unintelligible, or worse still of being declared irrational and mad.

If we are to determine and define the limited number of historical forms of rationality that human ingenuity has produced, it is essential to apply Weber's theory of ideal-types. The mass of empirical material in which rationality manifests itself, in usually imperfect ways, is so vast that no description can convey it unless it utilises a few clearly defined 'ideal' conceptual constructions as standards of historical comparison. Such ideal-typical constructions are derived from empirical reality, mainly from the ideas historically produced, but are nowhere exactly identical with such ideas. They are what Weber terms utopias. The attempt has been made in this work to construct conceptually a few such utopias of forms of rationality, in particular those which we have called Reason, Rationalism and Rationalisation. These forms must, therefore, be understood as sociological ideal-types which are nowhere to be found in actual discourses. Their function is solely that of sociological description and they are not intended as normative standards. They are to facilitate the new discipline of the sociology of philosophy.

The ideal-typical concepts of rationality are not a definition of rationality as this is philosophically understood. They cannot be used to decide substantively in a given discourse what is rational and what is not. Nor can they be invoked to decide in any given case what kind of discourse to rely on, and so what kind of rational form to invoke; as, for example, in solving a social problem whether to rely on the technical standards of natural science with its formal rationality, or the critical standards of a social science with its substantive rationality, or the traditional norms of empirical experience, or some kind of rational political process. It is not only possible but practically speaking imperative to reach a decision in any given case as to what is the appropriate discourse and form of rationality consonant with given ends and higher values; in this sense a normative comparison can always be made between forms of rationality. Our ideal-types might facilitate such a comparison and permit a better understanding of what is involved in making such a cross-rational decision, but they are not standards for making the decision itself. There are no such standards and philosophical definitions of rationality cannot provide any, for what is required in each case is a different and often unique argument mounted to settle the issue at hand. There are no algorithms or logical decision-procedures in such cases.

The sociology of philosophy is in no sense a substitute for philosophy itself, anymore than the sociology of science is a substitute for science; nor can it meet any of the expectations that are usually placed on philosophy. It forms the point of departure only for an investigation of the question of the end of philosophy. This is not the kind of question sociologists have ever asked. Only a few philosophers have faced up to its daunting challenge. Nevertheless, it is a question that touches on all our intellectual and scientific discourses. One of the key concerns of this work is the critical separation between philosophy and science that has developed in the disciplinary economy of the contemporary university. We shall also trace the historical antecedents of this separation at a stage when science and philosophy were still integrated. Our aim is not to write a history of philosophy and science but merely to outline a gradually opening rift that has become almost complete in our time. It is this that, sociologically considered, threatens the end of philosophy.

The main purpose of this book is to contribute towards the effort to avert this end. How this is to be achieved through an interrogation of the question of the end of philosophy itself will become clearer at the end of the book. So that beginning with the end of philosophy and taking it to its end we hope to redefine the ends of philosophy.

Notes

1. Richard Rorty, *Philosophy and the Mirror of Nature* (Princeton University Press, Princeton, New Jersey, 1979), p. 394.

2. Hans Küng, *On Being a Christian*, trans. Edward Quinn (Collins, Glasgow, 1978), pp. 26–7.

3. 1982 Power Lecture in Sydney, reprinted in *The Age*, 7 June 1982.

4. John Berger, *Ways of Seeing* (British Broadcasting Corporation and Penguin Books, 1981), p. 139.

5. Rorty, op. cit., p. 393. *Philosophy and the Mirror of Nature*.

6. Historically the professionalisation of philosophy has gone hand in hand with its transformation into an academic discipline dealing with the history of philosophy. The Right Hegelians and the neo-Kantians were particularly influential in effecting this transformation during the nineteenth century. See Rorty, op. cit., pp. 133–6.

7. Rorty, op. cit., p. 369. *Philosophy and the Mirror of Nature*.

8. See Paul Ricoeur, *Freud and Philosophy*, trans. Denis Savage (Yale University Press, New Haven, 1970), p. 33. 'These three masters of suspicion are not to be misunderstood, however, as three masters of skepticism. They are, assuredly, three great destroyers.' Ricoeur includes Freud rather than Wittgenstein, but the point holds for the latter as well. The difference between destruction and mere scepticism will be explored later in the work.

9. Jacques Derrida, *Writing and Difference*, trans. Alan Bass (University of Chicago Press, Chicago, 1978), pp. 79–80.

10. Ibid., p. 79.

11. T. W. Adorno, *Negative Dialectics*, trans. E. B. Ashton (Routledge & Kegan Paul, London, 1973), p. 3.

12. Ibid., p. 4.

13. T. V. Smith (ed.), *From Aristotle to Plotinus* (University of Chicago Press, Chicago, 1965), pp. 173–4.

14. See my book, *In the Beginning was the Deed: Reflections on the Passage of Faust* (University of California Press, Berkeley, 1982).

15. For a historical account of these two principles see *In the Beginning was the Deed*, ibid., Act I.

16. Adorno, *Negative Dialectics*, p. 33.

17. Ibid., p. 4.

18. 'Cybernetics', R.W. Marks (ed.), *Space, Time and the New Mathematics* (Bantam Books, New York, 1964), p. 189.

19. Ibid., p. 189.

20. Ibid., p. 189.

21. Karl Jaspers, *Leonardo, Descartes, Max Weber: Three Essays*, trans. R. Manheim (Routledge & Kegan Paul, London, 1965), p. 251.

22. Max Weber, *The Methodology of the Social Sciences*, E. Shils (ed.) (The Free Press, New York, 1968), p. 93.

23. Adorno, *Negative Dialectics*, p. 164.

24. Ibid., p. 166.

25. Max Weber, *The Protestant Ethic and the Spirit of Capitalism*, Talcott Parsons (ed.) (Unwin, London, 1967), p. 13.

Part One

METAPHYSICS, SCIENCE AND REDUCTION: A HISTORY

1 METAPHYSICS AND THE SCIENCES

1. A General Overview

Metaphysics and science are now totally at odds. Science shuns the few remainders that are still left of a once powerful metaphysical tradition, one that has been decisive for the history of Western science. Most scientific concepts had their origins in metaphysics. Metaphysical principles frequently were the sources of scientific theories.[1] From its inception metaphysics served the crucial function of establishing the fundamental intellectual relationships between the sciences, and maintaining thereby the unity of the sciences as the one coherent body of knowledge. This had already been systematically elaborated in the metaphysics and sciences of Aristotle, and remained so — major revisions of metaphysics and science notwithstanding — till the onset of Positivism in the modern era. Positivism marked a radical break in this tradition by promulgating an anti-metaphysical programme for the interconnection and unification of the sciences. This utopian logical programme has still not been realised; now it is losing its credibility, just as Positivism itself is becoming discredited. The sciences at present seem to be growing and doing well without benefit of philosophy. But, they are multiplying in an uncontrollable fashion and have become so fragmented that it is impossible any longer to relate them. This does not seem to bother scientists; preoccupied with their own substantive problems, they feel no need for the blessings of philosophy, and metaphysics is anathema to them.

The present mutual exclusion of science and philosophy is fraught with considerable danger. Science without philosophy is blind and cannot see where it is heading. Philosophy without science is dumb and cannot speak about anything real. The present divorce of philosophy from science has meant its separation from most areas of substantive knowledge, for nearly all such knowledge is now the province of one science or another. This is why it has become so important to concentrate on the lack of relationship between philosophy and science. Obviously, philosophy now also fails to relate to other concerns to which it was relevant in the past, such as morality, art and religion. But this is not crucial; unlike science such concerns are not decisive in the contemporary intellectual world. Philosophy has been partly responsible for this by downplaying them: in Positivist philosophy, for example, they are consigned to the realm of values in which they supposedly depend on nothing more than a subjective will or optional preference. This is a philosophical travesty that nobody takes seriously in practice, but it does point up the merely residual function now of such non-scientific concerns in the realm of knowledge.

This is one reason that this work concentrated more on the historical interaction between philosophy and science, than on other no less historically important intellectual spheres.[2] Metaphysics during its long history had no less influence on theology and moral casuistry (the impact of Platonism and Aristotelianism on Christianity), on the arts (especially poetry and music), on rational law (natural law doctrine), and the rational-legal legitimations of politics (social contract theory). Nevertheless, this work deals more with the sciences than with these other concerns because its focus is on the contemporary situation where science is pre-eminent. Philosophy will not survive if it has nothing to offer the sciences, even were it the case that it still had something to say in other cultural spheres.

The relationship between science and philosophy historically has been varied. Philosophy has played a different role in relation to the sciences in each major scientific epoch. One can distinguish at least three such major scientific epochs in Western history, each with a number of subsidiary phases. The first might be called the epoch of Aristotelian science which lasted from Aristotle, who first consolidated the Greek sciences, to Copernicus, who was both the last of the old and the first of the new cosmologists. During this long epoch of two millenia there were roughly three distinguishable phases of pre-modern science: firstly, ancient science — comprising also Alexandrian and Stoic science, which were partially distinct from the strictly Peripatetic; secondly, medieval science which was to begin with Arabic and then Christian scholastic; and thirdly, Renaissance science which was a summative and syncretist phase of its own. It led directly into the next epoch, that of modern or Newtonian science, which spanned the shorter period from Galileo to Einstein inclusive. This was the modern classical epoch, following the so-called Scientific Revolution, which Kuhn has described as that of paradigmatic science, calling the previous epoch — not altogether justifiably — pre-paradigmatic, or really pre-scientific. This epoch of modern classical science in turn breaks up into at least two phases: the first lasted from the Scientific Revolution to the Industrial Revolution, or more precisely till the time of the French Revolution; the second began with the institutionalisation of science in the early nineteenth century in the French *Grandes Ecoles*, and, more importantly, in the new German universities, and lasted till the onset of World War II. During World War II there ensued a wholesale mobilisation of science for the purpose of war technology and social welfare that has continued into the Cold War, and this development seems to have inaugurated a new post-Einsteinian epoch of science which has been dubbed Big Science.[3] It is a form of science associated less with any great individual names than with impersonal institutions of organised knowledge. The characteristic features of this science, marking its separation from classical science, have only recently begun to be explored by the new discipline of the sociology of science. The philosophy of science has, as yet, almost nothing to say about it.

Science is a very different kind of enterprise and practice in each major epoch. Different sciences arises or cease to be current depending on the general intellectual climate and overall disposition of the sciences. Music was a science within the medieval, but ceased to be one within the classical dispensation; grammar was a science within the first epoch of classical science, but was no longer one in the second when it was displaced by philology, which itself has given way to linguistics in the present epoch of science. Such harder disciplines as mathematics, physics and cosmology seem to show greater persistence and continuity, but even their history is now seen as broken up into almost separate sciences, which, some philosophers of science argue are incommensurable with each other. Ptolemaic cosmology, they contend, is not the same science as post-Copernican cosmology, and Newtonian physics is distinct from Aristotelian physics. Other authors distinguish further the subjects of the adjoining phases of the one epoch as separate sciences. In this vein, for example, Foucault separates the economics of the seventeenth and eighteenth centuries, calling it the analysis of wealth, from the political economy of the nineteenth century.[4] One need not accept Foucault's argument that a distinct episteme or intellectual structure governs the sciences of each separate phase, however, to agree with him that most sciences show marked differences even from phase to phase.

In the transition to a new epoch nearly all sciences change

drastically. The post-war period has revealed such marked changes in nearly all sciences that we feel justified in describing it as one of transition to a new epoch of science. The new features present in most sciences to which one can point to justify such a large claim are those of technification, formalisation, abstraction, problem-solving and finalisation.[5] Technification refers to the overriding importance of technology and to other kinds of technical procedures in Big Science. Formalisation is the tendency of many 'pure' sciences towards building axiomatic systems or, alternatively, to computer programming. Abstraction and problem-solving involve the redefinition of all difficulties as problems to be solved by reference to abstract models. Finalisation is a new term introduced in the sociology of science; it refers to the overriding importance of the external stipulation of ends and goals for further theory elaboration in a science that is already mature in that its fundamental theories are complete and fixed.[6]

It is possible to see even from this cursory glance that philosophy today cannot possibly fulfil a function in relation to contemporary techno-science like that of metaphysics in Aristotelian science, or that of epistemological philosophies (for example, Empiricism) in the first phase of classical science, or even that of Positivism in the second phase of classical science, during the nineteenth and early twentieth centuries. These diverse functions of philosophy are so distinct that there is good reason to maintain that something else is meant by the very word 'philosophy' each time. Philosophy as a traditional discipline does pride itself on its unity and continuity, largely because it keeps alive the great texts from its own past and because each new philosopher tries to align his own work with these classics. But if one looks behind this streak of traditionalism in philosophy — to which it owes so much of its dignity and mystique — it becomes apparent that what each new great philosopher actually does with philosophy is very different from what his predecessors, behind whose titles and words he disguises himself, were doing. Descartes might call his work *Meditations on First Philosophy*, but what he implies by this term is quite different from what Aristotle meant by *'proton philosophia'*; in other words, Cartesian metaphysics is no longer anything like Aristotelian metaphysics, which, in fact, it strenuously opposes on behalf of the new science. Similarly, Wittgenstein's *Tractatus Logico-Philosophicus* — the finest fruit of Logical Positivism, formed even before that school was mature — has little in common with Spinoza's work, whose mode of exposition and axiomatic method it so closely resembles that Moore was led to suggest the spinozistic title for the English translation. His *Philosophical Investigations* has even less in common with Husserl's *Logical Investigations* despite the short distance in space, time, mentality and culture that separates these two masterpieces of late German philosophy. Wittgenstein himself was no longer sure that what he was doing should be called 'philosophy', though he was adamant that it, nevertheless, was the 'legitimate heir to that which had previously been called "philosophy"'.[7] But even that tenuous claim to legitimacy is questionable if one compares the late Wittgenstein's relation to traditional philosophy with that of Husserl or any earlier great master like Kant. Since Wittgenstein, professional philosophy has become preoccupied with a narrow range of technical problems of its own and has further distanced itself from the continuity of its history. It has almost completely divorced itself from the living sciences of its time and so broken the long-standing relation between science and philosophy in Western thought.

The historical development of philosophy and science were mutually determining till the period of the Scientific Revolution, when modern science began to assert its autonomy. Before that, science had been subject almost completely to metaphysical controls. To begin with, in the first epoch of science, Aristotelian philosophy as metaphysics literally sought to be above and beyond physics, to exercise control over *physis*, that is, the natural world and all the regional sciences governing its knowledge. That such metaphysical control is doomed to failure if attempted in relation to modern science is evident from the total incongruity of Heidegger's project to place a new kind of *Ersatz* metaphysics over the sciences by giving the 'thought' of Being priority over all merely 'regional entities'.

> Only when science proceeds from metaphysics can it conquer its essential task ever afresh, which consists not in the accumulation and classification of knowledge but in the perpetual discovery of the whole realm of truth, whether of Nature or of History.[8]

Heidegger's philosophic design for the sciences was completely anachronistic; such ambitions had already been given up by philosophy from Locke and the Enlightenment philosophers onwards. Only in Hegel and the other German Idealists had there been an attempt to recover the full metaphysical function of philosophy. But this attempt, too, was bound to fail because of the way the sciences developed in the nineteenth and twentieth centuries during the second phase of modern classical science. It is a puzzling problem for the sociology of science and philosophy that such attempts to establish a metaphysics of science should continue to be made despite all the evidence of failure.

Following the Scientific Revolution, during the first phase of modern classical science, Locke had expressed what was to be the prevailing view of the role of philosophy in relation to the sciences when he referred to himself as the 'underlabourer' to the master builder Newton. Immediately prior to Locke, Descartes still held out larger ambitions for his philosophy; he sought to make it provide a grounding for the sciences by having it establish the first indubitable principles of scientific knowledge as well as the rational method of its development. But even his highly Rationalist philosophy had more of an epistemological than a metaphysical bent, though it could not and would not give up its claim to be a metaphysics. As we shall show, no epistemology, not even that of Hobbes or Locke with its thoroughly Empiricist disposition, could really free itself from metaphysics entirely. This only began to take place after Kant. Kant's 'Copernican Revolution' — which sought to found the sciences on the *a priori* categories of the understanding — completed the epistemological quest for the foundations of knowledge, and through its 'critique of pure Reason' or speculative thought began the process that would eventually separate scientific epistemology from any metaphysics. Though the epistemologically based Scientific Method was still inherently metaphysical in the first phase of modern classical science, it ceased to be so in the second phase when it referred itself to *a priori* categories or formal principles and eventually only to pure formal logic, and thus became methodology.

The role of philosophy in the second phase of modern classical science no longer required and was not dependent on metaphysical backing. This is the main reason why one philosophy after another could call for an attempt to carry through an end to metaphysics. This was most pronounced in the numerous, changing Positivist philosophies, succeeding each other from St. Simon and Comte through to Carnap and Popper. These could base themselves on a philosophical ideal of 'positive' science and seek to elaborate a purely logical methodology of science, that is, a logically foolproof method of validating, by either verifying or falsifying, all claims to scientific knowledge. The Positivists were not alone in demanding an end to metaphysics in the name of positive science; Marx and his followers did so too; or in the words of Marx himself: 'where speculation ends — in real life, positive science begins'.[9]

Throughout this second phase of modern classical science there were different kinds of attempts to end metaphysics by establishing anti-metaphysical philosophies on the foundation of the new sciences. The traditional relation was inverted: instead of science being based on philosophy, philosophy was now to be based on science. Thus, for example, experimental psychology raised hopes of establishing a purely scientific philosophy of mind and a rigorous science of ideas or an *'ideologie'*. Darwinist evolutionary theory gave rise to Social Darwinism, Bergsonism and indirectly also to Pragmatism. The new symbolic logic eventually led to Logical Positivism. Philosophies of Life developed out of a conjunction of biological, evolutionary and historicist sciences. Philosophies of the Unconscious both preceded and derived from the new psychiatries, above all from Freudian psychoanalysis and its close analogues. Philosophies of Language had an even more eclectic derivation from the various sciences of language, such as comparative grammar, philology and linguistics, as well as from attempts to found historical, cultural and hermeneutic sciences based on language or symbolic forms.

In reaction to these attempts to base philosophy on science, there also arose in this period philosophies that attempted to remove themselves from science completely. These were the moves towards a 'pure' philosophy: the neo-Kantian proposal for a purely formal philosophy of *a priori* categories or forms, the phenomenological project of a scientific philosophy or 'pure science' of 'essences', the existentialist philosophy of Existenz or Dasein, and finally also the attempt by linguistic analysis to found a pure philosophy on the usages of ordinary language. We shall have more to say on the significance and meaning of 'purist' philosophies' to which the work of Wittgenstein and Heidegger also belong. Purism in philosophy is closely associated intellectually with the tendency towards ever greater abstraction in the sciences and arts, as well as with the institutional need to establish a separate professional philosophy. Hence, the difficulties of purist philosophy are strictly analogous to those in these other spheres: they suffer from a rarification of substantive content or meaning that pushes them into empty

abstraction totally divorced from anything real. The professionalisation of philosophy has accentuated this tendency by institutionally
insulating it against critiques from the outside.

All this became more evident after World War II at the start of the
third epoch of science, when philosophy was almost exclusively an
academic discipline. Most of the older purist philosophies were well
adapted to take advantage of this situation, and most succeeded in
capturing all available chairs in their respective spheres of influence.
Thus, they were able to keep themselves intact because they were
insulated by their purism from the onslaught of the new technical
way of doing science, which destroyed many of the scientifically-
based philosophies of the previous period. Philosophies of Life
could not survive in the face of the new genetics, which also discredited evolutionary philosophies. Psychologistic philosophies could
not cope with the new emphasis on experimental psychology and
behaviourism, which put paid to all projects for a 'science of ideas' or
plans to formulate the 'laws of thought'. Philosophies of Language
were made increasingly more antiquated and redundant by such new
linguistic sciences as structuralist linguistics and transformational
grammar. By contrast, purist philosophies, which considered
themselves untouched and unmoved by anything that went on in
science, could resist attacks from the sciences — at the cost of
immuring themselves in the fastness of an academic department
where they had no contact with and no influence on anything else. It
is this situation of deepening academic 'solipsism', in which most
surviving philosophies find themselves, that arouses the fear that
philosophy will lose its *raison d'être* — and cease.

Philosophy is most in danger in the contemporary situation because
it seems to have lost one of its most important traditional roles, that
of defining and guiding the prevailing mode of rationality.
Philosophy has always seen itself as the determining and controlling
agency of the idea of Reason, which was meant to act as the standard
of rationality for the sciences and all other intellectual concerns.
And throughout its long history philosophy has tended to delude
itself that it is the same one standard that it is guarding, or, at least,
that it is the one continually improving standard. The unity and
continuity of Reason — of the Logos throughout all its translations
and transformations — is the implicit presupposition behind most
histories of philosophy, from Aristotle's initial attempt at the

opening to his *Metaphysics* to Hegel's explicit formulation of the idea of the unfolding of the Idea in his *Logic*. Many contemporary philosophers still believe in the indissolubility of this bond between philosophy and rationality and still see the main task of philosophy as upholding the unique and universal claim of Reason to be the norm of discourse and historical development. Both Toulmin and Habermas, among many others, have formulated new versions of this traditional assumption. But unfortunately their efforts are, to say the least, untimely for the sciences no longer look to philosophers to define for them their rational standards of procedure.

The rational standards of science in our time do not have much to do with philosophy. This fact suggests that rationality no longer means what it did in previous scientific epochs. It seems that the meaning and nature of rationality change from epoch to epoch in relation to the changes that take place in science and culture in general, and that rationality is a function of the overall character of the prevailing intellectual procedures. Far from constituting a uniform and universal superordinating standard for the intellect, rationality appears to be no more than a changing socio-historical symbolic or discursive form, depending for its formation on changes in those modes of knowledge over which it is supposedly set. Or to put it in contemporary jargon, it is more like a dependent variable. Philosophy's most important task has always been to sum up and prefigure such changes in the forms of discourse and knowledge by continually redefining the standards of rationality on which they can then be said to be based.

Thus what is called rationality in any given epoch is simply the philosophical formulation of the basic norms and procedures inherent in the discourses of that epoch. In the modern period the scientific discourses are decisive in constituting rationality. Frequently rationality is simply identified with a supposedly unique Scientific Method. Other definitions of rationality not based preeminently on science have also always been prevalent; those, for example, based on dialectical logic. Aristotelian logic or, more recently, Formal logic has also frequently been invoked as the touchstone of rationality, especially to counteract the influence of less formalistic modes of conceiving of rationality. Proceeding in this way in opposition to each other, philosophers have in effect defined a number of quite distinct modes or forms of rationality, almost invariably under the mistaken belief that they were disputing about the definition of the one and only universal Reason or Logos.

In the historical course of Western philosophy and science we can in very general terms distinguish at least three forms of rationality, each of which was to a greater or lesser extent dominant, though not exclusive, during one of the three epochs of science: viz. Reason, Rationalism and Rationalisation. These concepts can only be defined in the highest degree of generality; as ideal-types in Weber's sense they are sociological constructs, devised for the purpose of facilitating comparison and contrast so as to permit an understanding of actual instances of forms of rationality encountered in history. They are rarely if ever to be found completely instantiated in any one such concrete instance, each of which will appear as a crossing or mixture of the pure types. The justification for devising and employing such pure types is largely heuristic; they provide 'ideal' sociological standards of comparison against which historical forms of rationality may be seen, revealing their likenesses and differences. The differences will frequently be more important than the likenesses for they have more to teach us. Nevertheless, these ideal-types are not retrospective imaginary inventions; the construction of each one is based on actual ideals of rationality encountered in history, particularly in the history of philosophy and science. The sociological ideal-types are, of course, only abstractions from actual ideas.

Reason or the Logos was the dominant though not exclusive form of rationality during the first, metaphysically determined, epoch of science. It was throughout closely bound up with Platonic and Aristotelian metaphysics, from which it received its original formulation. As a mode of rationality it functioned by promulgating principles of categorial differentiation and ordering, continually subsuming lower concepts and categories under higher ones, and eventually building up a metaphysical system of the sciences through conceptual hierarchies in which Being became the highest category. Reason can be called logocentric in that it always strives to unify the world by the one universal Logos. It did not itself, however, remain the same from the start to the finish of its history; it received different definitions at different times, especially as it was translated from one major language of philosophy to another. It was Logos in ancient Greek philosophy, then Ratio in the Latin philosophy of the scholastics, and finally it became *Vernunft* in the neo-metaphysical Enlightenment German philosophy and among the Idealists. This last exemplification of Reason actually took place as a recessive strain in the second epoch of classical science when the dominant mode of rationality had already changed to Rationalism.

Rationalism, the next form of rationality, became predominant with the emergence of epistemology and Scientific Method during the Scientific Revolution, though its origins are earlier. It is a critical form of rationality which functions on principles of analysis and synthesis and aims for clear and perspicuous representations of reality. Beginning as the rationality of the new science, in the first phase of modern classical science, it was at first defined by the various conceptions of Scientific Method put forward successively by Bacon, Descartes and Newton; but eventually it was generalised to become the '*ésprit de raison*' of the Enlightenment. It transformed itself during the second phase of modern classical science, taking a developmental, progressivist form, and as such it persisted till the close of the classical epoch of science in the twentieth century. It has since come to be called by the Frankfurt school thinkers 'subjective' and 'formal' reason — and opposed by them to the supposedly more 'objective' Reason of metaphysics — partly because it was given its main definition by subjectivist philosophies from Descartes till Kant, the latter adding to it the formalist dimension.[10]

During the course of the second phase of modern classical science another mode of rationality began to dominate and gradually be defined: this might be called Rationalisation. It has also come to be known as technical or instrumental reason and as means–ends rationality (*Zweckrationalität*), and as such it can be identified with logic and techno-science. It is a calculating, systematising, formalising and organising mode of rationality, and it is also present outside science in social life for it is closely bound up with rationalising procedures, sociologically understood, as these were carried out in bureaucracy, economy, law and all other systematically organised and efficiency-minded enterprises. It has become dominant in science only during this third epoch, following World War II, through the widespread introduction of the procedures of technification, formalisation, abstraction, problem-solving and finalisation; and these also act as defining characteristics of Rationalisation in science. Positivist philosophy has provided a rationale for all these rationalising tendencies in science; it has also furthered the identification of rationality with Formal logic, completing a process which in some respects goes back to Aristotelian logic. At present the logical and calculating features of

Rationalisation are receiving their ultimate expression in the computer programming of intelligence.

Throughout history these three main ideal-typical forms of rationality in Western philosophy and science have been — sociologically considered — in constant tension with each other, maintaining a continuing dialectical struggle which received social as well as intellectual expression. It constituted a struggle for rational supremacy in which one or the other form of rationality might temporarily prevail at the expense of the others, becoming paramount throughout a given epoch or phase of science, but without ever totally excluding the others; for not even the near totalistic dominance of contemporary logistic Rationalisation has succeeded in completely eliminating the other forms of rationality. In the past there has often been a more even struggle in the battle for reason. The period of the Scientific Revolution saw the Rationalism of the new philosophies, Cartesianism and Empiricism, contending against the entrenched Reason of the old Aristotelian scholasticism and various humanist neo-Platonisms. However, when Rationalism eventually won out with the triumph of modern science and the epistemological philosophies, Reason did not disappear; it continued to flourish both in its antiquated versions in the universities and also in a redefined form as metaphysical *Vernunft*, eventually to stage at least one major come-back in *Naturphilosophie* and Idealism. Rationalism has persisted even during the present era of almost complete Rationalisation; and Reason, too, survives marginally in the last vestiges of traditional metaphysics.

There is in history no simple developmental succession outlining a sequence of rational forms, as, for example, from Reason through Rationalism to Rationalisation, which would make it possible to demonstrate an evolution or progress of rationality from lower to higher stages as Comte and succeeding Progressivists — including Habermas today — have tried to do. Rationality does not develop according to any schema or law of progressive stages; and the same is true for science, philosophy and the other intellectual modes on which it depends. One form of rationality does not arise out of and succeed another in any 'logical' way. In a certain sense, each of the three forms is coeval with the others. Rationalism did not emerge in direct succession to Reason at the time of the Scientific Revolution and Enlightenment, for early modes of Rationalism were already made available by the Sophists even prior to metaphysics and were subsequently developed further by the Sceptics, Epicureans and the scientists at Alexandria, as well as by late-medieval scientists at the University of Padua. The Reason of metaphysics was by no means the first form of rationality; it was itself only fully defined in a confrontation with the preceding pre-Socratic Rationalism begun by Socrates — who 'fought against the subjective, formalistic reason advocated by the other Sophists'[11] — and concluded by Plato and Aristotle. Rationalisation, too, does not begin *ab initio* in the contemporary period of rationalised science and society. Intimations of it are already present much earlier; the definition of rationality as calculation is already to be found explicitly set out in Hobbes who was himself, much taken with the formalisation of Euclidian geometry, which, of course, goes back to ancient science, as does formal logic. In a certain sense, then, each of the forms of rationality is age-old at least in Western civilisation, which is not to be taken to mean that they are perennial and unchanging. Rather, each can be studied from the beginnings of Western science and philosophy in terms of its own continuing transformations in relation to those taking place in the other opposed forms. Rationality has a history of continuing transformation and inner tension, which is the historical proof that it is neither uniform nor unique.

The history of rationality can briefly be told in terms of the continually changing relation between philosophy and science. It is a relation that underwent four major stages: after the first long period of unity of Aristotelian science there followed, with the Scientific Revolution, three secessions which split science and philosophy ever further apart until they became totally separate. Aristotle's work formulated and systematised a relation between philosophy and science that was based on the notion of *theoria* and was governed by the metaphysical idea of Reason. Notwithstanding numerous translations and transformations this persisted and maintained a unity of science and metaphysics that remained unbroken, despite periods of strain, till the Scientific Revolution when the first secession of science from philosophy occurred. Science or natural philosophy started to become an autonomous enterprise no longer overseen by metaphysics, with a redefined relation to a new philosophical epistemology based on an ideal Rationalism. Begun by Descartes and Hobbes, this first session was finally consolidated and completed by Kant who provided a critique of traditional metaphysics and specified a new role for philosophy as a foundational discipline. At the same time, though Kant was hardly aware of it, there began a second secession of science from philosophy as the second phase of the modern classical epoch of science supervened. The formation of new sciences of Man — anthropology, history, culture and language — challenged the Rationalist epistemological and foundational role of philosophy, which was still considered too metaphysical. On the basis of the new humanities and the older physical sciences there arose radical philosophies which attacked all earlier ones and inaugurated an iconoclastic climate of thought which spelled an end to metaphysics. This eventually paved the way for and helped further the third secession of science from philosophy which has occurred in the present epoch of techno-science and has brought about the total separation of philosophy and science.

The first secession of science from philosophy brought about a weakening and eventual destruction of traditional or Aristotelian metaphysics without eliminating every form of metaphysics, for the epistemological philosophies that arose in its stead had to remain themselves metaphysical. (We shall go on to show why this had to be so.) Only the second secession produced philosophies which could carry through an end to metaphysics as such. But this must not be taken to mean that reactionary metaphysical movements — for example, neo-Thomism — did not occur or could be prevented from arising, and in some respects even Idealism falls among these. The third secession of science from philosophy has gone further and now threatens the existence of philosophy itself, including such anti-metaphysical philosophies as Positivism which intellectually and ideologically sustained the new techno-science. Rationalisation at its most extreme seems to exclude every form of critical and self-reflective thought and so has no need for philosophy. It remains to be seen whether any role can, nevertheless, be found for philosophy in this new epoch of science.

To understand fully the present crisis of philosophy it is necessary to go right back to the very beginning, to the origin of metaphysics and the sciences, and then to follow through each of the three secessions of science from philosophy. The aim here is neither to make a critical study of all past philosophies nor to write an exhaustive history of philosophy. It is rather to undertake what might provisionally be called the sociology of philosophy, a relatively new sub-discipline developing from and modelled on the sociology of science and of knowledge in general. In keeping with this approach, in the first place the emphasis will be on an 'externalist' view of the function of philosophy in relation to the sciences. This will subsequently be complemented by a parallel 'internalist' study of the dialectic of change in philosophical rationality. The study of secessions will be completed (in the next chapter) by a study of reductions, for what appears 'externally' as a series of secessions can be seen 'internally' as a succession of reductions of philosophy. This is a historical *reductio-ad-absurdum* that threatens to bring the historical 'argument' of philosophy to a close.

2. Metaphysics as Queen of the Sciences

Neither metaphysics, strictly speaking, nor the sciences begin with Aristotle, or even with Plato. Nevertheless, we can take Aristotle as a starting point for he sums up most of the scientific achievements of his time, and formulates for the first time a systematic metaphysics designed to act as a foundation for the sciences. But first, what is the meaning of 'metaphysics'?

> . . . commonly in the Schools called *Metaphysiques*; as being a part of the Philosophy of Aristotle, which hath that for title: but it is in another sense: for there it signifieth as much, as *Books written, or placed after his natural Philosophy*: But the Schools take them for *Books of supernatural Philosophy*: for the word *Metaphysiques* will bear both these senses.[12]

Some, such as Hobbes, take the term 'metaphysics' as purely a bibliographic designation coined by subsequent editors (Andronicus is usually suggested) to refer to the book in Aristotle's opus that comes immediately beyond (*meta*) his book on Physics. But others, not only the scholastics, but such modern scholars as Jaeger, have maintained that the word must be taken literally to mean that the subject matter of the book on metaphysics is beyond physics. 'In truth, however, this word which was surely coined by some Peripatetic earlier than Andronicus, gives a perfectly just picture of the fundamental aim of "first philosophy" in its original sense.'[13] In this sense it is, strictly speaking, the super-natural philosophy, for the Greek *physis* is translated into the Latin *natura*, hence the meta-physical is the super-natural. Thus, Lady Macbeth speaks of the witches' 'metaphysical aid and supernatural soliciting'. Of course, the witches' crude sense of the 'supernatural' is not Shakespeare's, nor is it that of the philosophers who think of metaphysics as 'construed on the basis of physics'.[14] Physics is the science of the natural world; metaphysics is not the science of a world beyond, a supernatural world, but rather the science of the most fundamental principles that underlie the natural world. Metaphysics is, thus, the science of first principles, and Aristotle himself designates the subject mater of the book called *Metaphysics* as *proton philosophia*.

What did Aristotle mean by 'first philosophy'? It is first not merely because it is primary or fundamental, so dealing with first principles, but also because it is the science of all other sciences, the science of being as such and not merely some determinate part of being:

> There is a science which investigates being as being and the attributes which belong to this in virtue of its own nature. Now this is not the same as any of the so-called special sciences; for none of these others treats universally of being as being. They cut off a part of being and investigate the attribute of this part . . .[15]

And the reason 'it is the work of one science also to study the things that are, *qua* being',[16] is that there is for Aristotle a total unity of being. 'There are many senses in which a thing may be said to "be", but all that "is" is related to one central point, one definite kind of thing, and is not said to "be" by a mere ambiguity.'[17] That the verb 'to be' does not ambiguously fluctuate, even though 'there are several senses in which a thing may be said to "be"',[18] is not something that Aristotle or subsequent metaphysical philosophers seriously doubt, because there must be for them a total unity of being, a 'central point' to which everything relates. 'Hence to investigate all the species of being *qua* being is the work of a science which is generically one . . .'[19]

Modern Linguistic Positivists can indulge themselves in distinguishing multiple varieties of the meaning of 'being' — a conceptual activity which simply continues what Aristotle himself had already begun when he distinguished four basic senses of 'to be'[20] — yet, they cannot conclude simply from this that there is no being *qua* being or being itself. It is only because they do not require any 'central point', because they are fascinated by a heterogeneous variety of entities and a pluralistic universe that the different senses of 'to be' are indicative to them of a basic ambiguity of being. But for Aristotle 'being and unity are the same and are one thing'.[21] A thorough destruction of metaphysics would require the satisfaction of Nietzsche's self-declared aim:

It seems to me important that one should get rid of the all, the unity, some force, something unconditioned; otherwise one will never cease regarding it as the highest court of appeal and baptizing it 'God'. One must shatter the all; unlearn respect for the all, take what we have given to the unknown and the whole and give it back to what is nearest, what is ours.[22]

Such a destruction of metaphysics would at the same time constitute a destruction of Reason, or that mode of rationality that takes every particular as part of the All by 'ranking all concepts in order of their generality'[23] and deriving the lower from the higher. Once such an arrangement of concepts according to their logical priority is questioned, Reason cannot function as metaphysics.

This 'Respect for the All', for the unity of being and its centrality, characterises all metaphysics from start to finish and is inherent in the ideal of Reason. In the eighteenth century the special 'science' of being was separated off from all other regional philosophies and called by the new name of 'ontology', in which the basic sense of metaphysics as the 'logos' of 'being' was preserved even though this 'science' had already departed very far from its Aristotelian origins. Eventually for Hegel 'being' became merely the original abstract category of Logic; nevertheless, the unity and centrality of being are cancelled and preserved (*aufgehoben*) in his developmental progression from abstract and empty being to the fully realised being of the Absolute. And even though Heidegger insists that his 'fundamental ontology' is beyond metaphysics, in his thought, too, Being — as distinguished from beings or things that are — plays a unifying and gathering role like that it had performed all throughout the history of metaphysics and Reason.

The meaning of 'being' changes, as does the character of 'first philosophy', during the long course of metaphysical speculation. These changes begin in the very heart of Aristotle's own *Metaphysics*, as in this compendium of materials from different periods of Aristotle's development are deposited different strata of thought that only modern archeologists of the text can separate. According to Jaeger, the earliest stratum is that which arises 'out of the crisis of Plato's doctrine, and consists in efforts to rehabilitate the assertion of supersensible reality'.[24] At this stage metaphysics is itself more like a special science of the unmoved and transcendental which 'simply rests externally on physics, the science of the moveable and immanent';[25] it is merely the completion of physics, extending beyond matter and motion to supersensible substance and the first mover. As Aristotle puts it: '. . . but if there is an immovable substance, the science of this must be prior and must be first philosophy, and universal in this way, because it is first'.[26] It is in this way that at an early stage of his thought metaphysics and theology are identified, '. . . since it is obvious that if the divine is present anywhere it must be present in things of this sort'.[27] Jaeger argues that Book XII of the *Metaphysics*, commonly known as 'the theology', represents an early stage of his 'complete system of metaphysics *in nuce*'.[28]

However, it does seem as if already in Aristotle's developed conception it is possible to separate metaphysics from theology because the study of being is no longer focused on God as prime mover or super-sensible substance, and as Jaeger puts it, 'instead of them there appears the new subject of the morphology of being'.[29] This was crucial for unifying the sciences and placing them on metaphysical foundations. The point of departure for this morphology is substance (*ousia*) which is the primary being: 'if this is substance, it will be of substances that the philosopher must grasp the principles and causes'.[30] The interrogation of substance becomes the primary subject of first philosophy: 'the subject of our inquiry is substance, for the principles and causes we are seeking are those of substances'.[31] Aristotle goes on to examine the substrate (*Hypokeimenon*) of things so as to discover the different kinds of substance.

> The substratum is substance, and this is in one sense the matter (and by matter I mean that which, not being a 'this' actually, is potentially a 'this'), and in another sense the formula or shape (that which being a 'this' can be separately formulated), and thirdly the complex of these two . . .[32]

Starting with matter and form, Aristotle next defines essence, universal, potency and act which remained the key concepts of Aristotelian science. Jaeger states that 'by this analysis the mere "this-something-or-other" is differentiated into the form which determines matter, and in which universal conceptual thinking grasps the essence of the real, the latter being related to matter as act to potency'[33] — and this is also a way of defining science.

For Jaeger, it is this 'morphology of being' that is the keystone of Aristotle's philosophy and caps off the whole architectonic of his sciences, bringing them into an internal structural unity by means of its overarching concepts:

> The same fundamental conceptions persist like subterranean strata through several disciplines. Thus the conception of form penetrates psychology and logic and all the special sciences, while it also belongs to physics and metaphysics, that is to theoretic philosophy. . . . These common intellectual themes hold the disciplines inwardly together.[34]

Thus metaphysics provides the infrastructure of being, the systematic conceptual organisation of all the sciences that together cover the universe of knowledge. The unity and centrality of being is, therefore, no mere rhetorical figure of speech, but the exact definition of the meaning and role of metaphysics in relation to the sciences.

Aristotle's thought is certainly systematic, but this must not be taken to mean that he creates a metaphysical 'system' in the full sense in which this became current later. In fact, the idea of a fully enclosed, complete and internally coherent system was unknown to him; it was first developed in the Hellenistic philosophies among the Stoics and Epicureans. With these qualifications in mind, it can nevertheless be asserted that Aristotle was the first thinker to systematise the sciences, and that his creation of metaphysics is to be understood as serving this purpose. Seen in terms of its intellectual function, metaphysics is the systematic unity of the sciences. Aristotle himself was merely 'the compelling organizer of reality and of science',[35] not the founder of science. As a scientific innovator Aristotle only established the morphological sciences of form: the 'biological, morphological and physiological study of nature, or the biographical and morphological sciences of culture'.[36] Farrington, a writer not himself favourably disposed to metaphysics, nevertheless sums up Aristotle's achievement as follows:

> The conception was formed of an organic body of scientific knowledge, covering the whole field of human experience, in which the separate parts which made up the whole should be clearly separated from one another yet seen in their mutual relations. With this master plan before them his disciples continued his work, now reconsidering the basic principles of the whole structure (as when Theophrastus raised the whole problem

of the validity of the teleological principle), now defining the
limits of the particular sciences more clearly (as when Theo-
phrastus by his analysis of the nature of the parts of animals and
plants, separated the sciences of zoology and botany).[37]

Thus the contribution of the Lyceum to the sciences was at first in
keeping with Aristotle's own achievement. Later it very quickly
declined. Much later, in the period of Marcus Aurelius, Lucian the
satirist mocks the surviving Peripatetics for concerning themselves
with such seeming trivialities as the 'life-time of gnats', 'the pene-
tration of sunlight under water, or the psychology of oysters',
subjects which are not quite as funny to us as they must have been to
a literary Roman public unversed in any kind of natural science.[38]
But by this time Aristotelian science had long been taken over by the
scientists at the Museum in Alexandria.[39]
    However, despite the brilliant achievement of the Alexandrian
scientists after Aristotle, or perhaps precisely because of this, a rift
had already been opened up in the systematic metaphysical unity of
the sciences. Different sciences started to free themselves from the
control of Aristotelian metaphysics, as for example the physics of
Strato, the third head of the Lyceum, which reverted back to the
earlier mechanistic philosophies of Democritus for their basic
models. Was this already an early anticipation of the secessions of
science from philosophy to come two millenia later?
    Aristotle's achievement went further than metaphysics and the
natural sciences; to his credit there is also the formation of formal
logic and the organon or analytic method which was the predecessor
of scientific method. These departures were to be of crucial importance not only for science but for the definition of Reason, the traditional form of Western rationality. Without Aristotle the Greek
Logos could never have become Western Reason and would have
remained a largely speculative idea, somewhat on par with the *tao* of
China. Aristotle made the decisive identification of Being and
Reason, that is, he brought metaphysics and logic together. Before
Aristotle, Reason began to be differentiated only incipiently when
Herakleitus spoke of the Logos and Parmenides of the Nous for
these were still partly mythological. Both of these principles were
unified in Plato's intelligible Idea, whose developed architectonic of
the Form of forms provided the point of departure for Aristotle's
metaphysics of the Being of beings. And parallel with this
metaphysics of Reason, there was also the elaboration of Reason as

logic. The Logos, beginning as a simple principle of unity in the strife of opposites for the pre-Socratics, became the method of dialectics in Plato and the method of analytics in Aristotle, producing the two branches of logic which have persisted ever since. Metaphysics and traditional logic as two modes of Reason have been in the closest possible relation since Aristotle's identification of the rationality of being and the principle of the excluded middle.[40] This was upheld right through to Hegel's unification of the dialectic of concepts with the rational unfolding of the Idea and has persisted at least until the rise of mathematical logic, which is another kind of rationality. The unity of Reason and being has been a hallmark of all metaphysical thinking.

The historical realisation of Reason in society did not begin in earnest until philosophy had captured and transformed the educational institutions of the ancient world. A strong impetus for this came from the rediscovery in early Roman times of Aristotle's twin sciences of First Philosophy and Analytics. The practical expression of this purely intellectual work followed soon after in Roman grammar and law, and much later in Christian theology and Arab science.[41] Gradually, one by one the disparate dimensions of social being were subjected to and suffused by Reason. Thus, from its inception onwards Aristotle's organon and metaphysics became central to the whole rational history of the West. For it is no mere historical accident that it provided the instigation for the systematic renewal of study of the sciences during the early middle ages, and that it figured so prominently in the origin of the university, the new Christian institution of learning so different from the schools of the past. The Aristotelian problem of universals was the first major intellectual issue with which the university was concerned, and this launched the sciences on the further investigation of the universe. Universals, university and universe — these have more in common than their root word. For a long period these names spelled scholasticism, the bane of the early Renaissance scientists. But the overthrow of the scholars and dunces was by no means the end of Aristotle's influence or that of his metaphysics. Expelled from the natural sciences during the Scientific Revolution it maintained itself nevertheless in morality, poetics, logic and grammar. Science did not dare challenge these concerns, which remained the preserve of the antiquated universities; Hooke's draft Statutes of the Royal Society (1663) state expressly: 'The Business and Design of the Royal Society is: "To improve the knowledge of natural things, and all useful Arts, Manufactures, Mechanics, Practices, Engynes and Inventions by Experiments (not meddling with Divinity, Metaphysics, Moralls, Politicks, Grammar, Rhetoric or Logick).'"[42] Thus metaphysics as a specialised discipline, eventually to be called ontology, continued unchallenged, and remained practically unchanged from its Aristotelian origins; Kant complains that 'after so much pother and noise the science is still where it was in the time of Aristotle . . .'[43] The direct impact of Aristotle was still strongly felt as late as Hegel. Between these two great sign posts of the way of philosophy every other attempt at a metaphysics can be located. Each of these looks back to Aristotle's *Metaphysics*, and also, in a non-teleological sense, looks forward to Hegel's *Logic*, in which all past metaphysics are summed up and incorporated.[44]

However, to consider the history of metaphysics in the way that Hegel does is to do so from within that history itself and to locate oneself within that tradition. The issue of what is and what is not metaphysical presents itself very differently to someone within the tradition compared with someone outside it. The very question of what is metaphysics must be differently answered and 'metaphysics' variously defined depending on where one stands in this regard. Metaphysical philosophers consider metaphysical even those who themselves reject metaphysics. Thus, Empiricism and even Positivism are seen by metaphysicians to be based on implicit metaphysical premises which is a claim these schools deny. And to define metaphysics as the science of being *qua* being would not make sense outside the metaphysical tradition, in a discourse where the unity and centrality of being are rejected. Metaphysical philosophers interpret these denials as themselves constituting some kind of affirmation of being. In turn, anti-metaphysical philosophies treat as metaphysics that which metaphysicians would not consider a central part of the metaphysical tradition, The extent and bounds of metaphysics thus shift markedly depending on the standpoint from which they are being demarcated.

Even to raise the question of the end of metaphysics is already to take up a standpoint outside the metaphysical tradition, one which is only possible at a determinate historical juncture. It was only when a specific critical situation had arisen in history that the question of the end of metaphysics could make sense. It could only have been raised when not merely metaphysics itself but the cultural and civilisational forms tied to it had themselves reached their culmination. Metaphysics had often come under attack before, but the end of metaphysics could not have been seriously entertained until the whole of Western science had undergone a momentous transformation, replacing Reason with a different form of rationality.

3. The Inefficacy of Earlier Critiques of Metaphysics

Metaphysics was subject to attack as soon as it originated. The Atomists, Cynics and Sceptics of the ancient world kept up a sustained campaign against what they saw as dogmatic philosophy. But irrespective of how we now assess the cogency of their arguments, their strictures proved fruitless; the progress of metaphysics was not halted in its tracks, because the social conditions for a destruction of metaphysics did not obtain. On the contrary, the ancient world and later historical developments required metaphysics; the sciences in particular were in a state where they depended on a metaphysical order. It was not until social conditions enabled the development of the sciences in a direction where metaphysics was a bar that the arguments against it had their effect. This could not have happened until the Scientific Revolution brought about the first secession of the sciences from philosophy, which was eventually followed by the second secession that brought metaphysics to an end.

But to ascribe the ending of metaphysics to the two secessions of science from philosophy must not be taken to mean that the destruction of metaphysics was a mere external consequence of developments extraneous to philosophy itself. Arguments, or the rational aspect, and intellectual transformations, or the historical aspect, of social developments are not divorced from each other; one cannot treat the former as logical or conceptual and the latter as merely contingently empirical. Rationality functions both logically and historically. Thus the secessions of science from philosophy were at once dialectical and social changes. They expressed themselves in a change of problematic, in the emergence of new questions, methods and concepts and the suppression of old ones, which at its most dialectically explicit took the form of reductive arguments against a certain kind of metaphysics. These arguments were merely the most visible symptoms of the intellectual reductions going on underneath. On their own they could not possibly have brought about such drastic alterations in thought. They could be convincing only because changes in the problematic already laid the ground for their receptivity. And behind these changes there were new power dispensations in culture and society which institutionalised the new acceptations and rejections.

There is, thus, an inner 'socio-logic' to the destruction of metaphysics, which takes the form of conceptual changes and a dialectic of argumentation, as well as a sociology of external social developments. And so the following question arises: does this inner 'socio-logic' go back to the very first principles of metaphysics, and so was it derivable from first principles and predictable *ab initio*; or is it rather that each derivation and move is, so to speak, an historical surprise with no direct reference to or continuity with the origin? This question poses two ways of looking at the total history of metaphysics. It can be seen as a continuous development, as one single argument going back to the origins, in the way that Nietzsche and, following him, Heidegger and Derrida have presented it. Or, it can be seen as a series of discontinuous stages, each of which has no inherent connections with the others, as specific metamorphoses or breaks, in the way that Foucault reads the history of the sciences. Is the end of metaphysics inherent in its origin, or is it an abrupt closure occurring spontaneously?

Nietzsche and Heidegger maintain that metaphysics was doomed from the start because it arose out of an eschatological fault in the original philosophical thought which, like a Fall, condemned it to an inevitable decline and death. For Nietzsche this 'original sin' is traced back to Plato's inversion of 'this-world' of the senses and appearances and the 'other-world' of reason and the ideas, so that 'this-world' came to be denied and devalued. For Heidegger the eschatological fault lies in a forgetfulness of the ontological difference between Being and beings that goes back to Plato and Aristotle. Both Nietzsche and Heidegger trace out on the basis of the fall of metaphysics a resultant eschatological destiny in the history of the West that refers itself to an original teleology. This kind of historical scheme has come under severe criticism of late from such so-called post-Structuralists as Foucault, who deny the essential unity, the original destiny and the logo-centrism of history. History for these thinkers transforms itself through ruptures (*coupures*) in which one form of knowledge (*episteme*) shifts in its underlying and unconscious structures and gives rise to another form. Thus, the origin loses any privileged place; each such transformation is as original and total as any other.

According to Foucault, metaphysics came to an end as a mere by-product of the most recent of these epistemic changes, that which he locates as having taken place at the juncture of the eighteenth and nineteenth centuries. It was at this point that 'the entire field of Western thought was inverted'.[45] The inversion followed directly from a working out of the inner dynamic of the preceding so-called classical *episteme*, that which has held sway since the end of the Renaissance. As a result, metaphysics was brought to an end:

> Modern thought, then, will contest even its own metaphysical impulses, and show that reflections upon life, labour and language, in so far as they have value as analytics of finitude, express the end of metaphysics: the philosophy of life denounces metaphysics as a veil of illusion, that of labour denounces it as an alienated form of thought and an ideology, that of language as a cultural episode.[46]

Thus, according to this account, the end of metaphysics is not derivable from or continuous with its origin.

Foucault's theory of the epistemic changes from Renaissance to Classical thought and from Classical to Modern is closely related to the first and second secessions of science from philosophy. Each of these secessions must be accounted for as a unique and specific transformation taking place in the very depth of the thought of its period. Like any other revolutionary change, each of these intellectual upheavals of knowledge has its own specific configuration and takes place at a determinate period because of a confluence of unique local causative factors surrounding it. And just as it is absurd to try to trace back the French Revolution to the ancient Greeks and Romans, even though the revolutionaries saw themselves as latter-day Demostheneses and Brutuses; so it is equally absurd to account for the Scientific Revolution by reference to an original Thought or to some original Fall or misconception of Being, even though Bacon did write a *Novum Organon* and Descartes a *First Philosophy*. In this respect the approach adopted by Foucault to discount origins is quite correct.

However, in the history of philosophy there is an overall tradition despite even the most radical changes, as the above titles indicate, which ensures an appearance of continuity from start to finish of the same figure of thought. Metaphysics retains the identity it received from Aristotle at least till Hegel because Hegel and every metaphysician before him refer themselves back to Aristotle and take up at least in verbal formulation the old problems and concepts, no matter how much they change them in the process. There is even an inner 'logic' to the changes in this tradition because it takes shape as a continuing argument, a dialectic of debate from one major thinker to another. It would be too simplistic to see it as the one ideal conversation carried on in a realm of pure discourse, untouched by historical materiality as Oakeshott does.[47] But it would not be wrong to study the historically unfolding pattern of argument in which philosophy debates itself, not as a ghostly dialogue, but as a real flesh and blood dispute carried on by men with highly determined and limited conceptions at their disposal at any one time, and in specific social circumstances.

The end of metaphysics was caused by changes taking place outside metaphysics, in the sciences, in culture and in society at large. Nevertheless, it could not have been meaningfully realised without the kind of argumentation that only takes place as debate within philosophy. There had to be anti-metaphysical philosophies capable, by means of critical argumentation, of destroying the concepts and categories of metaphysics, even those which were first explicitly defined by Aristotle. The destruction of metaphysics had to involve a process of reductive rationality, and, as we shall see in Chapter 2, the arguments frequently took the form of a *reductio-ad-absurdum*. Metaphysics was literally reduced to nothing.

On the other hand, mere argumentation could not have brought about an end to metaphysics; on its own it could at best have established anti-metaphysical schools of philosophy alongside the metaphysical ones. The explicit arguments against metaphysics had to be backed up by a major shift in the disposition of knowledge, as occurred with the inauguration of new sciences, for metaphysics was not merely discredited, but rendered irrelevant. The secession of the sciences from philosophy had to take place simultaneously with the philosophic attacks on metaphysics before the metaphysical foundations of knowledge could be eroded and metaphysics destroyed. This can be demonstrated by means of comparison with the previous attempts to overthrow metaphysics, for these always proved unavailing. Even before the first modern moves against metaphysics, there had been numerous anti-metaphysical movements, some of which deployed a battery of arguments against it that were as sophisticated as anything delivered since. But they always failed; every time metaphysics emerged strengthened from the encounter. Metaphysics might have survived unscathed even the onslaught of modern philosophies if these had not been reinforced by the sciences and the whole panoply of modern culture.

From its origins metaphysics has carried with it a virulent bacillus, which, like the anti-body of a prophylactic inoculation, secured it against disease. For almost contemporary with Aristotle there came Pyrrho, the founder of the anti-dogmatic school of the sceptics. Of Pyrrho, Nietzsche, the great contemporary destroyer of metaphysics, has this to say in admiration expressive of a profound kinship:

> I see only one original figure in those that came after: a late arrival but necessarily the last — the nihilist Pyrrho: — his instinct was opposed to all that had come to the top in the meantime: the Socratics, Plato, the artist's optimism of Herakleitus. (Pyrrho goes back, through Protagoras, to Democritus.) . . . His life was a protest against the great doctrine of identity (happiness = virtue = knowledge).[48]

Beginning with Pyrrho, the sceptics systematically set about attacking all the other schools of philosophy, whom they castigated as dogmatic. For this purpose they employed a critical method of destructive reason that in refinement and self-reflexivity is as sophisticated as any since. They expressly spoke of themselves as destroyers, and their destructive impetus was directed against all first principles, causes and criteria, the main features of metaphysics; Diogenes Laertius reports that 'they would destroy the criterion by reasoning of this kind . . . causes too they destroy in this way'.[49] But they went on to attack Reason itself, for as Pyrrho puts it: 'reason disagrees with itself'. And not satisfied with that, they set about self-critically to destroy their own arguments by arguing that no statement is truer than another, that 'every saying has its corresponding opposite'.[50] They recognised the self-flexivity of destruction, insisting that 'even this statement has its corresponding antithesis, so that after destroying others it turns round and destroys itself, like a purge which drives substance out and then in its turn is itself eliminated and destroyed'.[51] They saw themselves as determining nothing, 'not even the laying down of nothing'.[52] Quite in the spirit of Wittgenstein, they held that they 'were merely using words as servants, as it was not possible not to refute one statement by another'.[53] So even the Logos is here challenged, in its very locus in language.

Theirs was the first rational refutation of Reason. But, inevitably, it was merely a pyrrhic victory which had to end in ultimate defeat. The sceptics avowal of non-conclusiveness, indetermination, suspension of judgement (*epoché*) and denial of knowledge was merely the negative side of the metaphysical or dogmatic affirmation of being, knowledge of truth, certitude of reason, etc. The sceptics were not like modern nihilistic anti-metaphysicians; they could not implicitly dispense with metaphysics as everything they had to say was a mere negation of metaphysical truths, thus dependent on and bound up with metaphysics. Despite their denials, they had to presuppose the very dogmas they were attacking. Their own thinking inevitably came to rest on common custom and belief, commonsense language and a simple practical attitude to the world not unlike that of Linguistic philosophy. They could not develop any alternative knowledge of the world, or any philosophy of language. Other philosophers saw them merely as expounders of paradoxes, and exponents of another school of philosophy rather than critics of philosophy itself, for they had no alternative institutional basis. Thus, metaphysics eventually absorbed scepticism and strengthened itself by elaborating new ideas and arguments to counter its critiques. The Platonic Academy which temporarily became sceptical returned to an even more dogmatic Platonism.

When ancient scepticism came to be revived during the Renaissance it was not as a mere school of philosophy. The humanists who were sceptics could make a much more effective attack on metaphysics and theology because they were in a position to invoke a new sense of Man which had arisen since the time of the ancients. Even though they still cultivated paradoxicality and the art of destructive argumentation, they did not have to rely on critical reason alone; they could refer themselves to what Auerbach calls a medieval sense of the creatureliness of humankind: 'unaccommodated man is no more but such a poor, bare, forked animal' (*King Lear*, Act III, Scene IV). Man is not the 'rational animal' of Aristotle; he possesses neither infallible reason nor even knowledge: 'man lacks certain knowledge for he lacks true being', as Montaigne puts it. Man's reasoning is simply intelligence to be used in the first place for practical purposes, or as Bacon asserts:

We are endowed with reason not for the sake of speculation or of spinning out theories about things beyond our reach: we possess reason for the sake of action. For man's essence is action and not mere thought.[54]

Prefigured in this is the early modern Faustian conception of Man. Montaigne goes even further and anticipates the whole modern reconception of human being in terms of language: declaring 'nous ne sommes hommes et ne nous tenons les uns aux autres que par la parole'.[55] This appreciation of language was taken up by Shakespeare, perhaps the most profound of the Renaissance sceptics, who was also so much more than a mere sceptic. Shakespeare carried out a dramatic revision of such key metaphysical notions as essence, nature, truth and reason, which in its depth and scope constitutes a critique of rationality unsurpassed until Nietzsche, if at all.

Despite its undoubted achievement and power, Renaissance scepticism was doomed to fail and paradoxically to further the very thing it was against. Renaissance humanism could not hold out against the new theologies of the Reformation and counter-Reformation; the humanists had no institutional backing or support apart from the odd secular prince. The humanist sceptics, faced with the certitude of theology, were forced into fideism. Thus, Charron, after he had carried through a critical destruction of metaphysics, scholastic theology and reason as such, then went on to an acceptation of the 'supernatural certainty of faith'.[56] After him Pascal — whose scepticism already touches on modern existentialism and anticipates Kierkegaard — was also driven to the leap of faith of a gamble on infinite odds. And, as in one direction scepticism moves towards fideism, in the opposite direction it just as surely moves towards the new Rationalism of the sciences, as the examples of Bacon and Descartes demonstrate.

'The *Novum Organon* has no other goal than to set against the sterile uncertainty of reason left to itself the fruitful certitude of well-ordered experience.'[57] Thus a rationalist Empiricism was born out of sceptical doubt. And out of the same doubt emerged the even more rigorous Rationalism of Descartes. 'From Descartes' point of view at any rate, the sixteenth century landscape is completely dominated by the sceptical element; and among the influences that Descartes has to contend with, in the first place, that of Montaigne is paramount.'[58] Descartes' *Meditations* opens with a recapitulation of all the sceptical arguments known to him, most of which had a long history going right back to Pyrrho, who had already said 'the senses are deceivers'. Descartes takes this scepticism to its logical conclusion and begins by doubting everything including his own existence, a doubt which none of the ancients could have entertained, with the possible exception of Augustine.[59] Out of the abyss of this ultimate scepticism he triumphantly derives his 'Cogito' affirming the certitude of his own being; he demonstrates that scepticism must refute itself provided it is pursued to the ultimate limit, and that out of it there must emerge a new certitude that is much more proof against doubt than the truths of the old metaphysics. With the 'Cogito' as his first principle he can proceed further with his 'meditations on first philosophy' — for this is what it is to be, a new First Philosophy. Metaphysics has been abandoned and re-established, lost and found. For once Descartes proceeds from the 'Cogito' to the demonstration of the existence of God and the external world, he ineluctably returns to most of the old metaphysical assumptions and even to scholastic proofs, which shows that he could not doubt metaphysics altogether, but had merely temporarily suspended judgement on it through a new sceptical *epoché*. The metaphysical Tradition was at this point still too strong to be abandoned completely.

For all this is no mere idiosyncrasy of Descartes' philosophy alone; it is an inherent feature of post-Renaissance philosophic thought. Hobbes, the great opponent of Cartesianism, and an even greater foe of traditional metaphysics — 'The particular Tenets of Vain philosophy'[60] — proceeds, nevertheless, like Descartes towards the semblance of a new First Philosophy. Hobbes, too, begins with sceptical doubt concerning Reason and the metaphysics of the schools, which he had inherited from Bacon. He, too, bases himself on the senses, on experience and the faculties of human nature. He proceeds from this empiricism towards a new materialism because he accounts for mind in terms of motions in the body. This permits him to link his 'motive' epistemology with the new Galilean physics of motion. But, almost surreptitiously, out of this physics he derives a new metaphysics: 'consequences from Quantity and Motion indeterminate; which being the Principles or first foundation of Philosophy, is called Philosophia Prima'.[61] Since the new physics is no longer Aristotelian it follows that this Hobbesian metaphysics of motion cannot be like the old one of the prime mover; though, as in Descartes, there are still many old remnants there, as when Hobbes speaks of the 'matter, form, power of a commonwealth' using the old categories once again.

But of far greater importance than these survivals of the old metaphysics was the emergence of a new epistemological metaphysics based on the new science.

4. The First Secession

The first secession of the sciences from philosophy brought about a total reconstruction of knowledge and supplanted the dominance of Reason by that of Rationalism, but it was inherently incapable of destroying metaphysics. The new sciences had to have an epistemological basis that would act as a new metaphysics. Its main logical features were a method of analysis and synthesis ideally culminating in a 'mathesis understood as a universal science of measurement and order',[62] a general theory of representation applicable to signs, ideas and all knowledge,[63] a distinction between primary and secondary representations, or qualities, and finally, and most crucially, a basic dichotomy of subject and object, Ego and world. These principles were common to all epistemological schools of philosophy; and out of them derive all the problems, issues and disputes in which these schools were engaged. Thus, for example, the basic question: 'how can the mind come to know the world?' is one that could only have arisen within the epistemological *episteme*, for it makes little sense in any other problematic of philosophy.[64] In the context of contemporary philosophy, it is clearly a metaphysical question, like most of the others arising out of the epistemological problematic; though it would not have been considered metaphysical by those philosophers themselves, such as Hobbes, who defined metaphysics only in terms of Aristotle and the schoolmen. In relation to a contemporary post-metaphysical outlook all such epistemological questions are metaphysical. Though it must not be assumed, as Burtt does, that any basic principles constitute a metaphysics, that 'there is no escape from metaphysics, that is, from the final implications of any proposition or set of propositions'.[65] If that were so, then every philosopher and scientist today would be a metaphysician, which can only be true in a very trivial sense.

The manner in which the new science and epistemological philosophy following the first secession were at once anti-metaphysical in their own estimation and metaphysical in ours can be gauged by considering Newton's assumptions. Newton rejects the old metaphysical basis for science. This is most evident in

Newton's frequent asseverations that *'hypothesis non fingo'*: 'hypotheses, whether metaphysical or physical, whether occult qualities or mechanical, have no place in experimental philosophy'.[66] What Newton is attacking is 'hypothesis' in the Aristotelian metaphysical sense of *hypokeimenon*, the underlying causes of things, not, of course, hypothesis in a modern sense. What he means to eschew is any speculation about fundamental natures, about substrata, essences or substances, and to declare that his physics is purely a natural philosophy which relies solely on mathematical deductive reasoning from experimental evidence. Nevertheless, Newtonian physics was itself committed to the new epistemological metaphysics, despite its seemingly 'positivistic' traits of seeking merely to establish mathematical relations and laws governing observable phenomena. His definitions of his basic concepts of mass, ether, space and time are all metaphysically conceived. Even more explicitly, Newton's physics leaves room for the hand of God which is necessary to keep his celestial mechanics in orderly motion — a watch-winder God, as he later came to be called — and it is meant to serve as a demonstration of God's providence. Newton has this theological bias in common with most scientists of the period; as Weber remarks: 'you will see what the scientific worker, influenced (indirectly) by Protestantism and Puritanism, conceived to be his task: to show the path to God'.[67] It was not until Laplace in his *Mecanique Celeste* was able to show that the universe could move and adjust itself by its own inherent laws, and that a watch-winder God was not necessary, that he could finally declare to Napoleon, *'Sire, je n'ai pas besoin de cette hypothese . . .'*, using the word now in its modern sense.

The secession of the sciences from philosophy was a difficult social and ideological undertaking, for institutionally it involved a bitter struggle with the universities, where Aristotelian metaphysics was strongly entrenched. It was a great liberating achievement, as one by one each of the natural sciences established itself as a separate discipline. What was at stake in this struggle, and how it was carried on, is well illustrated by Pascal's experiments with Torricelli's barometer. The scholastics of the Sorbonne and the neo-Aristotelian Jesuits following Suarez considered a vacuum impossible on metaphysical grounds. Everything was a plenum, nothingness could not be. The very possibility of a vacuum they associated with the dangerous atomism of Democritus and the 'atheist' Epicurus and such modern followers as Gassendi. The existence of a vacuum at the end of a glass tube, they had to deny, just as they had previously denied Jupiter's moons seen through Galileo's telescope. For Pascal the vacuum was real not only because he could experimentally demonstrate it and because it fitted in with his new physics, but also because he could make it the starting point for an anti-Jesuit Jansenist theology: 'nothingness' exists because Man is trapped between nothing and infinity.

The struggle between science and the metaphysics of the university was only over when in the newly established scientific institution its president, Fontenelle, could proudly declare:

> Jusqu'à présent l'Académie des Sciences ne prend la nature que par petites parcelles. Nul système général . . . L'espirit del l'Académie des Sciences a donc toujours été l'esprit d'expéri-ence, d'étude directe, d'observation précise, l'amour de la certitude.   D'abord   Cartésienne   elle   devint   ensuit Newtonienne.[68]

A systematic parcelling out of nature, subjecting each piece to the new scientific method and experimental control: such was the scientific undertaking freed from the influence of Aristotelian metaphysics. One by one all the old metaphysical concepts were abandoned or totally redefined. Motion, void, atom or particle, action, force took on a different meaning, even monad and entelechy were transformed; mathematical laws became paramount as the whole universe ceased to be a harmonious cosmos and became a law-governed totality determined in every point or particle. Thus, for example, the old Aristotelian *hyle* which had become *materia* for the scholastics gradually transformed itself into Kepler's 'plump matter', eventually to become Newton's 'mass', subject to precise measurement and calculation. Of course, Newtonian mass possessing a *vis inertiae* was no positivistic operational concept, but an inherent ultimate property of all material bodies, and so it could serve as the basis of a new mechanistic metaphysics. And something similar could be said of most of the other key concepts; they emerged from the old metaphysics to enter a new one. It was not until the Scientific Positivists of the late nineteenth century: Mach, Hertz, Frege, Weierstrass and ultimately the young Einstein, that the sciences were finally purged of all metaphysical notions and rendered axiomatic and functional. By that stage the parcelling out of nature was complete, and the new scientific regime of miniscule specialisations in gigantic institutions, which would make Fontenelle's Academie look like a club of amateur nature lovers, was already at hand.

Sociologically considered it was the emergence of a new educational institution during the Renaissance, the academy, that made it possible for the new sciences to defeat the universities, and thus enabled the first secession from philosophy. It was this academicism behind the sciences that produced the intellectual climate of the dawning Enlightenment. The *ésprit de raison* or Rationalism was a liberating force, in the first place only for thought, but eventually for culture and society as well. At first it acted as an agent of the absolutist state in its fight against the semi-feudal privileges and anarchy of the estates, and it helped to further a new rational order in politics, religion, economy and art. The old medieval unity of cosmos and society broke up as these were divided into numerous separate spheres each independently subject to a rational ordering. Politics were reconceptualised around the doctrine of *raison d'état* and the rational-legal principles of sovereignty, contract and representation. Rational religion moved towards Deism. A new classicism in the arts academically ordained new orders of style and decorum. In the hands of the ruling court and its aristocrats, Rationalism meant order and classicism. But it came to mean the overthrow of this order in favour of 'natural' freedom when the bourgeoisie found themselves too constricted in their capitalist pursuits by the ancient regimes. Partly as a result of this and other, more intellectual reasons to do with the second secession of the sciences, Rationalism was transformed to become progressive rather than ordering.

In itself Rationalism (*Verstand*, subjective reason, etc.) is not peculiar to the modern period; in its earlier forms it long pre-dates the Enlightenment and even the Scientific Revolution. Very early examples of it are to be found in ancient science and philosophy. A first incipient formulation as a basis for science is to be associated with the university of Padua between the fourteenth and sixteenth centuries, 'where Averroism was strong and logic was studied as a preliminary to medicine, not law or theology'.[69] Needham goes on to elaborate the 'methodological theory', 'called at Padua *regressus*', which 'showed some similarity to the eventual practice of Galileo'.[70] This so-called 'theory' is formulated by Needham as follows:

1. Selection, from the detailed phenomena under discussion, of features which seem to be common to all of them (analysis, *resolutio*), complete enumeration being recognized as unnecessary because of faith in the uniformity of Nature and the representativeness of samples.
2. Induction of a specific principle by reasoning on the essential content of these features (also *resolutio*).
3. Deduction (synthesis in thought, *compositio*) of the detailed consequences of this hypothetical principle.
4. Observation of the same, and perhaps also similar, phenomena, leading to *verificatio* or *falsificatio* by experience, and in rare cases, by arranged experiment.
5. Acceptance or rejection of the hypothetical principle formulated in 2.[71]

We can see here *in nuce* the basic principles of the later Scientific Rationalism.

Scientific Rationalism is in the first place a constructive, ordering method that functions on the basis of analytic and synthetic moments. In the first of its moments Rationalism breaks down its given object along structural lines: it anatomises the body, articulates speech or the deliverances of the senses into their basic elements, divides up space into quasi-geometric point particles, differentiates a continuous line of motion into instantaneous infinitesimal increments, etc. In the second of its moments Rationalism builds up the elements so analysed into an ordered complex representation, a rational map or picture of the object represented. Thus each of the sciences forms a systematic ordered arrangement of its subject matter, or a table in which its objects are represented and clearly displayed. Such a table might be an anatomical plan, a taxinomia, a scheme of human understanding, a system of co-ordinates, a calculus, or ultimately a universal mathesis. And all of these together, supposedly constituting the whole of human knowledge, 'may be divided in such a manner as I have divided them in the following Table'[72] — as Hobbes puts it.

This classical Rationalism of the first secession could not as yet do without a metaphysics. As a principle of knowledge it had a method of scientifically explaining everything except itself. Every object could be analytically and synthetically represented and so known scientifically and rationally, except for that knowledge itself and the rational method governing it. To explain this a new First Philosophy or metaphysics was required. This metaphysics could no longer be one of being, for the unity and centrality of being had been broken up; there was only the being of different kinds of objects. Instead there was a new unity and centrality of knowing how different objects were apprehended, which could give rise to an epistemological metaphysics. It is because of this feature that Rationalism has been called a mode of subjective rationality and contrasted with the supposed 'objectivity' of Reason.[73] But this is something of a misnomer prior to Kant.

A subjective interpretation of rationality only enters much later with Kant's move towards transcendental subjectivity.[74] Prior to Kant, the philosophic schools of Rationalists and Empiricists expounded an 'objective' metaphysics of Rationalism. Both sought to discover a universal order in objects themselves as these are rationally understood. The process of ratiocination as knowledge or understanding or perception has to mediate the presentation of this rational order, but it does not create it or impose it on things themselves. Things reveal themselves to be inherently rational when they are rationally understood. This understanding is only subjective in so far as it occurs in minds; otherwise it is a universal process. It was only Kant who first made understanding (*Verstand*) dependent on the subjective categories of the mind, the categories as schemata for synthesising the manifold of apperception. By so subjectivising all knowledge, ranging from phenomenal perception to the ascription of laws to all of reality, and by imposing limits to the free speculation of reason (*Vernunft*) Kant succeeded in placing rationality on a subjective and so, potentially, also a developing basis.[75] His philosophy is one of the doors through which history opens on a new progressivist Rationalism. It is Janus-faced, looking back to the physics of Newton and forward to the new science of sociology of Durkheim, Simmel and Weber. Though unable to give up the aspiration for a future scientific metaphysics, it is, despite itself, the transition to the second secession of the sciences from philosophy that brought metaphysics to an end.

5.   The Second Secession

The second secession of the sciences from philosophy resulted from those transformations that ushered in the second phase of classical science. Decisive changes took place in the natural sciences which made them further removed from the previous epistemological metaphysics: physics moved towards greater mathematisation and abstraction; mathematics, too, developed the abstractions of non-Euclidian geometry and symbolic logic; chemistry became atomic and biology cellular.[76] Of even greater importance for philosophy were, however, the new sciences of life, history, society, culture, or in short the sciences of evolution and Man. All this brought about the beginning of the end of metaphysics, or at least its transformation into a form which no longer had any direct relation to traditional First Philosophy. And, simultaneously, it brought about a transformation of Rationalism from its classical to its progressivist mode.[77]

Progressivist Rationalism is inherent in the post-Enlightenment ideal of rational Progress. Rationality is viewed in terms of one or another of the concepts of Progress, be it development, evolution, concrete realisation, or the stages of history or production. Progress is seen as inherently rational, and rationality is seen as the outcome of Progress; the one defines the other: Progress is the realised movement of rationality, and rationality is what is unfolded in the course of Progress. Thus the progressive unfolding of the stages of development of anything is always judged to be a rational sequence which, though not necessarily teleological, does move toward some goal or fulfilment. Rationality is inherent not so much in any ultimate culminating *telos* or end, as it would be in metaphysical thought, but in the very process of self-development, which is held to be governed by rational law. Rationality thus becomes subject to temporality; it is no longer manifest all at once, all there in the one ever-present order or structure; rather it presents itself successively over time through the propulsion of a creative Deed of ordering and structuring. It no longer simply 'is', it 'becomes': becoming, not being, is its quasi-metaphysical subject.

It is sociologically apparent why this should have meant an end to traditional metaphysics. Progressive Rationalism negated every fixed order so that no unity of being could maintain itself in the face of universal development and change. The earlier epistemological Rationalism still maintained, though in a greatly altered form, all the old metaphysical principles of Being, God, Nature, Human Nature, Essence and Truth. With the onset of Progressive Rationalism, all these were set in motion — first subjected to continual transformation, then finally abandoned. Being became Becoming, God became Progress or History, Nature became raw material for human activity, Human Nature became Man the chief active agent, fixed Essence was abandoned in favour of existence, and Truth was relativised in terms of sequential stages.

According to Marx, this intellectual revolutionising process was brought about by the material revolutionary inroads of capitalism and carried through by the bourgeoisie:

> Constant revolutionising of production, uninterrupted disturbance of all social conditions, everlasting uncertainty and agitation distinguish the bourgeois epoch from all earlier ones. All fixed, fast-frozen relations, with their train of ancient and venerable prejudices and opinions, are swept away, all new-formed ones become antiquated before they can ossify. All that is solid melts into air, all that is holy is profaned, and man is at last compelled to face with sober senses, his real conditions of life, and his relations with his kind.[78]

Among the ancient and venerable prejudices and opinions that were thus swept away, metaphysics would hold a prominent place. But the belief that such a clean sweep would force man to face with sober senses his real conditions of life rests on an historical empiricism that is no longer credible. We have learned to read the critique of ideology as itself an ideology. Marx's Progressivist Rationality is by no means the sober truth of historical reason.

Despite evident differences, Progressivist Rationality is a mode of Rationalism; for even though it is rationality temporalised, it is as law-governed, ordered and inherent in things or processes themselves as the earlier classical Rationalism. It is also method-bound and analytic; and though no longer simply presenting tabular analyses outlining a structural order, it is itself, nevertheless, given to tracing regular sequences of development and drawing up tables of stages. The new Rationalism is also self-reflexive and critical, like the earlier. The laws of Progress function as the rational standards by which everything traditional may be criticised, as did the laws of Nature earlier. The very same laws apply self-critically to the thought or science that discovers them, so that all new knowledge is viewed as the rational culmination at once of Progress and of self-consciousness. This self-conscious philosophic conception of Progressivist Rationalism was first elaborated 'idealistically' by Hegel, but it was eventually interpreted 'materialistically' and much more scientistically by Marx and even Comte.

Under the intellectual aegis of Progressivist Rationalism, there took place that disciplinary separation and definition of most of our sciences which we have called the second secession of science from philosophy. It was mainly carried through within the new German university system, which began with the foundation of Berlin University around 1806. At first it meant a greatly expanded role for philosophy, which temporarily became encyclopaedic, but the eventual outcome as one after another of the sciences broke away was the reduction of philosophy to the status of merely one among many other academic disciplines. As Ben-David and Zloczower see it, 'the German university system provided the basis for the great development of philosophy as a systematic discipline. But contrary to the intention of the philosophers, the university system made philosophy into just one of the academic disciplines, and added to it a great many new ones'.[79] These authors go on to explain the sociological processes by which philosophy first expanded and then contracted as it was broken down into specialised disciplines, all of which were at first 'closely connected with the ideological bias of German philosophy'.[80] That philosophy was predominantly Idealism.

Thus, in its opening phase it was not at all apparent that the second secession of the sciences from philosophy would also signal the end of metaphysics. On the contrary, it seemed as if Idealism meant the revival of metaphysics and speculative reason despite the earlier restrictions imposed by Kantian Critical Philosophy. The Idealist *Naturphilosophie* culminating in Hegel's *Encyclopaedia* was taken as indicative of the recovery of the hold of metaphysics over the sciences — an attempt at the comprehension and unification of all the sciences such as had not been seen since Aristotle. As we now know, all this proved short-lived and chimerical.[81] Hegelian Idealism collapsed — though it did not disappear for reasons we shall explore later — and metaphysics was under attack as never before. The new varieties of sciences, above all the historical sciences of Man together with new evolutionary sciences of Time, were in the process of breaking away from philosophy and they eventually excluded metaphysics completely from any hold on reality. They did so precisely by occupying the intellectual space that had previously enabled Rationalist metaphysics to function: the epistemological ground of knowledge, method and rationality. This ground now became the province of the new sciences of the mind, logic, language, culture and society. It was precisely the field of epistemology, the locus of classical Rationalism, that was subjected to a new scientific understanding.

Empiricism and Rationalism in philosophy were no longer needed. The formation of ideas was to be explained from now on purely scientifically by the new science of psychology. This at first took a purely mechanistic guise in Associationism, as in the work of Thomas Brown and Dougal Stewart (1804), but very soon became Phenomenological in the work of Goethe, and eventually spread over every area of human mind, including the unconscious. Its challenge to philosophy became total with the appearance of Fechner's 'Psycho-physics' (1860), 'which seemed to hold out the prospect of introducing into philosophical discussion the definiteness and methodical treatment which had done so much for the natural sciences'.[82] A similar challenge to any metaphysics of ideas was posed by another presumptive science, that of Ideologie as founded by Destutt de Tracy (1804). This 'science', castigated by Napoleon as the work of mere 'ideologues', had little success until it transformed itself into ideological critique as part of Marx's science of historical materialism, itself established on the basis of a criticism of the new science of 'classical' economics founded earlier by Smith and Ricardo. The social formation of ideas was also the subject of the new science of sociology founded by Comte. The almost simultaneous foundation of symbolic logic by Boole, computation by Babbage and the non-Euclidean geometries by the pupils of Gauss had an equally decisive effect on all Rationalist metaphysics of deductive reasoning from indubitable axioms and of intuited laws of thought.

But perhaps the innovations most destructive of every metaphysical epistemology were those of the new cultural sciences (*Geisteswissenschaften*), developed largely in Germany. By the early eighteenth century Vico had prefigured a thorough critique of the Rationalism of Descartes and the Empiricism of Hobbes by means of a cultural theory of language and the historical development of knowledge. Knowledge derived neither from abstract reason nor sensory experience, neither from intuited truths nor constituted ideas, but from the slow historical growth of cultural forms, above all, of modes of language. Vico's views were taken up by Goethe (who discovered his work in Naples on his first Italian journey) and also by Herder and Hamann, none of whom ever fully realised or acknowledged their debt to him. Together they laid the basis for most of our cultural sciences: from comparative literature to folklore, from philology to the history of knowledge, from cultural anthropology to a theory of world-history.

The emergence of philology alone had manifold consequences for philosophy, and perhaps the first man fully to grasp this was Goethe's friend Humboldt. (We shall see how his folkish view of language as the primary communal expression of a people, with its anti-individualist bias, anticipated Wittgenstein's so-called private-language argument against the Cogito.) Humboldt decisively rejected the classical Rationalist view of language as a set of signs whose function it was to represent ideas through an arbitrarily established relation of association — a view which his contemporary, Hegel, still held and which de Saussure was partly to revive in the context of a new systemic linguistics. He propounded instead a theory of the word as an expressive element within a language seen as an organic whole charged with '*energeia*'. This Aristotelian notion, which he acquired through Leibniz and endowed with his own 'activist' meaning, reveals lingering shades of metaphysics. Thus, activity, or the Deed, became explicitly the foundation of language, and so implicitly also of all meaning and reality, something which no philosopher at the time had yet formulated. To Humboldt and the other key figures of Berlin University, philology meant much more than the study of language in the sense that contemporary linguistics now propounds. Philology was for them the basic form of all humanistic scholarship; in his history of this period Merz makes apparent the importance of philology as the focus for scholarship throughout the German university system, a role that it has scarcely lost in Germany even today.[83] Hermeneutics has continued to be its basic philosophical quasi-epistemology; from Schleiermacher, a contemporary of Humboldt at Berlin, it was passed on to Dilthey, who first formulated it as a 'method'; from there it was taken up by Heidegger, and it is even now being continued by Gadamer, Ricoeur and even Habermas. Nietzsche, too, was trained in classical philology and its hermeneutic techniques and he taught rhetoric at Basel, all of which is clearly reflected in his first philosophic work, *The Origin of Tragedy*. Many of his later philosophic moves are strictly speaking philological: for example his questionable use of changing word-usage for evidence of the master–slave morality distinction, his more substantial linguistic critique of moral values, and also his suggestive remarks on the relationship between the philosophical categories and grammar, which we shall examine critically later.

After Nietzsche the idea of Language has continued to play an ever increasing role in philosophy. One might almost say that what Being had been to metaphysics, Language became to post-metaphysical philosophy. It gradually became the primary object of philosophical thought, and many philosophies explicitly considered themselves to be philosophies of Language.[84]

The turning towards Language in modern philosophy, which derived to a decisive extent from Goethe and his circle, also inaugurated a new conception of activity and time. All this is symbolically prefigured in Faust's translation of the gospel's 'In the beginning was the Logos' as 'In the Beginning was the Deed'.[85] The transformation of Logos into Deed captures symbolically the inner meaning of the move away from traditional metaphysics. However, for Goethe himself, the Deed was still not all that far removed from its theological sources; what he elsewhere called '*das lebendiges Tun*' was a creative activity that infused all things, since anything that ceases to act, and so to become, is nothing.[86] Goethe invoked one or another mode of activity to account for the developmental becoming of all things: individual moral character as well as the whole of a natural species, faculties and colours as well as forms of art, language and society — all were explained in terms of metamorphoses comprising stages of maturation and growth broken by abrupt changes of form. And behind every developmental drive there was an active energetic force propelling the process onwards; for just as the force of growth pushes the single shoot to become the plant and flower, so the force of life drives the original, simple *Urpflanze* to develop itself and diversify into the botanical plant kingdom, and this also holds for all living beings.

The Faustian Deed can be seen as the originating principle of a succession of philosophies, mainly German, which emphasised the Deed, Time and Language, in the way we have seen inaugurated by Goethe and his circle.[87] Here we shall concentrate on the four key thinkers who together point to the range and diversity of modern thought: Marx, Nietzsche, Wittgenstein and Heidegger. We have referred to them as Faustian philosophers because in each there is some individual variant of the Deed as creative activity, of Time as developmental history and of Language as the basic mode of meaning. The differences between them are, nevertheless, enormous, so much so that one might present them as polar opposites, and this is how they are usually seen, but the terms in which they differ are the ones we have identified as following on from the originating Faustian pronouncement.

In the original pronouncement the Deed appears in its most ideal rendering, for Goethe sees Nature's activity as equivalent to God's creation, in his own pantheistic interpretation of this. In the hands of Marx, however, it is stripped of any ideal theological pretensions and becomes productive human labour through which the human world is created and recreated. For Nietzsche activity is the expression of the will to power in both its natural and human manifestations; in the latter case, these are acts of making and breaking values. It is activity that is primary for Wittgenstein: 'language — I want to say — is a refinement, "in the beginning was the deed"'.[88] For Heidegger, too, speaking and language are fundamental activities for Dasein, but activity goes further than this since Being activates itself in disclosing and concealing itself and so temporalising itself as History, particularly as the history of philosophy.

Thus it is that language, in the context of creative activity and historicity, plays a key function in the philosophies of these thinkers. In Marx the role of language is crucial, though it is not fully developed (as we shall see in the next chapter). But Marx does insist that:

> We find that man also possesses 'consciousness' but, even so, not
> . . . 'pure' consciousness. From the start the 'spirit' is afflicted
> with the curse of being 'burdened' with matter, which here makes
> its appearance in the form of agitated layers of air, sounds, in
> short of language. . . .[89]

Thus, whenever he wants to underline the common and social character of any activity he invariably likens it to language, which he calls 'common consciousness' and considers the key mode of social relationship. In Nietzsche language is explicitly invoked as the ground of all values and ideas, so much so that he evokes a sense of man's entrapment in the 'prison-house of language'. However, the creative activity of the will to power is continually active in transforming language and the whole of human culture. Language for Wittgenstein determines the basic 'forms of life', which are given and so fundamental; but as these 'forms' change so does language; Wittgenstein imaginatively envisages such possible changes by conceiving of different language-games of imaginary tribes. For Heidegger language is ultimately a matter of 'poetic' creativity; in this respect he returns to the views of language of Humboldt and Hölderlin; language determines the being of things for things are only 'there' when they are named: 'language is the house of Being', as he puts it.

Such a total reconception of activity, time and language also entails a reconception of the nature of Man. Faustian Man emerges as something of an *alter Deus* or creator-god: he creates his own human world which is central to the world as a whole. Faustian humanism breaks the close attachment of human nature to Nature that characterised prior humanisms; Man is no longer an integral part of a natural order, or of a Great Chain of Being, or of a creatureliness governed by Providence; he is no longer a mere rational animal or thinking mind. Man also ceases to be a naturally positive being and becomes fraught with negativity, since as creator of his world he can also be its destroyer; and, indeed, destroying, annihilating, alienating and, in general, negating become even more characteristic of human activity than creating and positing. Man becomes the sustainer of death and nothingness, which is thus reconceived in its modern form as Nihilism.

Early in the Faustian period the idea of Nihilism had a negative critical charge. The term was invented by Goethe's friend Jacobi as a way of castigating the subjectivism of Idealists such as Fichte whose emphasis on thought and negation was perceived as totally annihilating by the more positively and religiously inclined thinkers. Later the term took on favourable connotations when such left-Hegelians as Stirner and Bakunin began considering themselves destroyers of decadent bourgeois society and referring to themselves as nihilists. Nietzsche derived the term from the political activities of the Russian nihilists, who by then had turned to 'the propaganda of the deed', but he deepened its meaning by his conception of the destruction of values. All subsequent thinkers of Nihilism have followed Nietzsche; Weber invokes it as part of his critique of rationalisation and Progress; Spengler, Jünger and Heidegger give it a more 'metaphysical' signification; Adorno and Anders apply it as an already known concept. These latter thinkers have emphasised that since nuclear weapons have made possible the self-annihilation of Man, the idea of Nihilism has been given a much more concrete meaning than it possessed before, and in the face of this possibility any thought of transcendence or metaphysical Being becomes meaningless in a far stronger sense than that invoked by the Positivists.

Throughout the period of the second secession and almost until now, one form of modern 'metaphysics' did, nevertheless, persist despite all the previously outlined anti-metaphysical currents, and that was Idealism. This was no mere reactionary historical revival, such as neo-Thomism, but a genuinely new development. It is very difficult to account sociologically for the fact that Idealism in philosophy, and partly in culture generally, should have arisen and continued during a period inhospitable to speculative thought. How was it possible that a neo-metaphysical trend in the sciences, called *Naturphilosophie*, as well as the associated philosophy based on the Idea or ideal Reason, should have flourished at a time when metaphysics was otherwise coming to an end? When it is recalled that Idealism was coeval with Positivism its seemingly anomalous historical character becomes even more pronounced.

The origin of Idealism in Germany is a little less surprising historically given the fact that, even during the first part of the nineteenth century, the modern economic, political and social changes that elsewhere spelled the end of more traditional modes of thought had not yet taken place there. Instead, religious revivals such as those of Pietism and Catholicism occurred, and the secular creed of nationalism was launched to develop a common German national consciousness and beat back French radicalism. All of these ideologies shaped the German cultural revival and determined the form that philosophy would take, predisposing it to speculative quasi-theological and historicising thinking with little practical relevance. But Idealism was no historical aberration peculiar to Germany alone, for after Hegel — when it largely declined in Germany as a result of socio-economic changes and the move to the natural sciences in the universities — it spread successively to France (Cousin and Proudhon), to England (Coleridge and Bradley), to America (Emerson and Royce) and to Italy (Croce and Gentile). Everywhere there were neo-Idealist revivals, even in this century: Lukacs, Adorno, Collingwood, Whitehead, Sartre and academic Hegelians such as Kojeve and Hippolite in France all kept it alive and testify to its continuing relevance.

According to Marx, Idealism is a form of 'German ideology' designed to mystify and disguise the real socio-economic conditions. But such a view is overly reductive and fails to account for the role Idealism continued to play in cultural trends in the arts, religion, law, morality and politics, which were not merely ideological in a narrow sense, and figured in the very movement he founded. It is true that Idealism was not generally out of touch with the more concrete historical realities and that it contributed little to the sciences; in that respect it was akin to movements in the arts which were free-floating and at a relative remove from their determining conditions. In its origins Idealism shared something with the contemporaneous revivals of neo-Attic classicism and neo-Gothic romanticism, the latter closer to Schelling and the former to Hegel; though both these opposed tendencies were closely related and came together in what one might call a common romantic-classicism. This artistic movement, like Idealism, had no direct bearing on economy or science, but it influenced deeply the cultural, moral and political climate.

Idealism is like an art movement; its thinkers freely dispose of ideas in a speculative way akin to the artist's handling of figures and forms. It is obvious that in Hegel's *Phenomenology* some of the main thought-themes are figures drawn from actual world drama, *Antigone* for instance, and the whole work is a dramatic odyssey not unlike *Faust Part II*. It has been said that it is history without names or dates, but moreover it is also history transformed into drama. Even in his most rigorous works, such as the *Logic*, it often seems that the metaphysical figures drawn from past philosophy are being rearranged and freely disposed in a new order. This could be done only because metaphysics had ceased to have any living reality or relevance for the sciences. In late Hegel and Schelling this 'art of ideas' subserved a conservative ideological purpose; the apotheosis of philosophy as Absolute knowledge or as Revelation provided the basis for an intellectualised Christianity.

Thus, Idealism as a movement can be located in the context of the historical revivals, particularly in culture and art, whose function was by no means simply ideological, but had deeper psychological roots. For as well as being oriented to the past, later Idealisms tended also to look to the future and develop utopian visions. Invariably it was the 'materialistic' present that was unacceptable. Psychologically speaking, the move towards Idealism is a sublimating and spiritualising tendency in reaction against an unacceptable material reality. The appeal of Idealism for radical intellectuals is that it provides them with a rationale for their own temporary failures in the assurance of a future that is on their side, that is, on the side of Spirit, Freedom, rational Progress, self-consciousness or whatever other ideal values they espouse. They could reconstitute in thought the existing reality and so gain a measure of intellectual control over it by affirming the superiority of thought as the rational element in existence. Idealism can serve as an inner rationalisation in Freud's sense to counteract the outer rationalisation of society in Weber's sense.

In its historical role, Idealism is at the opposite pole to Positivism, the dominant philosophy of the period of the second secession of the sciences. And just as Idealism was difficult to explain sociologically because it stood out so sharply against the main trends of its time, so Positivism by contrast seems all too easy to explain for it is in keeping with all these trends. Positivism is at one with the natural sciences, technology, the more scientistic social sciences, as well as with economy, positive law and the rational–legal state. During its history the changes within Positivism from one kind of school to another are also in keeping with the sociological make-up of their respective periods: the sociological Positivism of Comte was characteristic of the reformist bourgeois early nineteenth century; the scientific Positivism of Mach and Weber was characteristic of the industrialised state at the turn of the century; the Logical Positivists were symptomatic of the logical utopian plans made between the wars and in the immediate post-World War II period; and even Linguistic Positivism can be sociologically related to social developments in England. (In the next chapter we will examine these schools further in the context of an account of scientific reduction.)

Throughout its history Positivism was always closely involved with the sciences; it provided the dominant and generally accepted interpretation of Scientific Method, or methodology, as it was eventually called by the later Positivists. This Scientific Method became so pronounced an expression of the nature of science that already Nietzsche was impelled to speak of its ascendency as 'the victory of scientific method over science'.[90] This was not strictly speaking true, for Scientific Method bore little relevance to the actual practices of the sciences and had little effect on their inner development. Nevertheless, it acted as the prevailing ideology of science, one which is still dominant to this day, and as such it did help to legitimate and so further the changes that led to the new techno-science of the present. This was particularly the case when Logical Positivism was transplanted to the New World, where the decisive changes in the sciences that inaugurated the third secession took place.

6.   The Third Secession

The third secession of science from philosophy occurred when the sciences entered the contemporary epoch of Big Science, that is, science organised for the production of knowledge, frequently along industrial lines, with the result that it is symbiotically fused with technology and becomes techno-science. Its main characterising features, those which distinguish it decisively from the previous epoch of classical science from Newton till Einstein, are technification, formalisation, abstraction, problem-solving and finalisation. Technification means the predominance of technological instrumentation and routine technical procedures and methods over theory creation in the production of scientific results; this is evident both in the applied and pure sciences and has had the cumulative effect of breaking down this earlier classical distinction. Formalisation refers to the axiomatic elaboration of closed or already completed theories as formal systems; it is to be found mainly in the mathematicised, restricted sciences and in academic, 'pure' science generally. Abstraction results from the prevalence of constructive procedures and model building at a great remove from the actual objects to be explained and controlled. Problem-solving is the form that ·most scientific work takes, the aim being to find solutions to intellectually contrived problems resulting from theoretical or applied concerns. Finalisation (a term introduced by a new German school of sociologists of science) refers to the dependence of much contemporary science on externally stipulated ends and goals (final causes in Aristotle's sense) for the further development of theory, given that the autonomous goals of classical science have already been fulfilled in general terms and that consequently most fundamental theories are in a mature or completed form, leaving scope only for what might be called applied theories.[91]

These features also serve as defining characteristics of scientific Rationalisation (*Zweckrationalität*, instrumental or means–ends reason), the dominant form of rationality in our time. The distinctive character of this form of rationality was already evident to Weber well before the sciences assumed Big Science proportions. Weber distinguishes two senses of rationality:

> It means one thing if we think of the kind of rationalization the systematic thinker performs on the image of the world: an increasing theoretical mastery of reality by means of increasingly

precise and abstract concepts. Rationalism means another thing if we think of the methodical attainment of a definitely given and practical end by means of increasingly precise calculation and adequate means.[92]

These two senses of rationality correspond approximately to the difference between Rationalism and Rationalisation in our sense.

Rationalisation is a mode of calculating and controlling rationality, which is why technology is one of its paradigmatic manifestations. It is also evident outside science in systematic planning, bureaucracy and the organisation of monopoly capitalist or centrally-planned modes of production. Thus only the final stages of the whole historical process, which Weber rather misleadingly calls rationalisation throughout, actually amount to rationalisation in our sense of the term. This social process of Rationalisation explains the emergence of the new rationalised science; but at the same time its further course is itself explained by the inroads of this science into society; more and more dimensions of society become rationalised as they are based on scientific knowledge, frequently derived from the social sciences.

The simplest principle behind Rationalisation is that of recursive repetition and exact replication. Science is rationalised by becoming increasingly a matter of reliable repetition, as Whitley has observed:

> Generally speaking, the more control scientists can exert over their cognitive environment so that task outcomes are predictable and visible — i.e. *reliably replicable* — the lower is task uncertainty in that field. . . . Replicability is, therefore, seen as varying across sciences as a consequence of the degree of technical control achieved by a field and the amount of background knowledge which is taken for granted.[93]

Rationalisation as calculation and control works by bringing things down to standard, uniform units that can be reproduced and manipulated at will. Ultimately these will be the basic nuclear units: the nucleus of the atom, the nucleus of the cell, and the nuclear family, the basic social unit. Where something cannot be physically reduced to repeatable units, it is modelled as such, and by means of the model it is then suitably engaged and controlled.

Computer modelling is the most advanced form of rationalisation. To rationalise an activity ultimately means to programme it for a computer; and this means to reduce it to the most basic recursive units of information, ultimately the recursive repetition of the logical units 0 and 1. The attempt has been made to rationalise all activities in this way, including the most highly intellectual and creative ones, and a sub-discipline called 'Artificial Intelligence' has arisen for this purpose. To its advocates there are no limits to the possibilities of rationalisation; the question they raise 'is whether or not every aspect of human thought is reducible to a logical formalism, or to put it into the modern idiom, whether or not human thought is entirely computable'.[94] Weizenbaum answers this question firmly in the negative, and denounces this project as 'the imperialism of instrumental reason'; he also explicitly refers to it as 'a new rationality'.[95] He contrasts this rationality, which we have called rationalisation, with another kind that 'is not automatically and by implication equated to computability and to logicality',[96] and 'may not be separated from intuition and feeling'.[97] Apart from this Weizenbaum does not specify what other kind of rationality he has in mind, though Reason and Rationalism would both qualify.

These basic techniques of Rationalisation are not new. Babbage already had a plan for building a computer early last century, and analogous rationalising ideas for computable languages of signs were extant much earlier. Formal logic, the basic model of all such rationalising procedures, in some respects goes back to Aristotle. Nor are the rationalising processes in society new; most of them were already extant in the nineteenth century, if not before. This shows that there are no simple sequential stages in the historical development of rationality. One cannot treat Rationalisation as a higher stage evolving out of Rationalism, for many of the features of Rationalisation were already present even before Rationalism became the dominant intellectual ideal. Nevertheless, there was in actual fact an historical relation between these forms of rationality; the one helped pave the way for the other. The unintended historical effect of Progressive Rationalism in science and society was unknowingly to make it possible for rationalisation to take place. Rationalisation can be considered the unconscious 'Other' of progressive Rationalism.

There was a hidden nexus between the ideals of Progress and Rationalisation from the start. Progress furnished principles of development and liberation which overcame all traditional resistance; and so it enabled rationalisation to proceed much faster and to enter areas of life from which it had been excluded before. Every sphere of activity, every sector of society, even every individual or thing was freed from its place in any fixed order or hierarchy and allowed to develop autonomously according to its own laws. The idea of active self-realisation was the leading principle of the sciences and philosophies of the period and this fitted in well with the rationalising requirements of modern capitalism and of the State in freeing society from traditional restrictions. Active self-realisation was also applied to the autonomous development of each of the sciences; every science, freed from metaphysical surveillance, could separate itself functionally from every other science and proceed to investigate its own delimited field of research with its own methods and techniques. As a result, the eventual rationalisation of the sciences became possible, starting with their professionalisation.

Within the university rationalisation produced departmental separations as the universe of knowledge was parcelled out through a division of labour between the sciences. Philosophy was pushed into a specialised department of its own and gradually displaced from any substantive area of knowledge. It could only find room for itself in the temporarily unoccupied gaps between the sciences. This process had already begun much earlier during the second secession. As metaphysics was driven out from all natural and cultural reality by the new sciences, so simultaneously was room opened up between the sciences for new modern non-metaphysical philosophies to fill. But then these philosophies too were continually expelled by the formation of yet other sciences filling the gaps between the older ones. Still more specialised philosophies were devised to escape the newer sciences, and these, too, were then threatened by still further scientific developments. The structure of this total economy of knowledge following on the second secession does explain the bewildering proliferation of usually short-lived schools of philosophy whose ruins litter the historical landscape of the nineteenth and twentieth centuries. In most cases, each of these schools resulted from a specific configuration of sciences between whose interstices it was designed to fit. The total field of philosophy thus became fragmented and scattered as each philosophy could only be partial, and none could any longer hope for a general system to cover everything.

The process of fragmentation and displacement of philosophy begun earlier seems about to complete itself in this era of the third and perhaps final secession of science. There seems no place for philosophy at all among the technosciences in the technocratic 'multiversity', the current successor of the old university. It is temporarily tolerated as an antiquarian fossil only when it keeps to its own department. Outside it has no relevance. The sciences hem it in from all sides and remove the ground from any aspect of reality it might wish to occupy. The natural sciences deprive it of any say on the old philosophical issues, such as matter, space, time, the nature of life, or of the universe. The social sciences reject all its assumptions about history, language or knowledge. On behalf of a new discipline, the science of science, which is to take over from the philosophy of science, Elias pronounces the concluding expulsion of philosophy from science:

> Transcendental philosophers often claim that they can prescribe for sciences generally. Their claim ought to be firmly rejected. Theirs is an esoteric enterprise of no relevance to the work of social scientists, and probably not to that of natural scientists either.[98]

Bereft of all relevance to knowledge, philosophy seems about to come to an end. This final outcome is not, however, fore-ordained, nor is it completely necessitated by present intellectual conditions. It is true that the history of metaphysics is now a closed book. It holds for us no unrealised possibilities or undiscovered truths. For us the question 'what is metaphysics' can only be answered in the past tense: metaphysics is what it was. But this harsh verdict is not completely applicable to philosophy itself.

Notes

1. See the classic work, E. A. Burtt, *The Metaphysical Foundations of Modern Physical Science* (Routledge & Kegan Paul, London, 1964). A particularly striking example is the concept of 'mass', which derived from the metaphysical *hyle* via a long and involved detour, historically traced in the work of Max Jammer, *Concepts of Mass in Classical and Modern Physics* (Harvard University Press, Cambridge, Mass., 1961).
2. The other reason why this work will concentrate more extensively on philosophy and science is that I have already examined the relationship of modern philosophy to some of the other cultural spheres in *In the Beginning was the Deed: Reflections on the Passage of Faust* (University of California Press, Berkeley, 1982).
3. For a more detailed discussion of these epochs of science, in particular of the last mentioned, see my *The Ends of Science: An Essay in Scientific Authority* (forthcoming).

4. Michael Foucault, *The Order of Things* (Tavistock Publications, London, 1970), pp. 250–2.

5. For a more extensive discussion of these features and a further development of the arguments see my *The Ends of Science* (forthcoming).

6. The term was first introduced and explained by G. Boehme, W. van den Daele and W. Krohn. See their joint article 'Finalization in Science' in *Social Science Information*, 15 (2/3), pp. 307–30.

7. Quoted in S. Toulmin, *Human Understanding* (Princeton University Press, Princeton New Jersey, 1977), p. 146.

8. 'What is Metaphysics' in *Martin Heidegger: Existence and Being*, W. Brock (ed.) (Henry Regnery Company (Gateway Edn.), Chicago, 1970), p. 347.

9. Marx and Engels, *The German Ideology*, C. J. Arthur (ed.) (International Publishers New York, 1972), p. 48.

10. M. Horkheimer, *The Eclipse of Reason* (The Seabury Press, New York, 1974), pp. 3–11. The Frankfurt School thinkers conflate under subjective reason both the categories of Rationalism and Rationalisation, so that they treat subjective reason as also formal and instrumental reason; as Horkheimer puts it: 'as reason is subjectivized, it also becomes formalized' (ibid., p. 7). The effect of this conflation is very far-reaching; for example, it prompts them not to differentiate the Enlightenment and the contemporary technological world-civilisation.

11. Ibid., p. 10.

12. *Leviathan*, A. D. Lindsay (ed.) (Everyman, London, 1965), p. 367, chap. 46.

13. W. Jaeger, *Aristotle*, trans. R. Robinson (OUP, Oxford, 1962), p. 378.

14. Ibid., p. 379.

15. *Metaphysics* in *The Basic Works of Aristotle*, trans. R. McKeon (Random House, New York, 1961), p. 731, book IV, chap. I.

16. Ibid., p. 732.

17. Ibid., p. 732.

18. Ibid., p. 732.

19. Ibid., p. 732.

20. Cf. *Metaphysics*, book V, chap. 7 in *The Basic Works of Aristotle*, pp. 760–1.

21. Ibid., book IV, chap. 2, pp. 732–5.

22. F. Nietzsche, *Will To Power*, W. Kaufmann (ed.) (Vintage, New York, 1968), sec. 331, p. 181.

23. Horkheimer, *The Eclipse of Reason*, p. 181.

24. Jaeger, *Aristotle*, p. 196.

25. Ibid., p. 222.

26. *Metaphysics*, p. 779.

27. Ibid., p. 779.

28. Jaeger, *Aristotle*, p. 219. This initial close relation between metaphysics and theology has never been completely severed. It is always a very nice distinction to differentiate between being *qua* being and God, especially given the Old Testament characterisation of God as 'I am that I am' read as pure being by the Christian Theologians. Most theology, Christian as well as Muslim and Judaic — in so far as theology developed in these latter religions — was based on metaphysics, specifically that of Aristotle. The only other body of theological thinking, the Indian, was based on a metaphysics indigenous to Indian thought; though it is possible that it, too, was influenced by Aristotle and the Hellenistic schools. Heidegger goes as far as to consider all metaphysics basically theological, defining it as onto-theo-logy, or the logos-of the being of-God, and in this way he hopes to differentiate his own thought — which is directed to Being, but not God — as not itself metaphysical.

29. Ibid., p. 387.

30. *Metaphysics*, p. 732.

31. Ibid., p. 872.

32. Ibid., p. 812.
33. Jaeger, *Aristotle*, p. 375.
34. Ibid., p. 375.
35. Ibid., p. 406.
36. Ibid., p. 403.
37. B. Farrington, *Greek Science: Part Two* (Penguin, 1949), p. 47.
38. Cf. *Satirical Sketches*, 'Philosophies Going Cheap', trans. P. Turner (Penguin, 1961), p. 163.
39. See Farrington, op. cit., p. 15. 'From the Lyceum and its offshoot, the Museum of Alexandria, proceed in the two hundred years which separate Aristotle from Hipparchus a succession of great organized treatises on various branches of science — botany, physics, anatomy, physiology, mathematics, astronomy, geography, mechanics, music, grammar — which, largely modelled on the works of Aristotle himself and embodying and developing their spirit, constitute, with the addition of a few later contributions from men such as Dioscorides, Ptolemy, and Galen, the high water mark of the achievements of antiquity, and the starting point of the science of the modern world.'
40. '. . . it belongs to the philosopher, i.e. to him who is studying the nature of all substance, to inquire also into the principles of syllogism . . . and the most certain principle of all is that regarding which it is impossible to be mistaken . . . it is, that the same attribute cannot at the same time belong and not belong to the same subject and in the same respect . . .' (*Metaphysics*, IV, 3, op. cit., p. 736).
41. See De Lacy O'Leary, *How Greek Science Passed to the Arabs* (Routledge & Kegan Paul, London, 1949), p. 45. 'Christianity set a body of theological doctrine in the forefront . . . All this doctrine was strongly coloured by philosophy, much of it was simply philosophy expressed in theological terms . . . the eclectic philosophy to be derived from Plato and Aristotle . . . Perhaps the most salient point is the adoption of Aristotelian logic as the means of investigation and argument . . . the chief source of scientific and philosophical material received by the Arabs came through Christian influence.'
42. Quoted by Wolfgang van den Daele, 'The Social Construction of Science' in E. Mendelsohn and R. Whitley (eds), *Sociology of the Sciences Yearbook 1977* (Reidel, Dordrecht, Holland, 1977), p. 31.
43. *Prolegomena to any Future Metaphysics*, trans. Peter Lucas (Manchester University Press, Manchester, 1966), p. 137.
44. Hegel's own concluding summation of metaphysics is already prefigured in the *Metaphysics* of Aristotle. It, too, begins with a critical summarising history of the whole development of the basic principles of thought from the earliest thinkers, the Ionian 'physicist', down to itself. The history of thought is, thus, incorporated into the very thinking with which this history concludes. Hegel only had to historicise this organic, forming method of thought, and range over a much larger span of philosophical activity, to arrive at his own dialectical method of presentation.
45. Foucault *The Order of Things*, p. 317.
46. Ibid., p. 317.
47. See Michael Oakeshott, *Rationalism in Politics* (Methuen, London, 1962), pp. 197–206: 'The voice of philosophy . . . is unusually conversable, there is no body of philosophical "knowledge" to become detached from the activity of philosophizing . . .'
48. *Will to Power*, p. 241, sec. 437.
49. Quoted in *From Aristotle to Plotinus*, T. V. Smith (ed.) (Chicago University Press, Chicago, 1965), pp. 179–80.
50. Ibid., p. 173.
51. Ibid., pp. 173–4.
52. Ibid., p. 173.

53. Ibid., p. 174.
54. Quoted by A. Koyré in *Descartes Philosophical Writings*, E. Anscombe and P. T. Geach (eds) (Nelson, London, 1964), p. xii.
55. Quoted by A. Wilden (ed.), *The Language of the Self* (Dell Publishing, New York, 1975), p. 159.
56. Koyré, *Descartes Philosophical Writings*, p. xi.
57. Ibid, p. xii.
58. Ibid, p. xiii.
59. For the difference between traditional scepticism and the new kind deployed by Descartes see the comment by Richard Rorty, *Philosophy and the Mirror of Nature*, p. 94.

> I want to distinguish between 'mere', or Pyrrhonian, skepticism and the specifically 'Cartesian' form of skepticism which invokes the 'veil of ideas' as a justification for a skeptical atitude. 'Pyrrhonian' skepticism, as I shall use the term, merely says 'We shall never be certain, so how can we ever know?' 'Veil of ideas' skepticism, on the other hand, has something more specific to say, viz. 'Given that we shall never have certainty about anything except the contents of our own minds, how can we ever justify an inference to a belief about anything else?' For a discussion of the intertwining of these two forms of skepticism see Richard Popkin, *The History of Scepticism from Erasmus to Descartes*.

I believe this comment does not do full justice to Pyrrho himself or ancient scepticism in general, which in some respects was more radical than anything which succeeded it, including Cartesian doubt, as, for example, in its denial of reason and judgement.
60. *Leviathan*, chap. 46, p. 367, 1965.
61. Ibid., chap. IX, p. 42.
62. Foucault, *The Order of Things*, p. 56.
63. For the role of representation, or the 'mirroring of nature', see R. Rorty, *Philosophy and the Mirror of Nature*. A general theory of representation to cover all knowledge, language and politics was first developed by Hobbes. However, the problem of representation in science, art, theology, politics, etc. goes back to the Renaissance and beyond. Indeed, representation in a general sense is a key issue in the whole Western intellectual tradition. It is still the leading issue now in what can be called the modern crisis of representation in art, science and politics. See my paper 'Character, Action and Representation in Marx'.
64. See Rorty, *Philosophy and the Mirror of Nature*, p. 94.
65. Burtt, *The Metaphysical Foundations of Modern Physical Science*, p. 224.
66. Isaac Newton, *Principles*, II, 314.
67. Max Weber, 'Science as a Vocation' in *From Max Weber*, Gerth and Mills (eds) (OUP, Galaxy, 1958), p. 142.
68. Quoted in J. T. Merz, *A History of European Scientific Thought in the 19th Century* (Dover, New York, 1965), vol. I, p. 135.
69. Joseph Needham 'Mathematics and Science in China and the West' in B. Barnes (ed.), *Sociology of Science* (Penguin, Harmondsworth, England, 1972), p. 35.
70. Ibid., p. 35.
71. Ibid., pp. 35–6.
72. *Leviathan*, chap. IX, p. 41.
73. See Horkheimer, *The Eclipse of Reason*, chap. I.
74. For a succinct statement of the distinction between Kant's transcendental subjectivity and the prior philosophies of 'ontological knowledge' see P. Gajdenko, 'Ontological Foundation of Scientific Knowledge' in *Epistemological and Social Problems of the Sciences in the Early Nineteenth Century*, H. N. Jahnke and M. Otte

(eds) (Reidel, Dordrecht/Holland, 1981), p. 58. 'Only with Kant . . . for the first time the manner of cognition is not determined by the nature and structure of the recognizable substance but by those of the knowing subject, and the latter creates the object of cognition itself, as well as the means and methods of its construction.' Gajdenko, however, over-emphasises the role of ontology in the prior philosophy; he places too much weight on the ontological proof of God in Descartes, something which is totally absent in the Empiricists.

75. The move from Kant's universalistic transcendental subjectivity to the historicist subjectivity of Idealism is well brought out by Gajdenko in his 'Ontological Foundation of Scientific Knowledge', ibid., p. 61.

76. As regards mathematics, W. Scharlan has this to say: 'What we understand today as pure mathematics, namely, theoretical mathematics in which mathematical theories are developed for their own sake and then applied to particular mathematical problems for their solution, first existed around the beginning of the 19th century.' 'The Origins of Pure Mathematics' in *Epistemological and Social Problems of the Sciences in the Early Nineteenth Century*, p. 332.

77. A concise statement of this transition is to be found in the opening paragraph of the article by Michael Heidelberger: 'Some Patterns of change in the Baconian Sciences of the early 19th Century Germany' in *Epistemological and Social Problems of the Sciences in the Early Nineteenth Century*, p. 3.

> Gillespie once made the remark that the Encyclopedists boasted of having liberated science from metaphysics and that the generation succeeding them after the French revolution completed this emancipation by taking away from science even ontology — and not only that; any claim to grasp reality beyond controlled observation, experience and experiment became utterly impossible. For the generation of the philosophes science still was the source of gaining knowledge of the objective reality and, in turn, this knowledge was taken as the source for the enlightened perfection of man. In the post-revolutionary phase no effort was spared to make the sciences of the dynamic motor of human history and social development. The claims that science gains knowledge in the old sense of the word are coming to be forgotten, sometimes they are redefined and often negated. The ideal of an enlightenment through knowledge and cognition undergoes a profound change and it turns into the vision of progress by prediction and control.

78. See *Marx Engels: Selected Works*, vol. I, *Manifesto of the Communist Party*, 'Bourgeois and Proletarian' (Foreign Languages Publishing House, Moscow, 1951), p. 36.

79. J. Ben-David and A. Zloczower, 'The Growth of Institutionalized Science in Germany', B. Barnes (ed.), *Sociology of Science* (Penguin 1972), p. 50.

80. Ibid., p. 51.

81. This is, however, not to deny that *Naturphilosophen* produced some impressive results in many sciences. For an appreciation of these achievements see Michael Hamburger and P. Gajdenko in *Epistemology and Social Problems of the Sciences in the Nineteenth Century*, pp. 5 and 62.

82. Merz, vol. III, p. 179.

83. Merz, *History of European Scientific Thought in the 19th Century*, vol. I, chap. II.

84. For example, F. Mauntner, *Beiträge zu einer Kritik der Sprache* (Cotta, Stuttgart, 1901).

85. Goethe, *Faust*, Part I, 'Study', trans. P. Wayne (Penguin, Baltimore, 1962).

86. Goethe, the poem 'Eins und Alles' in D. Luke, ed., *Goethe* (Penguin, 1964), p. 274.

87. For a further exposition of this and succeeding points see my *In the Beginning was the Deed: Reflections on the Passage of Faust*, Act I.

88. *Culture and Value*, G. H. von Wright (ed.) (Blackwell, Oxford, 1980), p. 31.

89. Marx and Engels, *The German Ideology*, pp. 50–1.

90. Nietzsche, *Will to Power*, sec. 446, p. 261.

91. G. Boehme, W. van den Daele and W. Krohn, 'Finalization in Science' in *Social Science Information*, 1976, 15 (2/3).

92. Weber in *From Max Weber*, H. Gerth and C. Wright Mills (eds), p. 293.

93. R. Whitley, 'Sciences as Reputational Organizations' in *Scientific Establishments and Hierarchies*, N. Elias, H. Martins and R. Whitley (eds), *Sociology of the Sciences Yearbook 1982* (Reidel, Dordrecht, 1982), p. 335 and fn. p. 356.

94. J. Weizenbaum, *Computer Power and Human Reason* (W. H. Freeman, San Francisco, 1976), p. 12.

95. Ibid., p. 257.

96. Ibid., p. 255.

97. Ibid., p. 256.

98. N. Elias, 'Scientific Establishments', *Sociology of the Sciences Yearbook 1982*, p. 37.

2 THE END OF METAPHYSICS

1. The Socio-logic of Reduction

> For why has the advent of Nihilism become *necessary*? Because the values we have had hitherto thus draw their final consequence; because Nihilism represents the ultimate logical conclusion of our great values and ideals — because we must experience Nihilism before we can find out what value these 'values' really had. — We require, sometime, *new values*.[1]

The highest values and ideals of Western civilisation were enshrined in its metaphysics. According to Nietzsche these must reach their logical and historical conclusion, and by all accounts it looks as if metaphysics too has come to its end. It has been pronounced meaningless by some modern schools of philosophy, irrelevant by most others, and declared dead in nearly every contemporary mode of thought. It is now about to be consigned to the oblivion of history. Philosophy itself is not yet in quite that state, but seems to be approaching it. If philosophy, too, were to end it would be as the ultimate consequence of the end of metaphysics. The same historical process that brought about the closure of metaphysics would reach its logical conclusion in the end of philosophy.

This long 'argument' of history, which we studied previously, is a development that is social, and so to be studied sociologically, but also rational, and so to be investigated socio-logically. It can be called the sociological and socio-logical process of reduction. For if it were taken as literally the 'argument' of history then it would be a *reductio-ad-absurdum*, and its conclusion would be the *absurdum* towards which the *reductio* is tending. It is the same *absurdum* that had already received from Nietzsche the fateful name of Nihilism.

The socio-logic of reduction is the historical process inherent in Nihilism. It is to be found at work in philosophy just as much as in art, morality, religion and every other cultural sphere. However, its basic source is science; it most often emerges from science, and from there too derives the means for its reductive attack on the rest of culture. Ours is now a scientific–technological civilisation whose most basic mode of apprehending anything is through scientific reduction. However, not every mode of reduction is scientific; there are many other ways of reducing and these differ markedly from those deriving from science. Nevertheless, the scientific mode of reduction acts as the pre-eminent model for all others. It is of crucial importance for an understanding of the reduction of philosophy.

What we have previously studied as a process of secession of science from philosophy is equally, given its resultant diminution, a process of the reduction of philosophy. Indeed, secession and reduction are the sociological and socio-logical aspects of the same process: by focusing on its external relations it can be seen as secession; and by focusing on its internal relations, it can be seen as reduction. But the distinction is really only provisional and relative, for ultimately the internal and external perspectives are inseparable. The internal logic of ideas expresses itself as a rational argument on the level of discourse, but it is also a social and institutional process of negotiation whereby these ideas gain acceptation and become a consensus. Thus, secession and reduction are complementary concepts indicative merely of a shift of perspective in studying any one phenomenon: what is secession in the sociology of philosophy is reduction in the socio-logic of philosophical argumentation and dialectic.

The concept of reduction is well known in science and philosophy. It has already received extensive interpretation in philosophy, both in a positive and negative spirit. Negative interpretations tend to recognise the force of reduction but to interpret it critically: Nietzsche, for instance interprets reduction in science as nihilistic. The positive interpretation of reduction is by and large that given to it in Positivist philosophies, and can be dubbed reductivisim for short; it views reduction uncritically and welcomes it as a task to be accomplished. The schools of Positivism, especially Logical Positivism, propound a reductivist methodology for science and philosophy and make that the programmatic undertaking of their approach. The Logical Positivist reductivist methodology seeks to show that higher or more complex entities are nothing but lower or simpler ones, that ultimately all the sciences are reducible to the axioms of logic and the laws of physics — this is its version of the quest for the Unity of Science — and that anything not reducible is either not science or meaningless — the usual fate accorded to metaphysics and all contrary philosophies. This full reductivist programme is intended to carry through a literal annihilation of metaphysics in denying it any meaning or validity. As Wittgenstein declared programmatically in the *Tractatus*:

> The correct method in philosophy would really be the following: to say nothing except what can be said, i.e. propositions of natural science — i.e. something that has nothing to do with philosophy — and then, whenever someone else wanted to say something metaphysical, to demonstrate that he has failed to give a meaning to certain signs in his propositions.[2]

A negative and self-consciously critical interpretation of reduction does not aim to annihilate metaphysics in this reductivist fashion. It recognises the inherently reductive character of modern science and grants that metaphysics must inevitably suffer from this. However, it aims to subject metaphysics to a reduction that is destructive rather than merely annihilatory. Destructive reduction is a de-structuring method of critical analysis which seeks to expose the basis of metaphysics in language, its role in philosophic thought and its function in the history of science, and thus to reveal its hidden truth. Annihilatory reduction simply aims to expunge metaphysics without granting it any meaning, significance, function, value or truth. Much of what follows in this account of metaphysics will pivot on this crucial distinction between annihilatory and destructive reduction. To make clear this distinction it will be necessary to trace different modes of reduction, and that will involve specifying the innumerable changing meanings of this complex concept.

The concept of reduction is very old and well pre-dates modern science. Its initial use in the late medieval period was as a concept that was metaphysical, theological and logical. Subsequently the meaning of reduction changed drastically as a result of the Scientific Revolution and the first secession of science from philosophy. Reduction in science and philosophy came to mean something different again during the second secession of science from philosophy, and it was during this period that reduction first came to assume a Positivist meaning. In the contemporary epoch of science reduction has gone beyond the merely methodological intent of Positivism and become a technological enterprise, as for example, in the genetic reduction of life. It is this that threatens not only the existence of philosophy but existence itself. In what follows we shall explore these various stages of the reduction of reduction.

2.   Reduction in the First and Second Secessions

The word 'reduction', deriving from the Latin *re-ducere* to bring
back or restore, has many different meanings, most of which have
little to do with philosophy or science.[3] However, among the earliest
is the logical meaning of reducing one syllogism to another and the
method of disproof by *reductio-ad-absurdum*; both of these
meanings will be of considerable importance later in the history of
thought. But of even greater importance both for science and
philosophy was the use of reduction, together with the converse
expression 'expansion', in the context of a neo-Pythagorean and
neo-Platonic metaphysics that focuses on the figures of circle and
point, and has been extensively explored by Georges Poulet.[4] In this
thought, which goes back to Dante and beyond, God and the
universe made in his image are both circle and point: a circle whose
circumference is nowhere and centre everywhere and a dimensionless point, the immobile *nunc stans* of eternity. This figuration
and the ideas it carries were invoked by philosophers and poets from
the middle ages, Cusanus for example, throughout the Renaissance
and during the Baroque era which was co-extensive with the Scientific Revolution, and it has survived in literature right down to the
present day. As early as Pico de la Mirandola, it was applied to man
and the soul: in the words of Bérulle: 'Man is like a point and a
centre, to which all parts of the world are related.'[5] Thus the soul or
mind is a point which can expand to the infinite circle and take in the
All; or, conversely, it can contract the All and reduce it back to a
dimensionless point. Expansion and reduction are the two moments
of a systolic and diastolic rhythm in the soul mediating between
Being and Nothing: Nothing expands to encompass Being, and
Being is reduced back into Nothing.

In the Baroque poets and thinkers, on the very threshold of the
Scientific Revolution, this rhythm of expansion and reduction
becomes the motion of the mind from the infinitely large to the
infinitely small, or to quote Poulet:

> As the macrocosm is represented by the microcosm, and the
> rainbow by each one of the drops of water which compose it, so
> the immense sphere of the universe can be rediscovered, *reduced*
> but curiously like, in objects *which man's science engineers, in*
> *order to reproduce, on a small scale*, cosmic space or solar time.
> Astrolabes, terrestrial globes, planispheres, and clocks are

abridged universes, orbs in which the cosmos is drawn back to the miniscule.[6]

We have here the metaphysical and poetic origins of the Newtonian clockwork mechanical universe that was to dominate science in the modern classical era almost till Einstein and Quantum physics.

The universe of modern science and the basic idea of scientific explanation is founded on the concept of reduction. Poulet, quoting the Jesuit Father Binet, comments that

> . . . when Father Binet rejoices to see the Universe reduced to miniscule proportions, he rejoices as much to see it reduced to an abstraction. The globe has become globule, the form (spherical) has become a formule. A magical formule, since the globule contains the globe, and the Nothingness the All.[7]

Both the model and the formula of scientific representation are reductions. Reduction is the basic move in Descartes' conception of Scientific Method:

> We shall be observing this method exactly if we reduce complex and obscure propositions step by step to simpler ones, and then, by retracing our step, try to rise from intuition of all the simplest ones to knowledge of all the rest.[8]

Thus the scientific representation is reached through a reduction of what is pre-scientifically given or presented, and this is reduced so as to be represented in a rationally adequate form. Representation in general entails reduction in this early scientific approach to epistemology. Equally so, in Empiricist epistemology, as set out for example by Locke, ideas have to be reduced before they can be represented; complex ideas are reduced atomistically to simple ideas of sense.

The neo-Platonic and poetic sense of expansion and reduction does not disappear completely in classical scientific epistemology even though it is translated into the rule-governed method of analysis and synthesis. Much of the emotional feel and imaginative colouring of the poets is still retained by the scientists. Nevertheless, it is a different concept of reduction. It is in fact a concept and no longer a trope or figure or metaphor, as it had been earlier. It would be wrong to insist that science is bound to the original trope of reduction and base on this an argument that science is basically figurative or metaphorical. A concept can derive from a metaphor without itself remaining metaphorical. The concept of reduction as it is invoked in modern science has lost all meaningful connection with its originating metaphor, which has only been maintained in poetry, as Poulet's work shows. Metaphor and concept can transform themselves into each other, and even back again, but this is no reason to claim they are really identical. Hence, it is always essential to establish to what extent reduction is being used as a metaphor or concept or perhaps as an idea which is different from either of these. In this respect origins can be misleading; it is no less wrong to judge words by their origins than people.

Once reduction became a scientific principle — a rule of method — it lost its intimate connection with the theology and poetry of the infinitesimal point. But again, a transformation took place which at least in the first instance preserved something of the original meaning. Science took over the idea of reduction to a point by reinvoking the ancient Atomist hypothesis, and by reinterpreting atoms as point instants. Thus, instead of the poetic opposition of the microcosm-point to the infinite circle of the macrocosm, there came the analogous opposition of the point-atoms to the infinitely extended universe. Wedded to the mechanistic model, the point-atom became the most powerful reductive tool of science: every object could ultimately be reduced to a localised mass of swarming atoms obeying mechanical laws of motion in a geometric space extending to infinity. This scientific vision did not at first completely distinguish itself from its artistic counterpart, the Baroque vision of an unlimited space filled with moving particles such as globules or bubbles — the favoured images of Baroque poetry — so that as late as the eighteenth century Fontenelle could still present his view of the universe in these terms:

> One may therefore imagine that the universe as much as it is known to us, is an amassment of great balloons, great stretched elastic bodies bound one to another, which never cease to remain bubbles or balloons.[9]

Fontenelle's vision was already an anachronism in its own time, especially given its Cartesian predilections. As he himself came later to acknowledge, the more rigorous and quite unpoetic Newtonian mechanistic atomism won out against the earlier Cartesianism of vortexes, even in the French *Academie des Sciences*.[10] What made it so successful was precisely its reductive power. As a corpuscular theory it could even be adapted to light and optics, something that ancient Atomism was quite incapable of accomplishing. Ancient Atomism was already partially reductive in that it tried to reduce — though only in principle — objects of sense, such as colours and images, to the movement of atoms in a void. It could not provide an adequate account of all sensory perception for this required a representative theory incorporating the distinction of primary and secondary qualities. This distinction was inherently reductive, explaining the secondary qualities of colour, warmth, smell, taste, etc. in terms of the primary ones of size, shape and matter. Thus modern Newtonian mechanistic atomism was different in its reductive scope from its predecessor, Ancient Atomism. It remained the standard of reduction till well into the nineteenth century, providing the scientific basis for the new Materialist philosophy.

Newtonianism triumphed not least because, being reductive, it could oppose the anti-reductive tendencies of Aristotelianism, or science based on traditional metaphysics. Aristotle himself had already opposed the nascent reductive tendencies of the Atomists in order to develop a scientific mode that was sublimating: he sought to integrate the part into the whole, to discover functional and organic interrelationships in all of nature, and to explain all change and motion in terms of maturation, purpose and end. Aristotle eschewed mathematical and quantitative methods, utilising instead categorisation, systematic elaboration, logical consistency and teleological ends.[11]

The struggle between Newtonian and Aristotelian science might almost be seen as a world-historical instantiation of a universal propensity of the human mind towards two conflicting tendencies, reduction and integration or sublimation. As Jacobson put it:

> On the one hand, there is the propensity to reduce all complexity to the existence of simple indivisible elements capable of being counted, a vision of reality which seeks to reduce it to a dust-cloud of individuals. On the other, there is the propensity to think in terms of universal interaction and to regard as artificial every attempt to disengage definite individual phenomena from the universal flux.[12]

Modern science and philosophy had one by one critically to weaken and destroy almost every element of method and principle in Aristotelian science before it could take its place. It could not have succeeded in this without the support of a philosophy of reduction, though this was at first limited.

This was where the work of the new epistemological philosophers was auxiliary to that of the physicists. Philosophy assumed the role of what Locke called 'the under-labourer in clearing the ground, and removing some of the rubbish that lies in the way of knowledge', in the way, that is, of 'master builders' like the 'incomparable Mr. Newton with some others of that strain'.[13] Philosophy, no longer the queen of the sciences, was henceforth reduced to being their handmaiden; it was restricted to studying the formation of ideas, restricted, that is, to the basis of knowledge — knowledge itself became the preserve of science.

Locke more or less assumes a reduction of Aristotelian metaphysics and its substitution by epistemology; he does not give fully elaborated and explicit reductive arguments. The closest he comes to such an argument is to show how

> . . . it comes to pass, that one may often meet with very clear and coherent discourses, that amount yet to nothing . . . one may make demonstrations and undoubted propositions in words, and yet thereby advance not one jot in the truth of things: e.g. he that having learnt these following words, with their ordinary mutual relative acceptations annexed to them; e.g. substance, man, animal, form, soul, vegetative, sensitive, rational, may make several undoubted propositions about the soul, without knowing at all what the soul really is: and of this sort, a man may find an infinite number of propositions, reasonings, and conclusions, in books of metaphysics, school-divinity, and some sort of natural philosophy; and after all, know as little of God, spirits, or bodies, as he did before he set out.[14]

The terms Locke adduces are those derived from Aristotelian metaphysics and science. The argument he invokes to show the nonsense of such metaphysics is the forebear of Wittgenstein's later one in the *Tractatus*, which we have already quoted; it is in both cases an argument designed to show how a form of language may look like a sensible proposition and yet be bereft of meaning. The job of the real philosopher is simply to show that this is so, and the reduction of metaphysics supposedly follows in one easy step. The reduction in both cases depends on the representative theory of language, of which Locke is one of the originators and early Wittgenstein a late exponent. Locke devotes the whole of Book III, entitled 'Of Words', to it. It was an extremely influential theory throughout the age of Rationalism and remained so till our own time despite the inroads of philology and other ways of conceiving of language.[15]

The process of the reduction of Aristotelian metaphysics in the Empiricist tradition, which had started even before Locke with Hobbes, was eventually completed by Hume. By waking him from his metaphysical slumber, Hume in turn provided the impetus for Kant to carry through a reduction of dogmatic metaphysics which was deeper and more thoroughgoing than the shallow scepticism of Empiricism. Kant's critical philosophy made traditional metaphysical problems unanswerable, but at the same time showed why it is that they continued to be posed. For the first time he sought to explain the provenance of metaphysics in the very categories of pure Reason, that is, in the *a priori* tendencies of thought itself, in a way that neither the Empiricists before him nor the Positivists after him could attempt.

> Metaphysics as a natural disposition is real, but by itself . . . it is dialectical and deceptive . . . thus a critique, and only a critique, contains in itself the whole well-tested and proved plan, and indeed all the means to carry it out, according to which metaphysics as a science can be brought into being. . . . I guarantee that nobody who has thought through and grasped the principles of criticism even only in these prolegomena will ever turn again to that old and sophistical mock-science . . .[16]

Thus in Kant's critical philosophy we find the first attempt to carry through a genuine destruction of dogmatic or traditional metaphysics by providing an explanation of why metaphysics is necessary and why it is impossible in the way hitherto proposed by metaphysicians. Kant's foundational philosophy was subsequently taken up by the neo-Kantians and developed in an even more critical spirit to effect a thoroughgoing destruction of all metaphysics. But this was only possible because philosophy could be totally separated from science and pursued as a pure *a priori* foundational discipline after the second secession of the sciences.

The second secession of the sciences from philosophy produced a new kind of reduction more radical than any experienced in the strictly Newtonian phase of classical science. Paradoxically, many of the new sciences from which this new reduction stemmed began as anti-Newtonian movements directed against the reduction of the earlier science. This was the avowed aim of Goethe and his circle. However, these anti-Newtonian tendencies eventually merged with Newtonian ones. Thus, for example, in a way impossible for them to anticipate, Goethe and St.-Simon eventually joined hands in Darwin, whose revolutionary theory derived from both kinds of sources. Its reductive power was irresistible. For the first time Man himself could be reduced, if not right down to ape, at least to an evolved creature all of whose capacities and endowments had primitive origins. The reductive potential in all the other sciences of Man was thereby amplified and accentuated. Eventually Marx and Freud joined with Darwin in completing the reduction of Man. In our time this has been philosophically interpreted as the so-called 'death of Man' by Foucault and others.

Darwinianism set out in broad terms the reduction that other sciences carried out much more subtly. Both Marx and Freud reduced Thought, Subjectivity, the logical categories, and the *a priori* itself to historical and psychic factors respectively. And these in turn were themselves reduced to economic and unconscious motivations. In this way a reduction of the very premises of epistemological philosophy was attained. All knowledge came to be interpreted solely in historical, social and psychic terms — a reductive move that was strengthened and completed when the new sciences of language were absorbed into the other basic sciences of Man. Both Marxism and Freudianism, though linguistically based from the start, took a long time fully to absorb the lesson of language. In Marxism the dimension of language is only now coming to the fore in the revisions of Habermas; in Freudianism it was Lacan who first made language explicit.[17] We shall examine in the next section the reductive impact on metaphysics and philosophy in general of this discovery of language.

The other sciences, such as psychology, sociology, anthropology, economics and symbolic logic, which flourished after the second secession, had a lesser reductive impact individually, though together they reinforced each other and were no less decisive. Psychology in all its numerous forms — both mentalistic and behaviourist, introspectionist and experimental, Gestalt and

Stimulus–Response — had a reductive effect on the Cartesian conception of mind and subjectivity and on the notion of epistemology as a philosophical discipline. Later schools of psychology either dispensed with philosophy altogether or fed into cognate reductive philosophies, the so-called Psychologistic schools. Sociology played a similar role in relation to the various Positivistic schools which we shall presently examine. Sociology, too, had a reductive effect on philosophy in arguing that all philosophical categories and concepts were really social ones; and on the basis of this insight it developed as a sub-discipline the sociology of knowledge out of which would eventually derive the sociology of science with its own anti-philosophic critiques.[18] Anthropology was not significant for philosophy until much later, with the rise of Structuralism. Economics was of some importance early on, with Utilitarianism and then Marxism, but subsequent major economists did not seek to develop a general theory of Man or society and so were less philosophically relevant. Symbolic logic was crucial for the logical reductivism of Logical Positivism and the various constructivist philosophies of mathematics and operationalist philosophies of Scientific Method. Evolutionary theory and biology in general instigated philosophies ranging from Social Darwinism, Pragmatism, Bergsonism, and Nietzsche, to the cosmic speculations of de Chardin.

The full reductive effect of these new sciences could only be felt through the philosophies to which they gave rise. These philosophies made the reduction of metaphysics their primary aim; and they eventually succeeded in ending metaphysics, that is, in making metaphysical speculation impossible except as a reactionary throwback, such as neo-Thomism, neo-Hegelianism or the quasi-metaphysical neo-Kantianism. Another related effect of these sciences was indirectly to instigate the move towards pure philosophy, that is, philosophies which in self-defence against science and scientifically-based philosophies totally removed themselves from scientific knowledge. Such were the more formalistic varieties of neo-Kantianism, Existentialist philosophies from Kierkegaard to Heidegger, and Linguistic Philosophies from late Wittgenstein to the Oxford school. All these sought to establish a 'pure' philosophy free of both metaphysics and science. These became the favoured philosophies of academic philosophers after the third secession of science from philosophy. Thus the sciences gave rise to both 'pure' and 'applied' philosophies: those that kept themselves apart from science and those that were applications of scientific ideas to philosophical problems. And this in itself points to the secondary and frequently derivative nature of philosophy in this period.

Invariably each of the science-based philosophies had a reductive impact on metaphysical presuppositions, which in most cases were annihilated. The assumption of an absolute truth was relativised and truth itself was deprived of its essentialist character and made historical or practical or conventional. All absolute standards, above all those of natural law, were denied their validity and treated as no more than 'values' — a new concept of great reductive power. In many philosophies objectivity as such became a value assumption, so even scientific truth was relativised. *Telos*, purpose, potentiality, actualisation, and most other metaphysically-derived concepts were systematically eliminated from science and discourse, and even such Rationalist epistemological categories as cause and effect were subjected to reductive critiques.[19]

The witch hunt against metaphysics did not stop with traditional metaphysical or epistemological ideas; it eventually turned against all philosophies. The Positivists in particular inveighed against all other schools, levelling at them the charge of metaphysics. What this really meant was simply that the other schools were not rigorously enough reductive or that they retained concepts that the Positivists wanted to see eliminated. As in the arts, so in philosophy, the process of going one better in reduction was considered an advance and part of progress. And just as painting or music finally reduced themselves to the empty canvas or brute noises, so philosophies emerged that were stripped of everything but a few logical dogmas. The *reductio-ad-absurdum* was in all these cases complete; an elaborate Nothing was all that was left as 'our great values and ideals drew their final consequence' (Nietzsche). After that it seemed that silence was the necessary outcome in philosophy. For to 'say nothing except what can be said' (Wittgenstein) in science or practical life is really to say nothing in philosophy.

The reductive arguments deployed by Positivism in its final stages were the expressions of a minimalist philosophy that had succeeded in reducing itself to a few simple rules, the so-called logical principles of analysis. A few inflexible logical distinctions were enforced with utmost severity: the separation of the empirical from the logical or even conceptual; the division of the factual and the evaluative; the ban against inference from one to the other; and by the imposition of a hypothetico-deductive methodology, the separation of data from theory in science. In the very process of annihilating metaphysics and all opposed philosophies, Positivism had succeeded in reducing itself almost to nothing, and so inevitably in annihilating itself as well. This was not evident for a long time for it was an historical process that began with the second secession of the sciences from philosophy, at the beginning of the nineteenth century, and seems to be completing itself only now after the third secession, at the end of the twentieth century.

During this period Positivism went through at least four phases of self-transformation, each more reductive than the previous. Thus there were at least four distinct schools of Positivism: the first was the sociological Positivism of St.-Simon and Comte, taken up by Renan, Taine, Bernard, Durkheim and partly also by J. S. Mill and Spencer; the second was the Scientific Positivism of Mach, Frege, Hertz, Hilbert, the young Einstein, Pareto, Weber (despite his neo-Kantianism) and the legal Positivists like Kelsen; the third was the Logical Positivism of Russell, Schlick, the young Wittgenstein, the Vienna Circle and Popper (despite his own denials); and the fourth was the Linguistic Positivism deriving from Moore and the old Wittgenstein and exemplified by the Oxford school that was entrenched throughout the Anglo-Saxon world after World War II. Each of these schools was characteristic of the cultural mentality in the period during which it was prevalent. Sociological Positivism was expressive of the confident, progressivist spirit of the 'bourgeois' age in the nineteenth century. Scientific Positivism emerged out of the new scientific and technological advances, above all in Germany at the turn of the century. Logical Positivism was a quasi-utopian movement for logical renewal in the period between the two wars — analogous to the Bauhaus in art — when all the other philosophies and ideologies seemed to have failed and a new rational order seemed the only salvation. Linguistic Positivism emerged at the same time as the third secession of science from philosophy and became a professionalised 'pure' philosophy, no longer able or willing to grapple with the world; it reflected above all the dispirited post-war years of a declining England.

Sociological Positivism did not go all that far in reduction beyond Empiricism. But, unlike the latter, it was capable of reducing metaphysics by historically relativising it as a past mode of thought in a progressive sequence supposedly consisting of theology, philosophy and positive science. Positive science was taken to be the thought-form out of which Positivism would build a pyramid of exact knowledge at whose base were the mathematical sciences and whose crowning apex would be sociology, the science of Man and Society. From the point of view of subsequent Positivist schools, this early Positivism retained many metaphysical features, such as the attempt to found an ethic and even a new religion on a scientific basis.

The next school, Scientific Positivism, invented or enforced most of the fundamental logical distinctions, such as that between empirical and evaluative propositions or Facts and Values, according to which the separation of science and ethics was achieved. It was in conjunction with this school that systematic attempts were made to reduce metaphysics by eliminating it from the foundations of the sciences; this was to be achieved by purifying all basic scientific concepts of any metaphysical admixture, imposing a strict scientific methodology and as far as possible establishing each science as a self-consistent system. The greatest gains were made in logic, mathematics and physics: logic was formalised for the first time by Frege and joined on to mathematics proper; number concepts were defined and long obscure notions like 'infinitesimals' clarified; by an analogous move physics entered its final golden age when the old metaphysically-laden Newtonian concepts of absolute time and space were critically undermined by Mach and then eliminated by Einstein. Analogous gains were made in the social sciences, above all by the new *Verstehende Sociologie* of Weber, where value-neutrality and objectivity of explanation were defined and established. All these reductive efforts were to good effect, for without this severe destructive critique classical science could not have freed itself from the older Rationalist metaphysics and attained its final phase of achievement.

The Logical Positivists attempted to systematise these earlier achievements and construct out of them a fully rationalised world through the reduction of all discourse to logically ordered propositions. This reconstruction was to be carried through by means of a retranslation of scientific languages into new formal ones, which were to be logical calculi based on deductions from axioms or constructions from basic data. It was a logically utopian undertaking which in practice could never be achieved. But it had the annihilating effect of justifying every form of reductivism, both in science and philosophy.

Linguistic Positivism arose directly out of Logical Positivism when the attempt to construct formal languages and carry through strict logical reductions was abandoned and instead many of the techniques of logical analysis were applied to ordinary language, that is, to common speech forms. Abandonment of the still highly intellectual logical aspirations of Logical Positivism without any replacement resulted in all ideas of any complexity or difficulty being reduced to the level of common sense. Ideas were in effect discounted as a result of the pretence that all philosophical concepts, principles, theories, doctrines or values could be eliminated by language analysis supposedly carried out without presuppositions or theoretical assumptions. The effect of this procedure was to enforce the dogma that no philosophical truth is possible and that all the assertions of past philosophy are either truisms about ordinary language, misconceptions of it, or misguided plans to reform it. Even reductivism no longer had any meaning in this further reduction which brought the language of philosophy down to its zero degree. With the dominance of Linguistic Positivism and the onset of the third secession of the sciences, the end of philosophy has come close to being realised.

A fundamental problem in the Positivist programme is that of reductivism in contradistinction to reduction itself. The two concepts are rarely distinguished, least of all by the Positivists themselves. But such a distinction is of crucial importance in assessing the effect of Positivism on science and philosophy. Science, as we have recognised, is inherently reductive, a point already established by Descartes and maintained ever since. But science is only seen as reductivistic if interpreted along Positivist lines, especially according to the methodology developed by the Logical Positivists. Reductivism is the Positivist interpretation of reduction according to which to demonstrate that entity X can be reduced to entity Y entails as a necessary consequence that X can be deduced from Y. It is only in this reductivist sense that it is possible to say that 'X is nothing but Y'. This 'nothing but' locution is usually a sign of reductivism. As we demonstrate at length in Appendix 2, reductivism is a misconceived interpretation of reduction. In most cases of scientific explanation where X can be reduced to Y it does not follow that X can be deduced from Y; to give a simple example, water can be reduced to hydrogen and oxygen, but the physical properties of water cannot be deduced from those of the two gases. As we shall also show, reductivism does not allow for complementarity, another essential feature of science. All in all, it is reductivism, with its 'nothing but' propensities, that gives Positivism its annihilating edge, above all in its dealings with metaphysics. Reduction is, thus, not all of a piece, it has different modes and there are different interpretations of those modes.

3.   Annihilation or Destruction

Thus far we have dealt with reduction in general without distinguishing its different qualities or modes. The crucial distinction to be drawn is that between the two polar opposites of reduction: annihilation and destruction. This difference is fundamental not only to any understanding of the end of metaphysics but also to the whole issue of Nihilism.[20] Metaphysics can be annihilated, in the way that Positivist philosophies have done; or it can be destroyed in the way of the Faustian philosophers. The difference depends on the nature of the reductive act: annihilation merely rejects metaphysics by means of reductivist arguments that are external and do not touch on its inner meaning; destruction, by contrast, exposes the inner core of metaphysics by revealing the contradictions and suppressions on which it is based. The difference is that between de-structuring something so as to expose it for what it is, and merely denying it and so leaving it unanalysed and unknown. It is a little like the difference between treating a neurotic symptom by psychoanalysis, so as to reveal the complex that gives rise to it, and trying to remove it by aversion therapy or drugs. Even if metaphysics is considered a 'disease' of the Western mind or language, as Wittgenstein was wont to see it, the method of its dissolution is of greater interest than the mere fact that it might no longer trouble us after it has been treated.

Marx, Nietzsche, Wittgenstein and Heidegger were the great destroyers of metaphysics, Ricoeur, referring to Marx, Nietzsche and Freud and including Heidegger as well, speaks of them as such, and he could easily, without the least incongruity, have slipped in the name of Wittgenstein as well:

> These three masters of suspicion are not to be misunderstood, however, as three masters of scepticism. They are, assuredly, three great 'destroyers'. But that of itself should not mislead us; destruction, Heidegger says in *Sein und Zeit*, is a moment of every new foundation, including the destruction of religion, insofar as religion is, in Nietzsche's phrase, a 'Platonism for the people'. It is beyond destruction that the question is posed as to what thought,

reason, and even faith still signify. All three clear the horizon for a more authentic word, for a new reign of Truth, not only by means of a 'destructive' critique, but by the invention of an art of *interpreting*.[21]

Ricoeur's slightly too sanguine assurances derive partly from his using the term 'destruction' primarily in Heidegger's sense; as we shall see, that is a particularly equivocal meaning. Destruction can 'clear the horizon for a more authentic word, for a new reign of Truth' only if one can see it simply as preparatory to new creation, as those who accept Christian theology must. Whether there is anything 'beyond destruction' is still a moot question. And certainly, nobody now can see into this 'beyond' except, as through a glass darkly, with the gaze of faith.

However, what is indisputably true of 'destruction', as Ricoeur understands it, is that it does leave open possibilities of future growth; at least it does not close off the horizon of the future. In this respect, destruction must be distinguished from the opposed notion of annihilation, which does eradicate the very potentialities of renewal. Destruction and annihilation are both modes of the reduction of meaning, and so in that respect they are both nihilistic, but as we have shown elsewhere, they represent nihilisms of a fundamentally different kind. The act of *reductio-ad-absurdum* that both practise is indeed a reduction to nothing, yet it is a very different mode or 'quality of nothing' (*King Lear*, I, ii) that is invoked in each of these opposed actions. This difference relates closely to Nietzsche's distinction between passive and active, imperfect and perfect nihilisms, which we shall discuss in Chapter 3. It is also analogous to the distinction between 'destruction' and 'desolation' or 'devastation', which Heidegger invokes in the context of a discussion of the end of metaphysics:

> The completion of metaphysics sets beings in abandonment of Being. . . . In the future, this means the question of whether beings undermine and uproot every possibility of the origin in Being, and thus continue to be busy with beings, but also move towards the desolation that does not destroy, but rather chokes what is primal through organizing and ordering.[22]

The distinction is too fundamental to be more than merely broached here, to go into it in depth would require investigating the fundamentally opposed attitudes and relations to language, time and death that each sets up, which we have discussed in *In the Beginning was the Deed*.

Here we shall restrict ourselves to one key example: the difference between the ending of metaphysics as destruction and as annihilation, that is, between the treatment of metaphysics by our Faustian philosophers of 'Language' and by the Positivist philosophers of 'Logic'. Where philosophy is merely a canon of 'logic', or a 'methodology', there metaphysics tends to be annihilated. A metaphysics that is thus annihilated remains undestroyed; it is ignored and left in ignorance; it is, as it were, disposed of without being decently interred, its unhallowed corpse left to decompose and befoul the very intellectual air we breathe. Faced with Positivism, metaphysicians, have only been able to carry out a conservative rear-guard defence against the onslaught of this powerful logistical ideology. There is no way that they can engage with it, since it denies their language by declaring it meaningless and will not permit it to speak in its own defence. In the face of this logic of Rationalisation, traditional Reason is rendered speechless; it is silenced by being dismissed as a species of 'interesting' nonsense. The logical requirements of Positivism do not permit Reason to mean anything. Positivism asks crudely: 'what is this Logos? Is it an empirical, logical or evaluative proposition, and if it is none of these, what meaning can it have?' To a demand couched in these limiting terms the Tradition can have no reply. And so Positivism concludes: 'the Logos is a sign of great antiquity to which no meaning can be assigned at present'. Measured by the narrow and restrictive standards of the only allowable propositions of Positivism, the Logos can only appear meaningless. It is not allowed to bear any deep or silent meaning within itself that is not immediately visible on the surface, for there are no such meanings permitted in this logical methodology; all meaning must be 'clear', that is, intellectually perspicuous meaning. There can be no depth of meaning not immediately accessible to logical analysis; there can be no problems which, as Wittgenstein puts it, 'have the character of depth', reaching down to the very 'roots of language'.[23] In this way the Logos is annihilated, supposedly wiped out without any meaningful remainder. No attempt is made, or can be made within the Positivist terms of reference, to translate it or render it even historically meaningful.

The overall effect of the imposition of this logical methodology on language is that, in the guise of being clarified, it is instead simplified and rationalised. The logical categories of Positivism restrict meaning to that which can be defined and regulated in terms of rigidly sequestered types of propositions. The strict segregation of all sentences into the meaningful and meaningless, and then the subdivision of the former into the empirical, logical and evaluative categories — applied with full logical rigour, allowing for no exceptions, no intermediates, no syntheses — has the effect not only of simplifying, but of fragmenting discourse. The logical 'rule' proscribing inferences from propositions of one logical category to another means that the areas of knowledge governed by each can have nothing to do with one another; the formal logical-mathematical and conceptual disciplines are segregated from all empirical sciences, and both of these from moral, political and aesthetic value concerns. It has long been apparent that enforcing a rigid Fact–Value dichotomy on the social sciences produced highly restricted, crudely factual research, and there are analogous effects of imposing other Positivist categories.

The Positivist logical categories in themselves do not bear too much questioning, and can easily be destroyed by the application of a critique of logic based on a developed idea of Language. Such a critique in fact exists in all the Faustian philosophers, perhaps nowhere better than in Wittgenstein. The upshot of the Wittgensteinian critique of Positivism is that the three so-called logical categories of proposition — including the notion of a 'proposition' itself — are shown up as nothing but rationalised logical ideal-types constructed from simple language forms. They have no inherent primacy in language, but are derived from language by the idealisation of certain extreme, limit cases which have been removed from their meaning — giving context. Thus, for example, the Positivist notion of the empirical proposition is created by taking simple representative sentences such as 'This is red' or, even more precisely 'This that I seem to see is red' and treating these, in a logically idealised form, as touch-stones of all empirical reality; with the added demand that all language referring to things be capable of analysis into supposedly basic elementary 'data'. Wittgenstein has already developed all that needs to be said for a destructive critique of the notion of empirical 'data' of the senses, revealing it to be no more than a newly devised convention of language:

The 'visual room' seemed like a discovery, but what its discoverer really found was a new way of speaking, a new comparison; it might even be called a new sensation.

You have a new conception and interpret it as seeing a new object. You interpret a grammatical movement made by yourself as a quasi-physical phenomenon which you are observing. (Think for example of the question: 'Are sense-data the material of which the universe is made?')[24]

A similar 'grammatical' procedure goes into the inventing of the ideal-types of the logical proposition and the evaluative one as well: in the former case the 'grammatical movement' involves the idealisation of simple tautologous sentences like 'all bachelors are unmarried males'; in the latter, of sentences like 'I prefer X to Y'. Of course, there is nothing in itself wrong with such procedures, only with the purpose to which they are put. Such sentences do exist in language, but not as isolated instances that can be idealised into logical standards, for they function and derive their meaning from their relationship to the rest of language, where there are also sentences of quite different types. To deliver the Positivist logical standards over to such a destructive critique is not, however, to annihilate them. The logical categories of the 'logical', 'empirical' and 'evaluative' can be quite meaningful and useful if recognised and utilised as purely formal categories: that is, as ideal-typical logical abstractions that can be used as reference points and standards of comparison to gauge the degrees of similarity and difference of other types of sentences and meaningful expressions. Such formal categories are not without their purpose in analysis, provided analysis is understood not as a breaking up of the complex into the simple, but merely as a comparison of the difficult to the simple and easily surveyed, carried out for purposes of understanding.

As against these abstract categories of the logical, empirical and evaluative we might seek to develop comprehensive categories of Coherence, Reality and Significance, which can be referred either to concepts, or judgements, or whole systems. We can apply the well-established terms of philosophy to these categories and so interpret them in a new way: thus, systems of Coherence are called logics or mathematics, systems of Reality are called sciences, systems of Significance are called humanities; judgements of Coherence are called analytic, judgements of Reality are called synthetic, judgements of Significance are called evaluative; finally, concepts of

Coherence are called logical, concepts of Reality are called empirical and concepts of Significance are called values. Yet these domains of Coherence, Reality and Significance are not logically cut off from one another, for they are not logically separate types like the parallel positivist categories; quite the contrary, they are inherently bound up with each other, for even where there is a preponderant application of any one of these categories as the main criterion of truth to delimit a given domain, the others are not excluded; for they, too, must be invoked. Thus the truth of a scientific theory is not only judged by empirical verification or its representational fit (traditionally known as its correspondence with the world); it is also judged on its Coherence and Significance.[25] And similarly, the humanities as the domains of Significance also require their own standards of Coherence and of truth to Reality — not, in this case, the impersonal objective reality of Nature, but the 'meaningful' reality of human social life. Even a system of logic invokes questions of Significance (for what good would it be if it had no purpose or point?), and questions of reality (for does it not have to have some use or application in practice?). Concepts, judgements or systems that rely solely on one of these norms of truth, to the complete exclusion of the others, are merely abstracted limiting cases: limits to which one can approximate in theory but never quite attain in practice. The Positivist categories of logical, empirical and evaluative are in fact such limit cases.

Positivists can invoke their logical categories to annihilate metaphysics because metaphysical assertions do not fit these preordained logical compartments, not being purely logical, empirical or evaluative. The Positivists are unable to grant that such assertions are subject to higher criteria of Coherence, Significance and Reality. The Positivist categories are inapplicable, so these are misused if invoked to annihilate metaphysics. Metaphysics can, however, be destroyed. To show how this was done we shall briefly review the destruction of metaphysics effected in turn by each of our Faustian philosophers. In each of them there is to be found some version of the general thesis of the 'end of metaphysics', but in no case is metaphysics eliminated on logical grounds, or simply rejected as an outworn mode of thought, or as a series of historical 'mistakes', or as quasi-theological dogmas, or as pre-enlightenment prejudices, or — worst of all — as meaningless nonsense.

Metaphysics is uncomprehendingly annihilated from the outside, but to be destroyed it must be understood and exposed from within.

It is destroyed when it has its hidden basis revealed, the basis on which its existence as metaphysics depends but which it must repress in order to maintain itself and retain its own identity. This hidden basis — necessarily unrecognized in metaphysics itself — which modern philosophy uncovers is invariably language in one form or another. Behind the metaphysics of the Logos in all its modes — as Idea, Universal, Category, Substance, Subject — there lies as the real substratum the basic reality of language. For all these metaphysical notions are some form or other of language elaborated and disguised in an idealised manner. However, metaphysics might be said to be the necessary and unavoidable mystification of language; for it must be acknowledged that it is only through this round-about, disguised process that language could historically develop and finally be 'discovered' as what it is understood to be in modern philosophy and science. Thus metaphysics is the realisation of some partial aspect of language — its power of conceptualisation and abstraction, its creative potential, its form and grammar, its historical development as Reason — elevated into a metaphysical truth by being expounded as a doctrine of Form and Matter or Categories or Universals, etc. And to destroy this metaphysical 'truth' demands dis-covering what it is that the metaphysical idea is based on — and which it is unable to acknowledge — in order to remove its mystifying and disguising dress and reveal it in its naked truth as language.

Faustian philosophy breaks through to the hidden silence within the divine speech of the Logos, and it reveals that the silence within the Word is a human (all-too-human) silence of words. Once those words are spoken, and the silence within it is broken, the Word is destroyed. Language — that secret 'other' of the Logos — has the power to destroy it by revealing itself as its actual human reality, present within it from the very start, but necessarily repressed and unacknowledged. It is the darkness within the light of the Logos which the light comprehendeth not, and which it is unable to comprehend as long as it aspires to an illumination that is more than mere human enlightenment.

But we must beware of seeing this process of destruction in a wholly positive shallowly optimistic, Enlightenment way as a liberation to a new truth and unity of language. A paradoxical dialectic of Enlightenment ensures that once language destroys the Logos it also begins the process of destroying itself. The unity of all languages once guaranteed by the Logos as the centre of all Being — the unifying Word of all discourses — is a unity that is broken once the Logos is destroyed, for then its logocentric centripetal forces become ec-centric and centrifugal. A symptom of this is the fragmented, scattered state of our knowledge. Now there is nothing able to hold together our proliferating sciences and maintain their unity. The role that metaphysics once performed as the central discipline, from which derived the traditional criteria of Coherence, Reality and Significance, namely, *Unum*, *Verum* and *Bonum*, and which unified the sciences, is one that cannot be taken over by any modern philosophy. Metaphysical order and certitude are forever lost to us.

4. Philosophy as Language-Analysis

Marx was the first major thinker to have explicitly undertaken the destruction of metaphysics on the basis of a new conception of language; in this he anticipated the work of other Faustian thinkers, though it is not clear whether they took note of his pioneering thought. The destruction of metaphysics and the creation of a new concept of language went hand in hand in Marx's philosophy and that of the other Faustians. Language was dis-covered as its metaphysical cover was dissolved. Marx begins by noting that metaphysics is language concealed:

> The philosophers would only have to dissolve their language into the ordinary language, from which it is abstracted, to recognize it as the distorted language of the actual world, and to realize that neither thoughts nor language in themselves form a realm of their own, that they are only *manifestations* of actual life.[26]

In this passage there are already all the terms and turns that will play such a prominent part in subsequent Faustian destructions of metaphysics. Marx characteristically overreaches himself and speaks of a general 'dissolution of philosophy', not distinguishing too sharply between 'philosophy' and 'metaphysics', and he was unknowingly followed in this by the other Faustian thinkers, who frequently presented their critiques as attacks on philosophy itself. But this is a minor complication we shall resolve later. In this context, by the term 'philosophy' we simply understand those philosophies which are being dissolved as metaphysical, not including those which are carrying out the dissolutions. Marx uses the term 'dissolving' — also subsequently taken up by Wittgenstein — rather than 'destroying' — the term favoured by Nietzsche and Heidegger — but clearly these are cognate expressions.

Philosophy is to be dissolved by dissolving its 'language into the ordinary language, from which it is abstracted'. The term 'ordinary language' here appears in a significant formulation which in time will cause problems when it reappears again as 'ordinary language' philosophy. But this is not what is remarkable about the passage; rather it is Marx's suggestion that in the dissolution of metaphysics language dissolves back into language like ice into water. Or, in other words, that what is at play in the dissolution of philosophy is only the transformation from one state of language to another, from a frozen or 'distorted' to a more fluid or 'ordinary' form. The whole process is only a play of languages; there is no escape beyond, behind or beneath language. However, Marx himself was not fully aware of this point and imagined that language could in turn be dissolved into something more basic that he called 'life': '. . . neither thoughts nor language in themselves form a realm of their own, they are only *manifestations* of actual life'. Marx did not fully realise that life in its human dimensions cannot be divorced from language, and that language and life are conjoined at that level, rather than the former being a manifestation of the latter.

Marx imagined that language can be reduced to life because he thought he had already succeeded in reducing thought to language: 'Language is the immediate actuality of thought', he declared in an earlier passage.[27] This Hegelian-sounding sentence is actually the death knell of Hegelianism, which depends on the independence of thought, as in one way or another all metaphysical philosophy does. The philosophical problem of how thought relates to the world Marx reduced to a mere historical or even material problem of how language relates to life. 'The problem of descending from the world of thoughts to the actual world is turned into the problem of descending from language to life.'[28] This suggests a two-step descent: from thought to language, and from language to life. Though the last step is in some respects a false step, it, too, was repeated by subsequent thinkers. Nietzsche and Wittgenstein also frequently spoke as if 'life' was the final step out of language.

But irrespective of whether 'life' is or is not more fundamental than language, Marx interprets language as co-extensive with life. This effects a reconception of language which was to be extremely far-reaching. It meant that thought as philosophy was simply another mode of language. According to Marx, it was precisely that mode of language which was most intent on disguising itself and presenting itself as not language at all, but something higher — namely, independent thought. Thus 'the secret of philosophical language, in which thoughts in the form of words have their own content'[29] is that we fail to 'recognize it as the distorted language of the actual world'.[30] Philosophy is thus language that disguises itself as something sublime and other than language; it carries out the self-sublimation of language. For Marx this was merely one kind of ideological distortion, but for Wittgenstein it was much more, for on it depended not only the possibility of philosophy but also the possibility of a dis-covery of language as a consequence of the dissolution of philosophy.

Wittgenstein asks rhetorically: 'In what sense is logic something sublime?',[31] and his question is clearly meant to carry over to philosophical thought. The impression that it is something sublime arises from the fact that it has been formed through a process of the sublimation of 'ordinary' language. And like any Freudian sublimation, the sublimation of language also results from the 'striving after an ideal';[32] we have 'the preconceived idea of crystalline purity'[33] as our ultimate ideal in logic and philosophy. In some respects this sublimation of language is an ideological distortion of language in Marx's sense, but according to Wittgenstein the distortions, illusions and bewitchments of language are not simply the products of socioeconomic pressures or power realities. They are the ideological effects of language itself, 'produced by grammatical illusions',[34] or 'through a misinterpretation of our forms of language',[35] or because 'a picture held us captive'[36] or because 'we do not command a clear view of the use of our words'.[37] But ultimately the urge to sublimate language comes from language itself, from its 'deep disquietudes; their roots are as deep in us as the forms of our language and their significance is as great as the importance of our language'.[38] It is as if the neuroses of language itself give rise to problems which traditional philosophy tries to solve by sublimation, but which need to be dissolved by an analytic philosophy.

Wittgenstein rejected an explicitly Freudian reading of his 'language analysis', though he was not altogether averse to likening it in some respects to psychoanalysis. Nevertheless, his method of dissolving problems in philosophy is partly modelled on the resolution of complexes in psychoanalysis; and he explicitly states that in his philosophy 'there are indeed methods, like different therapies'.[39] Basic to all his methods or therapies is a move we might speak of without equivocation as a de-sublimation of language; but he thinks of it too simply as a return from the sublimated language of traditional philosophy back to 'ordinary' language. Wittgenstein himself puts it that 'what we do is to bring words back from their metaphysical to their everyday usage'.[40] And this is exactly what Marx undertook when he advised philosophers 'to dissolve their language into the ordinary language'.[41] However, much more is involved in this than a simple return or dissolution, and to explain it we shall have to turn to Freud.

The Freudian analogue of 'language analysis' is no more than a model and must not be taken literally; there were numerous models for philosophy and this is merely one that is particularly apt for modern philosophy (see Chapter 6). Something of it is already prefigured in Marx and Wittgenstein and there are other aspects of it in Nietzsche and Heidegger. Nietzsche — being a Freudian *avant la lettre*, and so uninhibited by any charges of unphilosophic influence — was much more explicitly able to express a 'psycho-analytic' orientation in philosophy. Sublimation and *ressentiment* are the two key concepts in his account of ideals and ideas, above all those which have their locus in metaphysics: 'the ressentiment of metaphysicians against actuality is here creative'.[42] As the mechanism of *ressentiment* is inversion, so it is by means of inversion that metaphysics primarily constitutes itself. The basic metaphysical inversion that Nietzsche identifies is that of the 'apparent' world and the 'true' world: in brief, this world is up-ended to figure as a mere 'apparent' world, and over against it is set a 'true' world which is supposedly the real world. The 'true' world is a sublime world and originates as the product of sublimation: 'what drives they sublimate'[43] he exclaims, speaking of philosophers. Elsewhere he explains:

> Many instincts — e.g. the sexual instinct — are susceptible of being greatly refined by the intelligence (the love of humanity, the cult of Mary and the saints, artistic enthusiasm; Plato thinks that the love of knowledge and philosophy is a sublimated sexual instinct). But its former direct action subsists, alongside.[44]

Blondel maintains that for Nietzsche as 'for Freud, primal repression (as well as regression or fixation) first makes sublimation possible'.[45] Nietzsche develops a view of repression as internalisation, but he does not refer it directly to language or metaphysics. We shall attempt to do so in what follows.

Basic to the psychoanalytic model of philosophy is the dual process of the sublimation of language into metaphysics and then its de-sublimation back into language again. That is to say, language is first concealed as metaphysics, then it is revealed as no more than language — the initial concealment making possible the subsequent revelation. The whole course of Western philosophy can be schematically set out in these terms as a sublimation of the word into the Logos; this was followed by the long history of the Logos as metaphysics in its various transitions and translations, first into logic and *ratio* and then into all the subsequent forms of Reason and Rationalism; finally came the de-sublimation of all these modalities of the Logos back into the word, but this time the word was conceived of in terms of the modern idea of language. This modern idea of language arose as a concept within philosophies that emerged out of the very metaphysical tradition they opposed and brought to an end. Without these philosophies there could have been no such conception, and in this sense language would not have been dis-covered. Thus the destruction of metaphysics through a de-sublimation of language is itself the very process of the discovery of language. Language had first to be covered over before it could be dis-covered.

Our Faustian thinkers were not fully conscious of the process of language discovery in which they were participating. They were not aware of the way in which their own work was a dis-covery of language in a sense quite different from that of merely finding something given and ready to hand. They failed to see that they were in effect creating a conception of language, or bringing it into explicit being; tending to assume rather that language was simply there like Life, that it was the ever-present source and original point of departure for all meaning: 'What we are given are forms of life', to paraphrase Wittgenstein.[46] But neither Life nor language are simply given. They have to be dis-covered and that also means, in a certain sense, created. This 'creation' takes place through a complex process of language analysis which has some close analogues in psychoanalysis.

Sublimation follows on repression in psychoanalysis, and so, too, in philosophy. The sublimation of language into metaphysics is at once also a repression of language into what might be called a social unconscious. Hence, the dis-covery of language can be likened to the return of the repressed to consciousness. And just as in psychoanalysis, where certain drives can be made conscious only because they were initially repressed and then brought back from repression, so, too, the consciousness of language had to be preceded by its prior repression. Language-analysis as a philosophical method or therapy is a way of deliberately bringing language back from its metaphysical repression into the consciousness of modern thought.

Thus, metaphysics — that is to say, the major part of the history of Western philosophy — was an inescapable stage in the self-conception of language without which no modern thought would have been possible. Hence it cannot be looked upon as any kind of error or mistake or misconception, unless one were to treat all of Western history as such. The Positivist assumption that metaphysics is in principle not essential, that the Western mind would have proceeded directly to the only correct methods of logic and science had it not been side-tracked on the metaphysical detour, is a grotesquely unhistorical conception of how thought develops and what are the presuppositions even of Positivism itself. It is another way of annihilating metaphysics by denying it any essential function in the history of thought.

Even Faustian philosophers are themselves not always alert to the difference between annihilation and destruction of metaphysics. There are passages in Marx, Nietzsche, Wittgenstein and Heidegger which must be read as expressions of pure annihilation that are contrary to the main tenor of their work. In some places Marx is intent on annihilating metaphysics as ideology, *tout court*, as in the following remark:

> Morality, religion, metaphysics, all the rest of ideology and their corresponding forms of consciousness, thus no longer retain the semblance of independence. . . . Where speculation ends — in real life, positive science begins.[47]

The last reference to 'positive science' sounds remarkably like a premonitory echo of the Positivism that Engels was later to preach, and gives the very strong impression that in these early remarks Marx is merely undertaking a quasi-positivistic annihilation of metaphysics. However, in direct contrast to such seemingly annihilating tendencies, there is Marx's life-long preoccupation with the philosophy of Hegel, whom he saw as the last of the great

metaphysicians. Marx's critique and re-working of Hegel constitutes a mode of destruction that functions as a translation of
metaphysics. The well-known Preface written late in his oeuvre
makes that point in his own words:

> The mystification which dialectic suffers in Hegel's hands by no
> means prevents him from being the first to present its general
> form of working in a comprehensive and conscious manner. With
> him it is standing on its head. It must be turned right side up again,
> if you would discover the rational kernel within the mystical
> shell.[48]

There is, of course, considerable controversy among Marxists as to
the nature of that rational kernel which the breaking of the mystical
shell exposes; in other words, what is it that is translated when
metaphysics is destroyed? What is at issue for Marxists is the nature
and role of the dialectic, which derives from traditional metaphysics
by way of Hegel, and which in its 'rational form' 'is in its essence
critical and revolutionary'.[49] The neo-Structuralists, such as
Althusser, have one way of interpreting it and the Frankfurt
thinkers, such as Adorno, quite another. There is no need here to
settle the issue of whether Marx's dialectic is 'in principle the
opposite of the Hegelian dialectic' because it is 'the transformation
of its structure',[50] or because this 'dialectic is the consistent sense of
non-identity'.[51] It is enough to point out that this critical dialectic is
itself a translation of the metaphysical one to show that Marx's
destruction of metaphysics is not mere annihilation.

Analogous doubts arise with respect to Nietzsche's treatment of
metaphysics. There are passages in his writings where he anticipates
the Linguistic philosophers, speaking as if metaphysics were nothing
but a tissue of conceptual errors: 'senselessness of all metaphysics as
the derivation of the conditioned from the unconditioned'.[52] If he
were to stop there, he would be saying no more than what Linguistic
philosophers have been repeating ever since. But then he goes on
with this remarkable elaboration, which shows that even the 'unconditioned' is not senseless:

> It is in the nature of thinking that it thinks of and invents the
> unconditioned as an adjunct to the conditioned; just as it thought
> of and invented the 'ego' as an adjunct to the multiplicity of its
> processes; it measures the world according to magnitudes posited

by itself — such fundamental fictions as 'the unconditional', 'ends and means', 'things', 'substances', logical laws, numbers and forms. There would be nothing that could be called knowledge if thought did not first re-form the world in this way into 'things', into what is self-identical. Only because there is thought is there untruth.[53]

Or in other words, it is the very nature of thought to require and presuppose the categorial forms which metaphysics goes on to affirm as absolutes; this position is not incompatible with Kant's except that Nietzsche considers the categories simply as fictions we cannot do without.

As early as *Menschliches, Allzumenschliches* he has this to say of metaphysics, and it separates him explicitly from the simple-minded positivistic anti-metaphysicians:

> *A few rungs back*: A degree of culture, and assuredly a very high one, is attained when man rises above superstitions and religious notions and fears, and, for instance, no longer believes in guardian angels or in original sin, and has also ceased to talk of the salvation of his soul — if he has attained to this degree of freedom, he has still to overcome metaphysics with the greatest exertion of his intelligence. Then, however, a *retrogressive movement* is necessary; he must understand the historical justification as well as the psychological in such representations, he must recognize how the greatest advancement of humanity has come therefrom, and how, without such a retrocursive movement, we should be robbed of the best achievements of man's existence up to the present age. In philosophical metaphysics, I now see ever-increasing numbers who have attained to the negative goal (that all positive metaphysics is error), but as yet few who climb a few rungs backwards; one ought to look out, perhaps over the last steps of the ladder, but not to try to stand upon them. The most enlightened only succeed so far as to free themselves from metaphysics and look back upon it with superiority, while it is necessary here, too, as in the hippodrome, to turn round the end of the course.[54]

In this passage Nietzsche sets out a programme which he would only accomplish later in fragmentary form, for nowhere does he present a thorough, overall treatment of metaphysics. It consists of two moments: the overcoming of metaphysics and the retrogressive movement away from mere overcoming — the few rungs back over the top of the ladder of progress. The first is what Nietzsche was later to call explicitly the destruction of metaphysics; the second is what he was to call a 'transvaluation of the highest values on the basis of the will to power'. The destruction and the transvaluation are both movements along the same circular course — 'as in the hippo-drome', a classical image Aristotle too had used, in referring to Plato's dialectic.[55] Both movements are involved in the Nietzschean translation of metaphysics, which is at once destruction and trans-valuation. Just exactly how he carries it through and what difficulties it entails, we shall see later by reference to his genealogy of Reason.

Wittgenstein's treatment of metaphysics can with considerably more justice than Nietzsche's be likened to the annihilation carried out by Linguistic Positivism, for the latter originated from his philosophy; yet his philosophy never took itself as annihilating. He never referred to his own work as in any sense constituting a 'revolution in philosophy' that would supersede past thought.[56] It was almost as if to dissociate himself in advance from any such claims that Wittgenstein declared to a friend many years before: 'don't think I despise metaphysics or ridicule it. On the contrary, I regard the great metaphysical writings of the past as among the noblest productions of the human mind.'[57] It is in this spirit that one must understand Wittgenstein's own dissolution of metaphysical problems in order to bring metaphysics to an end. For him, such problems are not mere superficial puzzles or conundrums or logical paradoxes; they are conceptual 'complexes' arising out of the deep anxieties of language itself.

> The problems arising through a misinterpretation of our forms of language have the character of *depth*. They are deep dis-quietudes; their roots are as deep in us as the forms of our language and their significance is as great as the importance of our language.[58]

It is because Linguistic philosophers treat such problems as if they were mere muddles or misconceptions of the conceptual forms of ordinary language that they only succeed in aggravating the difficul-ties, burying them even deeper in the 'unconscious' of language. It is as if they were providing aversion therapy where psychoanalysis is called for.

Wittgenstein's own approach to metaphysics is clearly destructive, even though he himself rarely uses that word, preferring instead the cognate term 'dissolution'. But there is one, somewhat uneasy passage, in which the word 'destruction' is invoked.

> Where does our investigation get its importance from, since it seems only to destroy [*zerstören*] everything interesting, that is, all that is great and important? (As it were, all the buildings, leaving behind only bits of stone and rubble). What we are destroying is nothing but houses of cards [*Luftgebäude*] and we are clearing up the ground of language [*Grund der Sprache*] on which they stand.[59]

The answer Wittgenstein gives to his own very challenging question is too pat and evasive, resorting as it does to the simple image of demolition that Locke had already employed in justifying an 'under-labourer' role for epistemology.[60] It is also reminiscent of a similar answer given to a similar challenge by Turgenev's character Bazarov, the first self-confessed literary nihilist:

> 'You repudiate everything or, speaking more precisely, you destroy everything. But one must be constructive too you know'.
> 'That's not our business now. The ground must be cleared first.'[61]

It is true that there are implict differences between these images: the Lockean English image of clearing work in preparation for the scientific 'master-builders' and the Russian image of clearing soil for new growth have none of the more resonant implications of the German 'making free the Ground of Language'. Wittgenstein's destruction is not 'demolition' to prepare new foundations, nor is it 'clearing' in that simple, young-nihilistic sense; it means removal of useless superstructures through a destruction of their foundations.

However, the answer Wittgenstein gives does not fully meet the challenge of the question, for while the assumption behind the question is that what is being destroyed is 'great and important', the answer speaks of it as 'houses of cards' (though *Luftgebäude* does carry the suggestion of superstructures). As we shall eventually see, this difficulty runs like a deep flaw throughout Wittgenstein's work, and can be focused in the question: What is it that Wittgensteinian analysis destroys, is it a 'house of cards' or something 'great and important'? One way of answering it is to say that there is something that was once 'great and important' but which has since become a 'house of cards'. In other words, metaphysics which was 'among the noblest productions of the human mind' now exists only as *Luftgebäude*. These are what Wittgenstein subjects to a deflating dissolution by bringing them down to earth, the ground of language. The problem of the 'cliché' — the useless 'dead' word, such as the decorative ornament left over from a once functioning style, as well as the 'shop-worn' philosophy — preoccupied Wittgenstein throughout his life, and he encountered it in all the spheres of his diverse activity: intellectual, artistic and moral. The destruction of 'dead' metaphysics — the clichéd words of once 'noble productions of the human mind' — is Wittgenstein's critical way of dealing with this problem in philosophy. But this answer is not altogether satisfactory for it leaves unclear whether the destruction is only of the dead remains of metaphysics or whether it is of their once living originals as well.

There is a similar ambiguity in Heidegger's notion of 'destruction'; it is not clear whether what is being destroyed are the latter-day elaborations of the traditionalists in philosophy or the Tradition itself. This ambiguity is unavoidable in Heidegger's philosophy because he has to rely on the very texts drawn from the traditional corpus that he seeks to subvert. His philosophical technique is to comment and elaborate on fragments of texts — frequently single sentences, such as those from the pre-Socratics — which he 'forces' to speak in his own way. If he were, therefore, seriously to undertake a destruction of the Tradition he would be undercutting the very basis on which he depends. Hence, he adopts all kinds of strategems of denying his destructive intent; he speaks of 'grounding primordially', eliciting the undisclosed sense, bringing back to origins or originary experiences, etc. We can trace the convolutions of these manoeuvres in texts from different periods and stages of his reflections on the history of metaphysics. Having introduced the term 'destruction' in his first major work, *Being and Time*, he then went on to reinvoke it in his subsequent works, revising it all the while without ever admitting that this was what he was doing, and instead weaving a network of ambiguities around it. As a result there arise in Heidegger's work two opposed senses of 'destruction': an 'original', radical meaning and a revised conservative one, and between these two extreme poles of meaning there are others with different nuances. In its original signification, 'destruction' figures as a quasi-phenomenological 'destruction of the history of ontology';[62] in its revised signification, 'destruction' brings an end to metaphysics only in the sense of delimiting it by a recollection of the history of ontology — and so in fact actually conserving rather than destroying it. This discrepancy between the early seemingly radical 'destruction' and the late conservative 'de-structuration' may reflect the intellectual distance separating Heidegger's hopes for and involvement with the apparent anti-traditionalist renascence of the German nation under Hitler, and the subsequent disappointment of his dashed expectations, which brought him back into the quietism of Tradition.[63]

The term 'destruction' is first introduced at its most radical in passages such as this:

> If the question of Being is to have its own history made transparent, then this hardened tradition must be loosened up, and the concealments that it has brought about must be dissolved. We understand this task as one in which by taking *the question of Being as our clue*, we are to *destroy* the traditional content of ancient ontology until we arrive at those primordial experiences in which we achieved our first ways of determining the nature of Being — the ways which have guided us ever since.[64]

The previous paragraph makes it quite clear that the tradition in question is the 'history of ontology' as the history of metaphysics; and a little later in the text, it is explicitly put that '. . . in our process of destruction we find ourselves faced with the task of interpreting the basis of the ancient ontology in the light of the problematic of Temporality'.[65] In direct contradiction to these seemingly unambiguous pronouncements there is a statement in the same text that seeks to restrict the 'destruction of tradition' only to tradition as it has been handed down to the present, namely to the traditionalism of the academic metaphysical philosophers of Heidegger's own time:

> But this destruction is just as far from having the *negative* sense of shaking off the ontological tradition. . . . This destruction does not relate itself towards the past; its criticism is aimed at 'today' and at the prevalent way of treating the history of ontology, whether it is headed towards doxography, towards intellectual history, or towards a history of problems.[66]

Thus the text as it stands in its late editions seems blatantly to contradict itself. In the very next breath, as it were, the text goes on unperturbedly to speak of carrying 'out this destruction . . . with regard to stages of that history which are in principle decisive',[67] which means that it must 'relate itself towards the past'.

The late Heidegger denies with some vehemence that he ever intended any such thing as a destruction of the decisive stages of the history of metaphysics. In the late 'Dialogue on Language' the following exchange occurs between a Japanese visitor and an 'Inquirer', who obviously speaks for Heidegger:

J: For this reason we in Japan understood at once your lecture 'What is Metaphysics?' . . . We marvel to this day how the Europeans could lapse into interpreting as nihilistic the nothingness of which you speak in that lecture. To us, emptiness is the loftiest name for what you mean to say with the word 'Being'. . . .

I: . . . in a thinking attempt whose first steps are unavoidable even to this day. It did, however, become the occasion for very great confusion, a confusion grounded in the matter itself and linked with the use of the name 'Being'. For this name belongs, after all, to the patrimony of the language of metaphysics, while I put that word into a title of an essay which brings out the essence of metaphysics, and only thus brings metaphysics back within its own limits.

J: When you speak of overcoming metaphysics, this is what you have in mind.

I: This only; neither a destruction nor even a denial of metaphysics . . .

J: . . . in fact you strive only for an original appropriation.[68]

It seems that what originally began as a 'destruction of the history of ontology' finally became an 'original appropriation'.

It is for good reason that Heidegger is so defensive about his notorious inaugural lecture: 'What is metaphysics?'. In that lecture he strives to ground science in metaphysics, but defines metaphysics in his own way as 'the enquiry into Nothing . . .';[69] this is what brought the charge of nihilism against him. There is no suggestion whatever in the lecture of any destruction or even overcoming of metaphysics. In fact, the lecture seems to represent a temporary regression back into metaphysics — as he himself puts it; 'metaphysics is the ground phenomenon of Dasein'[70] — but this is a position that he was shortly after quickly to abandon, probably under the instigation of his growing involvement with Nietzsche. However, in the 'Postscript' written much later, as usual Heidegger tries to bring the lecture in line with his later thought on metaphysics: 'The question "what is Metaphysics?" asks a question that goes beyond metaphysics. It arises from a way of thinking which has already entered into the overcoming of metaphysics.'[71] In this 'Postscript' he also defends himself against accusations of nihilism arising from his preoccupation with Nothing. It is likely that his extreme sensitivity to being branded a nihilist made him completely reconceive the whole project for the destruction of metaphysics: '. . . as in recent years, people do their best to show that this inquiry about Being brings only confusion, that its effect is destructive, that it is nihilism'.[72] Instead he embarked on an 'overcoming of metaphysics' which ends metaphysics only in the Hegelian sense of surpassing it: that is, deleting, conserving, and transcending it at once.[73] The term 'overcoming of metaphysics' Heidegger clearly derives from and refers back to Nietzsche, but he invokes it in the very opposite of the sense intended by Nietzsche. So much so, that Nietzsche's own 'overcoming of metaphysics' is read by Heidegger as itself being the last step within metaphysics, and Nietzsche the last of the metaphysicians:

> Was meint aber dann 'Ende der Metaphysik?' Antwort: den geschichtlichen Augenblick, in dem die *Wesenmöglichkeiten* der Metaphysik erschöpft sind. Die letzte dieser Möglichkeiten muss diejenige Form der Metaphysik sein, in der ihr Wesen umgekehrt wird.[74]

And because '*Nietzsche bezeichnet schon früh seine ganze Philosophie als die Umkehrung des Platonismus*',[75] it is Nietzsche himself who is last within the metaphysical tradition and Heidegger presumably the first outside it.

Heidegger's conception of the Nietzschean 'overcoming of metaphysics' as being itself the inversion of the original metaphysics of Platonism gives us the vital clue to what he himself means by calling the 'overcoming of metaphysics' its 'original appropriation'. Metaphysics, as an epoch in the history of Being (*Seinsgeschichte*), is the period of the fall away from Being into beings through the forget-fulness of the ontological difference between Being and beings and the resultant oblivion of Being.[76] This Fall, or fault in time, is the 'original error' of philosophy against Being. Plato was perhaps the first and Nietzsche 'himself only the last victim of a long process of error and neglect . . .',[77] hence neither he nor we are 'to blame that with all our effort, with all our chasing after the essent we have fallen out of Being'.[78] As Heidegger explains:

> And should we not say that the fault did not begin with us, or with our immediate or more remote ancestors, but lies in something that runs through Western history from the very beginning, a happening which the eyes of all the historians in the world will never perceive, but which nevertheless happens, which happened in the past and will happen in the future?[79]

It is this fault or original fall away from Being, which is also the fall into metaphysics, that Heidegger seeks to end; thereby to overcome metaphysics by once more repeating or recalling the original question of Being, which prior to the Fall had brought Western history into Being. Heidegger thereby hopes to inaugurate a new beginning, one that could not but be as momentous as the original one carried through by the pre-Socratics, with whom he identifies:

> To ask 'How does it stand with Being?' means nothing less than to recapture, to repeat [*wieder-holen*], the beginning of our historical-spiritual existence, in order to transform it into a new beginning. This is possible. It is indeed the crucial form of history, because it begins in the fundamental event. But we do not repeat a beginning by reducing it to something past and now known, which need merely be imitated; no, the beginning must be begun again, more radically, with all the strangeness, darkness, insec-urity that attend a true beginning.[80]

It is clear from this and other places that Heidegger's overcoming of metaphysics, or original appropriation, is to be a repetition of the origin of Being and is to bring about what he elsewhere calls 'a new dawn of Being'.[81] It is evident that this return to Being could only be an eschatological culmination of the original fall away from Being. The whole *Seinsgeschichte* is the readaptation of traditional and modern providential schemes, as Heidegger himself states: '*das Sein selbst ist als geschichtliches in sich eschatologisch'*,[82] and he calls it explicitly the *'Eschatologie des Seins'*. Hence it follows from his sense of Time and Being that the overcoming of metaphysics is clearly the fulfilment of an eschatological schema of Being, moving through the following five steps: origin of Being; Fall from Being into Metaphysics; the slow decline of metaphysics in the successive phases that is the history of ontology; the end of that history in the nihilism (Nothing) of Nietzsche; and finally the recall of original Being in the newly repeated beginning of Heidegger. In this schema simple quasi-dialectical patterns of turning, overturning and returning operate: thus Plato is the first erring turning, Nietzsche is the overturning of that turning (inversion of the inversion), and this enables Heidegger's own turn (*Kehre*) to be a Return (recall of the original).

What links all the twists and turns of Heidegger's original notion of 'destruction' and of his subsequent notions of 'overcoming' as 'recall' or repetition is a basic sense of a return to the Origin. So that the changes from one notion to another and the vagaries of his use of the term 'destruction' are prompted by and partly explained by his changing sense of what is Primordial or Original. In *Being and Time* the original is conceived of phenomenologically as primordial experience or root phenomena of existential being, such as *Dasein*, death and temporality. Hence, in accordance with this conception, 'destruction' figures as a kind of historical 'epoché' bracketing off the occluding tradition that 'blocks our access to those primordial "sources" from which the categories and concepts handed down to us have been in part quite genuinely drawn'.[83] Subsequently, when, following Nietzsche, Heidegger became more oriented to the pre-Socratic origins of philosophy, he reconceived the Origin as the original thought of Being. Finally, he made it his task to recall that Thought and the whole history of Being, and so repeat it in a new beginning. Hence, what had originally started off as a destruction of ontology became eventually a repetition of it.

Heidegger's 'destruction' of metaphysics is thus conservative rather than radical and far less decisive than that of Marx, Nietzsche or Wittgenstein.[84] Yet it is in one sense superior to any of the others: it provides a far more detailed and specific translation of the history of metaphysics, especially of the Logos and the Cogito. It is, therefore, itself part of the continuing argument of that history. Each destruction of metaphysics performed by these thinkers has its own unique strengths and weaknesses — those of Wittgenstein and

Nietzsche are analysed in the detailed studies following. However, it would be quite futile to attempt to collate or synthesise all these different achievements into one by adding their successes and subtracting their failures, since the very attempt to comprehend them together itself constitutes a different kind of destruction — in this case a destruction of Faustian philosophy. And this destruction, too, is a certain kind of translation. Our reading, for example, of two of these great destroyers is by no means neutral; it is a reading that alters what it comprehends — translates it in all the senses of that word.

The Faustian destruction of metaphysics is one of the greatest achievements of the modern mind, and as such it surely must rank with the very greatest accomplishments of the human mind. Yet it is an achievement of an extremely paradoxical kind, quite incommensurate with any that were accomplished within metaphysics itself. The end of metaphysics cannot be compared with any of the decisive stages that took place within its continued development. A similar paradoxicality pertains to all the great destructive achievements of modern culture in general. By comparison with this destruction one can begin to appreciate the nature and enormity of the failures of the parallel processes of annihilation. The annihilation of metaphysics at the hands of Positivism, for example, is a sheer denial of thought and amounts to a severance from and suppression of the whole philosophical past. And such forgetfulness of the past works back on itself and induces oblivion of the present as well. This reveals itself in the fact that Positivism is singularly lacking in self-knowledge, in any capacity to account for itself or its relation to that which it is denying; it is thus completely ahistorical.

It is this last point that constitutes the great problematic of destruction: what is the relation between the destruction and that which is destroyed? Perhaps nobody at present addresses himself more to this question than Derrida. In a paper entitled 'Structure, Sign and Play', he speaks of the paradoxical metaphysical circle within which 'destructive discourses' are trapped in their very attempt to destroy metaphysics, since 'it was within concepts inherited from metaphysics that Nietzsche, Freud and Heidegger worked', to mention but the key 'destroyers' referred to by Derrida.

But all these destructive discourses and all their analogues are trapped in a sort of circle. This circle is unique. It describes the form of the relationship between the history of metaphysics and the destruction of the history of metaphysics. There is no sense in doing without the concepts of metaphysics in order to attack metaphysics. We have no language — no syntax and no lexicon — which is alien to this history; we cannot utter a single destructive proposition which has not already slipped into the form, the logic, and the implicit postulations of precisely what it seeks to contest.[85]

Derrida's statement is in line with Heidegger and so is equally misleading. It is true in an obvious sense that most philosophical discourses originated from metaphysics — though by no means all, as some derived from artistic, scientific and religious discourses which had nothing much to do with metaphysics. From this simple fact Derrida illicitly moves to the conclusion that none were ever able to break free from their origins, that they were all for ever after trapped in metaphysics. Derrida seems to have fallen into the false genealogical argument that its origins are constitutive of and decisive for the whole history of philosophy, an argument that is otherwise against the 'structuralist' tenor of his thinking, which discounts origins. As Nietzsche at times insists, genealogy does not mean that origins are decisive for the whole nature and course of something; it is always possible for it to break free from its originating signification and assume a radically new meaning, and it inevitably will do so under the pressure of new purposes and uses. (But, as we shall see, Nietzsche frequently lapses into an eschatological search for origins against his own admonition.)

There is no set of maxims more important to an historian than this: that the actual causes of a thing's origin and its eventual uses, the manner of its incorporation into a system of purposes, are worlds apart; that everything that exists, no matter what its origin, is periodically reinterpreted by those in power in terms of fresh intentions; that all processes in the organic world are processes of outstripping and overcoming, and that, in turn, all outstripping and overcoming means reinterpretation, rearrangement, in the course of which the earlier meaning and purpose are necessarily either obscured or lost.[86]

As this quotation makes clear, origins are in no way decisive for the later meaning of something; this is determined more by its subsequent purposes and uses. As the original situation in which something arose changes and gives way to other constellations and complexes, it is almost inevitable that the thing in question will change its meaning, since meaning is a function of context not of derivation. Thus a word changes its meaning as the language of which it is a part transforms itself; the meaning of the word being determined by its relations to other words in the language and not by its own original or prior meanings. This holds good for the meaning of metaphysical and philosophical words, as for others. 'Genealogy' in this sense means tracing the sequence of changing meanings; it does not mean referring them all back to some archetypal meaning, some lost or forgotten *arche* which is supposedly the real original *Urwort*. Heidegger understood genealogy in something like the latter sense and strove always to recollect the original 'true' meaning, and Derrida seems to have fallen in with him in this extract.

Our own investigation into the genealogy of metaphysics and science has been guided by Nietzsche's admonition. We have sought to locate radical breaks where the meaning fundamentally alters and completely departs from the original or the prior meanings. It is precisely radical breaks of this order that we have located in the various secessions of science from philosophy, and the accompanying departures of anti-metaphysical philosophies from traditional metaphysics. Hence, we do have a language that is alien to the history of metaphysics, and we have concepts derived from outside metaphysics with which to attack it. The destructive workings of these concepts on metaphysics do not show that they were bound to it, or that they were themselves still metaphysical.

It seems that Derrida is arguing that even to deny metaphysics is already to affirm it, just as theologians used to argue that to deny God is nevertheless to affirm Him, so nobody can really be an atheist. An argument of this kind endows metaphysics with a privileged place analogous to that of God in theology. The 'unique circle' in which the 'discourses of philosophy are trapped', according to Derrida, would seem to be a magic circle formed by the spell that he himself has cast and which only he himself can dispel. It is not surprising that Derrida grants only himself and his predecessors the right to break the spell, step outside the circle and so 'step outside philosophy'. But to do so, he insists, in line with Heidegger, that one must once more return to origins, to 'the founding concepts of the whole history of philosophy':

Concerning oneself with the founding concepts of the whole history of philosophy, de-constituting them, is not to undertake the task of the philologist or of the classic historian of philosophy. In spite of appearances, it is probably the most daring way of making the beginning of a step outside of philosophy.[87]

And yet, paradoxically, it is not the philosophy of Heidegger but that of Nietzsche which according to Derrida goes furthest in taking this last step, for it is 'the joyous affirmation of the freeplay of the world and without truth, without origin, offered to an active interpretation . . .'[88] It is hard to see what 'an active interpretation, without origin' can mean in the context of a Heideggerian concern with foundational concepts.

At the end of another paper, entitled 'The Ends of Man', Derrida seems to have changed his mind as he once more raises these issues of ending. He explicitly contrasts there Heidegger's and Nietzsche's manner of 'deconstructing' metaphysics. Heidegger's manner of 'recalling' the 'founding concepts' is fated 'to constantly confirm, consolidate, or *relever*, at a depth which is ever more sure, precisely that which we claim to be deconstructing'; whereas Nietzsche's mode of overcoming metaphysics calls for a 'change of ground' that extends beyond 'the form of the house and the truth of Being', for 'Nietzsche called upon an active forgetfulness of Being which would not have had the metaphysical form which Heidegger ascribed to it'.[89] This seems to be Derrida's own final choice, despite his earlier inconsistent insistence that both modes of 'deconstructing' have to be utilised.

Derrida's vacillations, as he seeks to maintain a foot in both the Nietzschean and Heideggerian camps, do not of course vitiate his project for 'de-constituting the founding concepts of the history of philosophy'. This is an essential undertaking. Even if successfully accomplished, however, it does not constitute 'a step outside of philosophy', merely one outside of metaphysics. To step outside philosophy will require a different kind of turning, a move against the destroyers of metaphysics so as to destroy them in turn. Only when those who have reduced metaphysics are themselves reduced will the attempted *reductio-ad-absurdum* of philosophy be complete.

At the present stage of the historical argument against philosophy we stand, as it were, at the mid-point of this reductive process. The reduction of metaphysics has in principle been accomplished, though in what follows we shall complete it by de-constituting the two most crucial founding concepts of metaphysics: the Logos or the idea of Reason and the Cogito or the idea of mind and subjectivity. This will be carried through in the spirit of Nietzsche and Wittgenstein. But at the same time the reduction will turn against them. The very intellectual methods and means they provide for destroying the Logos and Cogito will be subject to a destructive critique by being turned against themselves. Thus the dialectic of self-negation will be constituted by these two destructive moments. Once this dialectic is complete in Part Two we will then see in Part Three whether indeed it has enabled us to step out of philosophy.

Notes

1. F. Nietzsche, *Will to Power*, W. Kaufmann (ed.) (Vintage, New York, 1968), preface, p. 4.

2. *Tractatus Logico – Philosophicus*, trans. D. F. Pears and B. F. McGuinness (Routledge and Kegan Paul, London, 1961), p. 151, sec. 6.53.

3. For an account of the various meanings of 'reduction' see Kenneth Burke, *A Grammar of Motives* (University of California Press, Berkeley, 1974), pp. 96–7. Burke points out that in one sense 'one can even be said to reduce a "lower" subject to a "higher" one, as Bonaventura, who rated theology as much higher than art, could write "On the Reduction of the Arts to Theology . . ."'. Ibid., p. 97. Reduction in the sense of contraction is a key term in Cabbalistic thought and goes back to neo-Platonism.

4. See Georges Poulet, *The Metamorphoses of the Circle*, trans. C. Dawson and E. Coleman (The Johns Hopkins Press, Baltimore, 1966).

5. Ibid., p. 7.

6. Ibid., p. 17.

7. Ibid., pp. 18–9.

8. 'Rules for the Direction of the Mind', Rule V; *Descartes Philosophical Writings*, trans. G. E. M. Anscombe and P. Geach (Nelson, London, 1964), p. 157.

9. Quoted in *The Metamorphoses of the Circle*, p. 31.

10. See his statement quoted in Merz, vol. I, p. 135.

11. See Jaeger, *Aristotle*, chap. XIII.

12. N. Jacobson, 'Continuity versus Discontinuity in Science' (manuscript 1960).

13. John Locke, 'Epistle to the Reader', *An Essay Concerning Human Understanding*, vol. I (Dover Publications, New York, 1959), p. 14.

14. *An Essay Concerning Human Understanding*, vol. II, pp. 299–300.

15. See Hans Aarsleff, *From Locke to Saussure: Essay on the Study of Language and Intellectual History* (University of Minnesota Press, Minneapolis, 1982), pp. 3–42.

16. *Prolegomena to any Future Metaphysics*, trans. Peter Lucas (Manchester University Press, Manchester, 1966), pp. 134–5.

17. The Marxist approach to language was brilliantly developed in the Leningrad school of critics, linguists and psychologists in the late 1920s founded by Bakhtin and including Volosinov, Medvedev and very likely Vygotskij, with whose work

Wittgenstein would almost certainly have been made acquainted on his visits to Leningrad in the 1930s. See in particular V. N. Volosinov, *Marxism and the Philosophy of Language*, trans. L. Matejka and I. R. Titunik (Seminar Press, New York, 1973). Unfortunately this work was suppressed during the Stalin years and only revived in the 1960s.

18. See in particular the attack on philosophy by Elias 'Scientific Establishments', N. Elias, H. Martins and R. Whitley (eds), *Sociology of the Sciences Yearbook 1982* (D. Reidel, Dordrecht, 1982), pp. 3–70.

19. See Paul Forman, 'The reception of an acausal Quantum mechanics in Germany and Britain' in *The Reception of Unconventional Science*, S. H. Mauskopf (ed.), AAAS Selected Symposium 25 (Westview Press, Boulder, 1979), pp. 11–50.

20. For further discussion see my *In the Beginning was the Deed*, Act II, Scene III.

21. Paul Ricoeur, *Freud and Philosophy*, trans. Denis Savage (Yale UP, New Haven, 1970), p. 33.

22. Martin Heidegger, *The End of Philosophy*, trans. J. Stambaugh (Souvenir Press, London, 1975), p. 66.

23. *Philosophical Investigations*, sec. 111, p. 47.

24. *Philosophical Investigations*, sec. 400–1, p. 121.

25. On this point see the philosophy of science of Kuhn and Polanyi. T. S. Kuhn puts it: '. . . since no paradigm ever solves all the problems it defines and since no two paradigms leave all the same problems unsolved, paradigm debates involve the question: "Which problem it is *more significant* to have solved?"' *The Structure of Scientific Revolutions* (University of Chicago Press, Chicago and London, 1962), p. 109.

26. *The German Ideology* (ed.) C. J. Arthur (New York International Publishers, 1972), p. 118.

27. Ibid., p. 118.

28. Ibid., p. 118.

29. Ibid., p. 118.

30. Ibid., p. 118.

31. *Philosophical Investigations*, sec. 89.

32. Ibid., sec. 98.

33. Ibid., sec. 108.

34. Ibid., sec. 110.

35. Ibid., sec. 111.

36. Ibid., sec. 115.

37. Ibid., sec. 122.

38. Ibid., sec. 111.

39. Ibid., sec. 133.

40. Ibid., sec. 116.

41. *German Ideology*, p. 118.

42. *Will to Power*, sec. 579, p. 311.

43. *Will to Power*, sec. 677, p. 359.

44. Quoted by Eric Blondel, 'Nietzsche: Life as Metaphor' in *The New Nietzsche: Contemporary Styles of Interpretation* (ed.) David B. Allison (New York, Dell Publishing Co., 1977), p. 154.

45. Ibid., p. 153.

46. *Philosophical Investigations*, p. 226.

47. *German Ideology*, pp. 47–8.

48. 'Preface to the Second German Edition of Capital', *Marx Engels: Selected Works* (Moscow, 1951), p. 414.

49. Ibid., p. 414.

50. L. Althusser, *For Marx: Contradiction and Overdetermination* (Penguin, Harmondsworth, 1969), p. 93.

51. Adorno, *Negative Dialectics*, trans. E. B. Ashton (Routledge & Kegan Paul, London, 1973) p. 5.

52. *Will to Power*, sec. 574, p. 308.

53. Ibid., p. 309.

54. Quoted in H. G. Schenk, *The Mind of the European Romantics* (Constable, London, 1966), p. 247.

55. Aristotle, *Nicomachean Ethics*, trans. J. A. K. Thompson, *The Ethics of Aristotle* (Penguin, Harmondsworth, 1963), bk. vi.

56. The title of a characteristic series of radio talks by the most prominent of the Linguistic philosophers in the fifties which captures something of the spirit of their pretensions. These were subsequently published under that title.

57. M. O. C. Drury in *Ludwig Wittgenstein: The Man and his Philosophy* (ed.) K. T. Fann (Dell, New York, 1967), p. 68.

58. *Philosophical Investigations*, sec. 111, p. 47.

59. Ibid., sec. 118, p. 48.

60. *An Essay Concerning Human Understanding*, vol. I, op. cit., p. 14.

61. *Fathers and Sons*, ch. X, p. 296.

62. Martin Heidegger, *Being and Time*, trans. J. Macquarrie and E. Robinson (Harper and Row, New York, 1962), p. 44.

63. For a political interpretation of the shifts in Heidegger's philosophy see: Pierre Bourdieu, *Die politische Ontologie Martin Heideggers*, trans. B. Schwibs (Syndicat, Frankfurt am Main, 1975).

64. *Being and Time*, p. 44.

65. Ibid., p. 47.

66. Ibid., p. 44.

67. Ibid., p. 44.

68. Martin Heidegger, *On the Way to Language*, trans. Peter D. Hertz (Harper and Row, New York, 1971), pp. 19–20.

69. Martin Heidegger, *Existence and Being*, trans. W. Brock (Henry Regnery, Chicago, 1970), p. 348.

70. Ibid., p. 348.

71. Ibid., pp. 349–50.

72. Martin Heidegger, *An Introduction to Metaphysics*, trans. R. Manheim (Doubleday, New York, 1961), p. 169.

73. In the late piece on Hegel: 'The Onto-Theo-Logical Nature of Metaphysics', Heidegger seeks to distinguish his own 'backtracking' from Hegel's 'sublation' or 'cancellation' but it appears to be a distinction without all that much difference.

74. Martin Heidegger, *Nietzsche*, vol. II (Neske, Pfullingen, 1961), p. 201.

75. Ibid., p. 201.

76. Martin Heidegger, 'Der Spruch des Anaximander', *Holzwege* (Klostermann, Frankfurt, 1957), pp. 335–6.

77. *An Introduction to Metaphysics*, p. 30. These lectures, delivered in 1935, were only published in 1953.

78. Ibid., p. 30.

79. Ibid., p. 30.

80. Ibid., p. 32.

81. W. J. Richardson, *Through Phenomenology to Thought* (Nijhoff, The Hague, 1963), p. 638.

82. 'Der Spruch des Anaximander', *Holzwege*, p. 301.

83. *Being and Time*, p. 43.

84. It might be more accurate to say with Bourdieu that he is a 'conservative-revolutionary' like so many of the Right-wing thinkers of his time.

85. *The Language of Criticism and the Sciences of Man* (eds.) R. Macksey and U. Donato (Johns Hopkins University Press, Baltimore, 1977), p. 250.

86. *The Genealogy of Morals*, trans. F. Golffing (Doubleday Anchor, New York, 1956), p. 209.

87. J. Derrida in Macksey and Donato (eds), p. 254.

88. Ibid., p. 264.

89. J. Derrida, 'The Ends of Man' in *Philosophy and Phenomenological Research*, XXX (1969–70), p. 57.

Part Two

DESTROYING THE DESTROYERS

3 THE GENEALOGY OF REASON: AN ATTACK

After all, am I a philosopher? But what does it matter?

Letter to Brandes

1. Reason and Philosophy

The greatest of struggles: for this a new weapon is needed.

The hammer: to provoke a fearful decision, to confront Europe with the consequences: whether its will 'wills' destruction.[1]

Nietzsche philosophised with a hammer; he wielded the hammer against philosophy itself. His destructive onslaught on philosophy was the most devastating it had ever sustained. He undertook to carry through a 'critique of philosophy as a Nihilist movement'.[2] According to Nietzsche, what makes philosophy nihilistic is its adherence to Reason and its attempt to impose Reason on the world. Reason, in the way the philosophers interpret and believe in it, 'is the greatest error that has ever been committed, the essential fatality of error on earth' (par. 584), and so the original cause of Nihilism. Hence, the destruction of Reason and the philosophy whose ideal values it enshrines becomes the supreme task for the thinking deed of destruction that seeks to complete Nihilism so as to get beyond it, to overcome it. The idols of philosophy must be smashed and this calls for philosophising with a hammer.

We shall attempt to deploy a hammer against this hammer in order to beat it back to the iron from which it was initially fashioned and fashion it anew. But before this can be attempted, and before a counter-critique to Nietzsche's critique can be undertaken, it is essential to expound his interpretation of the relation between philosophy, Reason and Nihilism.

'The faith in the categories of reason is the cause of Nihilism' (par. 12); and in the first place this is the faith of philosophy: 'one believed one possessed in them the criterion of truth and reality' (584). Out of this faith in Reason philosophy erects its conception of a true and real world where the categories of reason rule. This sets up a contrast to a world of illusion and mutability where Reason does not obtain.

Thus 'the philosopher invents a world of Reason, where Reason and the logical function are adequate: this is the origin of the "true world"' (586); and it is also the origin of the apparent world for 'one takes this world for the "apparent one" and the other world as "true"' (586). In this way the fundamental philosophical opposition of a true-world and an apparent-world is set up: 'the greatest error that has ever been committed, the essential fatality of error on earth' (584). It is philosophy's Fall from grace.

Historically considered, Nietzsche's account applies as a simplified picture to the metaphysical tradition. It fits best the Platonic conception of a true-world of intelligible Forms counterposed to an apparent-world of sensible things. Even earlier, however, the Heraklitean idea of a Logos prevailing through change and flux and the Eleatic idea of an unchanging Being are also expressions of a metaphysical true-world. Aristotle's constitution of metaphysics as the science of the categories of being established the categories of reason as the determinations of the true-world. Subsequent Christian theology, in so far as it was what Nietzsche calls 'Platonism for the people', elaborated this metaphysical true-world in moral terms by linking it to a theodicy of salvation and immortality. There is, therefore, some initial plausibility in Nietzsche's account.

Nietzsche develops it further by diagnosing its psychological aetiology, the psychological needs that metaphysics satisfies.

> Psychology of metaphysics: the influence of timidity. That which has been feared the most, the cause of the most powerful suffering (lust for rule, sex, etc.) has been treated by men with the greatest amount of hostility and eliminated from the 'true-world'
> . . .

> In the same way, they have hated the irrational, the arbitrary, the accidental (as the causes of immeasurable physical suffering). As a consequence, they negated this element in being-in-itself and conceived it as absolute 'rationality' and 'purposiveness' . . . (576).

Thus, in reaction 'man seeks "the truth": a world that is not self-contradictory, not deceptive, does not change, a true world . . .' (585). 'It is suffering that inspires these conclusions . . .' so that metaphysics 'is an expression of hatred for a world that makes one suffer: the ressentiment of metaphysicians against actuality is here creative' (579). Nietzsche's psychological explanation sounds convincing but actually explains little. Such crude wish-fulfilment motivations are not specific enough for the task at hand. Since pain, suffering, transitoriness, sex and death are universal human conditions it follows that these are no more linked to philosophy than to any other cultural response to the plight of mankind. Philosophy, which is a very rare product of human culture, must have more specific psychological grounds than the generalities Nietzsche offers.

Nietzsche is on the way to a better explanation when he refers philosophy to the striving for meaning, and in particular to the need to give the world a meaning. When such a need for meaning, due to specific cultural conditions, takes an intellectual form, philosophy can be one of its outcomes.

This meaning could have been: the 'fulfilment' of some highest ethical canon in all events, the moral world order; or the growth of love and harmony in the intercourse of beings; or the gradual approximation of a state of universal happiness; or even the development toward a state of universal annihilation — any goal at least constitutes some meaning (12).

However, among intellectuals and 'logicians' the tendency is to rationalise and systematise such a meaning and seek for 'some sort of unity, some form of monism' (12) for 'if the soul be that of a logician, complete consistency and real dialectic are quite sufficient to reconcile it to everything' (12). This is the kind of soul that 'has posited a totality, a systematization, indeed any organization in all events, and underneath all events, and a soul that longs to admire and revere has wallowed in the idea of some supreme form of domination and administration . . .' (12). This philosophical soul imposes on the world the categories of reason: 'aim, unity, being . . to project some value into the world' (12); and then proceeds to pass sentence on this whole world of becoming as a deception and to invent a world beyond it, a *true* world' (12).

According to Nietzsche, Nihilism must inevitably follow from this initial 'essential fatality of error', for as soon as these 'categories "aim", "unity", "being" which we used to project some value into the world' are pulled out again, 'the world looks valueless' (12). 'The feeling of valuelessness was reached with the realization that the overall character of existence may not be interpreted by means of the concept "aim", the concept "unity" or the concept "truth"'. Nietzsche's account at this point still sounds very general and vague but it can be made more specific by being referred to the history of philosophy. The categories Nietzsche adduces are roughly equivalent to the metaphysical categories '*unum*', '*verum*' and '*bonum*' or unity, truth and good as an end or aim. And their universal provenance in metaphysics is affirmed by the scholastic tag that Spinoza echoes: 'omne ens est unum, verum et bonum'. Theologically considered, they are the fundamental attributes of Being or God who is unity, true reality and the ultimate goal or aim to which everything tends. Hence the devaluation of these categories or their substitution by 'secularized' versions must be of momentous consequence; for what ensues when these categories are, as Nietzsche puts it, 'pulled out' is that the world can no longer be metaphysically or theologically interpreted. Such a 'pulling out' occurred during the course of the Scientific Revolution and was finally completed in the nineteenth century. In the physical sciences 'an essentially mechanical world would be an essentially meaningless world',[3] one without unity, truth and aim. Positivist philosophy seconded this denial and translated these categories into their 'logical' equivalents, the 'logical', 'empirical' and 'evaluative', which applied solely to propositions, not to the world. In short, there ensued the end of metaphysics and the death of God.

With that, Nihilism was at hand. For now the 'world looks value-less' because 'we have measured the value of the world according to categories that refer to a purely fictitious world' (12), the philosophers' true-world. Once this true-world is devalued, by being shown up for the fiction it is, 'the last form of nihilism comes into being: it includes disbelief in any metaphysical world and forbids itself belief in any *true* world' (12). But since this world acquired its value by reference to the true-world, once that had been denied it follows that this world was also denied any value. Hence the stage is reached where 'one cannot endure this world though one does not want to deny it' (12). Nihilism is where one 'judges of the world as it is that it ought not to be, and of the world as it ought to be that it does not exist . . . the pathos of "in vain" is the nihilist's pathos — at the same time, as pathos, an inconsistency on the part of the nihilists' (585).

For Nietzsche the overcoming of Nihilism consists in abandoning the inconsistency of the 'pathos of in vain' and instead affirming thi world with Dionysian joy, which, logically speaking, is no less of an inconsistency. Nietzsche is undeterred by this for he denies the passive, weak, imperfect form of Nihilism, that of the 'pathos of in vain', only to embrace it in its active, strong and perfect form. He calls himself 'the first perfect nihilist of Europe who, however, has even now lived through the whole of nihilism, to the end, leaving it behind, outside himself' (p. 3). For Nietzsche, 'nihilism, as the denial of a truthful world, of being, might be a divine way of thinking' (15), 'an ideal of the highest degree of the powerfulness of the spirit, the over-richest life . . .' (14).

This strong form of Nihilism constitutes an overcoming of philosophy:

> *Overcoming of philosophers* through the destruction of the world of being: intermediary period of nihilism: before there is yet present the strength to reverse values and to deify becoming and the apparent world as the only world, and call them good (585).

The way to achieve such a revaluation of the world is to 'realize how the world may no longer be interpreted in terms of these three categories' of reason, namely, 'aim', 'unity' and 'truth', for 'once we have devalued these three categories, the demonstration that they cannot be applied to the universe is no longer any reason for devaluating the universe' (12). It is we ourselves who have valued the world according to our created values, which we have 'falsely projected into the essence of things'; so our withdrawal of those values from the world in no way devalues the world. So that now 'one realizes that becoming aims at nothing and achieves nothing' (12), but this realisation far from being a cause of despair and of the pathos of in vain' becomes a root principle for the overcoming of Nihilism by going through with it to the end:

> Extreme positions are not succeeded by moderate ones but by extreme positions of the opposite kind . . . One interpretation has collapsed; but because it was considered *the* interpretation it now seems as if there were no meaning at all in existence, as if everything were in vain . . . [But] let us think this thought in its most terrible form: existence as it is, without meaning or aim, yet recurring inevitably without any finale of nothingness: '*the eternal recurrence*' (55).

With that formula Nietzsche brandishes his hammer, his 'great cultivating idea: the races that cannot hear it stand condemned; those who find it the greatest benefit are chosen to rule' (1053). But it is not merely destructive, it is also the formula 'toward a justification of life, even at its most terrible, ambiguous, and mendacious . . .' (1005); toward 'a Dionysian affirmation of the world as it is, without subtraction, exception or selection — it wants the eternal circulation — the same things, the same logic and illogic of entanglements' (1041). Thus Nietzsche has finally crossed over from the most fundamental Nihilism as 'a will to negation to the opposite of this . . .' and reached the 'highest state a philosopher can attain: to stand in a Dionysian relationship to existence . . .' (1041).

It is little wonder that Nietzsche considers himself 'something decisive and fateful that stands between two epochs'.[4] He has not merely placed himself at the decisive turning point of world-history but made that turning take place in himself and his work, for has he not 'even now lived through the whole of nihilism, to the end, leaving it behind, outside himself', and is it not in his formulation that 'a countermovement finds expression . . . that in some future will take the place of this perfect nihilism' (p. 3)? His world-historical vision of the origin, outcome and end of Nihilism is an eschatological schema premised on himself as its culmination. It has all the familiar eschatological turns: an Origin, Fall, Decline, End and Return. Though it presents itself as a genealogy of Reason and philosophy, it is clearly an eschatology.

The Origin is the pre-philosophical attitude to the world, such as that of Homer and the poets at the dawn of Western civilisation. At this stage it is this world of the senses, of suffering, change and death which is affirmed as the only world, as the true and real world. If there is another world it is an apparent world only, 'in fact the Greeks thought of, e.g. a shadow kingdom, an apparent existence, beside true existence' (586). But along came the philosophers who invented Reason and the categories of metaphysics and logic:

> And behold, suddenly the world fell apart into a 'true' world and an 'apparent' world . . . And behold; now the world became false, and precisely on account of the properties that constitute its reality: change, becoming, multiplicity, opposition, contradiction, war. And then the entire fatality was there:
> 1. How can one get free from the false, the merely apparent world? (— it was the real, the only one);

2. How can one become oneself as much as possible the antithesis of the character of the apparent world? (584)

This Fall can be seen in two ways: either as a fatal division of this world into a true-world and an apparent-world; or as the upturning and inversion of the original opposition of a real this-world and an unreal other-world into a 'real' other-world seen as a true-world, and an unreal this-world become a mere apparent-world. The Fall has both of these eschatological features of division and of inversion.

In both ways it is the original fault, 'the greatest error that has ever been committed, the essential fatality of error on earth' (584); and from it there can only ensue an inevitable Decline. This Decline constitutes the subsequent history of Western civilisation as a history of decadence. The Decline is a steady falling down from the high peak of Greek achievement. But there were rare superhuman efforts to stem the encroaching decadence; one such was the Renaissance. That effort was frustrated by the new moral decadence of the Reformation. Since then there has only been further deterioration to the End, which is Nihilism.

Nihilism ensues when the true-world is devalued and along with it the apparent-world, but it is realised that the apparent-world *is* this world. Hence nothing has any value and the world is meaningless. This conclusion follows necessarily from the initial false premise that sets a fictitious true-world over this world as a mere apparent-world. Once that false differentiation is made there is no preventing the degeneration of both worlds to Nothing. 'We have abolished the real world, what world is left? The apparent world perhaps? . . . But no? with the real world we have also abolished the apparent world!' This is the 'end of the longest error; zenith of mankind; INCIPIT ZARATHUSTRA'.[5] The final stage in the 'history of an error' in six stages has attained its climactic moment; the End is at hand.

Nihilism as the End is no final end since Nietzsche, the perfect nihilist, can accept the meaninglessness of the world and affirm it as 'eternal recurrence'. Hence, he succeeds in overcoming the Fall by reinverting the original inversion and placing this world back on its feet again as the only real and true world, and banishing the philosopher's true-world back into the underworld of fictions where it belongs. Thus he effects a revaluation of the false valuation resulting from the invention of Reason. Through Nietzsche himself, out of the End comes the Return. Return back to the Origin but also forward to a new innocence of Becoming, back to a master morality but also forward beyond good and evil, one step closer to the Overman. The eschatological cycle completes itself and begins anew.

That this genealogy of Reason is an eschatology can be further demonstrated by showing that it matches turn for turn the genealogy of morals; both are the same eschatology. The same turns repeat themselves around the tropes of Origin, Fall, Decline, End and Return; there is the identical pattern of version, inversion and reinversion. The genealogy of morals explains the Nihilism that stems from the Judeo-Christian heritage of Western civilisation, for, as he puts it, 'it is in one particular interpretation, the Christian-moral one, that nihilism is rooted' (p. 7); analogously the genealogy of Reason explains the Greek sources of Nihilism where it is the philosophers who are the main culprits. The moral interpretation of the world, as well as the rational, is a source of Nihilism.

At the start of the moral eschatology there is the Origin: master-morality. This is the right system of valuations, based on the power differential between a conquering race, the masters, and a conquered one, the slaves. In accordance with this power differential, the basic value term of this morality, 'the basic concept is always *noble* in the hierarchical, class sense, and from this has developed, by historical necessity, the concept *good*, embracing nobility of mind, spiritual distinction'.[6] The contrary term, bad, simply designates the other class, the slaves, from the point of view of the nobles; 'the words *kakos* and *deilos* (the plebian, in contrast to the *agathos*) emphasise cowardice and provide a hint as to the direction in which we should look for the etymology of *agathos* . . .'.[7] Thus, the master-morality is constituted by this value opposition of good and bad, one which expresses a natural and proper power relation between races.

The Fall ensues when the master-morality's good–bad is inverted and perverted into the evil–good of a slave-morality. That which the masters consider good the slaves interpret as evil, and that which the masters take as bad the slaves take as good. The basic concept in this morality is evil, a notion based on the reactive impulse to slander all that which is 'naturally' good. This is the reaction of the 'impotents . . . to damage the powerful and great of this earth',[8] their will to power expressing itself as *ressentiment*. 'It was the Jews who started the slave revolt in morals', who 'succeeded in avenging themselves on their enemies and oppressors by radically inverting all their values . . .'; they 'dared invert the aristocratic value equations good/noble/powerful/beautiful/happy/favoured-of-the-gods and maintain, with the furious hatred of the underprivileged and impotent, that only the poor, the powerless, are good; only the suffering, sick, and ugly, truly blessed'.[9]

After such a moral Fall there can only follow a moral Decline. Christianity, a religion invented by the Jews, purveys for over 'two millennia of history' the decadence of slave-morality; it is the source of infection for all the diseases of the West. It is the 'carrier of the levelling and retributing instincts' which 'represent human retrogression most flagrantly'[10] because they deny the natural power relations. These instincts triumphed over Rome and the Renaissance — a last, doomed, upsurge of the instincts for life of the natural masters. The same instincts, eventually taking a secular and even anti-Christian form, expressed themselves in the Enlightenment, the French Revolution, democracy, socialism and all the other manifestations of modern moral Nihilism. The slave-morality must Decline and come to nothing for it is anti-life; it must eventually negate and destroy itself because its secret impulse is will to death, will to nothingness.

Moral Nihilism is the End toward which the slave-morality has been striving all along. The inverted differential of power where the weak dominate the strong must in the end defeat itself for it is against the law of life. The slave-morality destroys itself when Christianity turns against itself:

> The end of Christianity — at the hands of its own morality (which cannot be replaced), which turns against the Christian God (the sense of truthfulness, developed highly by Christianity, is nauseated by the falseness and mendaciousness of all Christian interpretations of the world and of history); rebound from 'God is truth' to the fanatical faith 'All is false' . . . (p. 7).

The Christian sense of truthfulness does not of its own defeat the slave-morality; that only takes place when this sense of truthfulness turns against Christianity and establishes itself in the secularised form of Enlightenment, science, progress, and all the other post-Christian faiths. These faiths deny the Christian sense of evil; they reject the theology of guilt, sin, punishment as well as the anthropomorphic figure of the Devil. Instead they only affirm good in its various secularised forms. But this good, evacuated of its essential contrast in evil, loses its savour and sense. It is the faith of the 'last men'; 'the vermin man . . . tame, hopelessly mediocre and savourless . . .'.[11] The 'levelling and diminution of European man'[12] is complete.

'*Incipit Zarathustra*' once again as Nietzsche comes on the scene and begins the move beyond the good and evil of the slave-morality. Out of the End comes the Return, as beyond good and evil means a return back to the master-morality of good–bad. But the move back is also a move forward as the new masters are not the blonde beasts or barbarians of the past, but a new master race, the future rulers of the earth. Once again a morality is affirmed on the natural power differential of the strong and the weak; the natural herd animals will assume their rightful place as the platform on which will strut the nobility of world conquerors.

> And would it not be a kind of goal, redemption, and justification for the democratic movement itself if someone arrived who could make use of it — by finally producing beside its new and sublime development of slavery (— that is what European democracy must become ultimately) a higher kind of dominating and Caesarian spirits who would stand upon it, maintain themselves by it, and elevate themselves through it? (954).

But for these future master of the earth a new morality is called for, 'a morality . . . which desires to train men for the heights . . . a reversal of values for a certain strong kind of man of the highest spirituality and strength of will . . .' (957). Thus the original inversion of the slave-morality whereby good–bad becomes evil–good is itself inverted beyond good and evil to a new higher good–bad. The full eschatological logic of version, inversion and reinversion is thereby complete.

What historical validity or value has this kind of eschatological schematising? Let us briefly examine just one of its tropes, that of the Fall from master-morality into slave-morality. Does this correspond to anything one can actually find historically confirmed? It seems that one can historically locate it at the point when the Jews fell under Roman sway and became 'slaves' and then as a result Christianity arose, which subsequently spiritually conquered the Romans. But the Judaic conception of evil and of a morality in which this is the basic concept long predates that era; it is already fully developed in the book of Genesis, and is there throughout the Old Testament, which long predates any enslavement of the Jews; on the contrary, it reflects a period when the Jews themselves were a master-race of conquerors in Canaan. From the start Genesis is emphatic that the source of morality — of moral knowledge as conscience and consciousness — is some kind of a transgression or fall; and it sets out beside the Fall in Eden also the 'falls' of Cain and Abel, the tower of Babel and the Flood. In each case there is an original sin or transgression followed by a divine punishment; the original sins have to do with sex, violence, pride and turpitude and are followed by the punishments of guilt, homelessness, failure of communication and finally ecological social disaster. This morality is certainly different from that of the Greek Homeric ethos of warrior excellence or *arete*. However, it bears no relation to slavery or servitude; it is no less suitable for warriors and conquering people, which the Jews originally were. It bears no taint of *ressentiment*.

Nietzsche would have made a better sociological judgement had he continued as he began when he set out this distinction:

> In a tour of many finer and coarser moralities which have ruled or still rule on earth I found certain traits regularly recurring together and bound up with one another; until at length two basic types were revealed and a basic distinction emerged. There is *master morality* and *slave morality* — I add at once that in all higher and mixed cultures attempts at mediation between the two are apparent and more frequently confusion and mutual misunderstanding . . .[13]

Had Nietzsche continued to treat the distinction as one of two ideal-type concepts, whose use and historical reference was neither predetermined nor exclusive, but which functioned as comparative standards for the description of actual historically occurring moralities, then he would have saved himself from some of his worst excesses. Two such ideal-types would be particularly useful in an analysis of Christianity, a higher moral culture in which an admixture of simpler, more basic moral types is apparent. As we shall eventually show, features of the master-morality are by no means absent in Christianity, though overlayed by those of the slave-morality.

Nietzsche's thought was driven in a different direction because he was determined to identify slave-morality with the Jews. He was determined to see the Jews as '"a people born for slavery" as Tacitus and the whole ancient world says, "the chosen people" as they themselves say and believe . . .'[14] He maintains this despite the fact that they resisted Roman rule longer than any other nation: 'The Jews achieved that miracle of inversion of values thanks to which life on earth has for a couple of millenia acquired a new and dangerous fascination — their prophets fused "rich", "godless", "evil", "violent", "sensual" into one and were the first to coin the word "world" as a term of infamy.'[15] Which prophets, one would like to ask, those before or after the exile? But, of course, this hardly matters for Nietzsche, since what concerns him ultimately is to stage a moral world-drama in which the Jew is opposed to the Aryan, the born slave to the born master. Commenting on some of the most abhorrent regulations of the Indian Law of Manu, he concludes as follows:

> These regulations are instructive enough: in them we find for once *Aryan* humanity, quite pure, quite primordial — we learn that the concept 'pure blood' is the opposite of a harmless concept. It becomes clear, on the other hand, in *which* people the hatred, the Chandala hatred for this 'humanity' has been immortalized, where it has become religion, where it has become *genius* . . . Christianity, growing from Jewish roots and comprehensible only as a product of this soil, represents the *reaction* against the morality of breeding, of race, of privilege — it is the *anti-Aryan* religion *par excellence* . . . undying Chandala revenge as the *religion of love*.[16]

The genealogy of morals reduces itself ultimately to this apocalyptic ranting. Granted that this passage comes from a text only a few months removed from Nietzsche's collapse, nevertheless signs of apocalyptic madness are not absent from earlier texts. In this respect Nazi philosophy is quite continuous with Nietzsche's thought; it is simply its madness taken literally or with deadly seriousness and transformed into a mythology of race.

Throughout Nietzsche's thought genealogy continually degenerates into eschatology which eventually becomes mythology. Nietzsche is occasionally himself aware of the dangers of this slide and utters a word of warning, sometimes in the very midst of his own worst transgressions. Commenting on the genealogy of punishment he has this to say in a passage we have already referred to but which is worth quoting at length:

There is no set of maxims more important for a historian than this: that the actual causes of a thing's origin and its eventual uses, the manner of its incorporation into a system of purposes, are worlds apart; that everything that exists, no matter what its origin, is periodically reinterpreted by those in power in terms of fresh intentions; that all processes in the organic world are processes of outstripping and overcoming, and that, in turn, all outstripping and overcoming means reinterpretation, rearrangement, in the course of which earlier meaning and purpose are necessarily either obscured or lost . . . Thus the entire history of a thing, an organ, a custom, becomes a continuous *chain* of reinterpretations and rearrangements, which need only be causally connected among themselves, which may simply follow one another. The 'evolution' of a thing, a custom, an organ is not its *progressus* toward a goal, let along the most logical or shortest *progressus*, requiring the least energy and expenditure. Rather, it is a sequence of more or less profound, more or less independent processes of appropriation, including the resistances used in each instance, the attempted transformations for purposes of defence or reaction, as well as the results of successful counterattacks. While forms are fluid, their 'meaning' is even more so.[17]

Had Nietzsche taken to heart his own set of 'maxims' he would have been obliged to abandon all his eschatological tropes of Origin, Fall, Decline, End and Return. This would have left very little of his work unscathed. His search for genealogical origins would have to have been abandoned as irrelevant, for there are no such constitutive origins; behind every original an even more original one can always be found. In any case, origins are not constitutive of the nature of a thing, idea or institution, for that is determined by the context, social, cultural and historical, in which the thing, idea or institution finds itself. Thus, the thing acquires continually new meanings and identities as it enters into new constellations in different contexts, each time, as it were, acquiring a new origin as its old origins are forgotten, mislaid, eliminated or remain as purely vestigial survivals.

From this kind of critical approach a different genealogical thinking would have eventuated, one no longer given to looking for the *arche* of things, and so no longer prone to archaic thinking. It would also abandon the search for original faults or Falls, for primal divisions or inversions, for errors committed in the beginning to which the bad end of anything can be ascribed and for which its origi-nations can be blamed. For Nietzsche, history is always a matter of finding someone to blame for that which he dislikes in contemporary culture and society. The further back he can project the responsi-bility and culpability the better. He fails to heed his own warning that 'while the forms are fluid, their "meaning" is even more so'; the originators of a given set of forms are in no way responsible for what subsequently happens to them, for the original foundation did not necessitate the subsequent construction. Neither Greek Reason nor Christian morality were required to end up as nineteenth century Nihilism; their values did not need to be devalued. If they were in fact devalued, then this was due to other causes — about which Nietzsche has nothing to say.

Western civilisation has for Nietzsche an essential unity from start to finish. This is why he persistently casts his ideas into eschatological schemes. He refuses to realise the full meaning of his own judgement that history is 'a continuous chain of reinterpreta-tions and rearrangements, which need only be causally connected among themselves, which may simply follow one another". Hence, what takes place in Greek philosophy or Judaic morality is worlds removed from the nineteenth century and might have very little relevance to it. In fact, strictly speaking, the term Western civili-sation is a misnomer for a sequence of quite distinct and sometimes quite opposed civilisational forms. This has no essential unity, nor, therefore, any pre-ordained destiny.

The history of philosophy and rationality in the West has likewise no essential unity. It is broken up into numerous forms, strata, passages, and conflicting types. The history of Reason, as Nietzsche presents it, is at best only one strand among many others, and even in itself by no means a uniform process. This tendency to see the history of rationality as the one process of Reason, whether in a progressive or regressive sense, is a persistent failing in German thought, begun by Hegel and continued in a different spirit by Nietzsche, Heidegger, Adorno and Marcuse. Thus the *Dialectic of Enlightenment* is also an eschatological scheme that presents Reason as originating out of myth and returning back into myth again. As against any such unitary conception of Reason it is essential to deploy a genealogy of multiple forms of rationality, distinguishing at least Reason, Rationalism and Rationalisation, showing that these have multiple origins, developments, courses and ends, and concluding that the history of rationality is one of 'fluid forms' with continually changing meanings. Only in Max Weber is it possible to find the basis for such an approach to the history of rationality.

Nietzsche's approach to this 'history of an error', the 'fatality of error on earth', is inherently eschatological, for it is premised on an original inversion of this-world/other-world into an apparent-world/ true-world that is formally analogous to the inversion of good–bad into evil–good. As we have seen, this makes some historical sense when referred to Plato and Greek metaphysics. But it makes little sense to speak of metaphysics as a kind of error which might have been avoided from the start. He had forgotten his earlier admonition to the anti-metaphysical thinker who has 'overcome metaphysics with the greatest exertion of his intelligence . . . he must understand the historical justification as well as the psychological in such representations, he must recognise how the greatest advancement of humanity has come therefrom . . .'.[18] Thus the metaphysical conception of a true-world is the essential precursor of abstract conceptualisation and the development of the forms of rationality that made theoretical science possible. *Theoria* in philosophy paved the way for theory in science. However, Nietzsche believes the opposite:

> The road to science was in this way doubly blocked: once by belief in a 'true' world, and again by opponents of this belief. Natural science, psychology was (1) condemned with regard to its objects, (2) deprived of innocence (584).

But historically considered the road to science was only opened when the philosophers devised the idea of concepts and theories beyond the reach of the senses and commonsense. In the first instance this took the guise of a metaphysical picture; but the basic idea has never been abandoned, for even in a contemporary anti-metaphysical spirit some idea of a 'true-world' of scientific abstractions and mathematical formulation must still be retained. Nietzsche himself recognises that 'physicists believe in a "true" world in their own fashion' (636), though he thinks that thereby 'they are in error' (636). In a fundamental sense such an 'error' is not to be avoided in science, so in what way is it an error?

Nietzsche wants to link this *proton pseudos* with the contemporary fate of metaphysics and the devaluation of Reason. Because of his eschatological preconception, he believes that the origin and end of metaphysics are bound up with each other. But in a history of philosophy and Reason that is broken up into segments with numerous fits and starts and all kinds of arrivals and departures there need be no link left between beginning and end. The history of a thing can be like a rope with no single strand stretching from beginning to end, with no *roter Faden* of identity. It is fruitless, therefore, to scan the origins of metaphysics in order to explain why it had to end. The end of metaphysics and the philosophy of Reason were determined by factors of very recent provenance and nowhere in evidence at their beginning. Among such factors were the remarkable developments in the sciences in the last few hundred years. This leads to the kind of account previously presented in this work. To argue that these sciences themselves completely derive from and are an integral part of metaphysics is once again to conceive of Western civilisation as an essential unity synonymous with the history of metaphysics, as what Heidegger calls *Seinsgeschichte*. Such a conception has been strenuously avoided in this work in favour of one that gives sociological specificity to multiple developments and heterogeneous causes.

At the end of this work, in Chapter 6, we shall once again take up all these issues concerning the genealogy of Reason and provide a revalued reinterpretation of Nietzsche's key ideas on the subject. For it must not be assumed from the preceding or following criticisms of Nietzsche that what he has to say is to be dismissed or abandoned, that he is simply wrong or in error. On the contrary, his leading ideas can be reinvoked in another form to provide a different kind of genealogy of Reason. Thus, the concept of *ressentiment* and the master-morality, slave-morality opposition taken as an ideal-type, may be shown to be indispensible conceptual tools for the understanding of the origins of ethical rationalism in Judeo-Christian culture. And analogously, the opposition of the true-world to the apparent-world and the concept of sublimation are essential for any analysis in cultural depth of the origins of Reason and philosophy in the preceding Greek culture of Homeric myth. However, from this it does not follow, as Nietzsche supposed, that the beginning of Reason predetermines its end, namely, that metaphysical Reason and modern scientific Rationalisation are unified as the opening and closing stages of the one eschatological pattern. At the end of this work we shall provide a very different interpretation of the cultural meaning and relationship of Reason and Rationalisation.

2. Reason and Language

Nietzsche's search for the roots of Reason does not stop at historical eschatological origins, but moves further back into the primitive. For him the key to genealogy is etymology: 'The clue to the correct explanation was furnished me by the question "What does the etymology of the terms for good in various languages tell us?"'[19] Such a search for etymological origins means that the origin of things is pushed into the dim recesses of language prior to history. Archaism takes a further step back in its search for the *arche*. Heidegger followed Nietzsche's lead in this respect, but at least Nietzsche was a philologist; unlike Heidegger he did not invent his own etymology.

According to Nietzsche all possible philosophies have their genealogical origins in primitive language, above all in the Indo-Aryan language-family, specifically in its grammar:

> Under an invisible spell they always trace once more the identical orbit; however independent of one another they may feel, with their will to criticism or systematism, something in them leads them, sometimes drives them in a definite order one after another: it is precisely that innate systematism and relationship of concepts. Their thinking is in fact not so much a discovering as a recognizing, a remembering, a return and home-coming to a far-off, primordial total household of the soul out of which those concepts once emerged — philosophizing is to that extent a species of atavism of the first rank.[20]

Nietzsche's eschatology goes back to the primitive; he sees philosophy as a return to basic roots in the Indo-Aryan system of conjugation: 'The singular family resemblance between all Indian, Greek and German philosophizing is easy enough to explain.'[21] This philological myth of origins links up with Nietzsche's mythologising tendencies in general and adds a dimension of primitive thinking to his other more classically inclined symbols.

Philosophy and Reason, according to Nietzsche, have their identities fixed by the languages of the stone-age. The categories of Reason developed by the metaphysicians are no more than the grammatical substantives of primitive language:

> . . . we see ourselves as entangled in error, *necessitated* to error,

to precisely the extent that our prejudice in favour of Reason compels us to posit unity, identity, duration, substance, cause, materiality, being; however sure we may be, on the basis of strict reckoning, *that* error is to be found here. The situation is the same as with the motions of the sun: in that case error has our eyes, in the present case our *language* as a perpetual advocate. Language belongs in its origin to the age of the most rudimentary form of psychology: we find ourselves in the midst of a rude fetishism when we call to mind the basic presuppositions of the metaphysics of language — which is to say, of *Reason*.[22]

So the *proton pseudos* has also moved further back into the primitive, the idols of philosophy emerge out of the fetishism of language which philosophy has not been able to escape. Because of this fetishism of language the philosophers 'in India and Greece . . . committed the same blunder':

> At the beginning stands the great fateful error . . . the subjective *certainty* with which the categories of reason could be employed came all of a sudden in to philosophers' heads: they concluded that these could not have originated in the empirical world — indeed, the entire empirical world was incompatible with them.[23]

As an antidote to this fetishism of language on which Reason and philosophy depend, and as a 'basis for strict reckoning', Nietzsche resorts to the presumed certitude of the senses:

> Heraclitus too was unjust to the senses, which lie neither in the way the Eleatics believe nor as he believed — they do not lie at all. It is what we *make* of their evidence that first introduces a lie into it, for example the lie of unity, the lie of materiality, of substance, of duration . . . 'Reason' is the cause of our falsification of the evidence of the senses.[24]

It is rather surprising to see Nietzsche emerging in this late text as a staunch British Empiricist. It must be read as a temporary aberration on his part for it is against the tenor of the rest of his philosophy, especially of his perspectivism in knowledge:

> Against positivism, which halts at phenomena — 'There are only *facts*' — I would say: No, facts are precisely what there are not,

only interpretations. We cannot establish any fact 'in itself': perhaps it is folly to want to do such a thing.

'Everything is subjective', you say; but even this is interpretation. The 'subject' is not something given, it is something added and invented and projected behind what there is . . . (481).

The senses are as much a matter of interpretation as language and Reason: 'The development of reason is adjustment, invention, with the aim of making similar, equal — the same process that every sense impression goes through' (515). So it seems that the senses lie as much as language and Reason do. Nietzsche cannot derive from the senses any 'basis for strict reckoning' by which to condemn language and rationality.

Does it follow from this that there is no such thing as the fetishism of language? In an early text Nietzsche had put it more modestly that 'there is a philosophical mythology concealed in language'.[25] Many linguists, such as Whorf, have attempted to unearth the 'philosophical mythologies' of different languages, especially the Amerindian ones. Some have claimed that these encapsulate distinct world-views. It is unnecessary to dispute this claim, for what is at issue is merely the question of whether such philosophical mythologies determine the nature of philosophy and Reason. Philosophy and Reason are the products of developed civilisations, not of primitive tribes. Whatever effect its language has on the culture of a primitive tribe, it does not follow that it will have the same effect on a developed culture and civilisation. As civilisational forms, philosophy and Reason are quite impervious to transfers from one language to another. Western philosophy has been translated into numerous languages in its course, some, such as Arabic, outside the Indo-Aryan family. Nietzsche states that 'philosophers within the domain of the Ural-Altaic languages (in which the concept of subject is least developed) will in all probability look "into the world" differently and be found on different paths from the Indo-Germans and Moslems: the spell of definite grammatical functions is in the last resort the spell of physiological value judgements and racial conditions'.[26] If one takes this literally it is patently false, for there is no evidence that European Finns, Hungarians, and Basques have different philosophies or understand philosophy differently from Germans, or that Turks and Persians understand it differently from Arabs. The racial judgement Nietzsche makes is, of course, totally insupportable. The only way to take seriously

Nietzsche's statement is as the counter-factual conditional to this effect: if members of the Ural-Altaic languages had developed a separate civilisation (say, in the Urals) and invented philosophy, then this philosophy would have been markedly different from the Greek, and, furthermore, this difference would have been due to the difference in languages. Such a speculative judgement is historically unverifiable, being no better than a guess.

It is much more plausible to argue that civilisational differences are more important for philosophy and Reason than linguistic ones. The differences between civilisations are to some degree due to language, but much less so — since many civilisations had numerous languages — than to geographic, socioeconomic, religious and political factors. What distinguishes the European and Chinese civilisations and their philosophies and sciences cannot be traced to their languages. Far more important than language in this case is calligraphy, that is, the presence or absence of a phonetic script — an invention of the Semitic people who passed it on to the Greeks — without which the literate civilisation of the West is inconceivable and whose absence so hampered China. To argue thus is not totally to deny that differences of language in such cases 'colour' the quality of civilisations and their intellectual products, but exactly what this influence amounts to is notoriously difficult to establish. To grant this is a far call from Nietzsche's claim that philosophy and Reason are the outcome of a fetishism of language.

Nietzsche's proposals for overcoming the fetishism of language are even more revolutionary than Marx's proposals for defeating the fetishism of commodities. Nietzsche proposes a total restructuring of language and its rebuilding from the ground up.

> Philosophers . . . have not stopped to consider that concepts and words are our inheritance from ages in which thinking was very modest and unclear.
>
> What dawns on philosophers last of all: they must no longer accept concepts as a gift, nor merely purify and polish them, but first *make* and *create* them, present them and make them convincing. Hitherto one has generally trusted one's concepts as if they were a wonderful dowry from some sort of wonderland: but they are, after all, the inheritance from our most remote, most foolish as well as most intelligent ancestors. This piety toward what we find in us is perhaps part of the moral element in knowledge. What is needed above all is an absolute skepticism

toward all inherited concepts — of the kind that one philosopher *perhaps* possessed — Plato, of course — for he taught the reverse (409).

The radical nature of this proposal would take one's breath away were it not for the fact that there is no need to return to Plato to see it put into practice; since Nietzsche, the Logical Positivists and Wittgenstein in the *Tractatus* have not just spoken about a total reconstruction of language, but set about carrying it through. As it happens, all such utopian undertakings are the result of a shallow understanding of the nature of language. Despite his philological training, or because it never went beyond the premises of nineteenth century philology, Nietzsche, too, shows himself somewhat naive in his understanding of language. He imagines that our language has remained unchanged since our rude ancestors created it, and that we simply receive what has been passed on from primitive tribes. He does not grasp that the development of civilisation is a continuous process of language change, and that the concepts we inherit are far more the work of our fathers than our remote forefathers. Philosophers, perhaps more than anyone, participate in this process of civilisational language change; if they merely polished the concepts they received from the distant past, no science or any other new knowledge would have been possible. New concepts have been continually created and old ones reinterpreted, no concept has remained the same, for otherwise there could have been no change in our culture.

At times Nietzsche gives the impression of saying things which sound like the language philosophy of the late Wittgenstein, but in most cases this is a textual illusion deriving from his cryptic style.[27] An oft quoted passage to this effect is this:

Ultimate solution. — We believe in reason: this, however, is the philosophy of grey concepts. Language depends on the most naive prejudices.

Now we read disharmonies and problems into things because we think *only* in the form of language — and thus believe in the 'eternal truth' of 'reason' (e.g. subject, attribute, etc.)

We cease to think when we refuse to do so under the constraint of language, we barely reach the doubt that sees this limitation as a limitation.

> *Rational thought is interpretation according to a scheme that we cannot throw off.* (522).

The paragraph begins with a rendition in a jotted telegraphic style of Nietzsche's usual views about the fetishism of language which makes philosophers believe in the categories of Reason and project them into things. Wittgenstein, by contrast, holds the very opposite, namely that the ordinary forms of language are perfectly adequate as they are; it is only philosophers who misinterpret them and project their misconceptions onto language. Nietzsche wants totally to re-make language, not accept it as a gift from the remote past; Wittgenstein insists that we must leave it as it is, for 'what has to be accepted, the given, is — so one could say — forms of life',[28] and language can only change as our life changes. Nietzsche believes that the philosopher as heroic legislator can transform all our concepts and overcome nihilism; Wittgenstein holds that the philosopher can change nothing of any consequence: 'the sickness of a time is cured by an alteration in the mode of life of human beings and it was possible for the sickness of philosophical problems to get cured only through a changed mode of thought, not through a medicine invented by an individual'.[29] In all these respects Nietzsche is at the opposite extreme to Wittgenstein. Nietzsche maintains that the fetishism of language needs to be overcome; Wittgenstein sets out to fetishise language as a basic primitive given which must simply be accepted; 'It is not reasonable (or unreasonable). It stands there — like our life'.[30]

It might appear that the last two remarks Nietzsche makes in the long passage previously quoted are pure Wittgenstein, but that, too, is unconvincing if they are fully spelled out. Nietzsche's assertion that 'rational thought is interpretation according to a scheme that we cannot throw off' (522) seems to suggest the idea that language commits us to certain basic rational forms. But Nietzsche means it in a purely empirical sense for he treats all necessities and logical compulsions as factual impossibilities:

> We are unable to affirm and to deny one and the same thing: this is a subjective empirical law, not the expression of any 'necessity' but only of an inability (516).

This is not to say that Nietzsche means that the laws of logic are empirical regularities in the world, for he treats them also as imperatives: 'logic [is] an imperative, not to know the true, but to posit and arrange a world that shall be called true by us' (516). Nevertheless, they are empirical in the sense that we 'cannot throw them off' because our survival would be at stake:

> The subjective compulsion not to contradict here is a biological compulsion: the instinct for the utility of inferring as we do infer is part of us, we almost *are* this instinct — But what naiveté to extract from this a proof that we are therewith in possession of a 'truth in itself'! Not being able to contradict is proof of an incapacity, not of 'truth' (515).

By contrast, Wittgenstein treats rationality and logic, especially the making of inferences, not as a matter of 'biological compulsion' or pragmatic utility, but as a matter of the language-games utilised by different tribes, or really, by culturally diverse societies. Rationality and logic are founded on language-games which are not themselves either rational or logical, 'not based on grounds'[31] but themselves the grounds for rationality and logic. Such language-games can be 'thrown off'; they can change; we can imagine different ones. Wittgenstein is much more concerned with cultural disparities inherent in different logics and rational forms; Nietzsche is intent on supposed biological and pragmatic universals as laws of survival.

Nietzsche and Wittgenstein share a joint misapprehension that the metaphysical categories of Reason, such as those of Aristotle, are simply elaborations of the grammatical forms of language. They conceive of this differently, however; Nietzsche sees it as the result of a 'belief in grammar' which leads to the reproduction of the 'rude fetishism . . . [of] the basic presuppositions of the metaphysics of language — which is to say, of reason'.[32] Wittgenstein sees it as a falsification of the logical-grammar of ordinary language due to the philosophers' misconceptions. Neither fully appreciates the enormous intellectual distance separating metaphysical categories from grammar, regardless of whether this is correctly represented or misconceived. Aristotle's categories bear the same relation to the grammatical forms from which they take their bearing as does the calculus to counting on the fingers of the hand. Granted that if men did not count they could not have invented the calculus, but the calculus is neither a right nor wrong version of counting procedures. The metaphysical categories are not correct or incorrect versions of the rules of grammar, but highly intellectualised speculative constructions, idealised rational models, defined in terms of each other and designed to comprise a systematic comprehension of the sciences and the world. Likewise the laws of logic are not derivations of language rules, but abstract definitions of formal possibilities, highly intellectualised forms of rational discourse, integrated to make up a logical system. The rules of language are tacit, unclear, ambiguous, overlapping and frequently inconsistent with each other, for language does not ordinarily require any higher rigour or exactitude — for practical purposes it is all right as it is. But logic is a rational invention of norms in which each norm is related to every other and derives its meaning from that relation. The use and purpose of such a system is another matter; it is not to be used, as logicians imagine, to correct language but has technical uses in science and technology.

Nietzsche's attempts to reduce rationality and logic to primitive language is to be resisted. Language in itself is pre-rational in the sense that it only contains the preparatory forms and structures for the development of rationality. Rationality is, of course, not to be identified solely with its Western forms, such as Reason, Rationalism and Rationalisation; there are non-Western forms as well, such as Traditional rationality, and there are even pre-civilisational forms such as the Primitive rationality of tribal cultures. Such tribal modes of thought as magic, taboo and mythology which are from a Western point of view considered irrational and illogical — examples of savage thought — might nevertheless be said to embody norms of their own, such as those which anthropologists have sought to elicit and which we may dub Primitive rationality. But Primitive rationality is not inherent in primitive language as such; it is a cultural elaboration of language just as much as is Western rationality. The codes of sympathetic magic are forms of Primitive rationality, which are not given in language but are culturally defined and utilised, just as are those of logic (see Appendix 1).

3.   Reason and Power

Nietzsche's search for the primitive origins of rationality does not stop at language, but probes even further back for evolutionary stages prior to language itself.

Origin of the logical — Where has logic originated in men's heads? Undoubtedly out of the illogical, the domain of which must originally have been immense. But numberless beings who reasoned otherwise than we do at present, perished; albeit that they may have come nearer to truth than we![33]

What is one to make of this fantasy of prior beings who, reasoning otherwise than we do, were closer to the truth, yet who perished through evolutionary attrition? How does Nietzsche mean us to take his evolutionary parable?

Elsewhere in his work Nietzsche calls the rational forms 'errors' rather than 'truths' or approximations to the truth. What he means by this is that they are fabrications and fictions, something we create for a purpose:

> In the formation of reason, logic, the categories, it was *need* that was authoritative: the need, not to 'know', but to subsume, to schematize, for the purpose of intelligibility and calculation . . . No pre-existing 'idea' was here at work, but the utilitarian fact that only when we see things coarsely and made equal do they become calculable and usable for us. — Finality in reason is an effect, not a cause: life miscarries with any other kinds of reason, to which there is a continual impulse . . .
>
> The categories are 'truths' only in the sense that they are conditions of life for us . . . (515).

Beginning with the pragmatic view-point that the rational forms are utilitarian inventions, like tools and weapons, necessary to make life easier, Nietzsche ends up by treating them as biological needs and conditions of survival. He shifts from instrumentalism as utilitarian pragmatism to instrumentalism as biological evolutionism. This was characteristic of many thinkers in the period after Darwin. But Nietzsche took the evolutionary theory of rationality with extreme literalness, as we have seen from his evolutionist fantasy. What makes it a fantasy is that Nietzsche is incapable of distinguishing between the genetic evolution of species and the social evolution of groups. 'Whoever, for example, could not discern the "like" often enough with regard to food and with regard to animals dangerous to him, whoever, therefore, deduced too slowly, or was too circumspect in his deductions, had smaller probability of survival than he who in all similar cases immediately divined the equality.'[34] This is as much as to say that the capacity for deduction and rational thought evolves in the same way as teeth and claws and that swiftness of thought is no different to swiftness of foot. If that were the case then the lion's powers of deduction would be far superior to ours.

Why is it that Nietzsche is so oblivious of the differences between species evolution and social evolution, between the evolution of animal faculties and that of human society, its language and cultural forms, and finally, why does he not show an inkling of insight into the problematic issue of the separation of evolution and history? Nietzsche does not realise that it is not single individuals but human societies that adapt themselves to their given environment, each one differently, depending on its culture and history; and their rational forms develop not at a pre-historic stage but within history in culturally produced discourses, with all the resultant differences in the forms of rationality. Nietzsche is misled by his predilection for an instrumentalist biologism and by his philosophical prejudice for a reduction of knowledge to power. Thus he regards all forms of knowledge as 'forms of domination: the sphere of that which is dominated continually growing or periodically increasing and decreasing according to the favourability or unfavourability of circumstances . . .' (515). The rational forms are no more than instruments of domination, tools in the evolutionary struggle for survival and conquest. An analogously conceived instrumentalist biologism holds for all value spheres and meaning:

> That the value of the world lies in our interpretation . . .; that previous interpretations have been perspective valuations by virtue of which we can survive in life, i.e. in the will to power, for the growth of power . . . — this idea permeates my writings (616).

Thus, behind Nietzsche's instrumentalist biologism there stands his over-arching conception of the will to power and the perspectival theory of valuation and knowledge.[35] Nietzsche imagines that in the notion of power he possesses an objective criterion of epistemology which governs knowledge and ignorance, rationality and irrationality, truth and falsity, and that all are a matter of quanta of power which can be measured objectively: 'What is the objective measure of value? Solely the quantum of enhanced and organized power' (674). The next step is simply to construct epistemological value-meters, instruments for gauging quanta of power:

> Our knowledge has become scientific to the extent that it is able

to employ number and measure. The attempt should be made to see whether a scientific order of values could be constructed simply on a numerical and mensural scale of force. — All other 'values' are prejudices, naiveties, misunderstandings. — They are everywhere *reducible* to this numerical and mensural scale of force. The ascent on this scale represents every rise in value; the descent on this scale represents diminution in value (710).

This is no better than a philosopher's fantasy in the genre of science fiction. But it does serve as a *reductio-ad-absurdum* of the whole Nietzschean notion of quanta of will to power. If there were any such, then by any criterion of verification they would have to be measurable. But given that it makes no sense to measure quanta of power, it follows that whatever will to power means, it cannot be a matter of definite quanta. Hence, there is no way of assessing degrees of will to power and utilising this as an objective measure of knowledge, rationality and value.

Nietzsche pretends to a less objectivist assessment of will to power when he treats it as a synonym for life or some function of life, such as 'life-advancing, life-preserving, species-preserving, perhaps even species-breeding'.[36] On this basis Nietzsche claims to prefer false judgements to true ones: 'our fundamental tendency is to assert that the falsest judgements (to which synthetic judgements *a priori* belong) are the most indispensible to us, that without granting as true the fictions of logic, without measuring reality against the purely invented world . . . mankind could not live . . .'.[37] It seems that Nietzsche has a criterion for assessing judgements quite independent of the ones normally resorted to, say in logic, science or philosophy, for the purpose of distinguishing truth and falsity. Thus, for example, Nietzsche might be thought to be claiming that it is one thing to test scientific hypotheses for their truth or falsity by experimental and logical procedures and another to test them for their life-enhancing, life-preserving (or whatever) qualities; and furthermore, that he prefers the latter test rather than the former. But this, of course, is mere pretence for Nietzsche provides no independent way of telling whether a hypothesis is life-enhancing other than by testing it experimentally. In any case, to act on a false hypothesis, as Nietzsche well knows, would generally be disastrous for life — unless disaster were taken to be life-enhancing in some other sense. In general, then, the idea that will to power, or any of its life synonyms, is an independent means of assessing knowledge, rationality, value or validity is an unsubstantiated pretence. 'The criterion of truth resides in the enhancement of the feeling of power' (534) — perhaps, but what is the criterion of the enhancement of the feeling of power? Is it, in fact, any different from the criterion of truth, whatever it may be, in a given context?

This does not mean that what Nietzsche is saying concerning the will to power is vacuous, or that it is meaningless as the Positivist and Linguist philosophers would insist. It does have a meaning, but not the one Nietzsche supposes it to have. It is, as Danto puts it, a principle of 'Methodological Monism'[38] designed to unify the basic terms of all the sciences: energy, force, valency, growth, evolution, drive, struggle; these and many more are treated as manifestations of the one will to power, so that all spheres of being — the inorganic, the organic, the physiologic, psychological, social and cultural — can all be unified. This is the kind of unifying attempt characteristic of all metaphysics. Danto, in fact, believes that 'it is a metaphysical, or better, an ontological concept, for "will to power" is Nietzsche's answer to the question "what is there?"'.[39] Grimm takes up Danto's point and objects to it: 'Nietzsche does not intend to offer us a new metaphysical system . . .'; but he hastens to correct himself: 'it should be mentioned, however, that he very nearly does exactly that . . .'.[40] The reason he gives is that 'one of the fundamental differences between the will to power and the unified, homogenous, continuous, world-substances of traditional metaphysics is the fact that the will to power is discontinuous. It consists of discrete, separate power-quanta . . .'.[41] However, this is really a distinction without much difference for the so-called power-quanta are not independently measurable or ascertainable; they could just as easily be called energy-points, atoms, monads, or whatever other metaphysical entities are required. Nevertheless, it can be granted that Nietzsche's is a revisionist metaphysics somewhat different from the traditional varieties, and is so at least partly because it is confused with scientific ideas current in the late nineteenth century.

Grimm seeks to defend Nietzsche against the charge that he utilises an ontology that is circular, in that it presupposes itself and is thus no different to any metaphysics, by claiming that the principle of the will to power acts as a criterion for its own testing and potential refutability:

> Nietzsche's philosophical stature stands revealed to us in all its rigour and honesty when we realize that Nietzsche's reduction of

all other modes of philosophizing to interpretations and falsifications applies equally to his own thinking. The will to power is an interpretation, is a falsification, is a sublime illusion, and we need only add that Nietzsche would probably have maintained that it was so far the most efficacious interpretation advanced in enhancing and increasing the vital powers which we are.[42]

It seems magnanimous to allow this, but rather pointless, for once again we seem to be offered an independent criterion of value and validity which proves useless when we attempt to apply it. How is one to tell whether the doctrine of the will to power does in fact 'increase our vital powers', or enhance life, or do anything else of any efficacy; what would show this? If the Nazis had won, what would that have proved about the power of believing in the will to power? If believing in the will to power is to be judged by its results, over what time span is this to be determined? Are we to accept the doctrine of the will to power now on faith in the hope that this will prove efficacious thousands of years later? For, as Nietzsche puts it, 'it is nothing to be wondered at that a couple of millenia are needed to reestablish contact — a couple of millenia mean little' (1043)!

Nietzsche's hostility to metaphysics is by no means proof that he was not himself a quasi-metaphysician. As in many such instances hostility often betrays complicity. As he himself noted in speaking of the hostility to morals in the 'l'art pour l'art' aestheticism: 'but this very hostility betrays that moral prejudice is still dominant'.[43] In Nietzsche's hostility to metaphysics a metaphysical prejudice is also still dominant. A philosophical genealogy of the concept 'will to power' would show that its provenance was directly Spinoza's God as absolute power, Kant's Will as *noumenon* and Schopenhauer's Will as world. 'Schopenhauer's interpretation of the "in-itself" as will was an essential step; but he did not understand how to deify this will . . .' (1005). But a world-will is still a world-will regardless of whether it is despaired of or deified.

Like any metaphysical principle, traditionalist or revisionist, the will to power plays an important orientating and directing role in the economy of Nietzsche's thought. Deleuze writes in praise of it:

If the will to power is a good principle, if it reconciles empiricism with strict principles, if it constitutes a superior empiricism, this is because it is an essentially plastic principle that is no wider than its field of application; it metamorphoses itself within this field and

> determines itself, in each case, along with what it determines . . .
> it is always plastic and metaphorphic.[44]

It is impossible to see what will to power has to do with any kind of scientific empiricism, superior or otherwise, unless Deleuze means to coin a notion of super-empiricism on the model of surrealism. There is indeed something 'surrealist' about the will to power, since it is also a poetic principle that is 'plastic and metamorphic' or metaphoric. Chameleon-like, it can assume an infinite number of changeable forms: it is force, conflict, attraction and repulsion, now libido, now domination, and many others. It directs Nietzsche's attention and interest toward division, opposition, multiplicity, struggle and to non-resolvable contradictions and away from unities, identities, continuities, or the other predisposing prejudices of the older metaphysics. It is a polymorphic symbol of great plasticity, but no clearly specifiable meaning.

It is closely related to another of Nietzsche's polyvalent symbols: Life. Life, too, is a principle of great flexibility directing Nietzsche's ideas and valuations: 'the essence of life . . ., the intrinsic superiority of the spontaneous, aggressive, overreaching, reinterpreting and re-establishing forces'.[45] Nietzsche himself admits that Life acts as his model for the will to power:

> There is nothing for it: one is obliged to understand all motion, all 'appearance', all 'laws', only as symptoms of an inner event and to employ man as an analogy to this end (619).

> Life is a special case (hypothesis based upon it applied to the total character of being—) strives after a *maximal feeling of power* . . . the basic and innermost thing is still this will (Mechanics is merely the semiotics of the results) (689).

We might turn against Nietzsche one of his own sharpest remarks: 'What we find here is still the hyperbolic naiveté of man: positing himself as the meaning and measure of the value of things' (12).

The symbol Life pushes Nietzsche's metaphysics in the direction of the symbol Art. It leads him to an aesthetic perception of the world which he thinks is anti-metaphysical: 'An anti-metaphysical view of the world — yes, but an artistic one' (1048). The idea of an artist-god might not be one that metaphysics traditionally entertained, thus Lingis might in this respect be right when he claims that 'things are meaningful for Nietzsche in an entirely different way from metaphysical thought . . .'[46] But, nevertheless, an aesthetics of the world is no less speculative than a metaphysics; nor is it even more morally neutral. Weber, in fact, takes exception to it for this reason:

> Nietzsche occasionally gives voice to the conception of the 'artist-god' with the negative moralistic pathos which often betrays an embarrassing residue of bourgeois philistinism even in some of his greatest passages.[47]

Nietzsche dissents most strenuously from the Christian moral interpretations of the world and the idea of the creation of the world, only to lapse back into it as an aesthetic ideal: 'this, my Dionysian world of the eternally self-creating, the eternally self-destroying' (1067).

The aesthetic idea of creation and destruction gives Nietzsche a model for interpreting rationality and the modes of knowledge which is different from the instrumental biologism previously discussed. This aesthetic model holds that all cognitive terms are forms that are to be understood as no different from the forms of art. The model is bound up with his symbol of the Apollonian which emerged very early in his work and re-emerged briefly towards the end in his late notes. The Apollonian is closely allied to the rational, seen aesthetically: 'the eternity of beautiful form' (1049). Nietzsche develops this aestheticist rationalism in an early work, *Truth and Falsity in an Ultramoral Sense*, where all ideas are seen as metaphors created by man 'as an artistically creating subject'.[48] On this basis the rational forms become metaphoric abstractions, frozen metaphors or 'cooler ideas' to which man 'as a "rational" being submits his actions'.[49] 'Everything which makes man stand out in bold relief against the animal depends on this faculty of volatilizing the concrete metaphors into a schema, and therefore resolving a perception into an idea.'[50]

Unfortunately, much of what Nietzsche has to say about ideas in this work is secondhand Empiricism couched in an aesthetic style: Locke in metaphoric dress. Nietzsche simply translates the representative theory of perception and the representative formation of complex ideas into the language of 'metaphor' and 'translation'. Thus the relation of subject to object he calls 'an aesthetic relation': 'I mean a suggestive metamorphosis, a stammering translation into quite a distinct foreign language, for which purpose, however, there is needed at any rate an intermediate sphere, an intermediate force, freely composing and freely inventing.'[51] Nietzsche thereby endows the subject *qua* artist with far more creative latitude than Empiricism does, with its emphasis on the causation of impressions and reflection and on a quasi-chemical composition of ideas. Nevertheless, the very same difficulties that have always been laid at the door of the representative theory of perception and the representative composition of ideas apply to Nietzsche's aestheticised version as well. There is no need to reiterate all of these here, it is enough to press home the key one: namely, that Nietzsche leaves himself no way of comparing outer objects with inner ideas and so cannot say anything at all about their lack of match or otherwise.

The aestheticist approach to rationality fits no better than the instrumentalist one. Rational forms are forms of discourse that are neither like tools and techniques nor like art figures and *Gestalten*. A form in art or an artistic formula is an expressive means and serves a quite different purpose to a rational form or formula. The former are used to constitute works of art; the latter to assess validity and truth and so to constitute certitude and knowledge. These differences in usage make for great differences in meaning. Thus Nietzsche's treatment of rational forms as frozen metaphors is itself only metaphoric; apart from it being suggestive, it is impossible to say what it really means. Art and science are separate realms; the attempt to bridge them by applying the terms of the one to the other only leads to a false assimilation that hides the real differences without in any way relating the two human activities.

Instrumentalism and aestheticism in Nietzsche's treatment of rationality are not necessarily in conflict; both are species of formalism. Both are ways of denying the essentially discursive character of rationality, namely denying that in the first place it pertains to what is said; instead, they affirm the 'poetic' character of rationality as something that is made. Rationality as a fabrication and fiction or as a species of *technē*, is uppermost for Nietzsche, and the essential link of rationality to language, that is to logos and '*legein*' is lost. This is why he can so blithely assert that he prefers falsehood to truth when it is life-enhancing or works better. But actually, questions of truth and falsity simply fall away as all that matters for a fabrication is whether it does or does not work for a given purpose.

Nietzsche's instrumentalist and aestheticist approaches to rationality open the way dangerously to uninhibited Rationalisation and to an irrational poeticism, two seemingly opposed courses that are, nevertheless, complementary. To treat rationality instrumentally means taking the most efficient rational devices as the most rational ones, and that is a prescription for Rationalisation. This side of Nietzsche's philosophy opens the way to the unrestrained inroads of science and technology, to social engineering, physiological manipulation, racial geneticism, military discipline, organisational planning, and extensive class repression. On the other side, an aestheticist rationality opens the way to the irrationality of 'fashioning man according to the pleasure of a creative and profound will' (957), to the arbitrary 'legislation' of values by a great Legislator, to the sheer prescription and positing of meaning at will, and, most ominously of all, to barbarism with a 'classical taste'. 'Where are the barbarians of the twentieth century?' (868) he asked, and the answer was not long in coming. Rationalisation and aestheticist poeticism lead to scientism and mythology, the prescription for a twentieth-century barbarism which Nietzsche foreshadowed in a way he did not expect and towards which he contributed in a way he did not understand.

4.   Scientism and Mythology

Science and myth enter into a highly combustible combination when the myth of science is compounded with the science of myth, so that myths are taken for sciences and sciences are used for mythic ends. Nietzsche tried to give his myths and symbols a scientific meaning and validity. The eternal recurrence, he thought, was a cosmological principle based on the chance juggling of the finite number of atoms in the universe — since Einstein, an absurd idea. The Overman he took for an evolutionary hypothesis. The will to power was a matter of measurable quanta or a science of ergonomics. A future master race might be produced by eugenics. There is hardly a science that Nietzsche did not misuse and he invented a few pseudo-sciences of his own. In this respect he was very much a child of his age. At the same time some of his most novel and interesting ideas in the psychological and cultural sciences arise out of these scientistic lucubrations, as in this example:

> . . . there is neither an unegoistic action nor an entirely disin-
> terested point of view; they are both only sublimations in which
> the fundamental element appears almost evaporated, and is only
> to be discovered by the closest observation. All that we require,
> and which can only be given us by the present advance of the
> single sciences, is a *chemistry* of the moral, religious, aesthetic
> ideas and sentiments . . . [52]

Sandwiched between a conventional psychological egoism and a
purely imaginary 'chemistry' of ideas is one of the first references to
the important psychoanalytic concept of sublimation. In amongst
the chaff there is the grain of an important idea.

Like his instrumentalism and aestheticism, Nietzsche's scientism
and mythology also complement each other. From both together
there results a mode of thought that is archaicist and primitivist, as
exemplified by his search for ever earlier genealogical origins and his
recourse to overarching patterns of eschatological destiny. There is
a predilection in Nietzsche's thinking for logical schemas of mythic
inevitability, patterns of turning, upturning and returning. Logical
and mythical designs coincide so that the one kind of conclusion is
also the other kind.

This paradoxical relationship between science and mythology is
by no means peculiar to Nietzsche; it is one of the dominant features
of modernity. It received its classic critique from Adorno and
Horkheimer:

> In both the pregnancy of the mythical image and the clarity of the
> scientific formula, the everlastingness of the factual is confirmed
> and mere existence pure and simple expressed as the meaning
> which it forbids. The world as a gigantic analytic judgement, the
> only one left over from all the dreams of science, is of the same
> mould as the cosmic myth which associated the cycle of spring and
> autumn with the kidnapping of Persephone. [53]

However, as these authors present it, the conjunction of rationality
and mythology appears as solely a regressive phenomenon; they do
not sufficiently take into account its necessity for modern thought,
or the stimulus it provides for knowledge, no less than for art. The
elevation of myth into science is characteristic of such outstanding
scientific achievements as Freudian psychoanalysis and the
anthropology of Lévi-Strauss, as well as the more questionable

accomplishments of Sorel, Spengler and Klages. Nietzsche was perhaps the first major figure decisively to inaugurate this process, reversing a trend current in Western thought since Plato to separate Mythos from Logos. Nietzsche was among the first to realise that myth was as essential to modern thought as it was to art or culture in general. He was proved right, for without the recovery of mythic truths the greatest achievements of modern art and culture would have been unimaginable. In art alone, Romanticism, Symbolism, Art Nouveau, Expressionism and Surrealism are different modes and stages in the recovery of myth; a great many major artists and writers of the modern period were intensely preoccupied with mythic paradigms and concerned to recapture their truth. Drawing closer to the mythic was no irrationalist aberration for modern culture and thought, but a necessity in an age dominated by the sterile and sterilising effects of Rationalisation, technology, Positivism and other such scientistic impositions, with their accompanying restrictions and constrictions. It enabled culture and thought to come in touch with the impulses that Rationalisation had suppressed and repressed: the unconscious, the extraordinary, the dream-like, the child-like, the archaic and primitive. It made it possible for language to draw on a depth of meaning embodied in mythic traditions going back to pre-history, and thus partly to overcome the thinning, narrowing and diluting effects of intellectualism, formalism, logical exactitude and scientistic precision. It also seemed to be the only way of recovering the human universal among the mechanised trivia of modern everyday life. At the same time, this re-mythifying endeavour was accompanied by all kinds of spurious rationalisations — theories of race, the collective unconscious, the archetype, the archaic — which already directed it into some of its eventual misuses. In time these abuses of the mythical became horrendous precisely because they took a rationalised form. Revivifying myth quickly ossified into deathly mythological ideology, with the machinery of the state being placed at its killing disposal. Thus, the slaughterhouse of history was prepared among aesthetes in the salon and scholars in the study.

Nietzsche himself was in no way an accomplice in what was done in his name. But, he was reckless at a time when the dangers were not yet fully evident. He could indulge himself in an aesthetics of violence when it was not apparent that anybody would take it literally, rather than merely literarily. To us this is all too apparent, so much so that we need now to be reminded of the merits of myth before we forget them completely, to our own loss. Nietzsche's philosophy of Nihilism would not have been possible without his myths and symbols of the overcoming of Nihilism. His Zarathustran philosophy is a panoply of symbols and myths — 'to the sheep I am no longer a scholar', as he proudly declared.[54] Without that mythic turning it would have been impossible for him to have broken through and gone beyond the traditional categories of philosophy. For what sense can one make of Nietzsche's key discoveries within the concepts of traditional ontology, epistemology, aesthetics or ethics? Thus, for example, the distinction conveyed by the opposition of the two symbols 'Dionysian' and 'Apollonian' is not one that could be captured in fixed, rationally defined concepts. And similarly, the Eternal Recurrence is not primarily a scientific cosmological hypothesis about the successive states of the physical universe; it is far more a mythical principle which conveys a certain meaning that the universe might be said to have. Roughly put, it states: 'think of the universe as without goal or end, as if it were forever repeating itself, and think of its meaning as precisely this "meaningless" round — finally, think of yourself and this life in terms of that!'.

There is still an ever-present danger, to which he himself was not proof, of taking his myths for realities. But the two must not be confused. Thus it must be stressed that the myths of the Zarathustran philosophy of the overcoming of Nihilism do not constitute the overcoming of Nihilism. At best they point to a hope for the overcoming of Nihilism. They are a kind of poetics of the future. To take them as real or realisable prognostications, as Nietzsche himself frequently did, is to confuse poetry and reality. But even though such poetic truth does not have direct practical application, it can serve as the inspiration for making a practical effort, which it itself can only indicate, not exactly specify. The truth of the Overman — 'my concept, my metaphor for this [higher] type is, as one knows, the word "overman"' (866) — is not the truth of an evolutionary prediction about the future of mankind, even though this is how it is presented. It is a mythic truth which unfolds a certain kind of potential for overcoming Nihilism to those who are able to believe in it. In a Nietzschean 'politics' it would be analogous to the myth of the future proletarian revolution in Marx — both of these being the expressions of what Marx called a 'poetry of the future'.[55] Unfortunately, Nietzsche mistook his own myths for realities, and so gave himself over to all sorts of pseudo-historical, vatic pronouncements and admonitory prophesies of an apocalyptic kind. As we know now to our cost, what actually happened was far worse, and of a totally different character to what he foresaw even in his most blood-thirsty visions. As a political thinker Nietzsche was singly lacking in a sense of the realistic and practical — such as Marx possessed despite his revolutionary fervour — and it is this shortcoming that makes trifling, but dangerous, most of his political and practical proposals. His aversion to the herd and mob — in Shakespearean language actually the common body of humanity — which is the converse of Marx's belief in the proletariat, is partly the symptom of a refusal to countenance social practicalities and partly the failure to distinguish adequately art from politics. The mass of humanity is taken to be merely an inert lump, malleable material to be shaped according to the sovereign will of the great myth-making artist of history. Such a man is for Nietzsche an historical end-in-himself:

> To appraise the value of a man according to how useful he is to men, or how much he costs, or what harm he does them — that is as much — or as little — as to appraise a work of art according to the effects it produces (878).

But no man is a work of art, not even such a man as Goethe or Napoleon, for whose sake Nietzsche would be prepared 'to desire the anarchical collapse of our entire civilization' (877). A man cannot be separated from the effects he produces, for these are the consequences of actions for which he is responsible; so a man responsible for the 'anarchical collapse of our entire civilization' could be no Goethe or Napoleon; he could only be a Hitler. But, of course, no man could bring so much about by himself.

Nietzsche never adequately distinguishes aesthetic and social values; he speaks of the necessity of a new society and a new type of man as if it were the desirability of a new style of art:

> Overall view of the future European: the most intelligent slave animals, very industrious, fundamentally very modest, inquisitive to excess, multifarious, pampered, weak of will — a cosmopolitan chaos of affects and intelligence. How could a stronger species raise itself out of him? A species with *classical* taste? Classical taste: this means will to simplification, strengthening, to visible happiness, to the terrible, the courage of

psychological nakedness . . . To fight upward out of that chaos to
this form — requires a compulsion: one must be faced with the
choice of perishing or prevailing. A dominating race can grow up
only out of terrible and violent beginnings (868).

This passage brings out very clearly Nietzsche's propensity to discuss
the social problem of a whole civilisation as if it were a problem in
aesthetics. 'A species with classical taste' (868) — if that is the
desideratum then it hardly warrants a plunge into barbarism. And
why should classicism emerge out of barbarism better than out of
anything else; is there any precedent for this in history? Nietzsche
views the issue not sociologically or politically but aesthetically: the
idea of form emerging by compulsion out of chaos is what appeals to
him, on analogy with the formation of a work of art. But that is
hardly how social orders emerge. We who have now lived through
the barbarisms of the twentieth century do not feel ourselves one jot
closer to classical taste. We know only too well what the fake
classicism of a dominating race can amount to. We are no longer
willing to indulge in such historical experiments in a new barbarism
for the sake of dubious future aesthetic gains.

It was precisely for the sake of their aesthetic sensibilities that so
many after Nietzsche were prepared to follow him in indulging in
barbaric experiments. A new classical order, a new social order! —
these were their catch-cries. A re-mythification of art and society
was seen as the means of achieving this. That this re-mythification
was, in the first place, a re-barbarisation was acknowledged and
condoned. Under modern Rationalisation the mythical lends itself
very easily to a kind of civilised pseudo-barbarism, for all the means
of spiritualising or humanising myths have been eliminated. Modern
mythology leads to a reversion not only to pseudo-barbarism but
also to a pseudo-primitivism masquerading as the fundamental, and
a pseudo-archaism disguised as the original. Of real barbarism,
primitivity, or archaism there is under modern conditions no
question; modern society could hardly revert to tribalism to make
genuine primitivism possible.

This phenomenon of re-mythification, and the re-barbarisation
attendant on it, is an extremely important facet of Nihilism in its
early phases. For this is what it really is. It presents itself as an
attempt at the overcoming of Nihilism, but is actually only an inten-
sification of it. It is an attempt to escape the 'meaninglessness' of
Nihilism. As the loss of real meaning makes itself felt, every effort is

made to find substitute meanings, for few can bear to live in utter meaninglessness. Myths seem to afford a possibility of a recovery of real meaning; and so mythology appears as an answer to Nihilism, rather than showing itself as one of the modes of Nihilism. This is so because when myths are utilised as substitute patterns of meaning they are invariably intellectualised and rationalised. And in this form, as 'dead' meaning, myths become sources of sheer irrationality. But it is only this stultified mode of myth that is actually irrational, in itself myth is no more so than is poetry or music. Myth rationalised as mythology acts as an ideology.

The dangers of a recourse to myth becoming irrational, and so ideological, were evident to Nietzsche in his attacks on Wagner. Later Max Weber warned of it in his denunciation of pseudo-charismatic hankerings; though at the same time Weber was aware of the inevitability of the resurgence of myth in modernity: 'if one proceeds from pure experience one arrives at polytheism'; 'many old gods ascend from their graves; they are disenchanted and hence take the form of impersonal forces'.[56] Adorno and Horkheimer theorised this insight as a 'dialectic of Enlightenment'. Adorno went on to expose mythology as the 'jargon of authenticity', for not even a philosopher of Heidegger's stature is immune to the intellectualisation of myth in all its features: etymological archaism, philosophical primitivism, reintroduction of disguised theological meanings and eschatological schemas, a clever poeticising of language and a fetishising of concepts as symbols — much of this inspired by Nietzsche. But is this not characteristic of so many of the achievements of our time, ranging from *Decline of the West* to *Finnegans Wake*? In this respect all such works follow the lead given by Nietzsche in attempting to bring poetry back into thought and of putting philosophy in touch with the deeper meanings of mythic truth.

5. Mythology and Philosophy of Value

The impulse toward the formation of metaphors, that fundamental impulse of man, which we cannot reason away for one moment — for thereby we should reason away man himself . . . this impulse seeks for itself a new realm of action and another river-bed and finds it in *Mythos* and more generally in *Art*.[57]

Thus the thin stream of reason which had once flowed from the waters of myth is to return once more and be swallowed up in the ocean of its source. The philosopher is once again to rejoin the myth maker as at the start of Western civilisation. For despite Nietzsche's continuous assault on philosophy with his hammer, there is never any doubt that there is to be a future philosophy; he subtitles one of his works a 'prelude to a philosophy of the future', a philosophy 'beyond good and evil'.[58] A philosopher who is both artist and sage 'is again becoming possible in Europe — perhaps only for a short time' (987).

A new philosophy is for Nietzsche a matter of the creation of new values: 'the new values must be first created — we shall not be spared this task! For us the philosopher must be a legislator' (979). This task 'demands that he create values'.[59] Such creator-philosophers are distinguished from what he calls 'philosophical labourers after the noble exemplar of Kant and Hegel [who] take some fact of evaluation — that is to say, former assessments of value, creations of value which have become dominant and are for a while called "truths" — and identify them and reduce them to formulas, whether in the realm of logic or of politics (morals) or of art'.[60] These scholars are mere under-labourers for the great master-builders — 'their "knowing" is creating, their creating is a law-giving . . .'.[61] But philosophers who are 'legislators of such evaluations' (972) are perhaps not yet possible in Europe, after all, since 'the new philosopher can arise only in conjunction with a ruling caste, as its highest spiritualization' (978) and one is not as yet in evidence.

What does Nietzsche take himself to be if he cannot be one of the new value legislators rising with a ruling caste? He sees himself as their precursor, a free spirit in the benighted time of Nihilism presaging a new dawn, the avatar of his own Zarathustra preaching a 'gospel for the future' (p. 3). Nevertheless, his 'Dionysian affirmation of the world as it is . . ., is the highest state a philosopher can attain: to stand in a Dionysian relation to existence — my formula for this is *amor fati*' (1041). So he, too, is a philosopher who creates 'Dionysian value standards for existence', seeking 'in history the beginnings of this construction of reverse ideals (the concepts "pagan", "Classical", "noble" newly discovered and expounded —)' (1041).

Nietzsche begins the task of a 'revaluation of all values' which is both the conclusion of the historical process whereby the 'highest values devaluate themselves' (2), and at the same time a 'countermovement . . . that in some future will take the place of this perfect nihilism' (p. 3). In Nihilism 'the values we have had hitherto thus draw their final consequence' and 'we must experience nihilism before we can find out what value these "values" really had' (p. 4). Finally, 'we require, sometime, new values' (p. 4) — this is where the philosopher as legislator must 'behave as we have always behaved, namely mythologically'.[62]

Nietzsche's mythological philosophy is dominated by one key term: 'value'. This is his most plastic symbol, the master trope, which he turns and twists in all the ways his language permits: valuation, devaluation, revaluation, value-creation, value-destruction, value-positing, value-denying, inverse-valuation, etc., etc., — the whole philosophy is a play of value, a play on 'value'. Any kind of meaning, signification or form can be called a value, and then it can be troped according to all the pre-given value-turns. This permits an easy formulation of all the other aspects of the philosophy. Its eschatological patterns can be described in one or another variant of a version, inversion and re-inversion of values by the mere alteration of a prefix. Hence, just as all activity, effectivity, process and event is expressed in the monism of the will to power, so all meaning and signification is expressed by the monism of value.

This monism of meaning has its drawbacks. The term value was designed by Nietzsche as an omnibus designation to indicate a fundamental monistic unity in all meaning. As a result, the carefully contrived differentiations and nice distinctions developed in philosophy and elsewhere to express differences in modes of meaning become elided — somewhat as with Marx's term 'ideology'. One of the few distinctions Nietzsche allows himself to make is that between the positing and importation of values into things and their subsequent ascertaining and discovery.

> The ascertaining of 'truth' and 'untruth', the ascertaining of facts in general, is fundamentally different from creative positing, from forming, shaping, overcoming, willing, such as is of the essence of philosophy. To introduce a meaning — this task still remains to be done, assuming there is no meaning yet. Thus it is with sounds, but also with a fate of peoples; they are capable of the most different interpretations and direction toward different goals (605).

'Ultimately, man finds in things nothing but what he himself has imported into them: the finding is called science, the importing — art, religion, love, pride' (606). This distinction introduces a characteristic bias for it separates the few who create values from the others who merely discover what has been created. It is this bias that permits him to dub Kant and Hegel mere systematisers or scholars, not in the same class as the genuine artist-philosophers of whom he gives few examples; it makes him compare scientists unfavourably with artists. It also makes him view meaning-giving as value-creating, a highly individualistic activity, a matter of an individual heroic 'forming, shaping, overcoming, willing'. This creative emphasis derives from his even more fundamental doctrine of the will to power and must be subjected to careful critical scrutiny.

The mediating term linking the monism of becoming as will to power with the monism of meaning as value is perspectivism. All knowing is apprehending, a power relation whereby one centre as a quantum of power overcomes, appropriates or resists another. Hence all knowing is power-perspectival, an evaluation from a given point of view. A value is, therefore, a centrifugal projection of a power-interest extending from a centre to the things it is intent on appropriating. The term 'value' has its meaning in this relation to will to power and perspectivism, and stands or falls with them. Unlike other philosophies, such as Positivism, which also invoke the term 'value', Nietzschean values are not to be contrasted with other kinds of meaning functions, such as logical and empirical propositions; there is, therefore, no way of giving a meaning to 'value' independently of the quasi-metaphysics of will to power and perspectivism. What results from this is that the whole meaning-making function is conceived of as a kind of monadology of power-centres, each one with its own window on the world, valuing everything in accordance with its own needs and interests. Every individual creates its own meaningful world of values.

What results from this idea of value is that, despite Nietzsche's interest in language, there is absent any communicative conception of meaning, any recognition that meaning is a common creation by people in a group or society, or by the whole of mankind. The Wittgensteinian emphasis on language as common is missing: the idea that meaning is a social product that in some respects precedes the individual, who is born into an existing community of speakers or culture and has first to learn its language, to accept it without struggle or power confrontations, before he can begin to express his own power needs and interests, formulate his own values and see the world from his own perspective. The gift of speech is not something exacted through appropriation by means of power; it is something to be accepted from the givers just as is the gift of life itself. The community is in the first place a communicating body of people who live and speak together before each can even begin to struggle for himself. Nietzsche is predisposed by his basic metaphysic against any appreciation of the communal, social nature of meaning. It is his understanding of language, ironically, that predisposes him against this for he sees the inherited and acquired character of language in terms of the fetishism of language, its survival from our primitive ancestors, and this he wants to reject and overcome. He thinks the philosopher as creative individual can overcome the whole inheritance of the race.

Meaning-making for Nietzsche becomes a highly individualistic activity of the making and breaking of values. The heroic individual creator and destroyer is elevated to the position of a human-super-human artist-god — an Overman. Everything worthwhile in culture and society is ascribed by him to such titans. Humanity is merely a means to make such human gods possible and can be sacrificed indiscriminately for their sake. This is objectionable: not only are the moral valuations it entails on the whole abhorrent, but also its blindness to social and cultural achievements. There is no awareness on Nietzsche's part that meaning-making is usually a slow accumulation of changing significations — a process sometimes continuing over generations, and leading to changing forms of society and traditions. Even the greatest creator is born into an already existing tradition, just as he is born into a pre-existing language, and no matter how revolutionary his creativity he cannot change tradition unless he can win the co-operation of others to work with him. Together with others he always works within a social process which he cannot fully control, as one might a work of art, and whose outcome is usually unpredictable. The great man proposes but history disposes. Indeed a man can only attain creative greatness if he understands this and is not contemptuous of others; this is why Goethe insists that 'only by recognising limitation can one become a master'. A Nietzschean master who seeks to impose his will on others could never achieve anything.

A 'new value', to use Nietzsche's term, is created only when the work of a man passes through countless other hands and is modified and shaped by them in turn. In this way a tradition of received meaning is constituted. This is how all great religious, philosophical and artistic movements and political institutions were established. In all such cases, there was a complex and specific interplay between the leaders, their disciples and companions and the larger following, audience or public. Weber understood this extremely well and formulated his theory of the routinisation and institutionalisation of charisma to explain it. While not minimising the creative role of the great prophet, politician, artist or philosopher, this theory places it in a social context by relating the charismatic leader to his followers and showing that outside the follower's perception of him the leader does not have any charisma. Furthermore, the fluidity of a charismatic movement would disintegrate it and it would not last unless it were solidified through routinisation and institutionalisation over many generations. Only in this way can values be created and established as social meanings.

Nietzsche's individualistic, heroic approach to values informs his conception of history, especially the history of Nihilism. It leads him to imagine that Nihilism was brought on in the first place by a few individuals, a few philosophers and a few Christians, and that it can be just as easily overcome by a few individuals, himself and some legislator philosophers to come after him. The devaluation of values that the former carried through in order to bring about the eschatological Fall can be reversed by the revaluation of values whereby the latter will effect a Return. Thus, to himself as hero of the great revaluation, Nietzsche opposes his equally great antitheses, the great devaluators, Socrates and Christ. He becomes their inverse counterpart, the anti-Socratic and the anti-Christ.

Socrates and his pupil Plato he holds responsible for the devaluation brought about by the invention of Reason and the value-inversion of the opposition of a true-world to an apparent-world — the crime of philosophy. Christ and his apostle Paul he holds responsible for the devaluation brought about by Christianity and the victory of slave-morality, with its value-inversion of good–evil, over master-morality — the crime of morality. The whole of history is thus staged as a personal contest between a few artists of mankind in order to see who can create the more lasting and stronger values. The term 'value' lends itself well to this kind of play, for he can turn it as he likes; it is easy enough to speak of revaluing all values if one has already spoken of all values as devalued. Nihilism can be overcome with a change of prefix. The riddle of history can be answered in one word.

What are we to make of this kind of philosophy? It cannot be 'a prelude to the philosophy of the future'. It is more like a postscript to the philosophy of the past. If all philosophy, as Whitehead said, is a long footnote to Plato, then Nietzsche's is its brilliant codicil, or a kind of musical coda. Heidegger was partly right when he called it an inverted Platonism, not in the sense that Nietzsche would have understood, as a reinversion of the original inversion of metaphysics, but in the sense of returning metaphysics back to the mythology from which it derived. The artist whom Plato had originally banished from philosophy returned in the end to take his revenge.

Notes

1. F. Nietzsche, *Will to Power* (ed.) W. Kaufmann (Vintage, New York, 1968), par. 1054. All subsequent references to this work will be indicated by the paragraph or page from this edition in the text. All other references will be noted as usual. I have made extensive use of this work, compiled from Nietzsche's *Nachlass*, both because it bears more closely on the subject under discussion and also because I believe that Nietzsche is often truer to himself in his notes than in his published works. Just as the impressionist sketches of Constable are preferred to his finished paintings, so Nietzsche's jotted notes are often more honest and less pretentious than the works where he self-consciously addresses an audience. This is especially so with the works published in the last year of his sane existence where he sets out to lambast an unresponsive German public; there he is at his most truculent and least controlled. He often falls in with his own self-exaggerations, his humour lost in self-aggrandisement. In some places these writings already evince the incipient megalomania which was very soon to overpower him. It is from these that the Nazis derived their inspiration.

2. F. Nietzsche, *Twilight of the Idols*, trans. R. J. Hollingdale (Penguin, Harmondsworth, 1971), p. 37.

3. F. Nietzsche, *Joyful Wisdom*, trans. Thomas Common (Frederick Ungar, New York, 1973), par. 373, p. 340.

4. Letter to Seydlitz, 12 February 1888, in G. Clive, *The Philosophy of Nietzsche* (Mentor, New York, 1965), p. 92.

5. *Twilight of the Idols*, p. 41.

6. *The Genealogy of Morals*, trans. F. Golffing (Doubleday Anchor, New York, 1956), p. 162.

7. Ibid., p. 163.

8. Ibid., p. 167.

9. Ibid., pp. 167–8.

10. Ibid., p. 176.

11. Ibid., p. 176.

12. Ibid., p. 177.

13. F. Nietzsche, *Beyond Good and Evil*, trans. R. J. Hollingdale (Penguin, Harmondsworth, 1972), p. 175.

14. Ibid., p. 100.

15. Ibid., p. 100.

16. *Twilight of Idols*, p. 58.

17. *Genealogy of Morals*, pp. 209–10.
18. *Human All-too-Human*, quoted in Schenk, p. 247.
19. *The Genealogy of Morals*, p. 162.
20. *Beyond Good and Evil*, pp. 31–2.
21. Ibid., p. 32.
22. *Twilight of the Idols*, pp. 37–8.
23. Ibid., p. 38.
24. Ibid., p. 36.
25. *Wanderer and his Shadow*, quoted in *Beyond Good and Evil*, p. 191. See note 93 in Ch. 4 for an argument against this Whorfian thesis in linguistics.
26. *Beyond Good and Evil*, p. 32.
27. For an attempt to draw the parallels between Nietzsche and Wittgenstein, see Tracy Strong, *Freidrich Nietzsche and the Politics of Transfiguration* (University of California Press, Berkeley, 1975), pp. 78–86.
28. *Philosophical Investigations*, p. 226.
29. *Foundations of Mathematics*, p. 57.
30. *On Certainty*, sec. 559.
31. Ibid., par. 559.
32. *Twilight of the Idols*, p. 38.
33. *The Joyful Wisdom*, p. 156.
34. Ibid., p. 156.
35. For a very sympathetic exposition of these standard themes in Nietzsche see R. H. Grimm, *Nietzsche's Theory of Knowledge* (Walter de Gruyter, Berlin, 1977).
36. *Beyond Good and Evil*, p. 17.
37. Ibid., p. 17.
38. A. C. Danto, *Nietzsche as Philosopher* (Macmillan, New York, 1977), p. 216.
39. Ibid., p. 215.
40. R. H. Grimm, *Nietzsche's Theory of Knowledge* (Walter de Gruyter, Berlin, Berlin, 1977), p. 2.
41. Ibid., p. 3.
42. Ibid., p. 194.
43. *Twilight of the Idols*, p. 81.
44. Gilles Deleuze, 'Active and Reactive' in *The New Nietzsche* (ed.) D. B. Allison (Dell Publishing, New York, 1977), pp. 87–8.
45. *The Genealogy of Morals*, p. 211.
46. A. Lingis, 'The Will to Power' in (ed.) D. B. Allison, p. 45.
47. Max Weber, *The Religion of India*, trans. H. H. Gerth and D. Martindale (Collier-Macmillan, London, 1958), p. 169.
48. *The Philosophy of Nietzsche*, p. 510.
49. Ibid., p. 508.
50. Ibid., p. 509.
51. Ibid., p. 511.
52. *Human All-too-Human*, vol. I in (ed.) Clive, p. 549.
53. T. W. Adorno, *Dialectic of Enlightenment*, trans. John Cumming (Allen Lane, London, 1973), p. 27.
54. *Thus Spoke Zarathustra*, trans. R. J. Hollingdale (Penguin, Harmondsworth, 1961), p. 147. *Thus Spoke Zarathustra* is a mytho-poetic statement of Nietzsche's philosophy which always remains partially mytho-poetic even when he tries to present it in a different style in his later works.
55. Karl Marx, *The Eighteenth Brumaire of Louis Bonaparte* (Progress Publishers, Moscow, 1977), p. 13.
56. 'Science as a Vocation' in *From Max Weber* (eds) Gerth and Mills, pp. 147–9. For a full exposition of the role of myth in modern thought, see Chris Drury, *Myth and Modernity* (PhD thesis, Monash University, 1981).

57. *Truth and Falsity in an Ultramoral Sense*, cited in *Philosophy of Nietzsche* (ed.) Clive, p. 513.
58. *Beyond Good and Evil*, p. 18.
59. Ibid., p. 123.
60. Ibid., p. 123.
61. Ibid., p. 123.
62. Ibid., p. 33.

A PHILOSOPHICAL *WALPURGISNACHT*

'Those are the eyes of one that's dead I see'

1. The Dilemmas of Purism

Wittgenstein's late philosophy is one possible answer to the dilemma of how it is possible to philosophise at the end of metaphysics. In that respect it is analogous to Heidegger's philosophy. It is not clear, however, to what extent Wittgenstein was himself aware of this.[1] There is no doubt that he knew his philosophy was different in kind from any earlier; he also had a sense of the unusual historical situation in which his philosophy arose. The remarkable self-disclosures in the preface to the *Philosophical Investigations* leave no room for doubt about this. This preface relates to the rest of the text in precisely the way that the equally remarkable preface of the *Tractatus* relates to the text of that work. Both prefaces serve to place their respective texts in relation to an outside context. As Wittgenstein himself insists in a letter concerning the *Tractatus*: 'I would recommend you to read the *preface* and the *conclusion*, because they contain the most direct expression of the point of the book.'[2] The differences between the two prefaces are also worth dwelling on for they indicate the changed character and strange nature of the later philosophy: 'That the latter could be seen in the right light only by contrast with [*Gegensatz*] and against the background of my old way of thinking.'[3]

The preface to the *Tractatus* locates the text within the context of contemporary work on logic and reaffirms a positivistic anti-metaphysical stance: 'the reason why these problems are posed is that the logic of our language is misunderstood';[4] however, it is remarkable in that it deliberately seeks to underplay the importance of what the work might be said to accomplish in this respect in order to highlight the value of what lies outside the work — precisely that existential ethical-aesthetic problematic of life which 'we must pass over in silence'. By contrast, the preface to the *Investigations* distinguishes its text from the earlier *Tractatus* as well as from the linguistic philosophy then becoming fashionable and soon to become dominant in the English-speaking university environment, and finishes off by placing itself within the general historical context of the times: 'It is not impossible that it should fall to the lot of this work, in its poverty and in the darkness of this time, to bring light into one brain or another — but of course, it is not likely' (p. x). The contrast between that remark and this: 'the truth of the thoughts that are here set forth seems to me unassailable and definite' is a measure of the distance that has been travelled into the 'darkness of this time'.

Now the time is dark, the work is poor, the light flickering in one solitary brain is unlikely to light up any other.[5] It is a poor philosophy fit for an impoverished time — a '*dürftiger Zeit*' as Heidegger, following Hölderlin, was to call it. In the neediness of the time Wittgenstein takes a new vow of linguistic poverty, solitude and simplicity and dedicates himself to practising an asceticism of language with the attendant virtues of humanity, humility and purity.[6] This, it is implied, is one kind of philosophical practice possible in our time. The desire to inspire other minds to thoughts of their own, and so to different philosophies, is openly acknowledged, but Wittgenstein wryly refuses to believe this likely. For the darkness of the time refers not merely to the overshadowing of immediate circumstances — the war was just over and Wittgenstein felt himself and his work increasingly isolated — it also implies his historical judgement on the whole of the modern epoch.[7] The phrase gives emotional expression to Wittgenstein's awareness of modern Nihilism. This condition is passed over in silence within the text itself for it lies outside, in the sphere of life and time with which the work is not concerned, just as the sphere of action is outside the text of the *Tractatus*. Nevertheless, the later text, too, must be read within its silent context; the darkness of this time, which determines the possibilities of all writing and thought, is the indispensable backdrop for any understanding of the *Investigations*.

This work sees itself as a solitary light shining in the darkness, which the darkness comprehendeth not. But what is Light and what is Darkness for Wittgenstein? Light, which is the prime symbol of his philosophy, derives ultimately from the Christian tradition of *Lux aeterna*, though it has also been suffused with the secular colouring of Enlightenment illumination, of which this philosophy is itself perhaps the last glimmer. Wittgenstein's sense of Darkness is much harder to specify, but it is obvious that the darkness is there to show up the absence of Light, or because the Light is no longer communicable. Thus it cannot be said of Wittgenstein as it was said of Hegel that: 'in all his penetrating into the "realm of darkness", the young Hegel is already certain that reason can lead out of the darkness into the light because it itself is the light'.[8] Light for Wittgenstein is no longer universal Reason, so even if it finds its way into one brain it is not likely to be transferred to another.

Just as light is Wittgenstein's symbol of philosophical endeavour, so is vision his symbol of knowing and understanding. He continually speaks of rendering something visible or perspicuous, of gaining insight, of seeing something differently, of seeing continuities or connections, of changes of aspect, of clarifying problems, shedding a new light on difficulties, grasping in a flash, and so on. Indeed it sometimes seems that not merely his work, but his whole life was consumed by a passionate search for understanding, a quest for light and vision. (In this respect he was like Goethe, who also always strove for light and made this the basic formative principle of much of his work, above all of *Faust*. And Wittgenstein was continually fascinated by and preoccupied with Goethe's theory of light and colour.) Darkness as the obverse of light is thus the Other which the light is to dispel; it results from an inability to 'see', which he pictures variously as confusion, unclarity, the opaque, the tangled or twisted, as misinterpretation, misuse, abuse or no-use. The metaphorical web that he spins with these terms might be extended indefinitely, but, as we shall see, there is one form of darkness whose meaning it could not capture. For Wittgenstein saw as the prevailing 'darkness of this time' only the unclarity and confusion — cultural and social as much as philosophical — on which it was at least possible to shed light. The darkness of Nihilism, which resisted the light, he could not see.

Darkness in philosophy was for him merely the obscurity of philosophical problems, caused by a difficulty in seeing or orientating oneself. 'A philosophical problem has the form: "I don't know my way about"' (123). For him a problem could not be something constitutive, like a problematic, or something formed and sustained, like a contradiction. It had to be disposed of, seen through, illuminated and eliminated; and frequently this was done through examples that shed light on a difficulty; as a follower of Wittgenstein puts it:

Why so many examples? They speak for themselves . . .; each one acts as an analogy; together they light up the whole linguistic background with the effect that the case before us is seen in the light they produce . . . What is decisive is a new way of seeing and, what goes with it, the will to transform the whole intellectual scene.[9]

However, unlike the Linguistic philosophers, Wittgenstein did not expect any final dispelling of problems or dissolution of obscurities for he recognised that they are 'deep disquietudes; their roots are as deep in us as the forms of our language and their significance is as great as the importance of our language' (111). Nevertheless, in so far as these are 'problems arising through a misinterpretation of our forms of language' they only arise because of a failure to see what is there waiting to be seen. The sense of a problem as more than a misinterpretation, obscurity or blindness did not occur to him:

A main source of our failure to understand is that we do not *command a clear view* of the use of our words — our grammar is lacking in this sort of perspicuity. A perspicuous representation produces just that understanding which consists in 'seeing connexions'. Hence the importance of finding and inventing *intermediate cases.*

The concept of a perspicuous representation is of fundamental significance for us. It earmarks the form of account we give, the way we look at things. (Is this a 'Weltanschauung'?) (122).

'The concept of a perspicuous representation': is this, indeed, a *Weltanschauung*? — that is the question. For this question touches on the problematic nature of Wittgenstein's philosophical procedures. The primary issue it raises is whether the concept of a 'perspicuous representation' contains an implicit statement of the method behind the practice of problem dissolution. And if so, does this method involve a 'world view'? Is it a thesis in anything like the traditional sense? How can it be, since Wittgenstein asseverates that 'if one tried to advance *theses* in philosophy, it would never be possible to question them, because everyone would agree to them?' (128). Would everyone agree with the concept of a 'perspicuous representation'? So how can Wittgenstein be committed to a philosophical method, and even a *Weltanschauung*? His philosophy is a practice of philosophising: of shedding light on problems by making the grammar of language visible and so arriving at a perspicuous representation. As we have shown in Chapter 2, this does not mean that metaphysical issues are annihilated in the way Wittgenstein had proposed earlier in the *Tractatus*:

> The correct method in philosophy would really be the following: to say nothing except what can be said, i.e. propositions of natural science — i.e. something that has nothing to do with philosophy — and then, whenever someone else wanted to say something metaphysical, to demonstrate to him that he had failed to give a meaning to certain signs in his propositions (6.53).

A 'perspicuous representation' is not a method of annihilation in this sense; but neither can it be a method in the old sense, entailing a *Weltanschauung*. So what is it?

The concept of a 'perspicuous representation' emerges out of the mode of philosophical critique that Wittgenstein made peculiarly his own. This form of critique had its origins in the Enlightenment approach to philosophy as critique of representation or idea, but it is not to be identified with Kantian critique. It is not critique of Reason; it makes no judgements and sets no limits. Neither is it critique of Ideology or Culture. It is primarily a critique of language. As he stated in the *Tractatus*: 'All philosophy is a "critique of language" (though not in Mauthner's sense)' (4.0031); but we should add: not in the *Tractatus* sense either. Rather, it is a mode of critique that engages in 'a battle against the bewitchment of our intelligence by means of language' (109). And since the bewitchment of intelligence is caused by language — a misunderstanding of 'the workings of our language', which is overcome by 'recognizing those workings in despite of an urge to misunderstand them' (109) — it follows that philosophical critique is a battle against the bewitchment of language by language, carried out by means of language. That is to say, language itself gives rise to problems, which are metaphysical when they are deep enough, and these problems can only be overcome by another, a critical operation of language on language. Language entangles and then frees itself, and this process is called philosophy.

Wittgenstein's philosophy is critique of language in this sense. This is why he thinks he can practise philosophy in isolation and without recourse to the Tradition or to historical precedents: 'One might also give the name "philosophy" to what is possible *before* all new discoveries and inventions' (126). This startling remark — which seems to overlook the historically attested connection between philosophy and other intellectual concerns — reveals his desire for a form of philosophical critique that is neither conditioned nor constrained by history, and so may be carried out prior to all other theorising: an investigation into the foundations of mathematics and logic, for example, would dispense with abstruse mathematical or logical discoveries and inventions.[10] This, of course, must not be taken literally to mean that philosophy was already possible in the stone-age, but merely that a modern thinker can philosophise by disregarding scientific theories — as it were, bracketing them in Husserl's sense. In part this statement can be taken as a *cri de guerre* against all attempts in modern thought to ascribe inordinate philosophical importance to the latest scientific theory (Evolution and Formal Logic in his time). It expresses Wittgenstein's desire to defend the purity of philosophy against corruption by scientific methodologies. The main philosophical tendencies of the age: Positivism, Psychologism and Historicism, Wittgenstein saw as conspiring with these antiphilosophical trends.

There are some distant precedents for this attitude to philosophy in the history of philosophy itself. Wittgenstein's style of thinking is reminiscent of that of two classical thinkers, Socrates and Augustine, to whom he often refers; they too might be thought of as philosophising before all discoveries and inventions, and as requiring no more than the simplest language forms to do so. Wittgenstein's style reproduces both Socratic dialogue and Augustinian confession; he carries on an interminable debate with himself, the disputing parties being the various temptations to which a philosopher might be inclined; hence his characteristic opening gambit: 'I am tempted to say . . .'. So much so, that he frequently gives the impression of having internalised philosophical issues, almost as if they were personal worries to which he was obsessionally addicted. These 'problems are solved, not by giving new information, but by arranging what we have always known' (109) — which is reminiscent of Socrates' doctrine of knowledge as reminiscence; what is already known is rearranged, disposed of differently and the work of philosophy 'consists in assembling reminders for a particular purpose' (127). The difficulty of the work is that what is too well known remains for that reason unknown: 'the aspects of things that are most important for us are hidden because of their simplicity and familiarity (one is unable to notice something — because it is always before one's eyes)' (129). This reminded him of Augustine's dictum:

'What is time? When nobody asks me, I know, but when someone asks me I do not know' (89).

Basing himself on an unhistorical, idiosyncratic understanding of Socrates and Augustine, Wittgenstein strove for a philosophy of the simple; like them he was intent on practising a purifying mode of thought, but in another way and for quite different ends.[11] One might call this 'pure' philosophy a new philosophical ideal. It is an ideal that emerges out of Wittgenstein's practice, and not one that he first formulated and then tried to put into effect. The pure philosophy is one that is able to return to origins, to the *arche*, one that precedes theory because it only concerns itself with the most elementary things — initially with the simplest words of the language. In this way Wittgenstein sought to avoid all theoretical presuppositions and to remove his philosophy from contention, making it seem neutral and indisputable. But how is this possible?

Wittgenstein thought it was possible because, believing he had arrived at a mode of thought that involved no negation, he failed to realise the full destructive potential of his own philosophy. As we noted already, he was torn between seeing what he destroyed as something 'great and important' and seeing it as 'nothing but houses of cards'; the destructive act itself he saw as having solely a liberating function, as 'clearing up the ground of language' (118). In other words, destruction appeared to him solely as a mode of purification. In so conceiving of it he hid from himself the full nihilistic consequences of his dissolution of metaphysical problems. This is the blind-spot in his philosophical vision, the theoretical myopia which was built into everything he saw, and which he was, therefore, quite incapable of looking into or overcoming. It is not the kind of 'error' he could have recognised: being neither a blindness to what is obvious, nor a failure to resist temptation, nor anything that stemmed from personal shortcomings. To reveal this darkness within the light of his sight is to blind the whole vision. Wittgenstein saw light and darkness as mutually opposed; he could not see that the very light with which he attempts to illuminate the darkness is itself a darkness illuminated.

Wittgenstein was unable to see that his 'dissolutions' of metaphysical problems are not acts of purification but of reduction, like those which are encountered also in modern art and culture. They are philosophic manifestations of the general process of reduction that is modern Nihilism.[12] He could not conceive of a concept of 'dissolution' on this scale; the nature of his thinking made it unthinkable for him. And yet inherent in his practice of the dissolution of philosophical problems there is a much wider notion of dissolution than he could have appreciated.

Wittgenstein's view of dissolution as simply purification is encapsulated in the metaphoric structure of his language. When speaking of what he is doing he uses images of untying knots, relaxing cramps, dissolving complexes, treating diseases, as in the following: 'in philosophizing we may not *terminate* a disease of thought. It must run its natural course, and *slow* cure is all important.'[13] The resulting paradox is one that Wittgenstein only rarely confronts: namely, that the activity of philosophising should be everything, both difficult and intricate, and yet that the results of this activity should be nothing, for literally nothing is produced by so much effort. When he does confront it, by asking himself this very question, he does not face up to it as a serious objection, but tries to explain it away by means of his favourite metaphor:

> How does it come about that philosophy is so complicated a structure? It surely ought to be completely simple, if it is the ultimate thing, independent of all experience, that you make it out to be. Philosophy unties knots in our thinking, hence its results must be simple, but philosophizing has to be as complicated as the knots it unties.[14]

Implicit in this attempt by Wittgenstein to disarm the paradox are all his preconceptions about his philosophy. It is, he believes, primarily an activity from which there results no body of knowledge or doctrine or system or higher truth, as traditionally believed. Its results 'must be simple'; nothing but simplicity is allowed to be its outcome; presumably it is the simplicity of the 'perspicuous representation' of what is obvious and elementary. It is a complicated activity only because it seeks to undo the contortions in what might otherwise be straightforward: it unties the tangles of language, the complexes of thought, the knots in the understanding.

In his attempts to explain his philosophy Wittgenstein frequently also employs metaphors deriving from engineering and architecture — he was himself an engineer by training and an architect by avocation. If we pursue these further it will serve to locate his philosophy within certain tendencies in modern science and art. Using functionalist metaphors, he speaks of stripping away all that is mere ornament or picture, or pillar that is not loadbearing, or decorative knob not linked to the engine. The engineering emphasis is apparent in his instrumental view of language: 'Language is an instrument, its concepts are instruments' (569); and 'to understand a language is to master a technique' (199). Images of language as tools and machinery abound. The bias this produces is obvious; the instrumental view of language makes it appear rule-bound, determined, and narrowly functional and results in neglect of those modes of language for which mechanical metaphors are totally inappropriate.

Metaphors of functionality modulate Wittgenstein's language themes from engineering to architecture, and on to art in general. He approaches language as might a modern artist who was intent on achieving an utmost purity and simplicity of form. The house Wittgenstein designed in collaboration with Engelmann is characterised by an utmost restraint; all superfluous decoration has been removed in keeping with the style of their mentor Loos. The purism that characterizes Wittgenstein's approach to language was close to this in spirit. He faced the problem of freeing language from the dead remains of metaphysics and the burden of cultural history in much the way that purist artists set about removing the encrustations of dead historical styles, the relics of once living art, and reducing their material to the basic shapes and forms out of which they could then create a new beauty of utmost clarity and simplicity. Wittgenstein also had the example of the critic Karl Kraus to draw on in regard to language, for Kraus set out to expunge all clichés, the empty verbal husks of once living speech forms.

Wittgenstein thought of his philosophy in such artistic terms; he remarked that 'it was a question of changing the style of thinking . . . I am in a sense making propaganda for one style of thinking as opposed to another'.[15] It was this new style of thinking that required purification of language through the dissolution of the clichés of philosophy, the remainders of what had once been 'great and important', but which now figured merely as ornaments bereft of use. However, when he said 'what we do is bring words back from their metaphysical to their everyday usage' (116), he did not ask himself whether this metaphysical usage was the original one of the great philosophers, or that of their current philosophical imitators and expositors — in other words, whether he was attacking mere traditionalism or the Tradition itself. Like the poet Mallarmé he saw the philosopher's task as one of 'purifying the language of the tribe', but he tended to take this to mean that all language was to be brought down to the level of the language of the tribe, 'the language-game which is its original home' (116). As he emphatically put it: 'If the words "language", "experience", "world", have a use, it must be as humble a one as that of the words "table", "lamp", "door"' (97). In this it is evident that the desire to humble language all too readily turns into a secret wish to humiliate it.[16]

The quoted statement appears less outrageous if we remember that it is meant to deflate the old pretensions of philosophy and to de-sublimate the sublimity of metaphysical language. But it also reveals nakedly his unquestioned assumption that the meaningful, living word is always and ever the simple word, the word as it comes from the mouths of babes, from unsophisticated folk, from unthinking everyday-life situations, from primitive imaginary tribes, ultimately from people prior to history.

> I want to regard man here as an animal; as a primitive being to which one grants instinct but not ratiocination. As a creature in a primitive state. Any logic good enough for a primitive means of communication needs no apology from us. Language did not emerge from some kind of ratiocination.[17]

It would be a mistake to read this simply as a tendency to a kind of philosophical neo-Darwinianism. Behind it lie also the early-Romantic assumption of language as the primary, instinctive self-expression of a *Volk* (Humboldt) and the moral injunction to base language on the speech of simple, ordinary people (Tolstoy). Like the Romantics and the Tolstoyans, Wittgenstein tended to identify the primitive with the basic, the simple with the sound, the innocent with the spontaneous.[18] We find similar attitudes to language in the poets — Rilke for example — and also in Heidegger, in all those who seek to recapture a lost original, simple sense of words. For Wittgenstein, too, the recovery of the basic roots of words and the purification of language was not merely a matter of words, or even of art; it was a question of existential being, for in the purity of speech there lay for him the pledge of a purity of heart. The resuscitation of 'dead' language was simultaneously a re-animation of dead souls and a re-awakened sense of humanity. This purifying response, a kind of moral-aesthetic asceticism of language, is a poetic-romantic way of meeting the challenge of Nihilism. The annihilating and destructive tendencies of modern history are here met by a return to the unassailable root of things, to language that is basic, common, humble and original. The original in Wittgenstein is not the archaic reality, that which was once there and is no more; rather it is that which is always present, given at the root of life: the *arche*. This is why he can think of the original sense of simple words as always available, as only having to be searched for in order to be found. And just as the simple sense of words like 'table', 'lamp', 'door' is always there in that everyday life in which things have their humble uses, so he thought that the meanings of 'language', 'experience', 'world', must also be rooted there, for otherwise they would be transcendent and of no use. Thus he implicitly denied any independence to the intellect.

This purifying tendency, with its accompanying moral-aesthetic asceticism of language, has its own shortcomings in confronting Nihilism. It is a tendency to view this extraordinary condition as if it were mere decadence, corruption, disease or neurosis, something that could be cured or even avoided by a return to all that is wholesome and life-giving, as if this were always available to be returned to at will. But, paradoxically, the effect of trying to recover the simplicities of life is the opposite of what the purifiers expect: their efforts at purification result ultimately in a paring down to nothing. Thus, the artist or thinker who succeeds in dissolving the accumulated debris of the past, who has stripped away the conventional forms of culture, finds himself reduced to the barest and most basic of expressive means. Those who follow him and try to push the purifying process further are left with ever more limited resources, and eventually have nothing to work with and nowhere further to go. The whole point and value of the enterprise lies in the process itself, not in the pure end-product attained, for that is neither elemental nor original nor simple, in the sense the purists desire. The simple is just that, not a root starting point. This is why attempts to found schools on the work of the masters of purism has usually been so disastrous for their *epigoni*.[19] The achievement is the reductive process whereby the masters attained to their hard-won simplicity; their pupils, starting off with the mere end-products, can only repeat them or play formal games with them.

The dilemma of purism in thought and art is that in the end formal purity is achieved at the expense of content, simplicity at the expense of substance, and that from continual simplification impoverishment will finally result. As a trend, purism eventually works itself into a dead-end of minimal forms and barest expressive means, which are either too easy or too difficult to work with: too easy for those without conscience who are prepared to repeat mechanically the same few empty gestures, but too difficult for those who still try to win something rare or strange from the pared-down material at their disposal. The latter can only succeed in speaking in the most subtle of nuances, and these are not easily distinguished from the similar sounding sheer inanities pouring forth from their less scrupulous colleagues, and, certainly, there is increasingly less of a public able to make that distinction. The ultimate dilemma is thus a choice between degenerating into empty chatter or being reduced to silence. We find this dilemma exemplified at its most intense in the silence of Webern as against the cacophonies of the dodecacophonists, in the silence of Beckett as against the strident clamour of the avant-gardists, in the slender minimal line of Klee as against the loud colours and empty expanses of the minimalists. In thought we have an analogous relation obtaining between the simple quiet words of Wittgenstein and the noise of professional philosophers publishing apace in the same simplistic vein.

The purist turning in philosophy as exemplified in Wittgenstein's purification of language no longer leads anywhere, but it is not for that reason an error or an avoidable mistake. The only way out of it is to follow it through to the end. But one needs to know how it maintains its hold before one can work through it and abandon it. It is particularly tenacious because what seem like disqualifying failings are in fact its qualifying, if limiting, strengths. Such are its qualities of poverty, simplicity and humility; and such, too, is another feature which we referred to elsewhere when we spoke of Wittgenstein as a 'naif in the sense of the painters'.[20] The aptness of the metaphor depends, of course, on which painters one has in mind. It would be false if one thought of him as an untutored Sunday-philosopher; his perspicuous representations are not innocent, naive depictions, but essential insights into the inner-structure, the 'grammar' of concepts. They are naive in a way that invites comparison with the vision of Klee, which is highly sophisticated though it bases itself on the naive styles of Sunday-painters, primitives, folk-artists, children and madmen. Klee, like Wittgenstein, combines this kind of naiveté with a highly developed logical mind.

Like Klee, Wittgenstein bases his account of language on the language of those who are really naive and innocent — primitives, children, workmen, common people; it is language that might be found in the unreflective situations of practical activities and in everyday life. His most fundamental mode of language — the language-game — is an imaginary activity such as tribesmen playing at being workmen might act out, or as children might enact it. The opening of the *Investigations* is almost entirely made up of such language-games and comments on them. The language-game figures as something original, elemental and primitive, something that is beyond questioning or need for justification, as simply given:

> You must bear in mind that the language-game is, so to say, something unpredictable. I mean: It is not based on grounds. It is not reasonable (or unreasonable). It is there — like our life.[21]

But Wittgenstein's naiveté is not just one of subject-matter; it is one of method as well. Even to say this might appear a contradiction in terms, for how can there be such a thing as a naive method? It is true that naiveté manifests itself as a rejection of method, but that, as we shall see, is a kind of method in itself. True to type, Wittgenstein usually speaks scathingly of method and theorising in his prescriptions for his own philosophy:

> And we may not advance any kind of theory . . . (109). There is not *a* philosophical method, though there are indeed methods, like different therapies (133).

Wittgenstein does not classify 'perspicuous representation', for instance, as a method; he does not think of it as a method-bound or theory-guided mode of representation. Like all naive representation it is supposedly methodless — requiring no interpretative schemas, no hermeneutical theories, and no special concepts. He wanted 'to replace wild conjectures and explanations by a quiet weighing of linguistic fact'.[22]

> For 'naive language', that is to say our naive, normal way of expressing ourselves, does not contain any theory of seeing — does not show you a *theory* but only a concept of seeing.[23]

This may be described and philosophically understood apparently without reference to theoretical concepts, such as those deriving from the psychology of perception. The ordinary concept is simply there to be seen; he who cannot see it overlooks what stares him in the eye. Thus the whole practice of philosophy becomes a matter of direct sight:

> Philosophy simply puts everything before us, and neither
> explains nor deduces anything. — Since everything lies open to
> view there is nothing to explain. For what is hidden, for example,
> is of no interest to us (126).

This remark may partly be explained as an admonition against
searching for hidden essences in the metaphysical manner, or even
in that of Phenomenology. Wittgenstein's anti-method and anti-
theory stand is also justifiable in so far as it is intended to counter the
pseudo-metaphysical and pseudo-scientific pretences of many
modern philosophies, those for example found in Logical
Positivism, Historicism, and among Gestaltists, Structuralists and
others. In so far as he recognised that nothing can any longer serve
the role of metaphysics, his naive attitude is a post-theoretical rather
than a pre-theoretical one. After metaphysics philosophy must limit
itself, even at the cost of separating itself off from other theoretical
methods. '. . . our considerations could not be scientific ones . . .'
(109). He was 'honestly disgusted' with the indulgence of those
around him in pseudo-scientific pretensions, those, for instance,
who imagined that they could solve philosophical problems by
means of new theorems in Formal Logic.[24] Wittgenstein's naiveté is
one way of continuing to philosophise at the end of metaphysics; and
also a way of coping with the onset of Nihilism in philosophy. In this
respect his abjuring of method and theory is far from being simply
naiveté.

However, it falls down precisely in that he is naive about his own
naiveté. He did not and could not recognise that a naive approach is
itself a method, though not like any other, and that it does entail a
Weltanschauung in some sense. Since he could not make explicit the
methodological basis of his own naive practices, he was unable to
subject those practices to self-critical scrutiny. His philosophy
suffers from a complex failure of self-awareness for it is not self-
reflexive in the way that the very idea of philosophy demands. It
suffers from the in-built paradox of any naive approach; that it must
ultimately be naive towards itself no matter how it is otherwise
sophisticated. To expose that final naiveté is not just to break
through its inherent limitation; it is at the same time to destroy the
approach itself. Wittgenstein's philosophy, as we shall presently
show, can only be accounted for from a standpoint that goes beyond
its own terms of reference.

Wittgenstein's naiveté becomes evident as soon as we expose to critical scrutiny his problem-dissolving approach. This, he claims, calls only for 'methods like therapies'. But from where, one might ask, do the problems derive in the first place? They seem to come out of nowhere, supposedly 'arising through a misinterpretation of our forms of language' (111). No explanation is ever proffered as to why particular misinterpretations should have arisen (why not others?), or how they arose when they did. The question of the genealogy, formation and transformation, in short the history, of problems is never raised.[25] As philosophically and intellectually aware readers, we know what is tacitly understood: these are the problems of metaphysics, epistemology and other branches of philosophy as they arose and were developed in the course of intellectual history. To understand them we have to understand, as it were from the inside, issues that arose in the history of philosophy. In Wittgenstein's work this understanding must be assumed although it is nowhere explicitly given — if it resides anywhere, it is only in the man himself. [This is another reason why his pupils can make so little of his work.] Surrounding every problem dealt with in the work there is a contextual silence, therefore, about the real sources and nature of the problems that it naively accepts as given. Not only does the philosophy lack a theory of the formation and transformation of problems, as it were, a theory of the 'problematic', but it is precluded from providing this by the very nature of its 'methods like therapies'.

Of course, the degree and kind of this essential omission varies from case to case: sometimes it is a matter of ignorance on Wittgenstein's part, but mostly it is a theoretical suppression demanded by the approach itself. Thus, for example, we know, and Wittgenstein tells us as much, that by and large the logico-mathematical problems he deals with derive from his own previous work in the *Tractatus*, and so in turn from Russell and Frege, and eventually from the whole modern movement of Formal Logic. We know, too, that most of the problems he tackles in his philosophical psychology derive from the main modern schools of theoretical and experimental psychology: Sensationalism, Pragmatism (William James), Behaviourism (Watson), Gestalt, Learning Theory (Bühler). He states explicitly that it is the anomaly of 'experimental methods and conceptual confusion' (p. 232) which provides the instigation for his psychological investigations. Although he does not mention the actual theories and debates behind these experimental methods and concepts, they are implicit in what he does speak about, and so they can easily be filled in without altering his work. However, there is no way of deciding within Wittgenstein's own approach whether one way of formulating these theories and interpreting their concepts, and so of re-stating the disputes between the different schools is better than any other. Wittgenstein's work, that is, provides no way of making theoretical revisions, conceptual alterations and experimental improvements; it leaves the disputing theories more or less as they were even after its investigations.[26] All it manages in this respect is to restrict the area of dispute to psychology itself, and so prevent the issues invading other provinces of philosophy. This difficulty is even more pronounced when the problems he is dealing with derive not from easily understood modern sciences, but from the more difficult issues of metaphysics. Thus, there is no way of telling within his work whether a problem he investigates is the same as, of a later derivation, or modern version of a problem that one might encounter in a classic text. We are not provided with a method of reading those texts or interpreting the problems; we are supposed to accept them as self-understood.

And this contextual silence prevents Wittgenstein perceiving a further anomaly: having failed to see that the problems he investigates could only have emerged out of a long history of philosophical and scientific disputation, and are the outcomes of theory, he can claim that the dissolution of these problems also requires no theory and can be carried out 'before all new discoveries and inventions'. But how can such problems be understood before the discoveries and inventions that gave rise to them? There is, of course, a way of trying to resolve this anomaly in Wittgenstein's own terms: it might be said that, no matter what the theoretical origins of a problem, once it has arisen theory is no longer required, since the dissolution of the problem is not to be sought where it originates, but in the ground of everyday language. Thus, regardless of how and why the misinterpretation of our forms of language arises, the right interpretation lies in securing the 'command [of] a clear view of the use of our words' (122). In terms of Wittgenstein's metaphor, it might be said that no matter how our understanding became knotted, the untying of these knots only requires a skill in undoing the simple strands, and its sole result is a return to the simplicity of untangled language. This answer overlooks the fact that untying a knot involves the same movements as tying it, but in reverse; in other words, the dissolution of philosophical problems requires that one retrace the steps of their original formation; a complex is dissolved only when its constitution is understood. And unless one has a means of understanding how and why problems originate one has no way of dissolving them.

This Wittgensteinian answer also presupposes the possibility of an uncomplicated, un-theoretic and non-method-bound view of our words; it assumes that a 'perspicuous representation' of the grammar of language could be attained by means of a mere description of the uses of words. Over and over again Wittgenstein exhorts the philosopher just to describe, not explain or interpret:

> We must do away with all *explanation*, and description alone must take its place (109).

> Philosophy simply puts everything before us, and neither explains nor deduces anything (126).

Descriptions that are to be efficacious in removing the misinterpretations of language are to be secured by a direct view of the meaning of words. All that is required for the uncomplicated description that produces perspicuous representation is a naive vision: 'philosophy only states what everyone admits' (599) — and presumably, too, what everyone sees, for 'we want to understand something that is already in plain view' (89).

According to Wittgenstein the philosophical grammar of words also arises out of and makes use of sheer description: 'It only describes and in no way explains the use of signs' (496). And yet, at the same time, he distinguishes between conventional 'surface grammar' and philosophical 'depth grammar' on which the dissolution of problems depends:

> In the use of words one might distinguish 'surface grammar' from 'depth grammar'. What immediately impresses itself upon us about the use of a word is the way it is used in the construction of the sentence, the part of its use — one might say — that can be taken in by the ear. — And now compare the depth grammar say of the word 'to mean', with what its surface grammar would lead us to expect (664).

But if what is taken in by the ear, the grammatical expression as it were, is only surface grammar, what sense-organ is it that can take soundings and listen to the depth grammar below? In other words, is there a way of describing this 'depth grammar'? Can the grammar that constitutes the essence of a concept — 'essence is expressed by grammar' (371) — be grasped directly by looking into the ordinary workings of a word? Can such a linguistic '*Wesenschau*' be based on a 'quiet weighing of linguistic fact'?[27] Is the 'assembling of reminders' (127) all that is necessary? It is understandable that Wittgenstein should wish to counter such assertions as 'the essence is hidden from us' (92), which might be made in metaphysics or Phenomenology; but does he need to go to the other extreme and claim that everything 'lies open to view', so there is 'nothing to explain' (126)? If anything appears hidden, is it merely because of its 'simplicity and familiarity' (129)?

Wittgenstein insists that our 'naive language, that is to say our naive, normal way of expressing ourselves'[28] does not contain theories but only concepts, and presumably he would maintain that these are untheoretical, naive concepts. And he goes even further, saying that a naive concept can be understood and described in a naive fashion. But given that our 'naive, normal way of expressing ourselves' contains an indefinite number of features and, consequently, can be described in an indefinite number of ways, how are we to tell which of these features pertain to the concept and which do not? There must be some process of selectivity at work, some sense of what is significant and to what end, for otherwise the description could not even begin. In any case, we must have norms even to judge that something is part of our 'normal way of expressing ourselves'. We are reminded here of Nietzsche's dictum that in language, too, 'there are no facts, only interpretations',[29] that even the facts of everyday usage are not given as such, uninterpreted. Nor are what Wittgenstein calls 'forms of life' given in that sense.

The metaphor of 'depth' and 'surface' grammar also serves to mislead him; even if we allow that the surface grammar can somehow be recorded by the educated ear — though for this education we are indebted to the categories of Roman grammarians who devised a system of grammar based on Greek logic — yet from this it must not be extrapolated that there is a more essential grammar lurking beneath the surface, waiting to be described. Even if the conventional grammar is objectively descriptive, so that to give the grammar of a word does not alter its meaning or usage, it does not follow that the so-called depth grammar is equally objectively neutral and that to describe it leaves the concept untouched. For, if it constitutes an essential interpretation of the concept, it will by virtue of this fact alone be changing — defining, fixing, refining — the meaning of the word, and so altering its potential usage. We might go so far as to say that words have no depth grammar until philosophers interpret them, and so endow them with a grammatical 'essence'. In one form or another the making of essential definitions, and so the establishment of depth grammar, has been part of the process whereby philosophy acts on language; it has been going on ever since Socrates 'invented' the concept by asking for strict definitions of words. Philosophical investigation can never leave 'everything as it is', since conceptual investigation is always also conceptual alteration. Grasping a concept, 'seeing' a grammatical feature, illuminating a problem: these are not, as Wittgenstein imagined, neutral activities like seeing or illuminating an object.

Wittgenstein comes closest to understanding the nature of his own investigations into the meaning of words when he speaks of 'giving words a meaning':

> To say 'this combination of words makes no sense' excludes it from the sphere of language and thereby bounds the domain of language (499).

He realises that 'exclusion of a combination of words from the language' (500) is an interpretative move whereby certain words are assigned a sense. But he fails to see that the inclusion of a combination of words in the language is an equally interpretative move whereby certain words are assigned a sense. One does not establish whether a given question or problem makes sense by looking at the sentence in which it is formulated as a combination of words with pre-existent meanings and ascertaining whether these meanings can or cannot enter into this relationship; this assumes a logical atomism of sense that Wittgenstein abandoned together with the *Tractatus*. It is, rather, a matter of interpretation, of deciding whether the combination of words can be given a meaning, or put to some meaningful purpose. This is so even in the strict discipline of logic and mathematics: 'a mathematical question is a challenge. And we might say: it makes sense, if it spurs us on to some mathematical activity'.[30] And even more radically, 'we might then also say that a question in mathematics makes sense if it stimulates the mathematical imagination'.[31] In philosophy the question of meaningfulness is always a matter of interpretation. For example, Wittgenstein asks the question: 'does this mean that it is nonsense ever to raise the question whether dreams really take place during sleep, or are a memory phenomenon of the awakened?', and answers it by saying: 'it will turn on the use of the question' (p. 184). In other words, the question has neither sense nor is it nonsense prior to an interpretation of its use being considered. Meanings are not simply there to be put together in combinations, and so, for that matter, to be objectively observed and described. Meanings are made. Hence, a question that is meaningless in one context might be quite meaningful in another. And equally, the meaning of a word changes from context to context as it enters in different sentences into different combinations with other words.

That part of the meaning of a word which we define as its conceptual essence — which Wittgenstein calls its 'depth grammar' — is also labile. It changes as it is subjected to the process of description, for this necessarily entails definition. A definition describes the meaning of a word in such a way as to specify, and so alter that meaning. Without a definition, or something akin to it, such as a higher order conception or Notion, the meaning of a word cannot even be described. Even the description of the naive concept, the ordinary 'normal way of expressing ourselves', requires definitions or higher order forms of the same concept. It may be said that the act of describing does not change the naive concept — if for no other reason than that ordinary people being unaware of the conceptual description go on using the word in the same old way; yet the concept as a whole is changed, and those able to understand the conceptual description will also come to alter their ordinary usage, even if in ever so slight a way. This issue of the theory of conceptual description, which we might consider as a special branch of hermeneutics, is one that Wittgenstein left uninvestigated for reasons we have already given. He never considered the relationship between the 'naive' concept and higher order interpretative and definitional forms of the same concept. Because he took them to be different kinds of language-game, representing the general heterogeneity of language forms, he could not consider these relations of the different forms of the concept to each other. He did not ask himself how the primitive concept of primitive people relates to the simple, naive concept of ordinary people, or to the rudimentary concepts of their children; how these in turn relate to the more developed ideas present in the cultural elaborations of a language, such as its basic forms of thought and belief, and its ideological expressions; how these are altered by the fully developed concept or theoretical conception as this is formed in metaphysics, theology, science or criticism; and finally, how the fully defined concepts of thinkers and philosophers, their Notions, play a part in transforming this whole conceptual network. He did not realise that any one word may assume some or all of these conceptual forms in the course of its development, in accordance not with some predetermined scheme, but with the exigencies of history. A general theory of conceptual translation and change cannot be either Hegelian or Evolutionary, for it must account not merely for conceptual development or creation, but also for conceptual destruction. Wittgensteinian investigation is itself a specific mode of conceptual destruction as dissolution.

Wittgenstein was little able to appreciate this side of his work. He imagined that a conceptual investigation of philosophical psychology was possible which was not itself involved in psychological theory, one that could be carried out 'prior to all inventions and discoveries' in the science of psychology. We can now better appreciate the futility of attempting to cope with the conceptual confusions of a highly theoretical science by means of a naive investigation of ordinary concepts because this folly has since been repeatedly perpetrated by linguistic philosophers. And yet, we also know that Wittgenstein did contribute to alleviating the conceptual confusion in psychology; for example, his clarifications of the concept 'seeing' do serve a purpose in the psychology of perception. How could he have accomplished something that, judged by his own terms of reference, was impossible? If what he achieved was quite different from what he set himself to do, his own way of accounting for his work must have been misconceived. This failure of self-reflexivity is the self-limitation of his philosophy.

If we take the concept 'seeing' as indicative of this shortcoming, and turn to the passage where Wittgenstein begins his analysis, it immediately becomes apparent that in referring to 'two uses of the word see' (p. 193), he is not discussing two ordinary-language concepts. For one use of the word 'see' is immediately identified in quasi-technical terms as 'noticing an aspect', and he goes on to say that he is 'interested in the concept and its place among the concepts of experience' (p. 193). It is obvious that this is a new concept. And its home is not everyday language, but the science of psychological theorisation and experimentation, particularly of the *Gestalt* school. As Wittgenstein's investigation of this concept proceeds it becomes apparent that 'noticing an aspect' and the associated 'new' experience of a change of aspect — one which had not previously received attention — is the focus of a complete re-interpretation and re-ordering of the concept of 'seeing' in all its ramifications. All modes of seeing and their 'objects of perception' are being conceptually re-worked and re-arranged. We might claim, therefore, that unbeknownst to himself Wittgenstein succeeded in elaborating a new Notion (higher order concept) of 'seeing'. This would make his investigation a kind of conceptual creation. However, his redefinition was not sufficiently creative to inspire new departures in psychology; it was largely a re-ordering activity designed to place existing concepts in a clearer arrangement. And as we have shown, he carried this out in a piecemeal, *ad hoc* fashion, leaving implicit all the principles and norms of his revision. It would remain a philosophical task of quite a different magnitude to go through his scattered remarks on 'seeing' and elicit from them the theoretical practices that guided his procedures.

The main reason that Wittgenstein could not make explicit his own interpretative principles and higher-order concepts was his naive 'method' of 'methods like therapies'. He could say in general that 'concepts lead us to make investigations; are the expression of our interest, and direct our interest' (570), yet he would not specify the concepts that led him to make his philosophical investigations, that expressed and directed his philosophical interests. The knowledge-directing interests of his own knowledge remain unacknowledged. And this led him to deny to philosophy in general the capacity for formulating concepts of its own; it loses the right to a special language for itself. According to Wittgenstein philosophy arises out of a failure of language, not out of a special kind of language achievement. That philosophy requires special forms of concepts, that these are not the same as ordinary concepts, that philosophical words, like 'language', 'world', 'experience' can never have a use that is 'as humble a one as that of the words "table", "lamp", "door"' (97) — tells against Wittgenstein's conception of philosophy. If such terms were reduced to their ordinary language usage they would cease to carry out their philosophical function as higher-order concepts used to interpret lower-order ones. The de-sublimation of metaphysics must not be confused with the degradation of philosophy.

However, Wittgenstein does in fact accomplish that which he forbids himself. Does he not utilise his own special concepts of 'language', 'world', 'experience'; does he not formulate philosophical terms found nowhere else, such as 'language-game', 'depth-grammar', 'criterion-symptom', 'agreement', 'common-ness', and others? Are we, thus, to say that what he denies himself in theory he nevertheless attains to in practice? This would be too pat. Wittgenstein does have his own specialised terms, but these are never given adequate conceptual definition. His concepts are implicit in the texts, but not fully realised. Later we shall try to elicit them further and define some of them, but this task will take us beyond Wittgenstein's philosophy, where they are frequently no more than foci of analogy and illustrative example, and occasionally no better than extended metaphors, like the concepts to be encountered in such practical-critical fields as literary criticism.

Let us take, for example, Wittgenstein's key concept of the 'language-game'. He speaks of the 'extension of a concept into a theory (e.g. wish-fulfilment dream)';[32] we might speak analogously of the extension of a metaphor into a concept. The metaphor of language as a game juxtaposes the two terms in a series of extremely illuminating relationships, as in any fecund metaphor the ordinary meanings of both terms meet and generate new meanings — though these may degenerate with over-use, unlike a well-defined concept. The ground-analogy is that speaking a language is playing a game, or a set of such games if it is a complex language. From this, other extended analogies follow to set up a complex metaphoric web.[33]

He first introduces the term 'language-game' by way of the full-blown imaginary example of a tribe of builders acting out a single language-game of building which is like a single game a group of people might play. And as soon as one conceives of the example in this way, it becomes obvious that the language-game metaphor has been blown up into an impossible imaginary case. For such language-games are to be taken 'not as incomplete parts of a language, but as languages complete in themselves, as complete systems of human communication'.[34] 'Conceive this as a complete primitive language' (2). But how can there be a complete language whose sole function is to facilitate such activities as the passing of slabs and bricks between builders? If this were all they ever spoke about, or did, that appeared to be human, then what is to say that these creatures are people at all? They might be an unusual species of man-like bees, for, after all, bees also build and have a highly elaborate system of signalling for locating, communicating and gathering their materials, one which is much more involved than any of Wittgenstein's language-games. But clearly the signalling dance of the bees is neither a language nor a language-game. A language is a complex total system of intercourse and communication pertaining to a recognisably human mode of life: social, economic, cultural, artistic, or religious; in short, it must mediate and reflect on the activities of a recognisably human society, no matter how primitive. To the extent that a society is a unified totality, so too will its language be a complex unified system — there is, of course, great variety possible in the degree of unity, for this is culturally conditioned. No animal species can constitute a society, hence no animals can have a language. Wittgenstein has not taken his own dictum: 'and to imagine a language means to imagine a form of life' (19) seriously enough.

Wittgenstein is not unaware that his conception of the language-game is problematic and on occasions he asks himself a taxing question:

> (On language-game no. 2 [that of the builders]) You are just tacitly assuming that these people *think*; that they are like people as we know them in *that* respect; that they do not carry on that language-game merely mechanically. For it you imagined them doing that, you yourself would not call it the use of a rudimentary language.
>
> What am I to reply to this? Of course it is true that the life of those men must be like ours in many respects, and I said nothing about this similarity. But the important thing is that their language, and their thinking too, may be rudimentary, that there is such a thing as 'primitive thinking' which is to be described via primitive *behaviour*. The surroundings are not the 'thinking accompaniment' of speech.[35]

The answer goes part of the way toward remedying the deficiencies of Wittgenstein's original account of the language-game; but it is far from adequate. It is not enough that human surroundings should provide a context for the builders' language-game; what is required is that there should be other forms of language of which this is a part. Those people must be capable of engaging in speaking about other things apart from building. Their language might be rudimentary, primitive and much simpler overall than any known to us, but it cannot be merely a simplified fragment of our language; in its very primitiveness it must have *in nuce* some or most of the general forms possessed by our language: convivial, economic and cultural modes of speech, for example. Wittgenstein does not seem to be aware of the real meaning of 'primitiveness'; he confuses it with that which is partial or simplified, whereas the primitive is always complete in itself; a primitive tribe might be said to be lacking in certain developed forms, but its own forms are not themselves lacking in something, in the sense of being partial or fragmentary. Once again the identification of the primitive with the basic, elementary or childlike seems to have seriously misled him.

What has particularly confused him in this instance is, of course, the basic metaphor of language and game. It breaks down precisely because a game can be played on its own as a single, separable activity by different kinds of human being, or even by animals or machines. But a language is not a single activity, nor is it separable from the people whose language it is, nor is it easily transferable; and a language-game cannot exist on its own like a game, but only as part of a whole language. Ultimately then, either the language-game is merely a game and not a language, or it is a language, in which case it cannot be treated as if it were a game. Wittgenstein himself has said that 'An expression has meaning only in the stream of life',[36] and by analogy one can say that a language-game, too, only makes sense in the stream of a language. The language-games he imagines are easily recognisable fragments of our language, artificially abstracted from their total context. They are analogous to little plays in the theatre of the absurd, utilising a simplified variant of the Brechtian alienation effect for their construction. Any mode of social action, or any concept, can be dramatically enacted. But as any dramatist knows, each such piece of action can be staged in an indefinite number of ways because of the multivalence of all meaningful action. Special methods, values and assumptions are implicit in selecting one way of staging it as against any other, equally possible way. These considerations are not simply problems in dramaturgy, but issues in the rendering, describing and understanding of all social action, such as were raised by Weber in sociology. The whole problem of the methodology of language-game construction is one concerning which Wittgenstein had to remain silent, for had he raised it openly, his conception of the language-game would have been destroyed.

All the analogies that follow from the language-game metaphor have a breaking point of which Wittgenstein was unaware. As he likens the speaking of a language to the playing of a game, so he also likens the understanding of the meaning of a word to the ability to make a correct move in a game, explanation of the meaning of a word to explanation of the rules of a game, and in general, a child's learning a word to its learning the rules and moves of a game. Obviously, many of these analogies have a purpose in the context in which Wittgenstein makes them: they can be used to break down the empiricist philosophical conception that the meanings of words are mental 'ideas' or entities of a non-material kind; or they can serve to underline the importance of learning and training in acquiring understanding or knowing the meaning; or they can be used to distinguish between words and their uses, or uses and rules governing them. But all these analogies must break down somewhere because games are relatively discrete activities which are easily transportable from one context to another, whereas languages are cultural wholes or 'forms of life'. Games are easily analysable because they are usually made up of separable moves which are bound and governed by rules, and also prescribe the roles of the players. But words in a language are not in this way rule-governed; they are not like counters. As expressive means they may be infinitely varied and used in an indefinite set of different, totally unforeseen circumstances, for the only limitation on the use of a word is the intelligence, wit, ingenuity and creativity of its users. All language has this capacity to be infinitely generative with finite means. Speaking a language can only be likened to playing a game that is constantly altering in the course of play — an impossibility for games. People speaking to each other are playing a game only when they are making fixed moves, when their speech is ritualised or conventionalised, but if they are conversing or communicating freely they are making up new sentences, or utilising old expressions in a new way relying on understanding, tact, judgement, sensitivity to do so and not on rules or prescribed procedures. Rules play a minor part in speech, and sometimes none at all. Understanding speech is, thus, different to understanding a game; it means responding to the new and unforeseen, or devising questions and answers that are relevant to a particular situation; it does not mean producing stock reactions to the situation, no matter how clever such a reaction might be, as it does, for instance, in a game of chess. We could imagine a child who was a highly intelligent chess player but otherwise quite unable to speak or communicate. Learning a game is nothing like learning a language, for in learning a language a child is learning to become human. When Wittgenstein appeals to the supposedly simple, unambiguous facts of child-learning he is invariably imposing an interpretation on them to justify the analogy with the learning of games. What it is that a child learns when it learns to speak is a highly contentious issue in child-psychology, as Piaget has shown.

Wittgenstein tended to see game-playing as instrumental, and consequently gave his whole account of language an exaggerated techno-ludic emphasis.[37] His strong sense of rule-boundness and practicality made him restrict the idea of play to that of the purposive game. He was insufficiently alive to the play of language in discourse, dialogue and dialectic; it is perhaps too idealistic to say, as Croce did, that 'language is perpetual creation', but it is possible to say that it is perpetual play. Games are themselves but one limited instance of general play: consider the wealth of meaning the word 'play' drawn from its definitions as drama, ritual and ceremony, for example. A broad enough concept of 'play' might be adequate to comprehend language, but Wittgenstein was in no position to provide one. We would have to turn back from Wittgenstein to Nietzsche to find resources for such a concept.

Wittgenstein was deeply attached to the concept of the game because, like Goethe, he was intent on uncovering the *Urphänomena* of language: the basic, primitive, elementary roots of language, which are simply there as given, beyond all explanation or justification, and out of which everything else in speech develops. And the language-games conceived on the model of simple, discrete games seemed to satisfy this requirement for *Ursprachen*.

> Our mistake is to look for an explanation where we ought to look at what happens as a 'proto-phenomenon' [*Urphänomenon*]. That is, where we ought to have said: *this language-game is played*.
>
> The question is not one of explaining a language-game by means of our experience but of noting a language-game (654–5).

Thus, the language game is something ultimately elementary; 'it is there — like our life'.[38] Wittgenstein's insistence on having something that is 'simply there' is part of his refusal to countenance the need for interpretation and explanation. He had departed from the atomic propositions of the *Tractatus*, but instead of logical atoms

he devised for himself cultural simples or *Urphänomena*. Fundamental simplicity was indispensable for him.

This limitation notwithstanding, the game-metaphor did serve a
very useful purpose in the dissolution of the 'concept' in
metaphysics, which took the form of the universal, the essence,
nature, the real Idea. Initially the problem of 'essential nature',
arose for Wittgenstein as the issue of the 'essence of language', an
issue stemming from the *Tractatus* attempt to find a formal unity of
all possible languages:

> This finds expression in questions as to the essence of language, of
> proposition of thought. — For we too in these investigations are
> trying to understand the essence of language — its function, its
> structure, — yet *this* is not what those questions have in view. For
> they see in the essence not something that already lies open to
> view and that becomes surveyable by re-arrangement, but
> something that lies *beneath* the surface (92).

The solution of this problem first occurred to Wittgenstein in terms
of the game-metaphor. He saw the concept 'language' as analogous
to the concept 'game': just as 'game' refers to an indefinite set of
games joined together by an interweaving of family-resemblances,
in such a way that it cannot be defined in terms of genus and
differentia, so, too, 'language' is a non-essential unity made up of a
like set of language-games.

> Consider for example the proceedings that we call 'games' . . .
> What is common to them all? (66)

> We see that what we call 'sentence' and 'language' have not the
> formal unity that I imagined, but are families of structures more
> or less related to one another (108).

> Review the multiplicity of language-games in the following
> examples . . . (23) [a long list follows].

This destruction of the essential unity of the concept 'language'
was then extended and became a general tactic for the destruction of
metaphysical essences. Where philosophers had formerly searched
for essential unities and tried 'to grasp the essence of the thing'
(116), Wittgenstein was content to point out that these were 'game-

concepts' held together merely by a criss-crossing interplay of similarities with no such formal unity behind them.

But once again, even this, one of the outstanding achievements of modern philosophy, was won at too great a cost. In so deploying his game-concept metaphor to frustrate the search for essential unities, Wittgenstein had to forego the search for any unity whatever; everything became so heterogeneous to him that ultimately no definitions would be undertaken, no precise concepts specified and no theories developed. This view of language as made up of discrete sets of language-games that can occur in any combination discouraged effort to locate the structural unity of any given language. But language-forms differ from games precisely in that they cannot occur in any combination whatever; for instance, kinds of sentences adhere together in determinate ways, some presuppose each other, refer to each other, demand each other, whereas games have no such dependencies. Ultimately, the destruction of the essential unity of language only leads Wittgenstein into an atomism of discrete language-games, and this in turn deflects him from any theoretical attempt to specify the other kinds of unity of given languages. It even prevents him from realising that there must be a way of unifying games which would make it possible to develop a theory of games, and that concepts which are analogous to the concept 'game' must also be subject to some unity if a theorisation of them is to be undertaken.

That the destruction of essential unity does not preclude a conceptual unification sufficient for purposes of theory had already been realised by Max Weber in the social sciences, quite unbeknown to Wittgenstein. Weber had encountered a problem with the essential definition of social and historical concepts which was identical to Wittgenstein's problem with the concept 'language'. But he overcame this problem in a way that contrasts startlingly with Wittgenstein's merely analogical solution by means of metaphors and examples; Weber developed a new concept of the 'ideal-type', which was to be of far-reaching theoretical importance.

This is the problem as Weber perceived it:

Every conscientious examination of the conceptual elements of historical exposition shows however that the historian as soon as he attempts to go beyond the bare establishment of concrete relationships and to determine the *cultural* significance of even the simplest individual event in order to 'characterize' it, *must* use concepts which are precisely and unambiguously definable only in the form of ideal-types. Or are concepts such as 'individualism', 'imperialism', 'feudalism', 'mercantilism', 'conventional', etc. and innumerable concepts of like character by means of which we seek analytically and emphatically to understand reality, constructed substantively by the 'presuppositionless' *description* of some concrete phenomenon or through the abstract synthesis of those traits which are *common* to numerous phenomena . . .?[39]

Clearly, neither alternative is possible for reasons that we now understand much better as a result of Wittgenstein's illuminating game-concept metaphors; but Weber, too, had realised that such concepts cannot be defined in terms of an essential unity:

A 'definition' of such synthetic historical terms according to the schema of *genus proximum* and *differentia specifica* is naturally nonsense. But let us consider it. Such a form of the establishment of the meaning of words is to be found only in axiomatic disciplines which use syllogisms. A simple 'descriptive analysis' of these concepts into their components does not exist or else exists only illusorily, for the question arises as to *which* of these components should be regarded as essential. When a genetic definition of the content of the concept is sought, there remains only the ideal-type in the sense explained above. It is a conceptual construct [*Gedankenbild*] which is neither historical reality nor even the 'true' reality. It is even less fitted to serve as a schema under which a real situation or action is to be subsumed as one instance. It has the significance of a purely ideal *limiting* concept with which the real situation or action is *compared* and surveyed for the explication of certain of its significant components.[40]

This extract and the debate surrounding it provide a touchstone for testing Wittgenstein's attempts to cope with these problems of description by means of his game-concept and language-game metaphors. Certainly, Wittgenstein provides us with analogies that shed light on the difficulties, but light of itself is not enough; it may help us to see what the problem is about, yet it cannot show us how to solve it. Weber achieves more, for he establishes a new theoretical concept and a new method of theoretically describing and explaining social action and meaning in general. On this basis Weber founds a new science of sociology, whereas Wittgenstein founds only a new *ad hoc* practice for handling limited problems in linguistic analysis. Adorno spells out the profound philosophical consequences of Weber's destruction of essential unity and his formation of ideal-types: 'How objects can be unlocked by their constellation is to be learned not so much from philosophy, which took no interest in the matter, as from important scientific investigation'[41] — he means that of Weber. Adorno is being a little unfair to philosophers such as Wittgenstein who did take an interest in the matter, but basically his judgement holds.

On rare occasions it begins to dawn on Wittgenstein himself that his concept of the 'language game' is tending in the direction of an ideal-type:

> Our clear and simple language-games are not preparatory studies for a future regularization of language — as it were first approximations, ignoring friction and air-resistance. The language-games are rather set up as *objects of comparison* which are meant to throw light on the facts of language by way not only of similarities, but also of dissimilarities.
>
> For we can avoid ineptness or emptiness in our assertions only by presenting the model as what it is, as an object of comparison — as, so to speak, a measuring-rod, not as a preconceived idea to which reality *must* correspond (130–1).

If he had followed these insights, he would have realised that language-games are constructed as models of comparison, that they are, therefore, a species of ideal-type of language forms. Hence Wittgenstein is wrong to think of them as complete primitive languages, or even real parts of a language; they are not 'real' at all, neither as *Urphänomena* nor as 'simples' of language. Had he raised these issues, he would have had to ask himself how such ideal-types of language are constructed, according to what presuppositions, and on what criteria of Significance, Reality and Coherence. Unfortunately, everything in his naive approach militated against this kind of investigation of the method behind language-game construction.

2. Destroying the Logos and Cogito

The limitations of Wittgenstein's philosophical self-knowledge readily appear if one attempts to answer the vexed question of how his philosophy relates to the great Tradition of metaphysics.[42] He was aware, of course, that his investigations do have a bearing on the Tradition, but as this bearing was largely destructive he could not allow himself to confront the question openly. In revealing it we are exposing an inherent 'silence' in his philosophy that will eventually destroy it. However, to do so we must depend on his own words and thoughts to reveal what he did not say and what he could not think. And this paradoxical formulation identifies the chief difficulty, that of deciding where his words and thoughts leave off, and where others that take off from them begin. It is a question of the limits of his speech and thought, and like all boundaries limits are not absolutely exact; they always permit of an indeterminate no-man's-land between two fronts, for 'no single ideal of exactness has been laid down' (88). In this no-man's-land we now dwell.

We shall be exploring this gap between what he thought he was doing and what he actually did to the Tradition only in respect of the two topics that interest us here: those of the Logos and the Cogito. Several commentators have already noted that some of Wittgenstein's dissolutions of problems amount to critical arguments against aspects of the Logos and the Cogito. Thus, Bambrough sees the game-concept metaphor as an argument against traditional theories of universals or conceptual Realism, as well as against Nominalism;[43] and Kenny identifies the private-language argument as one directed against the Cogito.[44] But invariably such commentators have a traditional conception of what such an argument involves, so they believe that Wittgenstein is engaged in a conventional refutation of metaphysical ideas. They seem to assume that all philosophical arguments take place in a timeless realm of problems and issues, as if philosophers could talk to each other directly across the ages on matters of perennial concern. The commentators referred to above seem to think that Wittgenstein can argue with Plato or Descartes, just as Aquinas argued with Aristotle and Aristotle with Plato. They do not appear to be aware that the very meaning of 'argument', as well as its mode, style and procedure, are totally different in each of these historical cases. Philosophical argumentation is subject to historical changes and assumes many different forms; what is a compelling argument at one time is a fallacy at another, for there is no universally binding logic of philosophy; nor is there a mode of dialectic that is itself not subject to change.

At first sight even to say this might appear to fall into a trap of relativistic self-refutation, for is it not itself an argument, and how can it be subject to change? And in any case, what sense does it make to speak of the 'logic' of an argument that is subject to changing criteria of validity? Surely, canons of validity are given once and for all? Behind these questions there is the unquestioned assumption that argument, like all of logic, is based on an invariant Logos. But what if we can argue that there is no such Logos? Would it amount to making this very argument itself illogical and so self-refuting? It is in this way that the attempt to argue against the Logos brings itself into dispute; it is of necessity a self-referring argument for it refers to the nature of argument as such.

In order to begin we have to sidestep all these difficulties and simply presuppose the conclusion we intend to reach: there is no universal logic or Logos of all argument. Our own argument is thus itself ultimately circular, for to begin, it has to assume what it is required to prove. The advantage of making this crucial assumption is that it opens up the way to a critical study of how arguments function and what makes them valid. As Adorno insists, argumentation is indispensable to philosophy:

> The element of the *homme de lettres*, disparaged by a petty bourgeois scientific ethos, is indispensable to thought; and no less indispensable, of course, is the element abused by philosophy garbed as science: the meditative contraction — the argument, which came to merit so much scepticism. Whenever philosophy was substantial, both elements would coincide. At a distance, dialectics might be characterized as the elevation to self-consciousness of the effort to be saturated with dialectics (*sic*). Otherwise, the argument deteriorates into the technique of conceptless specialists amid the concept, as it is now spreading academically in the so-called 'analytical philosophy', which robots can learn and copy.[45]

A 'technique of conceptless specialists amid the concept' — thus Adorno castigates bad argumentation, and indicates the close relation between argument and concept formation. Wittgenstein, too, realised the connection, and in terms of it tried to account for how an argument moves from premises to conclusion and why it compels acceptance of this movement. Unfortunately, he restricted himself largely to proofs or arguments in logic and mathematics and left philosophical arguments virtually unexplored. Had he undertaken the latter, he would have been obliged to alter considerably his views on what it is to philosophise. But, fortunately, many of the points he makes about proofs may also be applied with slight modification to philosophy as well. For although the main difference is that arguments in philosophy are not as compelling as those in the strict disciplines, the latter cannot forcibly compel either, as is revealed by the fact that completely new modes of proof in logic or mathematics, like new theories in the sciences, do not at first command universal acceptance — there are always those who will refuse to acknowledge their validity. Philosophy does not, except in rare cases, provide proofs; it does provide compelling, and not merely persuasive, arguments, yet the difference between such arguments and proofs is a measure of the distance separating philosophy from science.

Wittgenstein explains proof in logic and mathematics in terms of concept creation achieved through the setting up of new conceptual connections. He asks two leading questions: 'Is a new conceptual connection a new concept? And does mathematics create conceptual connections?'[46] And he goes on to answer these questions in passages such as this:

> The mathematical Must is only another expression of the fact that mathematics forms concepts. And concepts help us to comprehend things. They correspond to a particular way of dealing with situations. Mathematics forms a network of norms.[47]

And in logic, too, 'the introduction of a new rule of inference can be conceived as a transition to a new language-game'.[48] This formation of new concepts is achieved through the establishment of new conceptual connections: 'I should like to say: the proof shows me a new connection, and hence it also gives me a new concept.'[49] This remark comes in answer to the question: 'An equation constructs a conceptual path. But is a conceptual path a concept? And, if not, is there a sharp distinction between them?'[50] The answer is clearly that there is no sharp distinction between them, for a new conceptual connection and a new concept merge fluidly into each other. Such connections are 'internal relations', or 'connections in grammar' that alter the concepts they connect, or, as Wittgenstein puts it, 'a mathematical proposition is the determination of a concept following upon a discovery'.[51] The discovery is that it is possible to connect concepts in precisely this way. As a result of the discovery the essence of the concept is changed, and so old concepts are altered or new concepts are created: 'The proof doesn't explore the essence of the two figures but it does express what I am going to count as belonging to the essence of the figures from now on — I deposit what belongs to the essence among the paradigms of language. The mathematician creates essence.'[52]

The Philosopher, too, 'creates essence', but in a quite different way, not rationally through a linear movement of proof between seemingly fixed termini, but dialectically in a conceptual passage whereby that which is being substantiated is also being constituted. In philosophy, argument and definition and concept formation form an intricate knot. Philosophy too, is a matter of 'grammatical movements' which establish new internal relations between concepts, and so create new concepts. The main difference between philosophical and mathematical concept formation is that the conceptual movement of the former does not compel one to follow it in the way the latter does. But even so, strictly rational arguments or proofs are not absolutely compelling either, for as Wittgenstein shows there is no forcible 'logical' compulsion to follow a certain conceptual path: 'Do not look at the proof as a procedure that *compels* you, but as one that *guides* you — And what it guides is your *conception* of a [particular] situation.'[53] A proof cannot absolutely compel because accepting it depends on a capacity and a willingness to follow it; the proof has to be grasped or 'seen', and a given person might be unable or unwilling to see it. '*In the course* of proof our way of seeing is changed';[54] and someone who refuses to have his way of seeing changed — perhaps rightly, for sound and proper reasons — will never accept the presumed validity of the proven.

In philosophy, too, accepting an argument is largely a matter of coming to 'see' something differently or 'see' a new connection, which is why the sign of assent is often the phrase 'now I see it'. The 'seeing' is not something separate from the argument, for it is the argument itself that leads to the insight by which it is comprehended. It is in this way that arguments obtain their power of illumination, of making something clear that was confused before. The sudden insight is not to be thought of as an isolated psychic phenomenon, anymore than an argument is to be thought of as standing on its own without preconditions or background. Particularly in philosophy, a new argument usually appears in the context of a new philosophical standpoint. A capacity to see the argument and accept it is part of accepting, or at least sympathetically considering, the new philosophy as a whole. To see through an argument and reject it is part of an even more complex dialectical playing off of one whole philosophy against another. An argument has to be seen or seen through because it is a showing or showing up of something: it is strictly speaking a demonstration. And to demonstrate is to expose a connection that was 'hidden' before. But to say that it was hidden is not to say that it was already fully there waiting to be uncovered. A hidden link is but 'dimly' there, only becoming present and showing itself when it is seen.

That is to say: to establish a connection by argument is both to invent and discover a link. We speak of making a connection where what is so made is created but not fashioned, and found but not stumbled upon. Two concepts can only be satisfactorily related by argument when features are present in them that lend themselves to the forging of a linkage; otherwise the connection is far-fetched and the argument unsatisfactory. But at the same time, the argument reflects back on the concepts and changes them in the very act of relating them. For, an argument does not merely attach itself to characteristics already fully present in concepts; it also develops implicit and incipient ones and renders them explicit. Thus arguing is itself part of the process of defining concepts. We do not only form concepts and then argue in terms of them, we also develop arguments and later realise to what concepts they lead: 'we formulate rules and only later do we see where they lead us', as Wittgenstein puts it.

But what is involved in a dialectical argument against a philosophical position? If one is restricted to the concepts and modes of argument of the position one is opposing then no fundamental argument against it can be launched; all one might do is point up an internal difficulty, or inconsistency, which can usually be corrected without giving up anything that matters. The radical way of launching the dialectic is to approach what one is against from a fully formed opposed position, and argue against it in terms of the concepts, theories and modes of argument that one has there evolved. One usually begins by restating the position opposed in one's own concepts. This does not mean that one simply imposes one's terms on it in any rough and ready way, for what is called for is an adequate 'translation', that is, a new rendering. This attempt can fail, and can be criticised in many ways. The most fundamental breakdown occurs where one's own concepts are not broad enough to comprehend all the wealth of meaning and precision of detail of that which they try to take in, so that what results is 'mis-translation':

distortion, simplification, arbitrary selection, misunderstanding and failure to grasp significances. But once an adequate 'translation' is achieved, an argument can follow through a critical placing of what has been thus 'read'. This critical placing may take innumerable forms: it might consist of pointing up 'mistakes' or such shortcomings as lack of breadth, lack of vision, lack of vital connections, far-fetched significances; or, conversely, what is opposed might be accepted but placed by showing up its partiality or limitation, so that it might be accommodated as merely a 'special case' within one's own broader approach. The two procedures are merely some of the simplest, most obvious movements and moments in a dialectical confrontation. The dialectical arguments that follow will be much more involved than these and much more difficult to analyse.

The account of argument given so far, which has been partly extrapolated from Wittgenstein's work, is of itself not adequate to account for the arguments against the Logos and the Cogito which we can also extrapolate from his work. For these arguments take a specifically modern form which is quite unlike any mode of argument to be found in classical philosophy, though there are distant premonitions and parallels among the sceptics and their critics. In logical form they are *reductio-ad-absurdum* arguments, but this does not mean that they bear any more than a purely formal analogy to the strict *reductio-ad-absurdum* arguments of logic, mathematics or classical philosophy. For these arguments are not simple demonstrations that something is absurd in the classical sense of being self-contradictory, incoherent, chaotic or irrational; rather they are modes of reduction to Nothing, of dissolution or destruction in a nihilistic sense. There are, nevertheless, intimate connections between the strict *reductio-ad-absurdum* arguments of logic and classical philosophy, those which can be extrapolated from Wittgenstein, and the historical *reductio* of this work itself. Each case involves a process of conceptual destruction, though the magnitude of what is being destroyed increases as the *reductio* is raised each time to a higher power. What we have said about the simpler *reductio* and philosophical argumentation in general might also be applied to the more complex ones, and ultimately to that performed in this work, provided these differences are understood.

But before we can even begin the presentation of Wittgenstein's *reductio*, there remains an awkward problem to be settled: how Wittgenstein could have confronted the Logos or the Cogito given that he had no way of interpretatively 'reading' the Tradition. He could only have been aware of the classical issues in one or another of their modern translations. The Logos he encountered largely through the philosophy behind the development of Formal Logic, such as the so-called 'Platonism' of Frege, Russell, Goedel, or the mathematician Hardy, as well as the Logicism of his own *Tractatus*. The Cogito he encountered as the 'realistic' solipsism of the *Tractatus*, which itself descended from the 'subjective' solipsism of Schopenhauer as well as the Subjectivism of nineteenth-century Psychologism and early Existentialism. As *In the Beginning was the Deed* shows both these philosophical tendencies reflect the overall translation in modern history of the Logos into Techno-logy and the Cogito into Subjectivity. The translation of the Deed into Activism is but implicitly present in the *Tractatus* as the silence of the ethical will, which is outside the world of facts.[55]

Thus, the *Tractatus* is the mediating text for understanding how and in what form Wittgenstein encountered the Logos and the Cogito in his later work. Even in its own right it is a remarkable text in the history of philosophy for in it one finds the prevailing tendencies of modern society and culture, viz. Technology, Subjectivity and Activism, brought theoretically to the point of extreme limit, precisely to that extremity where they begin to reveal their own nihilistic reality as Technocracy, Subjectlessness and Inactivity.[56] Wittgenstein's later philosophical revision was brought on in part by an instinctive realisation of this outcome and a recoil from it; and this led him to an asceticism of language and an emphasis on common life. The revision is not merely a matter of one thinker correcting himself, but it is the very self-critique of modernity in thought form. The *Tractatus* represents modernity taken to its self-cancelling extreme, the point where it beings to reveal its nihilistic counter-face; and the more fully developed Faustian philosophy of the *Investigations* is the retreat from the impasse of this extremity back to the life-giving origins and sources from which, supposedly, thought and language derive.

The roots of the *Tractatus* go back far into the history of philosophy, at least as far back as the new post-Renaissance philosophies of Representation. Representation became the basic issue in philosophy when scientific epistemology became pre-eminently a matter of mathematical representation, starting with Kepler and Galileo. Descartes and Hobbes made of representation the key issue in all method and knowledge, and as Foucault shows, it became the basic principle of all ordering thought during what he calls the classical age of the seventeenth and eighteenth centuries.[57] This is further illuminated by Heidegger's exposition of *re-presentatio* as the metaphysical operation establishing the subject–object opposition.[58] And it is well attested that the issue of mathematical representation was the starting point of Wittgenstein's thinking; he encountered it as a problem in mechanics through his reading of Hertz and in his own engineering work. He solved the problem of representation in the *Tractatus* only when he generalised it as a problem of all logic and language by means of his theory of picturing or mapping — the mathematical connotations are more important than the artistic ones — whereby the whole world is conceived of under the aspect of mechanics.

Thus in the *Tractatus* the classical philosophy of Representation is taken to its utmost extreme. It results in a picture of the world as a totally structured assembly of facts, reflecting an inexorable logic of propositions — 'logic is not a body of doctrine, but a mirror-image of the world' (6.13) — the very ultimate in the *logos* of *techne*. Identical with this world of utmost logical objectivity is one of utmost solipsistic subjectivity — 'I am my world (the microcosm)' (5.63) — the I of the solipsist has become co-extensive with the whole world. And, finally, there is an absolute separation of the world and the acting agent, the creator of society, culture, art and religion — 'the world is independent of my will' (6.373) — in the sense that all higher values merely show themselves through the world but are not in it, so they cannot be pictured in language or spoken about.

In this philosophy Technology, Subjectivity and Activism, taken to their utmost extremes begin to reveal their nihilistic consequences — in this lies the historical importance of a work that does not recognise history. The transformation can be studied in the very philosophical doctrines themselves. Thus, the propositions of logic once considered as deliverances of reason, laws of thought, or as the synthetic *a priori* — are reduced to senseless tautologies: 'tautologies and contradictions lack sense' (4.461); they 'show that they say nothing', and so are nothing. The constructive function of deductive reasoning is denounced as metaphysics, and is replaced by the mechanical operation of substitution whereby proofs are assembled through the derivation of complex tautologous propositions from simpler ones: 'proof in logic is merely a mechanical expedient to facilitate the recognition of tautologies in complicated cases' (6.1262) — shades of present-day computer technocracy.

Subjectivity becomes subjectless as the subject disappears into the 'limit of the world' (5.641), for the truth of the self is that which 'the solipsist *means* . . . only it cannot be said, but makes itself manifest' (5.62). This subjectless, unsayable solipsism means that 'the world is *my* world' (5.62): that 'the subject does not belong to the world: rather, it is a limit of the world' (5.632). So it is that 'solipsism, when its implications are followed out strictly, coincides with pure realism. The self of solipsism shrinks to a point without extension, and there remains the reality co-ordinate with it' (5.64). In an analogous fashion, the activite will become inactive, being quite incapable of altering the facts of the world, for if the will 'does alter the world, it can alter only the limits of the world, not the facts — not what can be expressed by means of language (6.43). Since nothing in the world has any value — 'in it no value exists — and if it did exist, it would have no value' (6.41) — it follows that the active will cannot endow value to anything in the world. It is only capable of changing the value of the world as a whole — a solipsistically limited whole — 'the effect must be that it becomes an altogether different world. It must, so to speak, wax and wane as a whole' (6.43). What is thus altered is only the total perspective on the world, and not anything in the world itself: 'the world of the happy man is a different one from that of the unhappy man' (6.43). This is a philosophical prescription for a quietistic inner-worldly mysticism with some affinities to that of Tolstoy. Thus, in the *Tractatus* a technocratic logic, a subjectless solipsism and an inactive mysticism are fused together to form the limit of the modern world.

But in thus driving the tendencies of modernity to their utmost extreme and arriving at their reversal in thought — at Technocracy, Subjectlessness and Inactivity — the *Tractatus* has despite itself already begun the act of destruction of the thought behind these tendencies. It has in effect already reduced itself to the absurdity of nothingness, and so prepared the ground for the *reductio-ad-absurdum* arguments that can be developed from Wittgenstein's later philosophy against the Logos and the Cogito, initially only in their modern forms as logicism and subjectivity (implicitly, perhaps, also against activism). The 'absurdity' of the *Tractatus* is thus the 'absurdity' of modernity expressed in its utmost consistency, extremity and purity. The *Investigations* both exposes that 'absurdity', and seeks to find ways to overcome it. But the means for doing so had already been prepared in the *Tractatus*, above all, in its foundations: the relationship between language and the world. No more than a shift in perspective and a change in the attitude on that key relationship were required for the move to the later philosophy: for whereas in the *Tractatus* it is language as a homogeneous calculus that mirrors the structure of the world, in the *Investigations* it is the world as structureless that takes on the features of the grammar of heterogeneous language.

This key reversal reveals itself very clearly in the *Tractatus* treatment of subjectivity, for already there the issue is considered as one of language: 'The world is *my* world: this is manifest in the fact that the limits of *language* (of that language which alone I understand) mean the limits of *my* world' (5.62). Thus, the subject is defined in terms of the limits of a language that is private — 'of that language which alone I understand' — so that a private-language is taken as the criterion of a solipsistic subjectivity. The terms of the later private-language argument are already there; all it will later require is their reversal, showing that such a language is impossible, to completely destroy the solipsistic subject, and so introduce a completely new approach to subjectivity.

However, before any such argument could be formulated a completely new notion of 'language' had to be achieved, once more on the basis of a critique of the *Tractatus* approach to language as logic. And it is only in terms of the new concept of language that the *reductio-ad-absurdum* arguments against the Logos and the Cogito can be devised. For what in effect these arguments show is that language is impossible when conceived of on the basis of a Logos or a Cogito, which means that either the Logos and the Cogito are impossible or that language is impossible, but since language is already given, the former must be impossible. This is the nub of the matter.

To begin, then, one needs to specify what language would be like if it were based on a Logos or a Cogito. Seen from the standpoint of a metaphysics of the Logos, words and sentences must reflect or correspond to '*logoi*' if they are to constitute a discourse capable of conveying any truth. Thus truthful speech as a whole mirrors a predetermined pattern prior to itself, a pattern that is a rational norm, one which might be found in universal or merely human reason. According to the metaphysics of the Cogito, words and sentences are only meaningful when they issue from and express 'inner' cogitations: thoughts or ideas that are prior to speech and which speech represents. Put at its simplest, the metaphysic of the Logos makes speech measure up to universal '*logoi*', that of the

Cogito makes it represent 'private' ratiocination. Paraphrasing that in our own terms it amounts to this: on the first conception 'true meaning' lies in some kind of logical universality; on the second, 'true meaning' lies in some kind of subjectivity. In both conceptions meaning lies outside the social practice of language.

Thus, in both metaphysics true or real 'concepts' are outside language. And this raises the critical question: is any such conception of a real 'concept', of a 'meaning' that is apart from language, tenable? Or, can there be a concept of a real 'concept' that is like the Logos or Cogito? The argument that there cannot be such a concept is one designed to show that there can be nothing else apart from language itself, and its purely humble and human surroundings, which determine meaning. If there can be no real 'concept' that is like a Logos or a Cogito, it follows that the metaphysical notion that there is a Logos or a Cogito loses its point, though it is not rendered meaningless.

The form of the argument is basically this: what is initially a metaphysical and ontological thesis is translated into a conceptual one by extracting the bearing it has on language. The conceptual thesis that results is then refuted by showing that it does not accord with our concept of language, and so *a fortiori* the initial ontological thesis is undermined, though in a way that Wittgenstein himself could not properly express. This basic form is common to both the argument against the Logos and the argument against the Cogito, though in their working out these will be very different arguments. We shall also refer to these arguments as the argument against the logos-concept and the argument against the cogito-concept. Thus the term 'logos-concept' is a complex expression referring both to the metaphysical notion that there is a logos, and to the 'translation' of this conception into conceptual terms; namely, that behind the words, thoughts and deeds of language there stand real 'concepts' that are '*logoi*'. Of course, the two senses of the term 'logos-concept' are so bound up with one another that they in effect constitute the one meaning; and this is equally true for the term 'cogito-concept'.

The central and crucial move in both arguments is a peculiar kind of *reductio-ad-absurdum*, largely derived from Wittgenstein, though the reader will not find these moves made in his writings as they are presented here. Wittgenstein was averse to deliberate arguments and preferred to make his case by a cumulative piling up of individual details. He was also averse to an explicit definition of presuppositions and concepts from which an argument could be launched. He was even against the formulation of contentious theses. Our arguments here are indeed contentious, for they derive from a concept of language which not everyone will accept and which certainly goes beyond any common agreement, or understanding, for that matter. These are not common arguments, but highly philosophical ones, for they operate on the level of metaphysics, though they are the opposite of metaphysical.

Before launching into the first argument itself a few words of explanation are called for. Nowhere in Wittgenstein will one find a systematically set out argument against the Logos. The argument here presented has been largely 'assembled' from all kinds of pieces culled from Wittgenstein. Even the word 'logos' itself does not occur in his writings, but something analogous is meant by a number of cognate expressions: for example, at one place he speaks of 'super-concepts', as in the following extract:

> We are under the illusion that what is peculiar, profound, essential, in our investigation, resides in its trying to grasp the incomparable essence of language. That is, the order existing between the concepts of proposition, word, proof, truth, experience, and so on. This order is a *super*-order between — so to speak — *super*-concepts. Whereas, of course, if the words 'language', 'experience', 'world', have a use, it must be as humble a one as that of the words 'table', 'lamp', 'door' (97).

Many of the key opposing moves of Wittgenstein's philosophy are to be found '*in nuce*' in this passage: there is the opposition of 'the incomparable essence of language' to 'words having a use', of the 'super-order between super-concepts' as against the 'humility of words', and the typical Wittgensteinian contrast between what seems peculiar, or profound, and what is down-to-earth. The idea of 'super-concepts' is amplified in the many other references to the 'essential', the 'ideal', the 'sublime', the 'unshakable', all of which are used to characterise what to Wittgenstein is one of the main illusions of philosophy: philosophers searching for a 'hidden essence of language' (92), their 'striving after an ideal' (98), that 'must be found in reality' (101) and that is 'unshakeable', with the result that in this way there is a 'subliming of our whole account of logic' (94), and consequently logic is taken as something sublime that lies at the 'bottom of all the sciences' (89). In a similar way the idea of a 'super-order' — or really a 'ratio' — is raised by Wittgenstein in numerous remarks: '. . . logic represents an order, in fact the a priori order of the world: that is, the order of *possibilities*, which must be common to both world and thought' (97), and again: 'these concepts: proposition, language, thought, world, stand in line one behind the other, each equivalent to each'. The philosophical views referred to here are in the first place those of the *Tractatus*, but it is clear that they also reach deep into the whole philosophical tradition — there are even hints of Plato, Aristotle and Kant — precisely that tradition which we have outlined as the Logos metaphysics.

To find something more approaching an argument against these metaphysical views we must look through the succeeding part of the *Investigations*, that dealing with 'understanding' and 'rule' (from approximately section 139 to section 242). One sees how this part, which deals at such great length with the seemingly trivial topic of how children learn to read and count, relates to the previously highly elevated discussion of philosophy and logic once one grasps that the whole matter of rule-following revolves around the notion of 'being logically determined': 'It was supposed to bring into prominence a difference between being causally determined and being logically determined' (220). However, many of the connecting links must not be looked for in the *Investigations*, but rather in the *Foundations of Mathematics*. They are the well-known topics concerning the 'compulsion' of a rule, the logical 'must', the 'inexorability' of logic, and the 'hardness' of logic, and these in turn link up with the other main matters dealt with there, such as inference, proof and necessity.

In the *Investigations* the whole intricate discussion opens innocuously enough with the question of what it is to understand the word 'cube'. Such an understanding might come to one by way of a mental picture of a cube, but the understanding cannot be that picture itself, for understanding is also a matter of using a word appropriately, and that calls for the 'mastery of a technique' (150). What relation is there then between something that actually occurs to one mentally, such as a mental picture', and the technique for the application of a word? Can this 'picture' logically determine an application: 'is there such a thing as a picture, or something like a picture, that forces a particular application on us?' (140). Wittgenstein considers this issue in connection with a case that makes it clearer and more perspicuous: the expansion of an arithmetic series: 2, 4, 6, etc., where the 'technique' is an ability to go on correctly and where what might spontaneously occur to one mentally is an image of the actual formula for the series in question. The idea that the formula forces a particular application on us can be expressed as follows: 'The way the formula is meant determines which steps are taken' (190). But to say that this 'meaning' determines a use is to suppose that there exists a pre-set correct path which the series has to follow if it is to correspond to this specific meaning of the formula as against another one. And this is as if one had 'the idea that the beginning of a series is a visible section of rails invisibly laid to infinity' (218). This idea derives from a sense that:

> 'All the steps are already taken', means: I no longer have any choice. The rule, once stamped with a particular meaning, traces the lines along which it is to be followed through the whole of space (219).

Wittgenstein retorts by asking in his own voice the pointed question: 'but if something of this sort really were the case how would it help?' This is the vital question, for implicit in it is the germ of the whole argument against the idea of the Logos.

One can see this better if the whole discussion is shifted from the terms of the *Investigations* to those of the *Foundations*: from 'what is it for a child to follow a rule?', to 'what is it for a mathematician to follow a rule?', that is, from following a simple numerical rule to following a chain of deductive inferences in validating a proof. The theme of 'being logically determined' is one that arises at both levels, the simple and sophisticated, as Wittgenstein makes evident by once more opening the discussion in the *Foundations* with the question: 'We use the expression: "The steps are determined by the formula . . ." How is it used?'[59] From that small beginning he gradually gets to all the deeper aspects of the 'inexorability of mathematics', such as 'how does it come about that the proof *compels* me?'[60] The discussion of this issue brings back all the notions already encountered in the earlier discussion of following a rule, and connects them with the issues closer to our main concern; as the following extract shows. It is from a dialogue between Wittgenstein and his interlocutor, one of his philosophical personae, a kind of naive *famulus* like Faust's Wagner:

Wag: But am I not compelled then to go the way I do in a chain of inferences?

Wit: Compelled? After all I can presumably go as I choose!

Wag: But if you want me to remain in accord with the rules you *must* go this way.

Wit: Not at all. I call *this* 'accord'. [Presumably referring to a continuation other than the accepted one]

Wag: Then you have changed the meaning of the word 'accord'.

Wit: No; — who says what 'change' and 'remaining the same' mean here? However many rules you give me — I give a rule which justifies my employment of your rules.

(Aside) We might also say: when we *follow* the laws of inference (inference rules) the following always involves interpretation too.

Wag: But you surely can't suddenly make a different application of the law now!

Wit: If my reply is 'Oh yes of course, *that* is how I was applying it', or: 'Oh! *That's* how I ought to have applied it!' then I am playing your game. But if I simply reply 'Different? — But this surely *isn't* different' — what will you do? That is: somebody may reply like a rational person and yet not be playing our game.

Wag: Then according to you everybody could continue the series as he likes; and so infer *any*how!

Wit: In that case we shan't call it 'continuing the series' and also presumably not 'inference'. And thinking and inferring (like counting) is of course bounded for us, not by an arbitrary definition, but by natural limits corresponding to the body of what can be called the role of thinking and inferring in our life.

For we are at one over this, that the laws of inference do not compel him to say or write such and such like rails compelling a locomotive . . .

Nevertheless the laws of inference can be said to compel us; in the same sense, that is to say, as other laws in human society . . .

If you draw different conclusions you do indeed get into conflict, e.g. with society, and also with other practical consequences.[61]

Wittgenstein's closing reference to the laws of society brings us to a higher sphere than that of logico–mathematical reasoning, and it is at this level that the argument against the Logos takes place. This is the cultural *niveau* of civilisation, of the historical development of concepts and techniques: the formation of the unified bodies of logic, mathematics, and science, and all the variety of classical cultural values. The same question arises on this level too: 'Is there something like a Logos or "ratio" that forces a particular kind of development on the history of our concepts?' The argument that there is no such thing follows the very same steps here as previously.

To be exact, the argument does not attempt to prove directly that there is no such thing, but rather that even 'if something of this sort really were the case, how would it help?'. For even if there were a predetermined path along which a concept had to go, if there were an 'ideally' rational way of unfolding a concept, it would still inevitably be the case that human beings would have to carry through this development. They would still have to choose this way rather than any other equally open to them. For it is men who would have to decide that one path is more rational than another, and they would have to have their own humble, human reasons for making that decision, and going in one direction rather than another.

But, of course, the lesson of the history of ideas and the sociology of science is that there is no such ideal rational path of development governing all human scientific enterprises and their concepts. The sciences could have developed differently within Western culture; and they in fact did so in other cultures — in China, for example; the same point holds good even for mathematical and logical techniques. And just as its past was not determined, so the future course of science is in no way logically pre-ordained: there is no universal Logos guiding it to its destination. Wittgenstein was much influenced in this respect by the cultural relativism of Spengler who went so far as to maintain that each civilisation has a mathematics and logic peculiar to itself. Whether such an extreme relativism is in excess of Wittgenstein's own implicit position is difficult to ascertain since he did not explicitly elaborate an historical approach to rationality. Some of his followers, such as Winch, have since put forward the view that each primitive tribe has its own language-game with a unique and peculiar standard of rationality — a relativism that is even in excess of Spengler's. (We will examine the debate surrounding this issue in Appendix 1.) This view is certainly not entailed by Wittgenstein's argument against the Logos. This requires only that there is no one necessary and universal rational course of procedure that must be followed by all rational individuals and societies in their historical development.

What would it be for men to choose to follow a conceptual path in accord with the metaphysical Logos? Even if there were such a path, following it would be as problematic as the very idea of the Logos itself. For what would they do other than we do at present, or have done in the past when we try to make our concepts as sound as possible for the human purposes for which they are intended? What would characterise a mode of human life capable of being guided by such transcendent norms? For us the existence of such a path is without significance, for no ideal conceptual path can compel us to follow it, anymore than telling a child the formula of a rule can compel it to follow it. For just as no 'flash of understanding', or anything else that might occur to one can contain its own application, so, too, no illumination by a metaphysical entity — no Platonic Form 'seen with the eye of the soul', no universal grasped by reason, no rationally agreed on convention, no law of reason or of nature — can exercise a 'logical compulsion' on anyone to whom such a thing might occur. No such thing can have the influence on human language that it is metaphysically supposed to have. Regardless of whether there are or were such things, language would still have to move in its humble, human way. But if such a thing can be of no human consequence then once again 'if something of this sort really were the case, how would it help?'. And, if it could in no way help, then what is the point of invoking it?

Here we have come to the very core of the argument. It is basically a sceptical *reductio-ad-absurdum* argument. This is the first time it has been used, though there are anticipations of it during periods of scepticism throughout the history of philosophy. I will give but two such instances, one very early, the other very late. The sophist Gorgias put it as follows:

If there is being, it is inaccessible and unknowable; if it is knowable it is inexpressible and incommunicable. Just as by their nature the senses of sight and hearing are restricted to their specific sphere of qualities; just as the one can perceive only brightness and colours, and the other can perceive only tones — similarly, speech can never transcend itself to apprehend something 'other', standing over against it, that is to apprehend 'being' and truth.[62]

Dilthey says something similar, but in a quite different way:

> If, behind the life which flows from the past through the present
> to the future, there were a timeless reality, then this would be an
> antecedent of life; for it would be, on this showing, something by
> which the whole ordered process of life was preconditioned; and
> then this antecedent would be precisely that which we did not
> directly experience [*was wir nicht erlebten*], and, therefore, only a
> realm of shadows.[63]

In Wittgenstein one finds echoes of both these ways of putting the
matter; for him, too, there is no getting above, beyond or beneath
language: 'your questions refer to words; so I have to talk about
words' (120), and the flow of life is also basic: 'What has to be
accepted, the given is — so one could say — forms of life' (226).

The fundamental steps of the *reductio-ad-absurdum* can now be
briefly summarised as follows. Postulate that there is such a thing as
a Logos in the way that metaphysicians require. If there is such a
thing then it ought to be possible for human beings to grasp it and be
guided by it. But what might that be? Wittgenstein does not deny
that one can grasp the meaning of something in a flash, but, he asks,
can anything that is grasped by someone ever exercise the kind of
logical compulsion that conforming to a rational order is supposed to
exercise? The answer is clearly, no! For no matter what might come
to one it would still need to be understood. Thus, one would need to
'read' it so as to know how it was to be followed, which steps or word
uses were in accordance with it and which went against it. Nothing
can have its own interpretation built into it, since everything can be
taken in different ways. An inherent possibility of ambiguity or
equivocation is the essential feature of everything that carries
meaning, of all signs, indicators and ultimately all languages. There
is no way of obviating this possibility in principle, for instructions
that spell out how something is to be understood can themselves be
taken variously. Of course, this does not mean that there is no way in
practice of eliminating ambiguities, nor that there is no obvious or
natural meaning of something; there are indeed ways of ensuring
that something is understood in the way we want it to be, but these,
though practically efficacious, can never be logically fool-proof.

To understand something in the way it ought to be understood is
to get it right. But what is right or wrong is determined within the
institution of language, or outside it by something such as a pre-

established norm. Language, as it is created and used by people, is the only guarantor of its own correctness. Whether something is right or wrong and how it ought to be understood is judged within human practices. And such practices are themselves assessed in relation to human requirements, which are in turn referred to the course of history in the nature of life. The fact that human beings can in general 'agree' in some of their practices and requirements is what ensures the universality of what they consider right, rational and true. Agreement here does not mean conforming to a contract or convention; it is the deeper accord of human life: 'not agreement in opinions but in forms of life' (241).

And so, the argument concludes: even if there were a Logos it could have no influence on human affairs; it transcends language and therefore cannot come to grips with it, so language must still pursue its own course. But anything that is thus without possible consequence is itself inconsequential. Hence, the initial postulate that there is a Logos has shown itself to be empty, a move explaining nothing. Thus the *reductio* is complete.

Once past this point in the argument Wittgenstein tends to 'dissolve' what he has shown to have no practical use, for to him that which does not do useful work in language remains merely as a functionless ornament, at best to be retained only as a decorative 'picture'. As we shall eventually see, this tendency is not to be unhesitatingly followed, for it encourages an inclination to overlook the historical role, and, hence, the efficacy of that which from a strictly practical point of view seems to be merely idling, and leads to forgetfulness of the historical impact on language of those metaphysical doctrines which are now found to be impractical. It is his somewhat narrow conception of practicality that needs to be called in question. This points also to a certain narrowness in his concept of language, which makes it difficult for him to acknowledge the role of metaphysical doctrines in the historical development of language.

Nevertheless this argument accomplishes much towards a definition of the concept of 'language' in that it links that concept to the concept of 'rule'; and, in turn, it links 'rule' to the concepts 'same' and 'agreement'. It is this conceptual network that the argument basically creates. It establishes essential connections (internal relations) between all of these concepts. Wittgenstein points up these interconnections in a number of remarks:

The word 'agreement' and the word 'rule' are *related* to one another, they are cousins. If I teach anyone the use of the one word he learns the use of the other with it. The use of the word 'rule' and the use of the word 'same' are interwoven. (As are the use of 'proposition' and the use of 'true'.) (224–5).

If language is to be a means of communication there must be agreement not only in definitions but also (queer as this may sound) in judgements (242).

As we shall soon see, the next argument against the 'Cogito' turns on this same conceptual network of 'language', 'rule', 'same' and 'agreement'.

The argument against the Cogito is to be found explicitly set out in Wittgenstein: it is, of course, the famous private-language argument. Once again, this argument, too, has been anticipated in the course of philosophical history. Perhaps the most remarkable anticipation is to be found in Humboldt, whom we have already mentioned as initiating the new Faustian conception of language:

We must free ourselves completely from the idea that it (language) can be separated from what it designates, as for example, the name of a man from his person, and that like a conventional cipher it is a product of reflection and agreement or in any sense the work of man (as we tend to think of concepts in common experience), *not to say the work of the individual.* Like a true, inexplicable wonder, it bursts forth from the mouth of a nation, and no less amazingly — though this is repeated every day and indifferently overlooked, it springs from the babble of every child; *it is the most radiant sign and certain proof that man does not possess an intrinsically separate individuality,* that I and Thou are not merely complementary concepts, but that if we could go back to the point of separation — they would prove to be truly identical, that in this sense there are spheres of individuality, from the weak, helpless, perishable individual down to the primeval clan of mankind, *because otherwise all understanding would be eternally impossible.*[64]

'Because otherwise all understanding would be eternally impossible' — this is also the operative phrase of the private-language argument. One can dimly see in the Humboldt extract that this is an argument against a Cartesian view of the privacy of language, and that it is also simultaneously an attack against a Cartesian conception of individual existence as 'intrinsically separate'. What it proclaims instead is the romantic idea of language as expression, bursting forth from the various 'spheres of individuality', from the single individual, to the nation and the 'clan of mankind'. The private-language argument, too, is based on the idea of language as expression, just as the previous 'Logos' argument was based on language as rational discourse. What it calls into question is the expression of thought — above all, the expression of that principal thought: the 'Cogito'.

Wittgenstein, however, first introduces the private-language argument in relation not to the expression of thought but to the expression of sensation. Unfortunately, this has made it more difficult than need be to see what is at stake, and has been the occasion of much misunderstanding. Wittgenstein himself makes considerable effort to avoid confusion by explicitly ruling out what he does not mean by the term 'private-language'. He does not mean a language of privacy, as, for example, one in which people 'spoke only in monologue' (243) to themselves, or even where an individual raised in isolation made up a language for his own private use; for in both these imaginary cases it is conceivable that the language should come to be shared, that others, too, could understand it, whereas the defining feature of the private-language is that no other person can in principle understand it. A private-language cannot be generally understood for it is conceived of as a language that lacks outward expression, making it comprehensible only to each private self. One can try to conceive of such a private-language by attempting to imagine a situation in which experiences have no outward indications, and hence can only be 'inwardly' named, each self naming its own experiences to itself and for itself alone, and thus forming its own private-language.

Wittgenstein introduces the argument by attempting to imagine such a case, which he first presents, and then follows with a dramatic disputation demonstrating its impossibility. Once more we shall set it out as a dramatic dialogue between Wittgenstein, or a person standing in for him, and his philosophical tempter, a kind of mephistophelian adversary. So, following the debate with Wagner we now have one with Mephistopheles.

Let us imagine the following case. I want to keep a diary about the recurrence of a certain sensation. To his end I associate it with the sign 'E' and write this sign in a calendar for every day on which I have the sensation.

Wit: I will remark first of all that a definition of the sign cannot be formulated.

Mephisto: But still I can give myself a kind of ostensive definition.

Wit: How? Can I point to the sensation?

Mephisto: Not in the ordinary sense. But I speak, or write the sign down, and at the same time I concentrate my attention on the sensation — and so, as it were, point to it inwardly.

Wit: But what is this ceremony for? For that is all it seems to be! A definition surely serves to establish the meaning of a sign.

Mephisto: Well, that is done precisely by the concentrating of my attention; for in this way I impress on myself the connection between the sign and the sensation.

Wit: But 'I impress it on myself' can only mean: this process brings it about that I remember the connection *right* in the future. But in the present case I have no criterion of correctness. One would like to say: whatever is going to seem right to me is right. And that only means that here we can't talk about right (258).

It is difficult to find our bearing in the argument that we have just heard. It seems extremely clear, and yet there is something obscure and odd about it. We are first asked to imagine a case which is described in concrete detail, and yet by the end of the description it seems that this case is conceptually impossible and inconceivable, so we have been put in the paradoxical situation of imagining a case that cannot be imagined. Little wonder, then, that the private-language argument has been subject to so many differing interpretations; and there is still no agreement even as to what it is about — not to speak of agreement as to its validity as argument.

The conclusion of the argument is also a little odd: it implies that 'E' stands for nothing at all, yet we began with the supposition that it stands for a 'certain sensation'. This implicit conclusion is made explicit by Wittgenstein later. He argues that if all that can be said about a sign 'E' is that it stands for a 'this' that I have now, and if all that is given to explain its meaning is a 'private' ostensive definition — an 'inner' pointing for oneself alone — then nothing has been said to give meaning to 'E', for such a 'private' definition is no definition. So 'E' stands for nothing since no meaning has as yet been assigned to it. And to the question: 'Then did the man who made the entry in the calendar make a note of nothing whatever?' he replies: 'Don't consider it a matter of course that a person is making a note of something when he makes a mark — say in a calendar. For a note has a function, and this "E" so far has none' (260). Hence, if the sign 'E' has no function in the language, then the purported sensation 'E' that the man is supposed to experience 'privately' is really, according to Wittgenstein, nothing but 'a beetle in a box' into which nobody else can look:

> The thing in the box has no place in the language-game at all; not even as a *something*: for the box might even be empty. — No, one can 'divide through' by the thing in the box; it cancels out, whatever it is (293).

But what could give the sign 'E' a place in our language? Wittgenstein has a clear answer to this:

> Let us now imagine a use for the entry of the sign 'E' in my diary. I discover that whenever I have a particular sensation a manometer shews that my blood-pressure rises. So I shall be able to say that my blood-pressure is rising without using any apparatus. This is quite a useful result. And now it seems quite indifferent whether I have recognized the sensation *right* or not. Let us suppose that I regularly identify it wrong, it does not matter in the least (270).

It would seem from this that sensation 'E' can, as it were, be made to come into existence as soon as it can be given physiological correlates, for example, rising blood pressure. But how peculiar this is that a sensation can be made philosophically respectable merely through the assignment of physiological correlates. After all, Wittgenstein has himself argued elsewhere that physiological correlates are not an essential part of mental experience: 'It is thus perfectly possible that certain psychological phenomena *cannot* b investigated physiologically, because physiologically nothing corresponds to them.'[65] So why should they make such an essential difference here?

However, there may be another way of taking this imaginary introduction of physiology: it may be argued that what matters is not that these are physiological correlates, but that they are an 'outward' expression of the 'inner' experience, no matter how indirect this expression may be. But if that is the argument, why does Wittgenstein speak of discovering this expressive mode by the use of an instrument, a manometer; how can the expressions of one's own 'inner' states be discovered? Certainly, 'an inner process stands in need of outward criteria' (580), but such criteria cannot simply be later-discovered physiological correlates. In any case, if the conclusion is simply this need for outward criteria, it makes a mockery of the whole argument designed to substantiate it. For why should rising blood pressure be more acceptable as outward criteria than the equally outward act of writing a sign 'E' in a diary? Why should not the very act of writing 'E' be itself the outward criterion?

On closer examination there does seem something wrong with the imaginary case by which 'E' is first brought to our attention. The conclusion is that such a case is really impossible, and yet we can imagine it only too well. A presumably normal man, one who is literate to boot, for he knows how to use a diary, makes a sign 'E', and explains that it stands for a sensation he has just had. Are we to tell him, as the argument requires, that he really had nothing at all, that his 'E' stands for nothing? Even supposing that this is a most unusual man, one who has never experienced bodily sensations before and never been taught sensation words in childhood, we can still imagine that one fine day he begins making the entry 'E' in his calendar, and explains that this stands for a sensation. Here it would be plausible to ask him what makes him say that it is a sensation. It might be possible to argue against his claim that it was a sensation by pointing out that sensation concepts require a certain type of behavioural expression as criterion, and that it was not enough to go by a mere written sign or verbal declaration. But it would not be possible to countermand his claim that 'E' stands for something that he experiences, if he claims and insists that it does. In any case what one would or would not say to such a peculiar man in such peculiar circumstances hardly carries any overwhelming philosophical consequence. This is surely not what Wittgenstein's argument is about; if it were it would be a mere oddity.

What we need to know at this point is: who is the man whom we are asked to imagine making an entry in his diary? And this is a way of asking against whom this argument is directed. If we can discover that, then we shall be closer to knowing what the argument is really about.

The *Investigations* opens with a long quotation from the *Confessions*, an extract in which Augustine pictures the soul of the human child as trapped in the internal solitude of its own absolutely private being. Through the senses of its body this '*anima*' looks out on the world as from windows in a prison. It sees its elders pointing at things and hears them uttering words, and it soon comes to know which words go with which things. And so it learns language. It learns the accepted words for its own 'inner' experiences in a similar way, by noting the words its elders apply to the 'outer' indications of these experiences. But no matter how much the soul learns to communicate with other souls it is ultimately always alone, and what it knows in the privacy of its own solitude it really cannot communicate, for all communication is nothing but an exchange of external signals whose real meaning cannot be shared. It is to this view of the human condition that T. S. Eliot, following Augustine, refers when he writes:

> I have heard the key
> Turn in the door once and turn once only
> We think of the key, each in his prison
> Thinking of the key, each confirms a prison.

In a note to this passage in 'The Wasteland' Eliot quotes from F. H. Bradley whose philosophy he had studied.

> My external sensations are no less private to myself than are my thoughts or my feelings. In either case my experience falls within my own circle, a circle closed on the outside; and, with all its elements alike, every sphere opaque to the others which surround it. In brief, regarded as an existence which appears in a soul, the whole world for each is peculiar and private to that soul.[66]

Thus, if one refers the private-language argument back to the opening passage from Augustine to which so much in the *Investiga-*

tions relates, it becomes apparent that this is not an argument about 'pain' or 'sensation' concepts, or even about mental concepts as such; rather, it concerns language as a whole. And thereby it is also an argument about the world as a whole, not merely about the 'inner' world. It asks: is all language necessarily private-language? And this is the same question as whether the world is for each of us necessarily a private world. But if this is what the argument is about, what does it have to do with a man making entries in his diary? And who, once again, can this man be?

It would be obvious who the imaginary man was, and why he was making entries in his diary, if instead of writing 'E', he wrote '*Cogito, sum*'. In other words, this is not an ordinary man we are asked to imagine, one who happens to make an entry in his diary — as it were, without ulterior philosophic motives. Rather, it is a Cartesian philosopher who does it in order to argue a philosophical case. The case that this philosopher wishes to argue by this means is Descartes' case. Descartes recounts how once in the depth of winter shut up by himself in a heated room he proceeded to meditate philosophically. First he resolved to 'pretend that nothing which had ever entered my mind was any more true than the illusions of my dreams'.[67] He pretends, that is, that he is an Augustinian soul. Modelling himself on Augustine, who had argued '*si fallor, sum*', Descartes continues as follows:

> Then, examining attentively what I was, and seeing that I could pretend that I had no body and that there was no world or place that I was in, but that I could not for all that, pretend that I did not exist, and that, on the contrary, from the very fact that I thought of doubting the truth of other things, it followed very evidently and very certainly that I existed; while on the other hand, if I had only ceased to think, although all the rest of what I had ever imagined had been true, I would have had no reason to believe that I existed; I thereby concluded . . .[68]

Now, the philosopher who writes 'E' in his diary is carrying out this kind of Cartesian pretence. He is pretending that he can imagine a word 'E' whose meaning is in principle only understandable by him. In order to do this he first has to pretend that he has experiences which he alone can know and name to himself. And this is tantamount to conceiving of himself in relation to the world in the Cartesian manner: he is an Ego in solitude, isolated from others and from a common world. Thus ultimately to pretend that one has a private-language is also to pretend that one has a private-world.

If this is what is at issue, then it is vital to distinguish and separate two quite different imaginary cases: that of the peculiar eventuality of a man who might, in all naivety, happen to write 'E' in his diary in the way described, and the quite common occurrence of a philosopher who does something like this self-consciously in order to demonstrate his philosophy. The first case is certainly an imaginary and quite unnatural situation, but one that is not simply a pretence; many things might be said about it, if it were to occur, none of them of any deep philosophical importance. The second case is by contrast an extremely interesting philosophical pretence, which presupposes adopting the Cartesian conception of individual existence. Wittgenstein to a certain extent confuses the issue by not distinguishing clearly between these two different cases, and by not making it obvious that in asking us to imagine the man who writes 'E' he is only thinking of this second kind of philosophical pretence. He has not distinguished sharply enough the metaphysical case of the Cartesian private-language from many other cases of languages of privacy. Such other languages of privacy might be real or imaginary, possible or impossible, but always for reasons that have nothing to do with the argument against the private-language. However, to say that Wittgenstein has not clearly and decisively distinguished the private-language from languages of privacy, is not to say that he has not distinguished them at all; on the contrary, he makes considerable effort to formulate such a distinction by imagining a people who spoke only in monologue, or individuals who invented their own languages. The private-language argument is, thus, an argument directed against a philosopher conceiving of himself as a Cartesian ego, and pretending to develop a language in the solitude of his own privacy.

It is a *reductio-ad-absurdum* that moves as follows.[69] Let us, for the sake of argument, assume ourselves to be Cartesian egos inhabiting our own private worlds. Can we in these Cartesian circumstances develop a private language? If it can be shown that even a single word is possible, then the case for such a language has been made. And the minimum that is required for there to be a single word is that something should be correctly named, that a word should be applied correctly on at least two separate occasions. Is this possible in the circumstances? If it is possible then a private language is possible. And if that were possible then there would be no

obstacles to such a Cartesian soul thinking to itself '*Cogito, sum*' —
and thereby the whole Cartesian philosophy could be launched.

It is in support of this contention that the Cartesian philosopher
introduces 'E', arguing as follows: 'I, as a Cartesian ego, experience
a sensation now and call it "E", later I have the same sensation again
and call it "E" again, I also write the sign "E" both times in my diary.'
It is at this point that the argument against the private-language
begins. Once more the whole argument turns on the conceptual
interrelation between 'language' and 'rule', 'agreement' and 'same'.
The argument amounts to a demonstration that any attempt to
deprive language of its connections with 'rule', 'agreement' and
'same' leads to its collapse. So that Descartes in 'destroying his
former opinions' through his critique of doubt, is, in effect,
destroying the basis for his own meditations. He is removing the
ground from the very archimedean point on which he hopes to rest in
order to move the world.

Wittgenstein's first line of attack is to show that 'sameness' makes
no sense if deprived of its tie to 'agreement'. What justification can
the man in the Cartesian predicament have for saying that he has the
same sensation again? If he says: 'Well, I believe that this is the
sensation "E" again', then the retort follows swiftly: 'Perhaps you
believe that you believe it' (260). If he says that he remembers it to
be the same, then he can similarly be asked what reason he has for
believing this memory to be correct, and the argument merely shifts
to questioning the standing of this 'private' memory. If he appeals to
a 'table (something like a dictionary that exists only in our imagination)' (265), which shows how 'E' is to be applied, then once again he
can be challenged as to what constitutes a correct use of this table.
Any such purely 'private' rule or test that he cares to bring up suffers
from the very same shortcomings; there can be no way of telling that
the rule or test is being correctly applied, hence there is no reason for
calling it a rule or test. In the absence of any kind of agreement with
other language users there can neither be any rule, nor any way of
ascribing 'sameness'.

But if a person cannot name the same thing twice, neither can he
name it even once. His naming procedure is 'mere ceremony', for 'a
definition serves to establish the meaning of a sign' (258), whereas
this attempt at a private ostensive definition does not establish the
meaning of anything. Thus, it would not even be possible to say that
'E' is a word for some sensation or other, not necessarily the same
one each time, for:

For 'sensation' is a word of our common language, not of one intelligible to me alone. So the use of this word stands in need of a justification which everybody understands. — And it would not help either to say that it need not be a *sensation*; that when he writes 'E' he has *something* — and that is all that can be said. 'Has' and 'something' also belong to our common language. — So in the end when one is doing philosophy one gets to the point where one would just like to emit an inarticulate sound. — But such a sound is an expression only as it occurs in a particular language-game, which should now be described (261).

This 'inarticulate sound' is like the silent pointing gesture that Antisthenes was finally left with in the face of the Heraclitean flux; it, too, is like a despairing gesture in an analogous Cartesian flux of private experience. For if it is not possible to name anything, then nothing can be identified, and nothing has being. Even the Ego loses its identity, as there is no way of establishing that it remains the same for any two moments running. Descartes' assurance that the deceiving demon can never 'cause me to be nothing, so long as I think I am something . . .'[70] is thus denied him. In fact, any kind of certainty is denied him. Certainty — the one thing for which Descartes strove — becomes impossible under the very conditions Descartes set up to attain it. The more Descartes removes himself from the real, everyday world, the more he retires into himself, the less he can achieve any kind of assurance. The whole Cartesian trial of passing through utter doubt to supreme certainty is self-defeating, for to doubt away the ordinary world is to doubt away the basis of any certainty.

The world of the Cartesian ego is thus *ex-hypothesi* a 'private' world in which both certainty and language are ruled out, for they become detached from this world of common humanity in which they have their life. Place a sign 'E' in the Cartesian world and it ceases to be a word. However, no such difficulties can arise in our world: a man using a sensation word like 'pain' does not face any of the arguments brought against the Cartesian philosopher using 'E'. There is no question of whether he has correctly identified to himself a 'private-item' given to him in his privacy. The whole issue of correctness resolves itself into one of agreement: whether he uses the word 'pain' in the way that is appropriate in the language. The word acts as a verbal expression of pain, which is usually not questioned provided we know that the man has learned to use the word properly. If it is doubted, then it is only questioned on non-philosophic grounds, such as: that he is absent-mindedly using the wrong word, or is malingering, or even that he has deceived himself that he is in pain, or in many other such conceivable ways. It is only the philosopher pretending to be a Cartesian Ego who can be asked sophisticated questions such as: how do you know you are using the sign 'E' twice in the same way?

Used by someone in the course of real life even the sign 'E' in the circumstances described would present no philosophical difficulties. If a man were spontaneously to tell us that he is experiencing a hitherto unknown sensation, which he has decided to call 'E', then even though one might question him closely to decide whether it was in fact an unknown sensation, in the end, if he insisted, we would have to grant him his right to make this claim. For it is certainly possible to conceive of experiences utterly different from the ones we now have. It is even possible to imagine a man, growing up in isolation, who has different experiences from us and develops his own language for them — in that sense a language that happens to be private to himself. This latter case might well be anthropologically impossible, and only conceived of as a 'miracle', yet no such arguments against it would have anything to do with the private-language argument. That argument is not directed at real people in this world, no matter how peculiar their circumstances; or, better put, it is directed at real people, but ones who pretend that they are unreal, as philosophers are prone to do.

With the collapse of the private language, the 'private' world that is co-extensive with it falls as well. For, if a private-item in a 'private' world is in principle unidentifiable and inexpressible then it can play no part in our language, and so, Wittgenstein concludes, it is no more than a useless philosophical 'picture' deriving from a 'grammatical fiction' (307): 'if we construe the grammar of the expression of sensation on the model of "object and name" the object drops out of consideration as irrelevant' (293). Thus, in this manner the whole 'private' world of the Cartesian ego drops out of consideration, too, as irrelevant. With that the *reductio-ad-absurdum* is complete.

If this argument is accepted, what follows from it is that the Cogito cannot be an absolute starting point from which to reconstitute everything. The Cogito as a thought cannot even be thought in complete 'privacy', for no thought can be divorced from a potential expression in language. All thinking presupposes language, even that which happens not to be expressed in words. Expression is what mediates between thought and actualised existence. It is through a mastery of the expressive means of language that a human being comes to think and develop his 'inner' soul and thereby transforms himself into a unique, individual existent. Thus, '*Cogito, sum*' can be translated to mean that through thought one develops one's individuality. And, in fact, the propensity to introspective thought, that Descartes justified philosophically and furthered historically, is closely related to the rise of later Subjectivity. The Cogito, in the setting of the Cartesian philosophy, is itself a new philosophical mode of self-expression, one that very quickly made its influence felt in areas of expression outside philosophy. Historically, therefore, the Cogito is a thought of great expressive power, establishing a new basis for individual existence. It was only with the rise of Faustian philosophy that it lost its intellectual hold, and we can no longer take it with full philosophical seriousness. It has already been historically discredited, so the argument against it presented here only completes an historical *fait accompli*. The effect of this on our sense of ourselves as individuals is part of the historical problem we are confronting now. How are we to repair the damage that the loss of Descartes' 'Ego' has done to ours?

On that thought we can now turn to a final reflection on both the arguments through which we have just passed. Where have they led us? Where are we now? An argument in philosophy, we said before, opens up a new conceptual path. Yet these arguments do not seem to have done that. On the contrary, it seems more as if they have blocked off old and well-worn roads by erecting barriers across them. Traditional philosophical approaches have gone the way of the Logos and the way of the Cogito, and have sought to go further in those directions. That is what we mean by calling them traditional. A tradition is formed through the continuous pursuit of an inherited direction; the great metaphysical tradition was formed in that way. But now we can no longer take that route. This tradition is no longer open to us, and it is our own arguments that have finally closed it off.

Thus, metaphysics is finished not because it has been completed, but because it has been finished off: it has been deprived of a living meaning, and that, for a cultural form, means that it has been destroyed. 'Because the destruction of the foundations necessarily brings down with it the rest of the edifice',[71] arguing away the Logos and Cogito brings down metaphysics. An abyss has now opened up, and everything rests on nothing. Wittgenstein would have been unconcerned by this, for he held that neither the world nor our thinking require foundations. His whole philosophy is explicitly anti-foundational. He showed that the old supports are now functionless, that their pillars and columns carry no weight, being merely decorative, ornamental trappings, left over from the old style. The abyss did not open up for him as it did for Nietzsche.

3. In the Aftermath of the Destruction

In these more speculative reflections on the *reductio-ad-absurdum* derived from Wittgenstein we spoke of carrying through a reduction of the foundations of metaphysics. But strictly speaking that is not correct. For as we originally said, the arguments do not apply directly to the metaphysical Logos and Cogito, but only to their translations into Language, to the Logos-concept and the Cogito-concept. These translations are renderings of the metaphysical doctrines into hypothetical theses about language, presupposing what language would have to be like if there were a linguistic equivalent of a Logos or a Cogito. And, of course, the argument is a way of demonstrating that these hypotheses are impossibilities. To remind ourselves once again, the first of Wittgenstein's arguments is directed initially against the inexorable 'iron-rails' of logical compulsion and against what he calls 'super-concepts'; and the second against the possibility of a private-language. There is nothing in any of this, as yet, about the Logos or Cogito of metaphysics. It is only when we fill in the silent or absent philosophical context that the connections begin to be made. Thus, the issue of 'super-concepts' relates to debates in modern logic concerning 'Platonism' or 'Logicism', and these we know on historical grounds to be derivations from the Platonic tradition and that of the Logos of metaphysics. Similarly, the private-language argument relates to debates on modern Subjectivity, on consciousness in psychology and absolute privacy, and these in turn refer back to the whole issue as this was initiated through Descartes' Cogito.

It is, therefore, only very indirectly that the demonstration of the impossibility of a Logos-concept or Cogito-concept as a thesis about language pertains to the destruction of the metaphysical Logos or Cogito. What it does is to show that these concepts have no relevance to language, and hence no role or utility in the whole framework of modern thought. And this serves to sever the metaphysical concepts from any conceptual connection to on-going thought in philosophy or science or the humanities, and to relegate them to a kind of invisible museum of dead ideas; in Wittgenstein's imagery, it is to treat them as ornaments, pictures without a use, knobs unconnected to the engine of Praxis. And this is in many respects a necessary move, for it prevents the ongoing development of sciences from being clogged up by the detritus of the past. But this purifying move also sterilises progress, and directs it into ever narrower intellectual channels, for it inhibits the development of any radically new forms of thought or of knowledge. Saying this should not, however, lead to the conservative conclusion that an attempt should be made to enrich the sciences with metaphysics, or that the Logos and the Cogito should be resurrected in modern meanings. Their destruction is final and irrevocable.

But it is a destruction which leaves their historical meaning untouched, and indeed preserves it as such. For the destruction — unlike an annihilation — does not show this historic meaning to have been an error, or prejudice, or myth, or mere confusion, or nonsense. Hence, the destruction, once accomplished, prompts an inverse move for the recovery of this meaning as, precisely, historical meaning. Nietzsche was one of the first to insist that the destructive course once complete must lead to a doubling-back — 'as in the hippodrome'[72] — over the same ground, so as to understand and recover what it is that has been destroyed. Heidegger has also complemented and completed his ontological destruction with a hermeneutic recollection; and Ricoeur has followed him in this. Both of them evince the hermeneutic hope that recalling the tradition, and especially its lost origins, will enable a new start to be made in thought. That, for instance, listening to the original voice of the Logos will permit a new 'gathering of language' and 'disclosure of truth'. We can have no such hopes if we appreciate fully the meaning of the meaninglessness of Nihilism. Nevertheless, an attempt at recovery of the past must be made, if for no other reason than to locate ourselves in terms of it and so to understand ourselves. Such recollection of the past will help us to recollect ourselves in the present, and thus to project ourselves better into the future.

Instead of hermeneutically evoking the lost Voice, we shall, more modestly, attempt to comprehend these concepts historically. Such comprehension involves special methods. To understand a given past concept that is as yet not understood, we must construct a mediating conception that can relate the past concept to an analogous concept of the present, thus comprehending both. The theory of how such mediating concepts are constructed and how they affect an understanding of the past, and show its present relevance, will be elaborated in Chapter 5. Here we can merely illustrate its procedures by sketching out an interpretation of the meaning of the Cogito.

What did Descartes achieve for thought when he propounded his Cogito, and how can it serve us today to try and recall this? The obvious answer is as simple as it is startling to us now: in establishing a new 'rational' epistemology based on the Cogito, Descartes was for the first time formulating a concept of Mind in the modern sense. In recalling that original concept we are reminding ourselves of the danger in which we place ourselves by dispensing altogether with the concept of mind — a danger incurred at first rather innocuously in Behaviourist psychology (including such philosophical-linguistic versions as Ryle's book entitled, with unconscious irony, *The Concept of Mind*), but much more threateningly in the current computer technology with its associated 'mindless' jargon. Descartes had the first intimations and made the first proper response to this danger.

In devising the Cogito Descartes was only marginally concerned with the threats of a then rudimentary technology; he was more intent on countering the dangers to thought and faith of pre-modern nihilism: the corrosive scepticism of the late Renaissance as this was exemplified in the greatest French writer of the time, Montaigne. In an even more potent form it is the nihilism manifesting itself in Macbeth's 'signifying nothing'. Descartes could only conceive of this nihilistic temptation, in keeping with his Jesuit training and religious orthodoxy, as emanating from a deceiving Demon, the Mephistopheles to his Faust, as it were. It is this Demon that Descartes had to fight off with the power of thought: '. . . let him deceive me as much as he likes, he can never cause me to be nothing, so long as I think I am something'.[73] The dread of Nothing takes for Descartes a pre-modern cast as fear of loss of self in deception, error, illusion and dream. The Cogito is the thought that saves him by enabling him to hold on to his Ego in a way that is irrefutable and unshakeable. Psychologically we might diagnose his invention of the Cogito as satisfying a need to seek safety and security in self-absorbed privacy and as a retreat from the dangers of the world and of human mutuality. Such an attempted escape into privacy from the uncertainties of the world bears in itself the seeds of even worse dangers to self and individuality, as the existentialist philosophers have since discovered.

As these philosophers have shown, Descartes confuses existence and mind:

> *I am, I exist*: this is certain; but for how long? For as long as I think: . . . I am, therefore, precisely speaking, only a thing which thinks, that is to say a mind.[74]

> I admit in myself nothing other than a mind.[75]

But as the existentialists have argued, 'existence' refers to individual being, whereas 'mind' refers to general forms of apprehension, and in particular to epistemology, the objective knowledge of things. Mind is constituted as the apprehending subject in opposition to the object (*Gegen-stand*). The concept of 'mind' does not answer the existential question 'what am I?', or explain what kind of being I am; though it is essential for any scientific epistemology as a means of distinguishing the subjective from the objective. It is largely for this purpose that Descartes devised it in laying the foundations of certain scientific knowledge. Prior to Descartes there was no such epistemology, and neither was there a proper concept of 'mind'. Renaissance philosophers invariably invoked one or another form of the 'soul', which was also invariably located in nature as a whole, as the world-soul, as well as in different levels of reality. The debates surrounding the soul were very varied, but at no time did they have the epistemological focus that Descartes was to give to Mind. As against the previous jumble of natural, vegetative, appetitive and intellectual souls, with all the attendant confusion of biological, physiological, medical, psychological and epistemological considerations, the clear-cut separation of mind from body-machine was an invaluable conceptual clarification and ordering. This simplification led, however, to the narrow intellectuality which many thinkers today reject, looking back longingly at the Renaissance profusion and confusion of concepts and metaphors. Descartes' achievement in philosophy is at one with the clarity and lucidity of French classicism, which is still a living tradition in France: 'There is no thought, perhaps, more alive today, than that of Descartes',[76] a judgement which might still be true in this context.

But how does all this derive from the Cogito? The Cogito must be understood in its context; it must be taken together with the sceptical argument from universal doubt, that precedes it and to which it is an answer; as well as with the definition of body as extension in opposition to thought, that follows it. In this context the Cogito inaugurates a fundamental conceptual transformation by which the concept of 'mind' was created. The argument from doubt is the instigator of this 'essential' change;

> . . . I see light, hear noise and feel heat. But it will be said that these appearances are false and that I am dreaming. Let it be so; all the same, at least, it is very certain that it seems to me that I see light, hear a noise and feel heat; and this is properly what in me is called perceiving and this taken in this precise sense, is nothing other than thinking.[77]

In the same way all experience is taken as 'thought' (*cogitatio*) in this sense: 'But what, then, am I? A thing that thinks. What is a thing that thinks? That is to say, a thing that doubts, perceives, affirms, denies, wills, does not will, that imagines also, and which feels.'[78] Later he even adds bodily sensations to thought: '. . . all those feelings of hunger, thirst, pain etc are nothing other than certain confused ways of thinking . . .'.[79] 'Thought' then becomes the defining criterion of 'mind', and the distinction between mind and body is taken as the opposition of thought and extension.

The previous extract reveals clearly the nature of the conceptual transformation that enabled Descartes to establish a clear-cut separation of mind and body. Instead of the normal 'I see light, hear a noise, feel heat', Descartes invents his new terminology of 'I seem to see light, hear noise, feel heat'; he invents what later came to be called the 'sense-impression' report. In this way the Cogito effects what Wittgenstein calls a 'grammatical' transformation in our everyday perception concepts and in 'mental' concepts in general; this move 'internalizes' their 'objects', the things perceived (light, noise, heat etc.) and changes them from actual objects to 'intentional objects' that are internal to the act of perception. It effects a similar grammatical change in all concepts that demand as their 'grammatical' accusative an object that is outside the mental act: '. . . when I will, fear, affirm or deny, I indeed conceive something as the object of the action of my mind . . .',[80] but not necessarily, it seems, as an actual existing object outside the mind. This 'grammatical' transformation is in effect, as we shall later characterise it, a change of essence of the concepts in question. In the case of perception concepts, it also creates the concept of the 'sense-impression', which is why Wittgenstein insists that 'the red visual impression is a new concept';[81] he shows how it arises out of a 'grammatical movement', but one which is also a new experience for it requires having 'discovered a new way of looking at things'. Wittgenstein likens this new way of seeing things to the invention of 'a new way of painting; or again a new metre, or a new kind of song' (401).

'Mind' taken as 'thought' first acquired from the Cogito two essential features, which it has kept since then: privacy and property. Privacy is that essential feature which arises from the 'grammatical movement' described above; it is the transformation of every 'mental' report into an indubitable avowal, so that every mental item (a thought, perception, or sensation) becomes private in that it is no longer open to public disproof or inspection — the mental statement becomes logically beyond reproof or observation. Property means the ownership of every mental item by an 'ego' or mind, so that it cannot 'grammatically' occur on its own independently of this bearer.[82] This belongingness of the mental arises directly out of the Cogito for it simply means that every 'I think, perceive, feel etc' is linked to an 'I exist', or really, 'I am a mind'. It is in this sense that the mind is understood as the Subject to which everything is subjected; as Heidegger points out, the Subject is what underlies everything (*subjectum*), it is the *hypokeimenon*, the new substance or sub-stratum. Thus in a paradoxical reversal the subjective becomes the objective, for it alone is treated as the certain and the substantial.

The objective itself takes on a new meaning: it is now no longer fundamental but defined as against the subjective. In Descartes it is extension as opposed to thought. From this emerges the sharp Cartesian cleavage between mind and body. This opposition is reinforced by characterising the one as the realm of freedom and the other as that of necessity; for the actions of the mind are free, while those of the body are strictly determined. Thus the body comes to be thought of as a machine in which the mind has to act, as it were, from another dimension. Just how two such divergent 'substances' can act on each other and causally interact has been one of the fundamental difficulties with Cartesian dualism all along. This, above all, is responsible for its present collapse.

But something can still be salvaged from the ruins. 'Privacy' and 'property' can still be taken as essential features of Mind. Wittgenstein makes strenuous attempts to translate them into a conceptual form as 'grammatical' features. 'The proposition "sensations are private" is comparable with: "One plays patience by oneself"' (248) — which is his metaphoric way of translating privacy. 'Property' he attempts to translate by reference to the idea of a person: 'Pain-behaviour can point to a painful place — but the subject of pain is the person who gives it expression' (302). And elsewhere he attempts to deal with the matter by recourse to everyday language:

Consider how the following questions can be applied and how settled:

(1)   Are these books my books?
(2)   Is this foot my foot?
(3)   Is this body my body?
(4)   Is this sensation my sensation?(411)

'Each of these questions has practical (non-philosophical) applications' (411). Unfortunately, we are not told how these 'practical applications' are to be interpreted, or what they mean, for this is not a non-philosophical matter. Thus, in taking 'privacy' and 'property' as conceptual features Wittgenstein is in effect also treating the distinction between body and mind as a conceptual distinction. Not that a conceptual distinction is a mere distinction between concepts as opposed to one between things — it is precisely a distinction between things, but one that is 'grammatically' expressed. Just what 'grammar' means for Wittgenstein we shall see later. However, from this it does follow that the sharp Cartesian dichotomy of mind and body as a distinction between two substances is no longer in force; it is replaced by a much more flexible differentiation of 'mental' and 'material' categories of concepts, which are logically distinct but also logically related. In this new conceptual rendering it is possible for the one to 'merge' into the other:

'I noticed that he was out of humour.' Is this a report about his behaviour or his state of mind? ('The sky looks threatening': is this about the present or the future?). Both; not side-by-side, however, but about the one via the other (p. 179).

This translation of 'privacy' and 'property' brings with it a corresponding reinterpretation of the causal relation between body and mind. Descartes himself had great difficulty in conceiving this interaction, and he insisted over and over again that the mind is not

lodged in the body as a pilot in a ship, or as a 'ghost in the machine' —
as Ryle's debunking of Descartes would have it. Yet, he still
conceived of it as a causal relation between two substances. Our
analogous problem is how to conceive of a causal relation between
two conceptually diverse kinds of entities, or how a cause can
operate — not across a substantial — but a conceptual gap. This
difficulty, too, Wittgenstein attempts to resolve through conceptual
clarification — not altogether successfully, for it is not an issue in
which clarification can be of much use.

This is also the case with a related difficulty, one that has become
very urgent of late, the issue of whether the human body, and in
particular the brain, can be looked on as a machine. Descartes' view
was that the body is some kind of material system which is in
principle determined, and therefore a machine. But can a brain be
considered a machine in the sense of a mechanical contrivance
designed for a purpose, in the sense in which computers are also
machines? Descartes himself gives an extremely cogent argument as
to why men cannot be considered machines

> . . . although they [machines] might do many things as well as, or
> perhaps better than, any of us, they would fail, without doubt, in
> others, whereby one would discover that they did not act through
> knowledge, but simply through the disposition of their organs:
> for, whereas reason is a universal instrument which can serve on
> any kind of occasion, their organs need a particular disposition
> for each particular action; whence it is that it is morally [sic!]
> impossible to have enough different organs in a machine to make
> it act in all the occurrences of life in the same way as our reason
> makes us act.[83]

This argument can be readily adapted to distinguish between a
computer and a brain in a way which has nothing to do with the
materials of their composition, or with their differing processes of
construction. A computer, too, needs 'a particular disposition for
each particular action' for it operates on a designed programme,
which, no matter how flexible, is in practice never as adaptable as
the human brain which is not only not programmed, but in a way is
the creator of all programmes. Thus there are also objections in
principle to be made against the possibility of devising a programme
— viz. a fully planned out and surveyable mathematical scheme or
model — which is as capable of acting 'in all the occurrences of life in

the same way as our brain makes us act'. Machines might indeed be devised to approximate as closely as desired to men, but the more they approach the brain the less they can be considered machines. For the more something behaves as men do the less is it in practice possible mechanically to compute and survey its workings as we might that of a machine.[84] As Wittgenstein saw it in Hegelian fashion, 'this is the case of the transition from quantity to quality' (284). There is a 'conceptual jump' that occurs when we treat someone first as a man, then as a machine:

> Seeing a living human being as an automaton is analogous to seeing one figure as a limiting case or variant of another; the cross-pieces of a window as a swastika, for example (420).

So it is conceivable that the same one thing could be treated in some contexts or for some purposes as a living being and in others as a machine, as sometimes happens when men are treated for neurological disorders. Such subtleties are beyond Descartes' grasp.

It is precisely difficulties of this kind, arising in the sciences, that make Descartes' concept of Mind inadequate for its intended task as the epistemological basis of science. But nothing radically new has been devised to replace it; we have as yet conceived of no fundamentally different way of conceptualising all these issues. The best we seem to be capable of is tinkering round with Descartes' concept, and the various adjustments that have been made to it since by a number of philosophers. Or, even worse, the concept of Mind is abandoned in one way or another: through the adoption of a mechanistic materialism, or behaviourism, or some version of 'vitalism'. This philosophical confusion reflects, and is reflected in, a confusion in the sciences themselves. Wittgenstein remarks on this: 'The confusion and barrenness of psychology is not to be explained by calling it a "young science"; its state is not comparable with that of physics, in its beginnings . . .' (p. 232). Unfortunately, this conceptual confusion cannot be resolved through conceptual clarification in the manner of Wittgenstein; to overcome it would require as great an achievement in conceptual creation as that of Descartes. Clarification can act as a temporary palliative to cope with individual difficulties as they arise; it cannot reach the root problem which is simply that we do not possess better concepts. Better concepts arise from better theories. And it is here that Wittgenstein's approach to philosophy in some respects perpetuates the existing problem, for he takes this to have been brought on by philosophical theorising, whereas really it is more the result of insufficient philosophical theorising. His anti-theory tendency in philosophy makes it difficult for his dissolutions of problems to be of really great moment in the sciences, though they are useful for some purposes.

Though the destruction of the Logos and the Cogito by argument was initially undertaken as a purely negative act of thought, it is not without positive effects, precisely on the very concepts of Reason and Mind that the argument seems bent on reducing. Rationality, once it has been divorced from the metaphysics of the Logos, may be placed on a much humbler, though solider, basis. And Mind, severed from the Cogito, may be redefined in a way more appropriate to the impasse of our sciences. Rationality and Mind need to be reconceived on the basis of the new conception of language that emerges from the very arguments against the Logos and the Cogito. Part of this reconception involves placing new limits on Rationality and Mind, for one of the key consequences of the *reductio* arguments against the Logos and the Cogito is the elimination of certain unlimited possibilities from language: the unlimited inexorability of logic and the apparent compulsion of Rationality in general, and the unlimited privacy of Mind and of Subjectivity in general. Both of these absolutes are shown up as metaphysical impossibilities, formal extremes that are beyond the bounds of significance in language. And showing this is, therefore, a way of drawing the limits, from within as it were, of both Rationality and Mind.

These limits of logical inexorability and mental privacy are the positive characterisations of language that follow from the negative reductions of the Logos and Cogito. The Logos and Cogito are placed outside the bounds of language. The *reductio-ad-absurdum* arguments that demonstrate this also show the circumscribed determinations of language in which these limits reveal themselves. For arguments, as we have said, are determined by the 'grammatical' internal relations of the concepts they utilise, and, working back, they in turn determine the grammar of those very concepts. The relation between arguments and concepts is inherently circular: an argument develops features implicit in a concept, the concept is established when the argument is successfully completed. Thus it is that our two previous *reductio* arguments depend on and in turn define a new concept of language. And this new concept establishes new limits to Rationality and Mind, limits founded on precisely those features of the concept which were established by the *reductio* arguments. For it is as a result of these arguments that the concept of language can be negatively defined as not 'extrinsically determined' by any transcendent order or form outside itself, that is, as not founded on a Logos; and, as not 'intrinsically based' on a private Cogito, that is, as not being a private-language. If we reverse these negative delimitations we arrive at the positive limits of language which reflect the limits of Rationality and Mind: language is not extrinsically determined, hence, it is arbitrary; language is not based on subjective privacy, hence it is common.

The arbitrariness and commonness of language are fundamental determinations of far-ranging scope and significance. Though both of these characterisations of language are to be found explicitly in Wittgenstein's work, neither is fully developed or completely comprehended. They are offered only tentatively as defining features, and appear more as side-effects or reactions to his predominantly destructive impetus, than as positively pursued affirmations. His aversion to 'theses in philosophy' inhibits him from developing either of them further. We shall have to proceed, as it were, behind his back and carry through for him what he could not do for himself.

The notion of arbitrariness (*Willkürlichkeit*) is introduced by Wittgenstein as a feature of 'grammar', but it is generalised to language as such:

> Why don't I call cookery rules arbitrary, and why am I tempted to call the rules of grammar arbitrary? Because 'cookery' is defined by its end, whereas 'speaking' is not. That is why the use of language is in a certain sense autonomous, as cooking and washing are not. You cook badly if you are guided in your cooking by rules other than the right ones; but if you follow other rules than those of chess you are *playing another game*; and if you follow grammatical rules other than such-and-such ones, that does not mean you say something wrong, no, you are speaking of something else.[85]

The implications of this remark are very far-reaching, as becomes apparent when we compare this use of the term 'arbitrary' with that introduced by de Saussure as the first principle of linguistics: 'the bond between the signifier and the signified is arbitrary'.[86] When de Saussure declares that 'the linguistic sign is arbitrary' he merely means that it is 'unmotivated, i.e. arbitrary in that it actually has no natural connection with the signified'.[87] The denial of any 'natural connection' between signifier and signified is thus no more than the expression of a linguistic Nominalism; it goes no further than this, does not affect the overall relation of language to the world, and so leaves the nature of logic, grammar and concepts in relation to things untouched. By contrast, Wittgenstein's use of 'arbitrary' is not indicative of any Nominalism, for it does not presuppose an atomistic relationship of individual words to things, or of signifiers to signifieds, but expresses the overall relation of language to the world. It is possible that Wittgenstein was inspired in this by the idea of 'arbitrariness' as free creative phantasy elaborated by Friedrich Schlegel, the early-Romantic critic in his 'On the Study of Greek Poetry'.[88] It was this romantic idea of arbitrariness in poetry that was attacked by Jean-Paul Richter as 'poetic nihilism'.[89]

Wittgenstein's notion of 'arbitrary' implies, as Schlegel's does, the free creation of the laws of language, but not by anyone for any purpose. It is meant to explain 'why the use of language is in a certain sense autonomous, as cooking and washing are not'. It is an autonomy of language that is expressed at its most fundamental in terms of the arbitrariness of grammar. Grammar determines 'the possibilities of phenomena' (90), and 'Grammar tells us what kind of thing something is' (373). If grammar is arbitrary, then it follows, paradoxically, that the possibility of things is also arbitrary. Wittgenstein puts this paradox in the form of a question:

> So does it depend wholly on our grammar what will be called (logically) possible and what not, — i.e. what that grammar permits? — But surely that is arbitrary! — Is it arbitrary [willkür-lich]? (520).

And since grammar for Wittgenstein also determines logical necessity and categorial truth, it follows that these, too, are for him in the last resort arbitrary:

> Consider: 'The only correlate in language to an intrinsic necessity is an arbitrary rule. It is the only thing which one can milk out of this intrinsic necessity into a proposition' (372).

The shock of this kind of pronouncement is only assuaged when it is recalled that as one of the outcomes of the destruction of the Logos, 'essential necessities' become dependent on language: 'Essence is expressed by grammar' (371), is Wittgenstein's rather cryptic way of putting it. 'Essence', a time-honoured metaphysical word, is coupled with 'grammar', another old word, but used in a modern sense, and the reverberations of this startling conjuncture suggests all kinds of new meanings. Essence in this new conjunction refers to the essential nature of concepts, their 'logical structure' which is expressed by grammar. Unlike the 'essence' of metaphysics, however, in this usage 'essences' are not fixed as universals or Forms, for essences change as concepts alter, essences are created as concepts are created — 'the mathematician creates essence'.[90] It is in this sense that essence, too, is arbitrary.

But what does 'arbitrary' mean? Wittgenstein has considerable trouble trying to explain it:

> The rules of grammar may be called arbitrary if that is to mean that the aim of grammar is nothing but that of language.
>
> If someone says 'If our language had not this grammar, it could not express these facts' — it should be asked what 'could' means here (497).

Clearly, 'could' cannot mean here that there is something there to be expressed but language is unable to express it. Hence, where a language does have a grammar that makes it fit to express a certain category of facts this is not because of any congruence, structural isomorphism, or other 'correspondence relationship' between its grammar and some purported logic of the world. Another remark about the grammar of colour concepts explains this point:

> One is tempted to justify rules of grammar by sentences like 'But there are really four primary colours'. And the saying that the rules of grammar are arbitrary is directed against the possibility of this justification, which is constructed on the model of justifying a sentence by pointing to what verifies it.[91]

Another remark puts the point even more bluntly:

> We have a colour system as we have a number system. Do the systems reside in *our* nature or in the nature of things? How are we to put it? — *Not* in the nature of numbers or colours.

Then is there something arbitrary about this system? Yes and
no. It is akin both to what is arbitrary and to what is non-
arbitrary.[92]

Wittgenstein is characteristically chary of the term 'arbitrary', and
is fearful of its nominalist and conventionalist implications. He does
not fully realise that it arises from the destruction of the Logos (for if
there were a 'nature of numbers or colours' verifying the grammar of
their concept, then there would be natures or essences or *logoi*
inherent in the world), and that it is, therefore, itself a philosophical
concept arising as a positive counter-image out of the negative
reduction. He persists in treating 'arbitrary' as if it were an ordinary,
simple, non-theoretical word. As a result he cannot distinguish
clearly between its specialised newly endowed philosophic meaning,
one that only emerges out of his arguments, and the meanings
carried over from other more ordinary contexts. He is unwilling to
define it as a new concept. And so, he is unable to see that this new
concept in turn changes the grammar of the concept 'language', that
this, too, is no longer simply a factually descriptive concept, but one
which is now explanatory, ordering and normative on the basis of
implicit standards of Coherence, Reality and Significance.

The same is true of the complementary characterisation of
language as 'common' which emerges as the positive counter-image
of the negative private-language argument. Wittgenstein cannot
clearly distinguish this new philosophic concept of 'commonness'
from the simpler concepts of 'ordinary language', 'everyday
language'; many of his followers completely identify the two and
even fail to register that there is a disparity there. He does not use
the word 'common' (*allgemein*) very often, but it is implicit
whenever he speaks of language as 'our language', which he almost
invariably does. For this 'our' does not refer to any one community
of speakers, or any folk, or national linguistic group, but rather
potentially to mankind as a whole, to all those for whom language is
comprehensible and who can participate in it. Language is 'our
language' in that it is 'common' also in a deeper sense, one which
emerges as the opposite of its being 'private' in the sense of the
private-language argument. It is with this sense in mind that
Wittgenstein does employ the word 'common' in one key passage:

What reason have we for calling 'E' the sign for a *sensation*? For
'sensation' is a word of our common language, not of one intel-

ligible to me alone. So the use of this word stands in need of a justification which everybody understands (261).

Here it is obvious that the commonness of language is affirmed in opposition to the mistaken notion of 'a language that is only understandable to me alone'. It arises as a positive affirmation out of the negative attack on the Cogito. 'Common' used in this sense is thus part of the loose network of philosophical concepts that Wittgenstein deploys, such as 'agreement' and 'rule', and with which it belongs as part of his unsystematic 'system'. Of course, its other connotations of 'ordinary', 'everyday', 'general', and even 'vulgar' are there, too, but they are not its essential meaning, merely the matrix of meanings from which the concept originates.

The definition of the grammar of the concept 'language' as arbitrary and common belongs to the Praxis approach to language. Wittgenstein also seeks to convey it in terms of his metaphor of the 'language-game', which is 'meant to bring into prominence the fact that the speaking of language is part of an activity, or of a form of life' (23). But because he has the literal sense of 'game' continually before him he keeps on confusing the arbitrariness and commonness of language with that of a game: as if language were arbitrary because one could change its rules at will, or common because more than one player was required. The deeper sense of arbitrariness as the creative free-play of language, and of commonness as the inherent mutuality of whatever meanings language produces Wittgenstein could not explore very far. A vision of language as the continual creation of essence in a mutual free-play is only partially realised in his work.

Despite this, a positive definition of 'language' does emerge, in reaction, out of Wittgenstein's negatively destructive critiques of the Logos and the Cogito: language is the key human Praxis which is open to the world and only limited by the two essential requirements of arbitrariness and commonness. There can be no determination of language that goes counter to its arbitrariness, as it were, its grammatical 'free will' (*liberum arbitrium*); nor can there be any private constitution of it that contradicts its commonness, as it were, its need for human mutuality. However, although arbitrariness and commonness set formal limits that no language can transgress, this does not mean that language is ever totally arbitrary or always totally common; these are limit-notions and not exhaustive characteristics. Indeed, there must be social determining conditions of language that are in various ways compelling; if there were not language would be a wholly free creation — which of course, it never is, not even as the language of music. In fact, the science of Linguistics is concerned with the discovery of the various determining conditions of language, among them some which are universal and govern all human languages. Even the earlier Whorfian hypothesis that each language is a unique cultural creation embodying the world-view of a given people — a language-relativist view derived from Nietzsche and close to Wittgenstein's language-game idea — is coming under attack as it is recognised that all languages are governed by similar requirements of human life.[93] And analogously, if language were always wholly common then it could in no way ever be private, which again is never so, since there can be all manner of privacy in language within the bounds of its commonness.

These limits of language reflect themselves in turn as limits of Rationality and Mind, in so far as these are mediated by language. Thus, there can be no logic that is inexorable, for this would deny the arbitrariness of Language; nor can there be a mode of Subjectivity that is totally private, for this would deny the commonness of language. But within these limits logic is indeed as compelling as it needs to be, and Subjectivity can be as private as desired; in other words, the arbitrariness of language does not make Rationality simply a matter of freely chosen conventions to be abandoned at will; and the impossibility of a private-language does not mean that languages that are subjectively private do not exist.

Indeed, these are precisely the accusations, arising out of misinterpretation, that have since been made against Wittgenstein, though he partly foresaw and tried to counter them. As we mentioned before, Wittgenstein guards himself against possible accusations that his denial of the possibility of a private-language also makes it impossible for there to be other languages of privacy by pointing out right at the very start of his discussion of privacy that 'we could imagine human beings who spoke only in monologue; who accompanied their activities by talking to themselves' (243).

In the remark preceding this he seems analogously to be defending himself in advance against the charge that his arguments against the possibility of a Logos make logic impossible:

If language is to be a means of communication there must be agreement not only in definitions but also (queer as this may sound) in judgements. This seems to abolish logic, but does not do so (242).

Some commentators have indeed taken it that Wittgenstein's resort to 'agreement' as a basis for logic does abolish it, for it seems to make of him a radical conventionalist for whom every single step in logic is subject to a separately agreed on convention, since at every step someone can 'choose' to go on differently.[94] The supporting evidence given for this assumption is that since Wittgenstein is not a Platonist or Constructivist or Intuitionist, he must therefore be a Conventionalist, the only one left of the standard positions. However, other commentators have gone on to point out that Wittgenstein's position is outside any of the previously known ones, that his stance is no more Conventionalist than it is any of the others.[95] Wittgenstein himself stressed repeatedly that the 'agreement' he is talking about is not 'in opinions but in forms of life':

So you are saying that human agreement decides what is true and false?' — It is what human beings *say* that is true and false; and they agree in the *language* they use (241).

Thus he is not saying that anyone can continue a series or a proof as he arbitrarily decides, or that a separate decision is required for each step taken, for there are strong compulsions and irrefutable reasons for continuing in the one correct way, and mathematicians are seldom in disagreement as to what that should be. What Wittgenstein allows for is the possibility of conceiving of other beings in other Societies proceeding in their 'logic' or 'maths' differently to us, and, therefore, to us, insanely:

But: if anyone believes that certain concepts are absolutely the correct ones, and that having different ones would mean not realizing something that we realize — then let him imagine certain very general facts of nature to be different from what we are used to, and the formation of concepts different from the usual ones will become intelligible to him (p. 230).

This statement raises a number of far-reaching questions about the idea of the universality of Rationality. Is Rationality, and more specifically the exact forms of Rationality such as logic and mathematics, an historically determined mode of procedure of Western man, or is it integral to the whole of humanity? Is the imagining of possible concepts other than our own rational ones simply a matter of conceiving of another civilisation, or does it call for imagining another world with other types of beings? And if the rational forms are an integral part of being human, then does it follow from this that Man is *zoon logon echon*, after all?

Wittgenstein seems to suggest that beings who behave in what is to us an irrational or illogical fashion cannot be said to have a language, and so cannot be said to be fully human either, for 'the common behaviour of mankind is the system of reference by means of which we interpret an unknown language' (206); and if there were a situation where we could not learn what seemed at first to be a language of a people because it was too irrational or illogical, then there would not be 'enough regularity for us to call it "language"' (207). Although, obviously, he would allow considerable divergence from our highly exact standards of Western Rationality, he does not specify what degree of difference could be tolerated before something could no longer be regarded as a language. What the 'common behaviour of mankind' is in respect of Rationality he does not spell out in any detail. However, we can partly divine it from his emphasis upon Praxis in determining whether something is a species of logic or mathematics, or whether it is a totally different activity. Thus he stresses that what distinguishes a mere formal system, or game of constructing symbols, or even a mathematical-seeming mode of decoration from a logical or mathematical practice of inference and computation, is the fact that the latter can be given a use in the world of practical activities. Applicability to the world is a decisive criterion of Rationality. The rational norms are precisely those without which human beings could not control or, further-more, dominate the course of nature or events. They reflect a technical cognitive interest in Habermas' sense.

Does it, however, follow from this that the world itself is rational or bound by Rationality? If it did, we would be once more back with the metaphysics of the Logos and the pre-ordained harmony between Nature and human nature, between Reality and Thought, and so on. But as Wittgenstein shows, it is ultimately a contingent fact, though one of utmost generality, that our rational norms do apply to our world, that we can rely on them in practice, and that they enable us to achieve control over things. It could be otherwise, a world is conceivable in which all our norms were useless and in which quite different procedures would have to be developed: it might be discovered that magical practices work much better. As Nietzsche insists, the world is rational not because it is a cosmos *per se*, but only because we have made it so, because we have imposed our norms upon it, and we find that by doing so we can as a matter of fact control the world. Or putting it another way, it is only contingently the case that our world allows itself to be dealt with by means of the modes of rationality that humanity has historically devised.

To accede to the destruction of the Logos is, thus, in no way to weaken the force of logic or rationality; the dissolution of the forms of the Logos — Ideas, universals, essences, natures — does not deny the power of the concept, nor the compellingness of rational argument. It is a measure of Wittgenstein's achievement that he confronts the Logos precisely in its own seemingly impregnable fastness of logic and mathematics by showing that even these are not founded on anything transcendentally ultimate. Neither is this to deny the historical truth that most of the western norms of Rationality had to develop on the basis of the metaphysics of the Logos. As we now know, these same rational norms, as the forms of Civilisation in Alfred Weber's sense, have since also been accepted by people who do not share in the Western cultural heritage. Rationalization in Max Weber's sense has become the common historic fate of all mankind, for it is an historic 'project' to which all men have to 'agree' if they wish to participate in the domination of nature and of each other. By contrast, the specific cultural forms of Western Reason are by no means so prevalent or compelling. Thus the norms of philosophical Reason are neither universally practised nor accepted. This historical difference is due to the fact that Reason in philosophy or culture calls for a certain kind of openness and a willingness to follow the course of an argument, which is not like the inexorable compellingness of an argument in logic or mathematics. Reason and Rationalisation call for very different kinds of 'agreement'.

'Agreement' of one kind or another there must always be. When Nietzsche states that 'rational thought is interpretation according to a scheme that we cannot throw off',[96] this 'cannot' must not be taken absolutely. It is true, however, that if we were to throw off all possible proto-rational schemas, we would cease to have any language, and no longer be human. As long as men remain human they will tend to adopt some ordering schema or other in dealing with the world, for this is an inherent feature of language. Language with its sameness of meanings, concepts, identities, formulae for equivalence, always imposes some order on the world; not so much because the world is an Order itself, or because language is structurally isomorphic with it, but merely because this is a way of dealing with the world that human beings can develop — the way they have developed over the course of history, ever more successfully, given their purposes. Men thus devise ever more complex forms of order and discover regularities in the world, recurring patterns, which more or less, and for given ends, fit those forms of order.

Wittgenstein might have been right to doubt that his approach to Language constituted a new *Weltanschauung* — though he did so for the wrong reasons, maintaining that investigations of language 'change nothing, leave everything as it was'. In another sense, it is a new *Weltanschuung* since it does literally change our view of the world. For to allow for the possibility of language being an arbitrary and common Praxis, the world must be viewed as open — and this is, of course, a grammatical remark in Wittgenstein's sense. The openness of the world is simply the reflection in grammar of the arbitrariness and commonness of language; what it means is that the world can have no determinate Being: not a Logos, nor Ratio, nor Idea, nor Order, nor any of the other metaphysical determinations of Being. The openness of the world means also that it can accommodate all possible modes of language, there can be no such thing as a language that does not suit or fit the world. To say this seems to deny Truth and objectivity, and obliterate the distinction between reality and illusion, but actually does not do so, for these norms can still be judged by reference to the comprehensiveness, scope of disclosure, utility, and other such criteria by which the truth of one language is preferred to that of another. For although no language can in principle embrace all of the world — each is self-limiting since it only discloses at the cost of concealing — yet some languages are more comprehensive than others, if only in the sense that they comprehend others as sub-languages within themselves. The scope of a language is a reflection of the scope of the social and cultural form of life from which the language derives; one that is more mutual and more embracing will produce a language of greater comprehensiveness. The 'grammatical' characterisation of human being as mutual is itself a reflection of this commonness of language. When Schiller stated that 'out of the wholly common is man made, and custom is his nurse', he forgot to add that without language there would be neither custom nor commonness. And yet, as we shall see, neither man nor language is wholly common, since each man can also be a separately existing individual and some languages can be private.

The possible languages of privacy, located within the limits set by the private-language argument — provide an alternative basis for Mind and Subjectivity, which seem themselves almost to have become impossible after the destruction of the Cogito. Wittgenstein never investigated actual languages of privacy; he merely allowed for their possibility through imaginary anthropological examples, such as that of the tribe of people who speak to themselves in monologue, and other such Robinsonades of language. What it means for someone in our society to speak to himself in monologue, in a way that other people fail to understand, he never considered. But such are the real uses of languages of privacy that we encounter, and in our world they are becoming more widespread as the individual is increasingly reduced to his own private existence.

A language of privacy is, at its simplest, one that cannot be publicly understood or employed in public discourse; at its most extreme, it is one that has ceased to be in any way common or shareable with others. However, of course it would have to originate from, and so still be based on, forms of language that were common, for otherwise the private-language limit would apply to rule it out as impossible. But a language might leave its common origins far behind, and push ever further into privacy. Languages of privacy can be inifinitely varied. Among the simplest are secret languages which can only be understood among a small group of initiates; some of these languages are only trivially private because they are no more than codes or jargons, but there are also secret languages that are more profoundly private because they deal with intimate knowledge or arcane mysteries. A large sub-species of languages of privacy are those which demand extraordinary private experiences to be understood: such are the special languages of love, or of mysticism, or of the 'unspeakable' experiences of death. The languages of madness are a species of private language that are on the border between language and sheer nonsense, for sometimes a madman's gibberish can still be understood like a language and sometimes it is mere symptoms to be read clinically.

The fact that it is always at least in principle possible for someone else to understand a language of privacy is what distinguishes it from the limit case of the private-language. Nevertheless, some such languages can approximate as closely as possible to the limit case.

Some of the languages of modern literature are fully comprehensible to their authors alone, some of the experiences on which they are based are virtually incommunicable, and frequently they approximate to languages of sheer madness. But usually it is possible to offer some way of interpreting even extreme literature, and so of making it understood. This does not mean that it can ever be publicly understood, or made universally intelligible; if this were possible it would not be a language of privacy, since such a language defies every attempt at translation into a public language. A language of privacy can be understood by others, but only in private, only, that is, if as private individuals they are able and willing to enter into the special world of private experience which the language inhabits and transform themselves so as to be able to acquire its language. The individual must realise in himself the particular mode of private existence in order to acquire the language of that privacy. Such spheres of privacy develop themselves in every society in opposition to its public spheres, and so languages of privacy are universally present; it is only the form they take which varies depending on the nature of this opposition.

In the modern world, under conditions of Nihilism, the formation of private spheres has assumed unparalleled urgency and importance, and together with it the quest for new languages of privacy. In a world where even basic 'natural' languages and public languages requiring a public in the old sense are being eroded by the impersonal 'languages' of communication technology, the only recourse to personal truth or self-expression is to be found in languages of privacy. The sociological process whereby personal identity is forced out of the official world and into a private world has its exact correlates in language. And the process of the annihilation of 'natural' language is itself the correlate of that whereby Nature in general is de-natured by being transformed through technological domination into a product. Natural languages are only suffering the fate of human nature itself. In such a situation the individual is forced to protect his individuality in private, and to resort to languages of privacy in order to do so. Today we speak, as 'we live, as we dream — alone'.[97]

Our artists have know this predicament for some time. Public art has long ago become a monstrosity, and only 'in private, pianissimo'[98] can the artist still say anything. The artist has had to opt for a 'lonely discourse'[99] in music as well as in words. This is why artists have developed what Adorno calls the 'hermetic work of art', one that creates its own private world. In the hermetic works of Kafka and Beckett the lonely discourse of art has been taken to its ultimate conclusion, into silence and death.

The language of these writers exemplifies at its most extreme the process whereby the individual can only discover his own existence through a process of self-estrangement from the outside world, first by alienating himself from public life and society and eventually from mutual relations to other men. His language thus departs increasingly from common and even 'natural' language. It becomes a language only comprehensible in private by those who have themselves experienced a similar process of self-alienation, and who exist in a situation of solitude and loneliness. To follow the writer on his lonely path into privacy is the cost exacted from those who wish to understand his works. Taken to its ultimate conclusion, this path leads to self-extinction and death, for individual existence discovered in privacy must wither and be lost if it cannot return to something humanly common and sustaining. But the return journey from this new 'heart of darkness' is being made increasingly difficult by the fact that there is almost nothing common to which to return. So the individual is trapped between the nothingness of himself inside him and the Nothing of his world outside.

'Nearly all my writings are private conversations with myself. Things that I say to myself tête-à-tête.'[100] Like the work of other writers of his time, Wittgenstein's philosophy is in many respects a philosophy of solitude, a 'lonely discourse' expressive of the alienation of the individual from the world. It, too, is a hermetic work composed of inner dialogue: an intense self-questioning inside one 'solitary brain', whose insights or illuminations he despairs of ever conveying to any other. In the 'darkness of this time' it is all that seems possible to him in continuing to philosophise. Nevertheless, his philosophical language of privacy is gradually coming to be understood by others. And if it were to 'stimulate someone to thoughts of his own',[101] as he hoped despite his own misgivings, then his work would continue in the way he meant it to do.

Notes

1. Wittgenstein saw philosophy as an endemic 'disease of language' from which mankind would one day be cured, not through further philosophising or any other purely intellectual endeavour, but rather through a changed way of life:

The sickness of a time is cured by an alteration in the mode of life of human beings, and it was possible for the sickness of philosophical problems to get cured only through a changed mode of thought and of life, not through a medicine invented by an individual.

Ludwig Wittgenstein, *Remarks on the Foundations of Mathematics*, trans. G. E. M. Anscombe (The MIT Press, Cambridge, Mass., 1967), p. 57.

Till that time philosophy would continue to 'scratch the itch': 'philosophy hasn't made any progress? — If someone scratches the spot where he has an itch, do we see some progress? . . . And can't this reaction to an irritation continue in the same way for a long time before a cure for the itching is discovered?'

He obviously would have preferred the itch to stop sooner rather than later:

I am by no means sure that I should prefer a continuation of my work by others to a change in the way people live which would make all these questions superfluous. (For this reason I could never found a school.)

Ludwig Wittgenstein, *Culture and Value*, trans. P. Winch, (ed.) G. H. von Wright in collaboration with H. Nyman (Blackwell, Oxford, 1980), pp. 86 and 61.

2. Quoted in Paul Engelmann, *Letters from Ludwig Wittgenstein — with a Memoir* (Blackwell, Oxford, 1967), pp. 143–4.

3. Ludwig Wittgenstein, *Philosophical Investigations*, trans. G. E. M. Anscombe (Blackwell, Oxford, 1953), preface, p. X. All subsequent references to this work will be indicated in the text by the section number or page number.

4. Ludwig Wittgenstein, *Tractatus Logico – Philosophicus*, trans. D. F. Pears and B. F. McGuiness (Routledge and Kegan Paul, London, 1963), preface, p. 3. All subsequent references to this work will be indicated in the text by sentence number or page number.

5. For a sense of Wittgenstein's conception of the darkness of the times, namely, of modern Nihilism, see his preface to *Philosophical Remarks*, a work midway between the *Tractatus* and *Investigations*, reprinted in *Culture and Value*, op. cit., p. 6. The key idea of an end to culture and the arts in an age of technological civilisation is derived from Spengler. In this respect Wittgenstein seems also have had some knowledge of Nietzsche, whom he occasionally mentions. See particularly the comment in *Culture and Value*, p. 9, where he explicitly compares himself adversely to Nietzsche in relation to this issue:

There are problems I never get anywhere near, which do not lie in my path or are not part of my world. Problems of the intellectual world of the West that Beethoven (and perhaps Goethe to a certain extent) tackled and wrestled with but which no philosopher has ever confronted (perhaps Nietzsche passed by them).

6. The extent to which these themes of philosophy reflect Wittgenstein's own character traits and his personal predispositions is apparent from many biographical recollections. See in particular: Ludwig Wittgenstein, *Personal Recollections*, (ed. R. Rhees (Blackwell, Oxford, 1981).

7. See in particular *Culture and Value*, p. 56.

The truly apocalyptic view of the world is that things do *not* repeat themselves. I isn't absurd, e.g. to believe that the age of science and technology is the beginning of the end for humanity; that the idea of great progress is a delusion, along with the idea that the truth will ultimately be known: that there is nothing good o desirable about scientific knowledge and that mankind, in seeking it, is falling into a trap. It is by no means obvious that this is not how things are.

8. Werner Marx, *Heidegger and the Tradition*, trans. T. Kisiel and M. Greene (Northwestern University Press, Evanston, 1971), p. 56.

9. F. Waismann, 'How I see Philosophy' in (ed.) H. D. Lewis, *Contemporary British Philosophy*, Third Series (Allen and Unwin, London, 1956), pp. 481–3.

10. See also an analogous remark in *Remarks on the Foundations of Mathematics*, p. 157: 'Even 500 years ago a philosophy of mathematics was possible, a philosophy of what mathematics was then.' Wittgenstein is clearly not thinking of the kind of philosophy of mathematics that was actually historically possible in the fifteenth century given the mentality of the age. Had he thought it through he might have said that fifteenth-century mathematics is sufficient for his purpose as a philosopher even in the twentieth century.

11. For a sense of Wittgenstein's appreciation of Socrates and Augustine see M. O'C. Drury, 'Conversations with Wittgenstein' in Ludwig Wittgenstein, *Personal Recollections*, pp. 104 and 131.

12. For a full treatment of dissolution and reduction as nihilistic processes see *In the Beginning was the Deed*, op. cit. A literary treatment of dissolution as a general cultural condition is given by D. H. Lawrence in his major novel *Women in Love* (Heinemann, London, 1964), p. 164: 'Dissolution rolls on just as production does . . . It is a progressive process — and it ends in universal nothing'

13. Ludwig Wittgenstein, *Zettel*, (eds.) G. E. M. Anscombe and G. H. von Wright, trans. G. E. M. Anscombe (Blackwell, Oxford, 1967), sec. 382.

14. Ibid., sec. 452.

15. *Lectures and Conversations on Aesthetics, Psychology and Religious Belief*, (ed.) C. Barrett (Blackwell, Oxford, 1966), p. 28. Note also his remark in *Culture and Value*, p. 79: 'I find scientific questions interesting, but they never really grip me. Only conceptual and aesthetic questions do that. At bottom I am indifferent to the solution of scientific problems; but not the other sort.'

16. Marcuse makes this very sentence the point of departure for his attack on Wittgenstein, commenting that 'the almost masochistic reduction of speech to the humble and common is made into a programme'. He rightly goes on to object that 'the words with which philosophy is concerned can therefore never have a use as humble . . . as that of the words "table", "lamp", "door"'. Herbert Maercuse, *One Dimensional Man* (Sphere Books, London, 1968), pp. 144–5.

17. Ludwig Wittgenstein, *On Certainty*, (eds.) G. E. M. Anscombe and G. H. von Wright, trans. D. Paul and G. E. M. Anscombe (Blackwell, Oxford, 1969), p. 62.

18. Wittgenstein's remarks in *Culture and Value* abound with these attitudes. See, for example, his remark: 'All great art has man's primitive drives as its groundbase' (p. 37). His tastes in the arts reflect these values. Leavis, noting his extreme fondness for works such as Dickens' *The Uncommercial Traveller* and *A Christmas Carol*, comments rather uncharitably: 'cultivated as he was, his interest in literature had remained rudimentary'. See *Personal Recollections*, op. cit., p. 79. However, a better and fairer explanation would be that his literary sense was bound to these values which, obviously, Leavis does not share.

19. Those who have followed Wittgenstein closely have undoubtedly suffered from his purism. Wittgenstein himself was aware this might happen. See *Culture and Value*, p. 61: 'Am I the only one who cannot found a school or can a philosopher never do this? I cannot found a school because I do not really want to be imitated. Not at any rate by those who publish articles in philosophical journals.'

20. See *In the Beginning was the Deed*.

21. *On Certainty*, sec. 559.

22. *Zettel*, sec. 447.

23. Ibid., sec. 233.

24. *Lectures and Conversations on Aesthetics*, p. 28.

25. In one of the few comments on this issue, Wittgenstein states that

philosophical problems have in fact no history, they are perennial and always the same because they are inherent in the unchanging nature of language, which presumably also has no history:

> People say again and again that philosophy does not really progress, that we are still occupied with the same philosophical problems as were the Greeks. But the people who say this don't understand why it has to be so. It is because our language has remained the same and keeps seducing us into asking the same questions.

Culture and Value, p. 15.
   26. Wittgenstein was aware of this himself:

> Nothing seems to me less likely than that a scientist or mathematician who reads me should be seriously influenced in the way he works . . . What is needed here is artillery of a completely different kind from anything I am in a position to muster . . . I ought never to hope for more than the most indirect influence.

Culture and Value, p. 62.
   27. *Zettel*, sec. 447.
   28. Ibid., sec. 223.
   29. Nietzsche, *Will to Power*, sec. 481.
   30. *Zettel*, sec. 696.
   31. Ibid., sec. 697.
   32. Ibid., sec. 449.
   33. For an elucidation of the metaphor see Farhang Zabeeh, 'On Language Games and Forms of Life' in *Essays on Wittgenstein*, (ed.) E. D. Klemke (University of Illinois Press, Urbana, 1971), p. 358.
   34. Ludwig Wittgenstein, *The Blue and Brown Books*, (ed.) R. R. (Blackwell, Oxford, 1958), p. 81.
   35. *Zettel*, sec. 99.
   36. Quoted in N. Malcolm, *Ludwig Wittgenstein — A Memoir, with a Biographical Sketch* by G. H. von Wright (Oxford University Press, London, 1962), p. 93.
   37. Farhang Zaheeb ventures this criticism but he blames only Wittgenstein's *epigoni* and tries to exonerate Wittgenstein himself, see *Essays on Wittgenstein*, p. 372:

> Wittgenstein's pre-occupation with the pragmatic dimension, which was due mainly to the language game — instrument analogy, led some of his disciples to be dazzled with the analogy — the analogy which in due course made them meaning-blind — as if the deposit of words and rules of grammar or of logic are by themselves of no significance, since they are in the long run tools in the hands of all speakers. Wittgenstein himself was conscious of the pitfall of his analogy.

But the quotation he addresses (Inv. 569) in fact shows nothing of the kind. He seems to have misunderstood what Wittgenstein is saying in this instance.
   38. *On Certainty*, sec. 599.
   39. Max Weber, 'Objectivity in Social Science' in *The Methodology of the Social Sciences*, (ed.) E. A. Shils (Free Press, New York, 1968), pp. 92–3.
   40. Ibid., p. 93.
   41. Adorno, *Negative Dialectics*, p. 164.
   42. His ignorance of metaphysics was in some respects astounding. He himself

tells Drury in 1948: 'Here I am a one-time professor of philosophy who has never read a word of Aristotle!' *Personal Recollections*, p. 172.

43. R. Bambrough, 'Universal and Family Resemblances', in *Modern Studies in Philosophy*, (ed.) G. Pitcher (Macmillan, London, 1968).

44. A. Kenny, 'Cartesian Privacy' in Pitcher, pp. 352–70.

45. Adorno, *Negative Dialectics*, pp. 29–30.

46. *Remarks on the Foundations of Mathematics*, p. 188.

47. Ibid., p. 194.

48. Ibid., p. 190.

49. Ibid., p. 154.

50. Ibid., p. 154.

51. Ibid., p. 127.

52. Ibid., pp. 12–13.

53. Ibid., p. 122.

54. Ibid., p. 122.

55. See *In the Beginning was the Deed*, Act III.

56. See ibid. for an account of this paradoxical dialectic whereby Technology, Subjectivity and Activism become Technocracy, Subjectlessness and Inactivity.

57. See Michel Foucault, *The Order of Things* (Tavistock, London, 1970), Chapter 3. Foucault's account of representation is, however, restricted to what he calls the classical episteme; he does not explore the subsequent role of representation because he denies its further relevance beyond the classical age ending with the eighteenth century.

58. Martin Heidegger, *The End of Philosophy*, trans. J. Stambaugh (Souvenir Press, London, 1975), pp. 28–9.

59. *Remarks on the Foundations of Mathematics*, Chapter 1, p. 2.

60. Ibid., Chapter 1, sec. 33, p. 13.

61. Ibid., pp. 33–4.

62. Diels, *Fragmente der Vorsokratiker*, 76B, pp. 553–4. For another translation see Kathleen Freeman, *Ancilla to the Pre-Socratic Philosophers* (Blackwell, Oxford, 1956), p. 129.

63. W. Dilthey, *Gesammelte Schriften*, vol. 5, quoted in H. A. Hodges, *The Philosophy of Wilhelm Dilthey* (Routledge and Kegan Paul, London, 1952), p. 15.

64. Wilhelm von Humboldt, 'Vorstudie zur Einleitung zum Kawi-Werk', quoted in E. Cassirer, *Philosophy of Symbolic Forms*, trans. R. Manheim (Yale University Press, New Haven, 1957), vol. I, p. 156.

65. *Zettel*, sec. 609.

66. F. H. Bradley, *Appearance and Reality*, p. 346, quoted in T. S. Eliot, 'The Wasteland', *Collected Poems 19 9–1962* (Faber and Faber, London, 1963), p. 86.

67. R. Descartes, *Discourses on Method and other Writings*, trans. F. E. Sutcliffe (Penguin, Harmonsworth, 1968), p. 53.

68. Ibid., p. 54.

69. The idea that the private-language argument is a *reductio-ad-absurdum* was first put forward by Norman Malcolm. See 'Wittgenstein's Philosophical Investigations' in *Wittgenstein: The Philosophical Investigations*, (ed.) G. Pitcher (Macmillan, London, 1968), p. 75.

70. Descartes, 'Meditations on First Philosophy' in *Discourse on Method and Other Writings*, p. 103.

71. Ibid., p. 95.

72. *Human – All-Too-Human*, sec. 1, par. 20, quoted in H. G. Schenk, *The Mind of the European Romantics* (Constable, London, 1966), p. 247.

73. 'Meditations', p. 103.

74. Ibid., p. 105.

75. Ibid., p. 111.

76. A. Koyré 'Introduction' in *Descartes Philosophical Writings*, trans. E. Anscombe and P. T. Geach (Nelson, London, 1964), p. VII.

77. Ibid., p. 107.

78. Ibid., pp. 106–7.

79. Ibid., p. 115.

80. Ibid., p. 115.

81. *Zettel*, sec. 423.

82. For the word 'property' in this philosophic sense see Shakespeare's 'The Phoenix and the Turtle':

Property was thus appall'd
That the self was not the same

The Riverside Shakespeare (Houghton Mifflin Company, Boston, 1974), p. 1797.

83. 'Discourse 5' in *Discourse on Method and Other Writings*, p. 74.

84. This argument was first suggested by von Neumann and has since been also taken up by Marvin Minsky. See Jeremy Bernstein, *Science Observed* (Basic Books, New York, 1982), p. 122: 'What would it mean to understand the mind? It is difficult to imagine that it will consist of an enumeration of the component parts. Even if we had a diagram containing every one of the billions of neurons in the human brain and the billions of interconnections, it would stare at us as mutely as grains in a desert . . .'.

85. *Zettel*, sec. 320.

86. F. de Saussure, quoted in *The Structuralists: From Marx to Lévi-Strauss*, trans. R. and F. M. de George (Anchor Books, Doubleday and Company, New York, 1972), p. 72.

87. Ibid., p. 73.

88. Quoted in D. Arendt, *Nihilismus: Die Anfänge von Jacobi bis Nietzsche* (Jakob Hegner, Köln, 1970), p. 46.

89. Ibid., p. 46.

90. *Remarks on the Foundations of Mathematics*, p. 13.

91. *Zettel*, sec. 331.

92. Ibid., sec. 357–8.

93. Whorf's ideas were nurtured by German philology, including those of Nietzsche. The main evidence against Whorf in contemporary linguistics comes from the structural similarities uncovered in different languages that are geographically widely removed from each other. Thus the colour spectrum is not divided arbitrarily, despite the presence of diverse colour concepts in different languages, but according to fixed principles of differentiation present universally. So, too, the grammars of different languages are far less arbitrary than Wittgenstein imagined, no more arbitrary than cooking and washing customs. See Keith Allan, 'Language, Conception and Perception: Evidence of the ways in which speakers come to terms with their Environment' (unpublished paper, Monash University). Whether there are universal deep structures of grammar as Chomsky and Lévi-Strauss maintain is another matter, which need not be debated here.

94. M. Dummett, 'Wittgenstein's Philosophy of Mathematics', *Philosophical Review*, vol. LXVIII (1959), pp. 324–48. Reprinted in Pitcher.

95. B. Stroud, 'Wittgenstein and Logical Necessity', *Philosophical Review*, vol. LXXIV (1965), pp. 504–18. Reprinted in Pitcher.

96. Nietzsche, *Will to Power*,

97. Joseph Conrad, *Heart of Darkness*.

98. Max Weber, 'Science as a Vocation' in *From Max Weber*, p. 155.

99. T. Adorno, *Philosophy of Modern Music* (Sheed and Ward, London, 1973), p. 43.

100. *Culture and Value*, p. 77. Note, too, the remark on p. 53 where he compares himself with Lenau's Faust in his loneliness, or isolation.

101. *Philosophical Investigations*, preface.

Part Three

PHILOSOPHY AND RATIONALITY

5 THE ENDS OF PHILOSOPHY

1. How to continue to Philosophise?

> A living philosophy which today does not depend on the security of current intellectual and social conditions, but instead upon truth, sees itself facing the problem of the liquidation of philosophy.[1]

Since the end of metaphysics some philosophies have indeed been 'facing the problem of the liquidation of philosophy' — not only those which depend upon the truth, as Adorno sees it, but also those which reject any such dependence. For these philosophies, Philosophy itself has become the main problem. It has only succeeded in staving off its end through numerous delaying tactics. Ever newer forms of metaphysics were discovered in order to be destroyed, so that philosophy could keep going. And when these gave out the old destructions were re-enacted to the point of self-parody. But how much longer can this go on? Philosophy has turned to the sciences to give itself some semblance of relevance and substantiality, but the scientists have turned away and will have nothing to do with it — the epithet 'philosopher' has become an insult among them. Philosophy has turned to the arts to put itself beyond the reach of scientific derision, but artists are less and less disposed to have anything to do with thinkers; they call them 'intellectuals' and leave it at that.

It seems philosophy has nowhere further to turn; it has come to the end of its tether. Like a character from Beckett it cannot go on — yet it does. Every attempt to bring it to a stop only helps to perpetuate it. Indeed, the end of philosophy has so often been mooted that the continual repetition of the threat has come to seem like a self-defeating prophecy. This work too began with that threat, but has postponed carrying it out till the end. Will it too prove guilty of arousing dire expectations that it is itself specifically designed to forestall?

We are not alone in having to face this accusation: the charge can be laid at the door of just about every major modern thinker. Each one promised to end philosophy, yet continued to philosophise without evident embarrassment. Marx, Nietzsche, Wittgenstein and Heidegger, all proclaimed the end of philosophy in one sense or another, yet each also provided a loophole in the final closure to enable himself to slip through and continue philosophising, though he might not have called it by that name any longer. So philosophy was repeatedly declared dead, yet allowed to live on incognito under an assumed name, given a new identity and made to migrate to another intellectual clime. It has been called dialectical materialism, or the transvaluation of all values, or conceptual analysis, or simply Thought — heavily capitalised. Has it, indeed, over-capitalised on its past deposits of thought, and is it now a bankrupt living on debts to the past? A conservative metaphysician would think that this is all there is to it, but those who are beyond metaphysics know that it is not quite so simple — there are evident complications which must be brought out.

Marx undertook to carry through 'the negation of philosophy, of philosophy as philosophy', yet this negation hardly freed him from philosophy. He pronounced his final verdict on philosophy in no uncertain terms:

> Where speculation ends, where real life starts, there con-
> sequently begins real, positive science, the expounding of the
> practical activity, of the practical process of development of men
> . . . When reality is described, a self-sufficient philosophy loses
> its medium of existence. At best its place can be taken by a
> summing-up of the most general results, abstractions which were
> derived from observations of the historical development of men
> . . . But they by no means afford a recipe or schema, as does
> philosophy, for neatly trimming the epochs of history.[2]

The philosophy in question is in the first place Hegel's, though Marx's judgement is on philosophy in general. Yet Marx was by no means content to bury Hegel as a 'dead dog' and as late as *Capital* he could still 'flirt' with the Hegelian philosophy. There is, of course, continual and continuing dispute as to the nature of the philosophical elements in Marx. There are those, such as Lukacs and the Frankfurt school, who see this philosophy as a direct succession from Hegelian dialectics; and others, such as Althusser and the neo-Structuralists, who deny this and instead derive from Marx a new philosophy of dialectical materialism which they view as the philosophical counterpart of the science of historical materialism. But regardless of whether Marxism is negative dialectics or dialectical materialism it remains philosophy.

Nietzsche railed against philosophy more vehemently than Marx:

> The history of philosophy is a secret raging against the precondi-tions of life, against the value feelings of life, against partisanship in favour of life.[3]
>
> . . . It is a miserable story: man seeks a principle through which he can despise men — he invents a world so as to be able to slander and bespatter this world: in reality, he reaches every time for nothingness and construes nothingness as 'God', as 'truth', and in any case as judge and condemner of *this* state of being—[4]

He believed all philosophy to be tainted with the Nihilism inherent in metaphysics. Thus, the overcoming of metaphysics must also be the ending of philosophy. All the philosophies of the past, and certainly those starting with Socrates, the first philosophical decadent, were to be destroyed. The contamination of thought by morality, which philosophy brought about, was to be ended. But did this mean that there was to be no more philosophy in the future? Far from it:

> Genuine philosophers . . . are commanders and legislators: they say, thus it shall be! They first determine the Whither and For What of man, and in so doing have at their disposal the preliminary labour of all philosophical labourers, all who have overcome the past. With a creative hand they reach for the future . . . their 'knowing' is creating, their creating is a legislation, their will to truth is — will to power.[5]

The 'new philosopher can arise only in conjunction with a ruling caste, as its highest spiritualization'.[6] 'The philosopher must be a legislator', but also 'a great educator, powerful enough to draw up to his lonely height a long chain of generations . . .'.[7] Nietzsche's own work is the preparation for the education of these educators; it is for them that he writes. It is itself, therefore, a philosophical propaedeutic, and so cannot but be considered philosophy. It seems, then, that Nietzsche, too, is saying, 'Philosophy is dead! Long live Philosophy!'.

Wittgenstein advised in his *Tractatus* that 'the correct method in philosophy would really be the following: to say nothing except what can be said, i.e. propositions of natural science — i.e. something that has nothing to do with philosophy — and then, whenever someone else wanted to say something metaphysical, to demonstrate to him that he had failed to give a meaning to certain signs in his propositions'.[8] Philosophy is, he says, rendered impossible by the very logic of language itself, for it seeks to represent that which can only show itself. By this criterion even Wittgenstein's own propositions, if understood correctly, are 'nonsensical'.[9] However, by the time of the *Philosophical Investigations*, as the very title itself indicates, philosophy had become possible once again, though the emphasis is on 'investigations'. What these philosophical investigations have to do with traditional philosophy is far from clear, and not well understood by Wittgenstein himself. 'Ludwig Wittgenstein's reply to critics who complained that what he was doing was "not philosophy", was to answer "Maybe not, but what I am doing is the legitimate heir to that which has previously been called philosophy".'[10] But what legitimates this heir? Perhaps it is only that these philosophical investigations are concerned with treating the problems arising out of traditional philosophy. The treatment of such problems is interminable, so there will always be the need for further philosophy.

Heidegger's philosophical legitimacy seems much better substantiated than Wittgenstein's. He seems the inheritor of the very Tradition he sets himself to destroy, for he invoked all its holiest names and noblest words, from Being onwards. Nevertheless, like Nietzsche he, too, insists on the 'overcoming of metaphysics', though he means it differently; he even speaks explicitly of the 'end of philosophy':

We are asking:
1. What does it mean that philosophy in the present age has entered its final stage?
2. What task is reserved for thinking at the end of philosophy?[11]

It is soon apparent, however, that by 'philosophy' Heidegger only means 'metaphysics', so the question of the end of philosophy is only that of the end of metaphysics: 'What we say about the end of philosophy means the completion of metaphysics.'[12] But he does extend the scope of metaphysics by treating nearly all modern philosophies — except his own Thought — as metaphysical: 'All metaphysics, including its opponent, Positivism, speaks the language of Plato.'[13] Accordingly, even Nietzsche and Marx before him, both of whom 'reverse Platonism', precisely for this reason do still belong to the metaphysical tradition; the reversal of metaphysics is itself metaphysical.

To Thought, as opposed to mere philosophy, Heidegger assigns the task at the end of philosophy of initiating a '*first* possibility for thinking apart from the *last* possibility which we characterized (the dissolution of philosophy in the technologized sciences), a possibility from which the thinking of philosophy would have to start, but which as philosophy it could nevertheless not experience and adopt'.[14] In earlier writings Heidegger was much less tentative about what Thought could accomplish. In this piece 'the thinking in question remains unassuming . . ., [being] content with awakening a readiness in man for a possibility whose contours remain obscure, whose coming remains uncertain . . .'.[15] This 'preparatory thinking' prepared for future Thought by a return to the original thought of the past, to the origins of philosophy prior to Plato, above all to Parmenides and *alytheia* or Truth. '*Alytheia* is named at the beginning of philosophy, but afterwards it is not explicitly thought as such . . .'[16] Heidegger means to rethink it again originally, to 'think *alytheia*, unconcealment, as the opening which first grants Being and thinking and their presencing to and for each other'.[17] This shows clearly that the basic eschatological thought has remained unaltered in Heidegger from beginning to end of his thinking, for every ending for him is but a return to the one original beginning, the root source from which all beginnings start: 'The quiet heart of the opening is the place of stillness from which alone the possibility of the belonging together of Being and thinking, that is, presence and apprehending, can arise at all.'[18] Unfortunately, when he comes to spell out specifically what this 'quiet heart of opening' discloses, Heidegger relies on his own philological contortions of word play, curious etymology and poetic metaphor.[19] For Heidegger, too, then, there really is no end to philosophy, even at the end of metaphysics.

Marx, Nietzsche, Wittgenstein and Heidegger: each one provides for himself a way out of the closure of philosophy, a rationale for continuing to philosophise even at the end of philosophy. But if these rationales are now highly suspect, what then? Does this mean that there is now no way of going on? We have set ourselves in this work to push such questionings to their conclusion in order to see whether any of the ways of philosophising still claimed to be open can in fact be followed. The overt aim of the work has been to show that there are no such openings left for philosophy; but its actual intention is to have this argument refute itself. The work tries to prove what it wishes to have disproven in the hope that the attempted proof constitutes a disproof of itself. This is what makes it a self-destructive argument, a *reductio-ad-absurdum*. Out of the utmost sceptical doubt, driven to the point of nothingness, it tries to wring something for philosophy; as in the tradition, scepticism is to be granted its Pyrrhic victory, which is also its defeat.

The main ways of continuing to philosophise have been rendered questionable by the destructive critiques in the body of this work. By implication some of these critiques also apply to the contemporary followers of Marx, Nietzsche, Heidegger and Wittgenstein. Here we shall briefly examine the neo-Nietzscheans of the school of Paris, the neo-Marxists of the Frankfurt school and the neo-Wittgensteinians of the school of the two Cambridges. In a later section we shall separately consider such hermeneuticist neo-Heideggerians as Gadamer. Each of the above schools has split up into an aesthetic wing and a quasi-scientific one, the one side seeking to push philosophy in the direction of literature, the other in the direction of the sciences. In the school of Paris such Deconstructionists as Derrida and de Man take the former tack, and those who follow Foucault the latter one; in the Frankfurt school there is an analogous opposition between Adorno and Habermas; in the school of the two Cambridges Cavell, and in a different way also Feyerabend, stand opposed to Toulmin and Kuhn. Each of these wings takes a different view of rationality, as we shall show. However, there is no clear-cut division between scienticists as rationalists and aestheticists as anti-rationalists; there are those, such as Adorno, who seek to maintain the autonomy of philosophy in a nice balance of art and science. Others, however, have already resigned themselves to the demise of philosophy and turned away from it to the history of science or the science of history, or alternatively to the art of criticism or the criticism of art.

In an article on Nietzsche, de Man puts it quite explicitly: 'philosophy turns out to be an endless reflection on its own destruction at the hands of literature'.[20] The reflection is endless because the destruction is 'a rhetorical mode . . . unable ever to escape from the rhetorical deceit it denounces'.[21] Philosophy, on this account, is trapped in figures of speech. Philosophy cannot get beyond or behind language, seen as figural and rhetorical, to some external realm of reference, to Truth, Being, or even Society; it is inextricably caught in language, that is, in the art and artifice of words. Hence, it is consigned to literature, the primary mode of the figural disposition of words. Like Polonius we ask: 'what is the matter?' in the book of philosophy, only to be told that it is 'words, words, words'. If it is nothing but words, 'this is the same as saying that it is structured as rhetoric. And since, if one wants to conserve the term "literature", one should not hesitate to assimilate it to rhetoric, then it follows that the deconstruction of metaphysics, or "philosophy", is an impossibility to the precise extent that it is "literary".'[22] So philosophy lives on because it is literature; it cannot be finally destroyed because the destructive attempt is itself a literary trope doomed to continuous self-repetition. But once one is aware of the internal irony of this literary game, why one should keep on playing it out is not explained.

Deconstruction is Derrida's term for the literary trope of textual decomposition. In practice it amounts to an aesthetic-critical way of uncovering and teasing out the basic ground-figures on which the discourse of a text is constructed. If the text is a philosophical one, the deconstructive activity seeks to find behind the argumentative rational surface of the discourse a partly concealed figure that is invariably ambivalent and works ironically against the seeming rationality of the surface. Such a figure may be a complex metaphor, such as the *'pharmakos'* in Plato's texts, which is ambivalently poison-medicine, scapegoat-saviour, victim-hero. All of Derrida's so-called anti-concepts are metaphors of this type: for example, supplement, margin, hymen, *parergon*, *differance*, writing. When the technique is applied to a metaphysical text the aim is to show that the central terms of the text, which supposedly denote real entities, essences or presences, are mere products of the structural play of the differences of the terms in the text, the *differances*, and that they are, therefore, meaning-empty rather than full, and indicate absences without any centre. For Derrida everything is text, either as pre-text, con-text or inter-text, for everything is 'writing', or what he calls *'arche-ecriture'*, so that language, too, is basically a writing rather than a speaking. Thus, Derrida takes literally, if this word any longer makes sense in the context, Freud's metaphor of the psyche tracing itself out like the toy called the mystic writing pad; perhaps 'tracing' would be a better word than 'writing', with its misleading connotations of an artificially devised script, for what Derrida has in mind. His own writings are increasingly becoming re-writings of other texts, thus *Glas* combines parallel commentaries on Hegel and Genet, and the reader has to fill in the correspondences and absent–present relations between them, one of which is Sartre. The most obvious literary model for this layered text is *Finnegan's Wake*, and, as in Joyce, multilingual puns figure prominently: Hegel, *aigle*, *eigen*, and so on. Like Joyce, Derrida seems much influenced by Renaissance thinking on signatures, letters, writing, marks, traces.

Foucault turns his back completely on this kind of philosophy, probably seeing it as a reactionary retreat to the Renaissance 'writing of things' — as in the book of the world — preceding classical discourse.[23] He also partly rejects philosophy in general: 'if philosophy is memory or a return of the origin, what I am doing cannot, in any way, be regarded as philosophy . . .'.[24] The archeology of knowledge has no need of philosophy for: 'instead of travelling over the field of discourses in order to recreate the suspended totalizations for its own use, instead of seeking in what has been said that *other* hidden discourse, which nevertheless remains the *same* (and instead of playing endlessly with *allegory* and tautology), it is continually making *differentiations*, it is a *diagnosis*'.[25] It is perhaps a little difficult to detect who or what this is directed against, but the general thrust is clear. For Foucault, not the elusive text but the material document is the object of knowledge, not the *arche* but the archive is its source. Not writing as rhetorical free-play, but language as the medium for the trans-mission of power in society is what is to be diagnosed. Language that gives rise to discourse, like the steam that powers the locomotive of society, is studied in respect of its rarification and condensation, its exteriority and accumulation; and, like the route traversed, it is surveyed in terms of 'the concepts of discontinuity, rupture, threshold limit, series and transformation'.[26] Hence, even though he claims that he has 'never presented archeology as a science, or even the beginning of a science . . .',[27] and that he has 'tried to reveal the specificity of a method that is neither formalizing nor interpretative . . .',[28] nevertheless the overwhelming impression is of a scientific undertaking. One feels oneself enclosed by the language of the interior of laboratories, pathology-chambers, documentary archives.

However, in Foucault's late work not even the neutral archeology of knowledge suffices to eradicate the last traces of philosophy in discourse, he aims for a 'political history of truth' as his own work becomes less scientific and more political. He sees truth as a product of power, and derides the view that 'truth does not belong to the order of power, but shares an original affinity with freedom: traditional themes in philosophy, which a "political history of truth" would have to overturn by showing that truth is not by nature free — nor error servile — but that its production is thoroughly imbued with relations of power'.[29] As in Nietzsche, will to truth is will to power, except that power is taken also in a Marxist manner. As in Marx, power depends on production; not the production of commodities, however, but rather, the production of discourse. Unlike Marx, Foucault does not subscribe to a progressive series of modes of production, nor to any evolutionary view of Progress, but he does consistently plot a series of historical stages or 'epistemes' separated by ruptures or revolutionary breaks. These are not Marx's ancient, feudal, capitalist and socialist stages of production, but rather temporal divisions into periods of medieval-renaissance, classical, modern and even post-modern. He seems an evolutionist *manqué*, *malgré lui même*. In his pre-1968 writings there is some apocalyptic suggestion that after the 'death of Man' there is to be a new post-modern stage superior to that of modernity, that 'something new is about to begin, something we glimpse only as a thin line of light low on the horizon'.[30] Later that suggestion disappeared as his work became more practically oriented and more concerned with prisons and sexuality, that is, with more immediate issues of personal liberation, which he pursued until his untimely death.

The school of Paris and the Frankfurt school, even though both are concerned with liberation, have little to do with each other; nevertheless, it is perhaps not altogether coincidental that in the latter, too, divisive tendencies towards art and science are now quite apparent. To exemplify the aesthetic trend we must return to Adorno for no one has continued that side of the school. Habermas, once his symbolic heir, has gone the other way and lacks an aesthetic dimension. These two aspects of the school, for so long contained together in its best work, such as the *Dialectic of Enlightenment*, seem now irreconcilable.

Adorno sought to balance out the respective claims of art and science in philosophy, but in his own philosophical work the tendency is indubitably towards art. As he himself puts it: 'as a corrective to the total rule of method, philosophy contains a playful element which the traditional view of it as science would like to exorcize'.[31] But it soon becomes obvious that this is more than just an element in his philosophy, since philosophy is dialectics and dialectics is a matter of language — which for Adorno is an aesthetic dimension — and so also bound to rhetoric. 'Dialectics — literally, language as the organon of thought — would mean to attempt a critical rescue of the rhetorical element, a mutual approximation of thing and expression, to the point where the difference fades'.[32] The critical rescue of the rhetorical element — that of language play and free creation — opens up the utopian possibility of the coincidence of word and thing, the ultimate dream of art.

This is what Adorno calls 'cognitive utopia',[33] the aesthetic promise of perfect expression, of the reconciliation of concept and object as well as subject and object; the adequation of name and thing, named in accord with Benjamin's demand for an eschatological fulfilment of language in art. 'Utopia would be above identity and above contradiction, it would be togetherness of diversity.'[34] Such a togetherness of diversity can only be attained in and through art; and for Adorno only in an art that bans images, in a poetry that is the opposite of '*ut pictura poesis*', perhaps only in music, for 'it is only in the absence of images that the full object can be conceived'.[35] Utopia is not 'to be positively pictured';[36] it is conceptually ineffable, intimations of it are only to be had in imageless art. So, too, the horrors of the modern world are not to be conceived, but registered in art. In the face of these horrors, 'what art, notably the art decried as nihilistic, says in refraining from judgement is that everything is not just nothing'.[37] Art has the last and first word in Adorno's philosophy and the major claim to truth.

In Habermas it is science that seems to be increasingly winning out over philosophy, even though, as one commentator puts it, he tries to locate himself 'between science and philosophy'.[38] He also undertakes to relate this science to politics, to combine an 'empirical philosophy of history with a practical (political) intent'.[39] This empirical philosophy of history has become an evolutionary systems theory as the influence of Parsonian functionalism, Piaget's neo-structuralist learning psychology and other developmental, Ego and social psychologies are combined with a Marxism reconstituted into an evolutionary science.[40] The main stages of human progress are conceived of as stages of learning maturation through which all societies have to pass, at their own speed and with divergencies of cultural variations, much in the way that children have to pass through Piaget's learning stages. These stages apply to all the human social and cultural dimensions, to the cognitive, psychological, practical-moral, and aesthetic. For Habermas the world divides into three fundamental dimensions determined on the basis of the developed, rational, categorial distinctions between the natural world that is known instrumentally, the social world that is known communicatively, and the inner, subjective world that is expressively known. For each of these he supplies tables setting out the main stages of rational development over the whole course of human progress. This evolutionary progressive pattern must apply to every society, since each one has sooner or later to come up against the same set of predicaments or problems, that is, critical developmental junctures which it either solves and so advances, or fails to solve and so becomes retarded. History is the school for the education of mankind. Habermas' approach seems highly reminiscent of that of Hobhouse, whom he does not seem to know, an earlier exponent of social evolution and moral progress, as in his main book, *Morals in Evolution*.[41]

However, what distinguishes Habermas' work from all earlier evolutionists is his emphasis on language, or, more specifically, what he calls the universal pragmatics of communicative actions. What he aims for in this respect is to undertake 'the reconstructive procedure of sciences that transform a practically mastered pre-theoretical knowledge (know-how) of competent subjects into an objective and explicit knowledge (know-that) to an extent sufficient to make clear in what sense I am using the expression *formal analysis*'.[42] The scientific intent is clear, since Habermas aligns himself with 'the Chomskian program for a general science of language as the rational reconstruction of linguistic competence'.[43] He, therefore, aims to extend the programme of scientific linguistics and complete it with a parallel science of universal pragmatics, the science of speech-acts, working on the assumption that 'the competence to employ sentences in speech acts . . . communicative competence has just as universal a core as linguistic competence'.[44] The issue remains, however, not whether there is a universal core to speech-acts, for it is possible, perhaps, to discover universally prevalent features of all language use — such as the distinction between questions, statements and commands — but rather, whether such discoveries are of any scientific importance. It is possible that they will prove merely trivial as compared with the richly structured resources of phonetics and grammar, available in every language and the subjectmatter for the already developed science of linguistics. Alternatively, if the results of the putative new universal-pragmatics of speech-acts are not merely trivial specifications of the most general possible features of all speech, and if these results prove to be of sufficient significance to lead to the discovery of things we do not already know, then what is to guarantee the formal scientific character of such an interpretative procedure? It might well be argued that the findings so far of speech-act theorists such as Austin, Searle and others are either trivial or non-scientific. Why should all language know-how or 'pre-theoretical knowledge' be transformable into 'an objective and explicit knowledge' capable of sustaining a science? Might not non-scientific interpretative approaches be better suited to the investigation of language beyond the limited extent already reached by linguistics? Wittgenstein never claimed scientific status for his linguistic investigations; he thought they amounted to no more than 'assembling reminders for a particular purpose', where it was the purpose that mattered not the reminders, yet he did uncover features of language that no science could have discovered.

Thus it is ironic perhaps that the innovative influence that Wittgenstein has exerted on the school of the two Cambridges has largely gone into the philosophy of science. Beginning with his oldest disciples, such as von Wright and Toulmin, other younger Wittgensteinians have carried through a veritable transformation in the philosophy of science, giving it a strongly historical emphasis, remote from former concern with methodology or even the contemporary methods of the sciences. Beginning with Hanson, then Kuhn and finally the 'maverick' Feyerabend, the philosophy of science has become a specialist historical academic discipline. Hanson, an acknowledged Wittgensteinian, took up his remarks on aspect switches and applied them to scientific observation. Kuhn, as Toulmin has shown, took up Wittgenstein's term 'paradigm' and charged it at first with revolutionary impetus, which he has since modified, as he himself puts it, into 'a view of scientific development that is fundamentally evolutionary'.[45] Feyerabend has taken up Kuhn's early view of epistemic breaks, and has pushed it to the extreme of maintaining the total incommensurability of rival major theories. This he has sought to buttress with Wittgensteinian ideas of language-games as distinct 'forms of life' or incompatible language-worlds. As he puts it, 'it was Wittgenstein's great merit . . . to have emphasized that science contains not only formulae and rules for their application but entire traditions. Kuhn has expanded the criticism and made it more concrete.'[46] Feyerabend himself develops the more aesthetic aspects of Wittgenstein's philosophy in his approach to scientific traditions, which he considers as not much different from artistic traditions. For him scientific forms, like forms of art, do not cumulatively add up to any evolutionary rational progress.

This is precisely the line that Toulmin develops: 'the evolution of human understanding, as represented by the historical growth of concepts'.[47] The concepts Toulmin is concerned with are mainly those of the sciences. In respect of these he is a rational progressivist; he sees the natural sciences as the ones that have attained 'disciplinary maturity'[48] and the social sciences and other disciplines as lagging behind, but potentially capable of eventually catching up. Rational progress comes about through the evolution of concepts, and this he takes in a literal Darwinian sense, unlike Habermas, for whom evolution means historical development in stages; Toulmin applies rigorously the ecological-biological model to history and speaks of population selection, adaptation, lines of descent of intellectual disciplines seen as species, and gives genealogical tables of concepts seen as kinds. There is some licence in Wittgenstein himself for treating history as natural history, but he never speaks of the natural history of concepts. Thus, Toulmin's view of epistemology, and perhaps the whole of philosophy, is that of a quasi-scientific evolutionary history, and this he considers 'a new theory of human understanding'.[49]

As he puts it, 'this means treating society as a historical species developing more or less "compactly" in response to changing historical demands'.[50] He recommends 'paying proper attention to the population mechanisms by which representative sets of institutions, practices and concepts are transformed in the transition from one temporal cross-section to the next; and the criteria for deciding whether, having regard to the "demands" of the relevant situation, these changes took place in a more or less "well-adapted" manner".[51] Unfortunately, the two key terms 'demands of the relevant situation' and 'well-adapted manner' cannot be given any definite meaning in 'discussions of social, cultural and intellectual change'[52] to which they are referred. To view a social phenomenon or historical event as well-adapted explains nothing, since every such entity that actually occurs is adapted to its situation and meets its demands, for otherwise it would not have happened. Survival of the fittest in this context means simply the survival of those that did survive, since there is no independent way of specifying fitness. With natural species it is possible to specify the conditions that make for survival or extinction quite independently of whether a given species does or does not meet them. Clearly, scarcity of food in the environment, space, breeding rate and physical characteristics play a leading part in whether a given species thrives or becomes extinct. In the case of concepts, institutions and customs it is not possible to specify independently conditions which will select some and not others; all are equally suitable for any historical purpose one cares to envisage. Toulmin thinks he can specify such conditions of selection in the 'problems' that concepts, institutions or customs are best fitted for solving or overcoming. But no human problem is simply given; it has to arise within a specific and often unique historical and conceptual context; it has to be interpreted or defined as problematical before it can be said even to exist and need to be solved; and, so, it itself depends on the very social setting and language that will provide its potential solution. There are no problems which are given by nature or by history to humanity as such to be overcome; men have to create the problems they wish to solve, and in different societies they create different problems for themselves. This is perhaps the ultimate argument against all evolutionary approaches to history.

By contrast, as we have seen, Feyerabend denies any evolutionary rational progress in science or in any other mode of human knowledge. Like Kuhn, he insists on changing 'paradigms' or basic cosmologies which cannot be measured by any 'universal and stable rationality',[53] since they 'involve a changing rationality'.[54] He sees Man as 'the inventor not only of laws, theories, pictures, plays, forms of music, ways of dealing with his fellow man, institutions but also of entire world views, he is the inventor of entire forms of life'.[55] The scientific forms, like the forms of art, simply do not add up, but remain separate dramatic figures, play-worlds which we either accept or reject *in toto*. Feyerabend has radically extended Wittgenstein's notion of the language-game, and has taken literally his fictive anthropology of tribes speaking such language-games, with the result that he interprets scientific theories as the language-games of 'tribes' of scientists, each with its own procedures for establishing truth and falsity. He is thus compelled to deny that science has a different kind of history from myth, religion, artistic traditions or any of the forms we generally consider irrational. Science is seen as simply the mythology of modern man. His position is at the opposite extreme to Toulmin's.

Cavell too has aestheticised epistemology, but in a different way, since he is not concerned with science but with art. The traditional epistemological problem of how we know other minds becomes for him an existential issue of interpersonal acknowledgement; thus the problem the epistemological sceptic raises is the same one that the tragic dramatist represents:

> . . . both skepticism and tragedy conclude with the condition of human separation, with the discovery that I am I; and the fact that the alternative to my acknowledgement of the other is not my ignorance of him but my avoidance of him, call it my denial of him. Acknowledgement is to be studied, is what is studied, in the avoidance that tragedy studies.[56]

Philosophy and art are, thus, ultimately identical, and the discourses of epistemology and drama come to the same; the philosopher's 'problem is to discover the specific plight of mind and circumstance within which a human being gives voice to his condition'.[57] As a result it becomes very difficult to specify the precise status of this key term 'acknowledgement': is it the ordinary social term where what is acknowledged is someone's claim to something or the status of a person; or a literary-critical term referring to a certain kind of attitude; or a psychiatric term for a certain state of mind; or 'the sort of concept Heidegger calls an existentiale';[58] or a conceptual term for the essential 'grammatic' features of concepts in Wittgenstein's sense? Cavell seem to want it to be all of these at once. Perhaps the story of Pygmalion brings out why 'acknowledgement' cannot have all these senses at once: Pygmalion certainly acknowledged the statue as living, but he failed to ascertain the grounds for such an acknowledgement — he was too little of a philosophical sceptic. In other words, the issues that scepticism raises are not the same as those which tragedy represents; for whereas tragedy is concerned with how one human being is to relate to another, scepticism asks in a purely rational spirit what human beings are as contrasted with other things. Cavell cannot, therefore, convincingly 'juxtapose'[59] a philosophical essay on 'other minds' with a literary one on love and separation in *Lear*, and read the play as providing an 'answer' to the problem of the existence of an external world; one which is strikingly like Cavell's own previously presented answer to the problem of other minds: 'the world is to be *accepted*, as the presentness of other minds is not to be known, but acknowledged'.[60]

In all of the separate schools thus far outlined there seem to be similar themes emerging. On the scientific wing of each school the issue of evolution, or at least of stages of historical development, is common to Toulmin, Habermas and, in a somewhat disguised way, even to Foucault. On the aesthetic wing, the issue of rhetoric has re-emerged, after a long historical abeyance, in Derrida, Adorno and even Feyerabend. Are we witnessing the convergence of philosophy onto a few broad issues? It hardly seems so, since each school deals with these issues in its own way. But neither can it be a sheer coincidence. Perhaps it is partly to be accounted for by an issue common to all thinkers now, namely the problem of rationality, which has reached a critical stage not only in thought but also in all other dimensions of social and cultural life.

The contemporary debate concerning the state of philosophy is increasingly being fought out on the issue of the nature and status of rationality. As might have been expected, those who see philosophy in scientific terms, with some notable exceptions, favour rationalism and rational progress; they usually insist on the full panoply of rational argument, logic and conceptual definition. Whereas those who favour a philosophy tending more to art and literary criticism seek to sever the bonds of philosophy and rationality, to be sceptical of the claims of reason altogether and to conceive of philosophy more in terms of rhetoric and figurative language. It is not surprising that rationality in philosophy should be the issue in an age when rationality has been almost completely appropriated by the sciences and philosophy is threatened with exclusion. Some philosophers have accepted this as a *fait accompli* and separated philosophy from rationality; others have sought to recover for philosophy a rationality equal to that of the sciences. Both courses are open to criticism, for though philosophy cannot be as strictly rational as the sciences, neither can it forgo all claim to rationality. It must seek a rationality of its own.

Among the contemporary schools the most intense attacks against rationality in philosophy have come from the neo-Nietzscheans. Both wings of the school of Paris have on different grounds sought to deny the traditional philosophical claim to Reason, and have referred themselves to Nietzsche for support. But there is a difference between the two sides: Foucault with his scientific leaning not surprisingly appears as an exponent of many kinds of rationalisation, whereas Derrida emerges as an anti-rationalist.

In his account of Aristotle's logic, Derrida is quite explicit that the categories as figures (*skhemata*) are inherently the same as figures of speech or tropes, and that rationality, too, is ultimately a matter of figures.

> Categories are figures (skhemata) by means of which being properly speaking is expressed insofar as it is expressed through several twists, several tropes. The system of categories is the system of the ways in which being is construed. It relates the problematic of the analogy of being — its equivocality and univocality — with the problematic of the metaphor in general. Aristotle links them together explicitly by affirming that the best metaphor is prescribed according to analogies of proportionality. This would suffice to prove that the question of metaphor is no more marginal to metaphysics than metaphorical style and figurative usage are accessory embellishments or secondary aids to philosophical discourse.[61]

It is immaterial to us in this context whether this is an adequate reading of Aristotle. It reveals what Derrida understands as metaphor and how he uses it to justify his practice of reading philosophical texts as if they were literary. He has a transcendental notion of metaphor; he does not consider it as merely a figure of speech or even as a linguistic form, but regards 'metaphor as the very structure or condition of possibility of all language and concepts'.[62] Hence, all of rationality — logic, method, science — is in the last resort metaphorical. This transcendental notion of metaphor derives from Heidegger's insistence that 'poetry' and 'thought' are more fundamental to language than mere linguistics. Derrida tries to combine this Heideggerian view with Nietzsche's early view that language is basically metaphoric because it involves the transference of a word from one thing to another. The root meaning of 'metaphor' is what he had in mind. In later Nietzsche this metaphoric view of language is abandoned in favour of a perspectival and pragmatic approach which sees language as the creation of fictions useful from the point of view of power centres. Derrida quotes Nietzsche approvingly to this effect:

> Logic is only slavery within the bounds of language. Language has within it, however, an illogical element, the metaphor. Its

principal force brings about an indentification of the non-identical; it is thus an operation of the imagination. It is on this that the existence of concepts, forms, etc. rests.[63]

Derrida tries to square Nietzsche's view of logic as based on identifying what is different with Heidegger's very different view of language as founded on a primordial poetry and thought. As so often in his writings, he wants to give allegiance to both at the same time. So he treats both as 'textual strategies' to which he can turn at will. Derrida, like Nietzsche, 'must resort to philosophical schemes (for example the arbitrariness of the sign or the emancipation of thought from a given language)' in 'his critical campaign against metaphysics'.[64] De Man, by contrast, seems content with Nietzsche alone; for him truth and rationality are metaphors in the figurative linguistic sense; he quotes with approval the early Nietzsche as saying that 'truths are illusions whose illusionary nature has been forgotten, metaphors that have been used up and have lost their imprint and that now operate as mere metal, no longer as coins'.[65]

Foucault follows not the early Nietzsche of rhetoric and metaphor, but the late Nietzsche of the will to truth as will to power. On this view, concepts, logic and rationality as such are instruments of utility and power. Foucault expresses himself strongly against any transcendental Reason: 'the essential task was to free the history of thought from its subjection to transcendence'.[66] Nevertheless, he is in favour of many of the forms of rationalisation in the sciences, such as formalisation and strict method; he prefers stricter sciences — biology, economics and linguistics, for example — to such humanistically inclined ones as psychology or sociology, which he considers not even sciences but mere 'positivities', destined soon to disappear. In other words, he proposes to rationalise the sciences so as to eliminate from them not merely metaphysics, but any trace of humanism as well. Foucault, however, does not think of rationalisation as a progressive historical process; he implicitly denies that such a process is possible He thinks in terms of discontinuous stages, or 'epistemes', following each other like tableaux on a stage, each its own presentation, not necessarily related to what came before. On these grounds, it seems that he would deny any continuous history of rationality. His view begins to approach from the opposite direction that of the early Kuhn and Feyerabend.

Both Foucault and Kuhn take off from Bachelard's theory of epistemological ruptures. Kuhn elaborates this in a neo-

Wittgensteinian way in terms of paradigm changes, whereas Foucault works on the basis of a Lévi-Straussian Structuralism. Thus Foucault always treats clusters of sciences as comprising the one epistemic structure, whereas Kuhn considers each individually, since a paradigm can only belong to the one science. Both refer scientific rationality and truth to power; Kuhn does so sociologically by reference to the group-power of 'invisible colleges' of scientists, whereas Foucault, as we have shown, understands power more as do Marx and Nietzsche. Feyerabend goes even further than early Kuhn in the direction of scepticism when treating rationality. He even treats his own arguments as rhetorical ploys in a manner worthy of the ancient Sophists and Sceptics whom he admires: 'An argument is not a confession, it is an instrument designed to make an opponent change his mind.'[67] It seems, then, it does not really matter whether the argument attains a true conclusion provided it serves its persuasive purpose. Other neo-Wittgensteinians have argued for complete rational relativism; for example Winch, who on anthropological grounds considers each tribe to have its own language-game with its own norms of correctness, and so, therefore, its own standards of rationality.[68]

The older Wittgensteinians have tended to be overly rationalistic, and some have fallen back into traditionalist or positivist stances. Toulmin has gone in a different direction, in keeping with his evolutionist approach. Rationality for him is the capacity to change and adapt, presumably in an evolutionary progressive direction; and, as we shall see, he can provide no way of knowing which this is to be. He repeatedly insists that it is not any set of concepts, methods, logics, or any other fixed procedures that make a scientific discipline rational, or, for that matter, the whole development of science rational. Rather, it is the capacity of the particular discipline, or science as such, to abandon any given intellectual tools when they prove ineffective and to evolve new ones better fitted for solving the new problems. Thus, the rational progress of science is the succession of changing problems and their changing solutions. What is a problem and what is its solution is to be decided by the acknowledged scientists.

This account of problems and their solutions is itself problematic. How is one to tell whether the problems and solutions put forward by scientists in fact advance science in a rational way or whether they turn science in a regressive or even irrational direction? In other words, what is to ensure that a change of scientific procedure is an instance of greater rational flexibility, rather than an abandonment of rational standards altogether, especially in view of the fact that scientists are frequently themselves in disagreement on this matter at a period of theoretical innovation? Toulmin provides two further positive conditions for ascertaining what is the satisfactory solution of a problem: that the solution should meet practical demands, and that it should prove fruitful in the future.[69] Unfortunately, neither of these stipulations removes the evolutionary impasse. 'Being more fruitful in the future' is a present prophecy and not a criterion for deciding at present which is the more rational solution. And 'meeting practical demands' reintroduces 'verificationism' in the guise of practical utility. As we have already indicated, rationality cannot be determined by reference to problems and solutions because problems only exist within a pre-established framework, rational or otherwise. It is our accepted standard of rationality that determines what is a problem for us and what is an adequate solution, not vice-versa. Biological evolution offers no analogy: such 'problems' are not given by nature; nor are there universal problems common to all humanity. Toulmin's approach to rationality has to make both these assumptions:

> It assumes, for instance, that men's lives do face them, in certain significant respects, with some very general but common problems, regardless of the milieu; and that these shared problems call for the development of corresponding sorts of techniques, concepts and procedures. It, assumes furthermore, that men's collective rational enterprises can legitimately be regarded as so many attacks — whether in parallel cultures or successive epochs — on those common problems.[70]

Neither assumption is, however, warranted, for each takes for granted an extremely dubious view of history, which at best applies only to material developments. Technology is perhaps partly explicable in this way, not science.

In the Frankfurt school, Habermas seems to be impelled to a similar view of the universality of the problems that societies have to face as they develop. He identifies basically two types: those of an instrumental-technical nature and those of a communicative nature. The solutions to the former give rise to instrumental rationality, which is embodied in purposive-rational action, 'that is, in technologies, strategies, organizations and qualifications',[71] as explained by the theories of Marx and Weber. The solutions to the latter give rise to communicative rationality, which comprises 'the rationality structures that find expression in world views, moral representations, and identity formations, that become practically effective in social movements and are finally embodied in institutional systems . . .'.[72] Habermas thus believes in rational progress in all aspects of human history: in morals, politics, law, art and even the development of personality. The highest stage of rational progress has been reached in the modern period when 'for the first time, the universalistic potential already contained in the rationalised world view could be set free . . . the unity of theoretical and practical reason then became the key problem for modern world interpretations, which lost their character *as* world views'.[73]

The rational progress of Man is propelled by the reason inherent in all language and communicative action: 'in action oriented to reaching understanding, validity claims are "always already" implicitly raised . . . In these validity claims communication theory can locate a gentle but obstinate, a never silent although seldom redeemed claim to reason, a claim that must be recognised de facto whenever and wherever there is to be consensual action.'[74] These 'latently available structures of rationality are transposed into social practice'[75] through the learning process which all of mankind has to pass in resolving the problems and crises of evolutionary development. Habermas does not wish to deny the possibility of differing cultural contents in such resolutions, but he insists that 'every culture must share the formal properties of modern rationality if it is to attain self-consciousness, sublimation or reflexive awareness'.[76] There is, therefore, in Habermas' project to develop a new theory of communicative rationality more than a hint of Hegel in modern guise: reason is the driving force of history and what it attains to is ever greater self-consciousness.

Habermas' communicative rationality must also be seen as an attempt to redeem rationality from the strictures of the earlier Frankfurt school thinkers, who attacked it as instrumental rationality, modern rationalisation and the logos of *techne*. It is true that despite their wholesale critique of the 'nexus of rationality and social actuality, and what is inseparable therefrom — that of nature and the mastery of nature',[77] Adorno and Horkheimer were committed to 'a positive notion of enlightenment which will release it from entanglement in blind domination'.[78] Their own work was devoted to this positive notion of enlightenment by furthering critical reason in the form of negative dialectic. However, in his final work (bearing that title) Adorno had already greatly reduced his expectations in this respect; and Horkheimer shared this pessimism, for they both wrote in a joint new preface to the *Dialectic of Enlightenment* that their 'prognosis of the related conversion of enlightenment into positivism, the myth of things as they actually are and finally the identification of intellect and that which is inimical to the spirit, has been overwhelmingly confirmed', and they add that their 'conception of history does not presume any dispensation from it . . .'.[79] Critical reason itself is no longer exempt from the new ideologies, which as linguistic jargons invade all of consciousness. True reason and real enlightenment are now put off into the indefinite future as mere utopian possibilities.

Since it is realisable only in utopia, rationality becomes an aesthetic matter for Adorno. The utopian intimation of rationality survives in the present horrors of modern rationalisation only in its most basic form as discrimination, which 'provides a haven for the mimetic element of knowledge',[80] that is, the aesthetic element. Discrimination is the irreducible minimum of all knowledge and rationality; 'a discriminating man is one who in the matter and its concept can distinguish even the infinitesimal, that which escapes the concept . . .'[81] Without this element 'the unleashed rationality would be irrational'.[82]

> In the total process of enlightenment this element gradually crumbles. But it cannot vanish completely if the process is not to annul itself. Even in the conception of rational knowledge, devoid of all affinity, there survives a groping for that concordance which the magical delusion used to place beyond doubt.[83]

The utopian promise of that concordance when 'the mimetic element blends with the rational one'[84] is retained only in discrimination.

Thus, in the Frankfurt school, too, as in all the others, there is now a deep ambivalence on the subject of rationality. Each school divides into a scientistic and an aestheticist faction. The mutual interrelation of reason and art, of discursive argumentation and aesthetic model, in philosophy is no longer understood or practised.

2. Philosophical Functions

Philosophies that seek to collapse language into rhetoric or poetics are in danger of losing all claim to rationality and degenerating into an intellectualised mode of literary criticism, if not into bad art. Just as those philosophies which try to rationalise philosophy by making it rigorous and subject to logic and scientific method are in the complementary danger of becoming secondary sciences, as the fate of Positivism has shown. Philosophy must sustain both sides of its contradictory being. A philosophy without such rational means as the argument, the definition and strict concepts is quasi-aesthetic and bereft of all compellingness. On the other hand, philosophy cannot do without what Adorno calls the aesthetic elements of form and expressive language, for otherwise it becomes an intellectualised system, or what is really a mere systematic table of concepts incapable of expression.

Given, then, that philosophy cannot simply appropriate scientific rationality for its own use, where is a distinctly philosophical form of rationality to come from? It must start from the reflexive moment of philosophy itself — in this present predicament, from the self-critical effort philosophy must make to think through its own failure. As Horkheimer put it, '. . . in such self-critique reason will remain faithful to itself'.[85] In this way modern philosophy at the very moment of faltering remains true to the primary impulses of rationality towards reflexivity and self-recollection, which are no longer sustained in the prevailing scientific Rationalisation. The very impossibility of continuing to philosophise becomes the source of the critical resources of a rationality that may provide a way of continuing to philosophise. Out of its own failure philosophy has to derive the means of sustaining itself; it must capitalise on its own bankruptcy and, like Falstaff, 'turn disease into a commodity'.

Philosophy remains rational so long as it continues critically to reflect on its own inability to sustain its claim to a higher Reason. The self-critique of philosophy is no longer the critique of Pure Reason, it is the critique of Reason itself. That critique begins with the attack on the categories of Reason launched by Nietzsche and continued by Wittgenstein, and it concludes with the attempt to destroy philosophy itself. We have sought to radicalise this procedure and turn the destructive thrust back on the destroyers themselves. Their attempts to continue philosophising have been shown to be impossible; their assumptions concerning values or language have been undermined; thus once the destroyers have been themselves destroyed, it seems that there must be an end to philosophy.

But it is precisely by pushing philosophy to the end that philosophy rediscovers its ends. The germ of a new possibility of philosophical rationality lies in the destructive critique of philosophy. 'It is a critique of philosophy, and therefore refuses to abandon philosophy.'[86] The destructive critique of language-forms by the methods of conceptual dissolution, deconstituting, reducing, etc. holds in its workings the key to a new mode of self-critical rationality. We have shown how this destructive rationality functions in the *reductio-ad-absurdum* arguments against the Logos and the Cogito, the fundamental principles of Reason and Rationalism. This reduction is no longer to be taken in the classic sense of deriving a conclusion that is absurd, in that it is counter to Reason; but, rather, in a modern sense of absurdity, that is, as a reduction to Nothing in a nihilistic signification. It still remains a rational mode, even though it is an argument against Reason, for it exemplifies the reflexive workings of the self-critique of philosophical rationality. Beginning as a critique of the language of metaphysics and as a destruction of metaphysical concepts, it can be further generalised into a critique of language in general.

The importance of such a critique of language is not merely, as Wittgenstein supposed, of internal relevance to philosophy alone, serving to dissolve the puzzles and temptations that befuddle the ordinary clear-sighted understanding; it is, furthermore, as Nietzsche knew, part of the ongoing critique of culture that is one of the expressions of modern Nihilism. Nietzsche took on this destructive function as his own primary task; the critique of language was for him a matter of destroying the ideals and idols that figured as the values on which the languages of Western decadence were based. Thus, his view of language critique was over-simple — just a destruction of values — even allowing for the complexities of the eschatology of inversion and re-inversion by which he explains how this takes place. Nietzsche thought it was simply a matter of exposing the lies of Western civilisation — the fictions of metaphysics and religion imposed by philosophers and priests — by revealing the realities they subserved, primarily the will to power. His notion of destructive critique is, thus, at one with all the other modern techniques of exposure, such as demystification, unmasking and ideology-critique; and all of these misinterpret themselves and misconceive their own procedures. They all assume that basic reality is given, but hidden or disguised by some covering 'lie'; all that is needed then for reality to be 'discovered' or revealed is for the lies to be 'uncovered' or exposed. What this reality amounts to differs from 'exposeur' to 'exposeur'; for Nietzsche it is this-world of appearance, temporality, mortality and the body. But, as we shall argue, these are far from simply being 'there' or 'given'; in this respect they are like the reality of language, which was not really 'there' until it was 'discovered' in the very process of the destruction of metaphysics, behind which it had been hiding.

The destruction of metaphysics is simultaneously the exposure of the idea of language; but this exposure is not the revelation of a pre-existing reality of language, there all the while simply waiting to be found. The discovery is at the same time a kind of constitution, in that it is only the conceptualisation and awareness of language that makes it real. It is true of all symbolic realities that they are not real until they are realised. Prior to their realisation they can only be said to be potentially there without as yet having any actuality. Language in the sense in which we understand it now was only potentially given prior to the modern realisation which constituted it. And this constitution could only have been achieved through the deconstitution of metaphysics. Metaphysics hid language because it was itself a form of language mystified and sublimated, whose self-reflexive purpose it was to hide from itself that it was nothing but a disguised form of language. And so, too, metaphysical Reason was the idealisation of the rational language forms; the Logos was words taken as the Word. It was only with the destruction of the Logos and of metaphysics as reflecting a higher order of reality that its being as language could have been grasped. In this process language itself was grasped; it revealed itself for the very first time. Language could only have been realised through a process which first required it to be disguised as metaphysics and then required this disguise to be destroyed — so language would stand revealed. It was covered over only to be discovered, but prior to the discovery it was not yet there. Its truth is a lie belied.

All such symbolic realities can only be discovered in the negative, that is, through a process of negation whereby they are first denied, or acknowledged in denial — only then, when the denial is in turn denied, to be revealed or acknowledged positively. This denial may take many forms; it may be an ideological masking, a conceptual sublimation, or idealisation, or a symbolic substitution, or rejection, or any of the other modes of negation that such diverse thinkers as Marx, Nietzsche and Freud have identified. The negation of the denial, or the exposure of 'truth', is the work of the relevant mode of critique. The various kinds of critique go under the well-known names of ideological demystification, de-sublimation, dissolution, destruction, deconstitution and deconstruction. Each of these exemplifies a different form of modern critical rationality. Every such form of rationality constitutes its entities as negative realities through its act of critique. It forms 'nothings' through its reduction, which is, thus, literally a *reductio-ad-absurdum*.

This process of critically constituting by deconstituting has its close analogues in the psychoanalytic conception of the workings of the psyche, which, as we shall later see, provide a close parallel to the workings of language in general. In the psyche the realities of the repressed unconscious only reveal themselves through the exposure of their own censored, disguised and distorted manifestations, in conscious phenomena such as dreams, symptoms, parapraxes. The exposure of the repressed takes place in the negative through a kind of critical working-through of the manifest content to reveal the latent one. But in so far as the unconscious content is merely latent, it is only potential; it becomes actual through the very process whereby it is made conscious. The return of the repressed in analysis is a formation of that which is as yet unformed but struggling to achieve form. Language plays a crucial role in all this, as Lacan has made us aware. And this is why, as we shall show later, there are such close analogues between psychic repression and exposure and symbolic repression and exposure, and also between the return of the repressed and the discovery of the hidden. These will enable us eventually to take psychoanalysis as a model for language-analysis.

Language-analysis or the critique of language is the main mode of the operation of critical reason in philosophy. In elaborating it we are discovering a new form of critical rationality, and simultaneously a new way of philosophising. This discovery, as we have shown, proceeds directly from a self-critique of philosophy, which begins with the destruction of metaphysics and goes on to a wholesale questioning of the possibility of philosophising as such. By reflecting on its end philosophy can rediscover its ends. Such self-recollection might be exemplary for culture as a whole, just as the self-critique of philosophy might be developed into a self-critique of society at large. Language-analysis need not stop with the critique of higher concepts, but can be expanded into a critique of all our symbolic forms, as we shall go on to show in Chapter 6.

Philosophy alone can perform this function, though it need not be the professional philosopher who carries it out. Some are even now fulfilling it who would not deign to call themselves philosophers. Their work must be discovered by being identified for what it is and assigned its proper designation, which is in itself work for a philosopher. Even within the confines of academic philosophy departments there is much that can be done. The traditional pretensions of the university to universal Reason — which academic philosophy backs up — need to be exposed from within, and its new statist role revealed beneath the trappings of traditional decorum.[87]

This critical role of philosophy is merely the prelude to its other ends. The critical function of language-analysis both presupposes and develops into another of the ends of philosophy; this takes the dual form of translation and mediation. Mediation, a term derived from the now nearly defunct tradition of dialectical Reason, indicates another form of philosophical rationality, one which gives philosophy a new function to perform in mediating between the specialised sciences. For this, translation is indispensable since direct communication between the sciences is now impossible; their 'languages' are too far removed for direct accessibility.

Any kind of criticism already presupposes some mode of translation, for even the initial comprehension of the terms to be criticised requires some degree of transmission of meaning. Language-analysis cannot even begin if what is to be analysed is not first understood in some preliminary manner by being transposed into terms that are already known and familiar. This transposition is analogous to translating from one spoken language into another. But this is no more than an analogy, not the equivalence Steiner claims it to be when he insists that 'a human being performs an act of translation, in the full sense of the word, when receiving a speech-message from any other human being',[88] and that 'inside or between languages, human communication equals translation'.[89] Steiner makes it his key point by not distinguishing the various senses of 'translation' — failing, that is, to discriminate between such distinct notions as understanding, rendering, interpreting, transposing and philosophically translating or mediating. These are all closely related to each other, as well as to translating in the literal sense, and shedding light on the one activity also illuminates the others, but they are not all identical; the differences are equally important and need to be shown up. Ordinary interlingual translating is merely a model for philosophical translation. Translating on this higher level is not simply a matter of finding in one given language the already available terms most appropriate for those of another language; rather it requires creating intermediate concepts able to comprehend those to be understood. This is what brings philosophical translation close to dialectical mediation.

To treat all translating as literally the translation from one language into another, as Steiner does, must inevitably mean ending up with a last terminus of translation, and this would have to be a private-language. For, ultimately, if every act of understanding requires an act of translation in this sense, then even the understanding of one's natural language will call for a translation which can only be into a private-language. Steiner comes to this conclusion himself:

> Thus, in a general sense, though not in that of the Wittgenstein-Malcolm argument, there is 'private language' and an essential part of all natural language is private. This is why there will be in every complete speech-act a more or less prominent element of translation. All communication 'interprets between privacies'.[90]

Unfortunately, if all communication without exception interprets between privacies then the private-language in question is of the Wittgensteinian kind. For, if even communicating in a common language means translating, then it can only be translating into a private-language understandable to oneself alone. And, thus, the private-language argument can be applied explicitly, for the regress of translations must continue: the private-language, too, must be understood, and if that understanding is in turn another translating, then there will have to be another language of second order privacy into which it can be translated . . . and so on relentlessly.

One must therefore conceptually distinguish literal translation from one language into another from other senses of translation, in particular from reading and philosophic translation. Nevertheless, an overall theory of translation must cover all these modes, or, as Gadamer puts it: 'the many-layered problem of translation became for me the model for the linguisticality of all human behaviour in the world'.[91] The central issue in this many-layered tier is that of reading as translation; reading a text that is not immediately comprehensible calls for a mode of translation since to be understood the original text has to be transposed into another, the gloss, in which the understanding is expressed. Many schools of modern philosophy have explicitly or implicitly elaborated theories of translation, either under that name or a cognate term; one could refer to the phenomenological, hermeneutic and structural-linguistic approaches, as well as to the various related dialectical schools ranging from neo-Hegelianism to the Frankfurt school. The two diametrically opposed theories of translation are the hermeneutic and the structural-linguistic; they adopt contrasting approaches to the reading or decoding of texts in particular. Both these theories bring out important aspects of reading, but both exaggerate and seek to make their chosen features explain everything. Another theory will be required to embrace both, and this we will call the comprehending approach to reading.

Steiner is the exponent of a hermeneutic approach to reading as translating: 'it must remain a selective, highly intuitive proceeding, at the very best self-conscious of its restricted, and, in certain regards, fictional status. It hinges, in Schleiermacher's phrase, on the "art of hearing".'[92] As its name indicates, this approach derives historically from biblical interpretation, and has since been elaborated largely in the German tradition, first by Schleiermacher, then by Dilthey, Heidegger and finally Gadamer, its leading contemporary exponent. According to Gadamer no reading can even begin without prejudices or pre-judgements: '. . . the historicity of our existence entails that prejudices, in the literal sense of the word, constitute the initial directedness of our whole ability to experience . . . they are simply conditions whereby we experience something — whereby what we encounter says something to us'.[93] These prejudices are derived from the tradition in which the interpreter happens to stand, and which he cannot, therefore, completely rule out. He cannot eliminate them; he can merely modify his prejudices by altering his traditional inheritance. From these prejudices derive the initial assumptions and presuppositions as to the meaning of something with which the reading of a text begins. The act of reading can, however, correct and change the initial assumptions, and so modify one's prejudices; for an assumption is like a question posed to the text which can, as it were, receive a reply from the text, and according to this reply it will need to be adjusted to make it fit the text better. Heidegger has dubbed this process the hermeneutical circle, for there is no escape from it if one wishes to understand.

Thus, all in all, hermeneutics is a tradition-bound approach that regards reading as an ideal conversation between reader and text or present and past — an art of listening to the lost voices of traditions.

The structural-linguistic approach to reading is, by contrast, not a conversation but a decoding. The text is approached with a ready-made, preconceived code or schema of interpretation and is read in terms of it. The chosen code might be a set of general principles adapted from linguistics, such as the Russian Formalists deployed; or a structural schema of binary oppositions such as Lévi-Strauss uses; or a structuration of ideology such as Marxist critics apply; or an 'episteme' in Foucault's sense. Barthes reads with the aid of a compound code made up of five constituent ones: respectively, the proairetic (code of action), the semes (code of semantic units), the hermeneutic (code of truth), the cultural (gnomic codes of science), and the symbolic.[94] These codes apply not merely to the Balzac story of which Barthes gives his reading, but supposedly to any and every story and piece of writing. The codes produce what Barthes calls a 'structuration' out of which 'the text is woven'.[95] They enable him to read the text by reconstituting its basic 'narrative grammar'. This approach is the latest and most intricate version of reading deriving from Russian Formalism.

The hermeneutic and structuralist approaches to reading and translation have complementary problems. The trouble with the latter is that it takes its codes as fixed, like laws having universal validity: texts exemplify historically but do not alter the codes themselves. They are, as it were, the *a priori* of reading, for the interpreter already knows them prior to encountering the text he will read in terms of them. The text can only confirm the code; and ultimately this means that it cannot teach the reader anything new about reading. Reading cannot be a communication through which we alter and shape ourselves. And this is precisely what the hermeneutic approach brings out so well, for it does allow mutual interpenetration between reader and text. In hermeneutics there is no invariant fixed code that is pre-given; instead, there are pre-given prejudices that vary with the tradition. The weakness of this approach is that it makes for a subjectivity determined by arbitrarily given traditions. One's prejudices are fixed by the tradition one accidentally happens to have derived from; hence, divergencies of traditions begin as differences in the initial prejudices of readers and end up as irreconcilable differences in the reading of every text. Two readers from opposed traditions will read everything starting from opposed assumptions. Though the hermeneutic approach envisages an interpersonal dialogue to resolve such differences, it is clear that such a dialogue cannot overcome basic background conflicts. For if what is at stake are whole traditions which determine the prejudices and assumptions of reading, such disputes will be interminable. Every major difference in reading — since according to hermeneutics it involves opposed traditions — is also in practice unending. The traditions can continue dialoguing for a very long time, but unless one reader accept the other reader's prejudices there will be no way they can settle a dispute in their reading. Reading can function as a conversation provided the partners share the same tradition, and in that sense speak the same language, but if that differs the conversation cannot go on.

Given these problems with hermeneutics and structuralism, it is essential to develop an alternative theory that retains the strengths of both but avoids their weaknesses. Such an approach can be derived by adapting Weber's theory of ideal-type concepts which was initially devised to enable historical understanding. A reading requires the construction of a code that is akin to a constellation of ideal-type concepts, each especially created to translate the terms of the text to be read. But such a code is like a one-time pad to be used only once, since each new species of text will require the construction of a new code. No code for reading can ever be universal. The ideal-type interpretative concepts constituting the code will be composed in many different ways: they might be adaptations of our current concepts, such as concepts derived from our sciences or other rational types; they might be composed from a partial reading of numerous texts from the one period; or they might be highly aesthetic and sympathetic 'depictions', or scholarly reconstructions. A splendid instance of the latter is the reading of the Greek term '*metis*' by Vernant and Detienne; they construct an ideal-typical comprehending concept of '*metis*' on the basis of partial readings of a whole range of ancient texts from Homer through to Oppian over a span of ten centuries.[96] Frequently such ideal-typical constructions will be characteristic exaggerations and simplified departures from the intricacies of meaning of the texts themselves, for this will permit easy surveyability and make possible comparisons between one composed version of the concept and another. The very fact that both are constructions, and not renderings of the 'true meaning', means that a relatively impartial, 'objective' assessment of the essential logical features of both is made possible. Disagreements can be discussed and more easily settled than on any hermeneutic reading. For example, anyone disagreeing with the interpretation of *metis* can much more easily point to the grounds of his objection in ancient texts than he could with Heidegger's reading of any of the Greek concepts. It is also much easier to change and adjust such an ideal-type rendering before or after the reading of any specific text because the elements that have gone into its composition can be analysed and separated out. Hence, much of the subjectivity of hermeneutics is avoided.

An actual reading of a specific text is achieved by applying the code of ideal-type comprehending concepts to it in order to elicit the congruences and incongruences between text and code. Unlike the codes of structuralism, which must by definition fit the text and where what does not fit is discounted, this process of reading seeks to elicit the resistance of the text to the preconceived code imposed on it. What are sought are precisely the points where the code does not fit the text, so that thereby areas of incomprehension will be opened up which will require changing the code in order to achieve understanding. A code is like a beam of light which not merely illuminates one area, but shows us where the shadows lie which will need further illumination. In understanding, the areas of darkness are as important as those of light. This is why each code works only for one kind of text, and in rare instances even only for a single text. The power of a text is to be judged by its capacity to resist the initial decoding and force us continually to alter our concepts in order to come to terms with it. This is how we come to learn from the texts of the past; not merely by inheriting traditions that we understand, but also by grappling with traditions we no longer understand, and allowing them to shape us. A really great text will never be fully decoded; hence, never completely comprehensible, it remains like a dark enigma against which we are continually impelled to test our interpretative powers. Such texts are like sphinxes to our understanding: their riddle will never be fully resolved. For no matter how much light we throw on them, this only creates newer and deeper areas of darkness. In such cases understanding is measured by how much is yet to be understood. The texts of Shakespeare have this kind of power over us. The extraordinary failure of our understanding of such rare texts is itself the supreme achievement of our understanding, and it is only revealed by an approach to reading as translating which is as much intent on what is not yet understood as on what is understood.

Translation is a matter of understanding. But where understanding becomes critical engagement, translation gives way to
dialectical mediation. Understanding and mediation are extreme
versions of each other; if what is understood is also critically
grasped, this makes it a matter of dialectics, but if what is mediated is
simply rendered understandable, this makes it a matter of translation. Thus, for example, the interlingual mediation between
different scientific languages or theoretical systems is an extreme
mode of dialectics. It is mediation between 'languages' that have
become incomprehensible to each other, and so it involves translation; however, when this translation produces an understanding that
gives rise to critical comprehension of the one language by the other,
it becomes a dialectical mediation. Thus, in any really complex act of
understanding there are two moments, the translating moment that
aims for a neutral understanding, and the mediating moment that
enters into a dialectical debate with what has been understood. By
and large, dialectics deals with contradictions arising within the one
language where there is no problem in understanding what the
contradiction is about. Two contradictory positions in the language
of metaphysics have no major difficulties in understanding each
other and entering into mutual debate. Hence, the dialectical
function of philosophy is usually distinct from translation, which one
might, therefore, refer to as a separate function. Traditionally
understood, theories of dialectics have not involved translation.
This is so from Plato's dialectic till Hegel's; only in the negative
dialectics of Adorno has understanding also become an issue.

Adorno's conception of negative dialectics as critical reason
contains within itself also the two other distinguishable functions of
philosophy: destructive criticism and recollection or concrete
philosophising. The first is what Adorno calls 'the logic of disinteg-
ration' as a way of distinguishing negative dialectics from Hegelian
dialectic:

> But such dialectics is no longer reconcilable with Hegel. Its
> motion does not tend to the identity in the difference between
> each object and its concept; instead, it is suspicious of all identity.
> Its logic is ore of disintegration: of a disintegration of the
> prepared and objectified form of the concepts which the cognitive
> subject faces, primarily and directly.[97]

Adorno defines his dialectics as 'the consistent sense of non-identity'.[98] He means by it that mode of thought that opens up and explores the gap between the concept and its non-conceptual Other. Negative dialectics reveals the inadequacy of the concept, or the totality of concepts in any system, to completely cover the object — that is, the inherent inadequacy of thought itself: 'The name of dialectics says no more, to begin with, than that objects do not go into their concepts without leaving a remainder, that they come to contradict the traditional norm of adequacy.'[99] This points to an inherent contradiction that cannot be sublated or overcome, as Hegel thought it could, in Absolute Knowledge, that is, in a dialectic based on the principle of Identity.

Adorno's view of contradiction is, thus, the opposite of Hegel's; contradiction 'indicates the untruth of identity, the fact that the concept does not exhaust the thing conceived'.[100] As against Hegel, Adorno maintains that contradiction is not merely a matter of thought, but of reality itself, that it is inherent in things themselves in so far as they are the products of an antagonistic totality: '. . . the object of a mental experience is an antagonistic system in itself — antagonistic in reality, not just in its conveyance to the knowing subject that rediscovers itself therein'.[101] Contradiction, he insists, is real, it is not just a cognitive law. Hence, it is also possible to overcome it in reality through the ending of the antagonistic totality. This is the hidden utopian dream in Idealistic dialectics and all identitarian thought, even in formal logic, 'the pledge that there should be no contradiction, no antagonism'.[102] Thus, even negative dialectics sees itself as the outcome and expression of 'the wrong state of things' and it looks forward to its own dissolution; 'the right state of things would be free of it: neither a system nor a contradiction'.[103]

The end of dialectics is to end itself: 'it dismantles the coercive logical character of its own course . . . .'.[104] It 'serves the end of reconcilement'.[105] Only 'reconcilement would release the non-identical, would rid it of coercion, including spiritual coercion; it would open the road to the multiplicity of different things and strip dialectics of its power over them'.[106] This is what Adorno means by 'cognitive utopia', not merely that utopia represents social reconciliation, but that it also represents the reconcilement of subject and object, concept and thing, language and reality. Through reconcilement thought would attain to the Other as the non-conceptual, the unutterable. The Other is Nature under the aspect of non-domination, that Nature which is left over as the remainder in all dominating concepts and systems, and is now unexpressed and inconceivable, but which awaits expression and conception in utopian reconciliation. And, as we saw previously, hints and intimations of this 'cognitive utopia' are, for him, now to be had only in art.

It would be merely a pointless disagreement to castigate Adorno's vision of utopia as utopian. The hope for utopia might, after all, be necessary 'for the sake of the hopeless'. Rather, it is what underlies this utopian hope that is questionable: Adorno's preconception of the relationship between Nature and language and between contradiction and antagonistic reality. According to Adorno, the necessity for dialectics is due to antagonistic reality, so the overcoming of antagonistic reality in utopia entails the self-cancellation of dialectics and the reconciliation of Nature and language. This means that he does not ground contradiction in the very nature of language itself; for Adorno, at least in aspiration, language in cognitive utopia might be a non-contradictory medium of expression capable of fully conveying Nature and the Other without loss or remainder. But if this view of language is impossible, if language is itself inherently contradictory, and if it is, therefore, incapable of being a pure expressive medium able to convey Nature whole and as it is without distortion or remainder, then the utopian hope for the abolition of contradiction would be tantamount to a hope for the abolition of language itself and with it all of human knowledge. This kind of redemption of language would be no more than a mystic aspiration.

The issue is whether contradiction is inherent in language itself by its very nature, or merely in an antagonistic reality which can be overcome. In what follows it will be contended that language is no mere transparent medium of expression conveying a pre-existing Nature, but that since it structures reality it also determines what is Nature for us; always in terms of some symbolic form or other, and always in opposition to other symbolic realities, such as the opposition of Nature and culture. Nature in itself outside of any symbolic system is not an object of human knowledge, not even in any 'cognitive utopia', for as soon as anything becomes an object of knowledge it is already symbolically determined by language. And language necessarily structures itself and, therefore, its objects — and so all of Nature — on contradictions. Language structures itself on patterns of exclusion and inclusion, of what is spoken and unspoken, and of what is conscious and unconscious. If the notion of the Other is to be given any meaning, it cannot be the Other as

Nature in itself, for that goes beyond all conception and beyond language itself; it can only mean the Other as an aspect of language, as that which is unconscious and unspoken in language. And this unconscious dimension is no more than a language-effect itself; it results from the inevitable self-obscuring of language as a symbolic system of exclusions. Reconciliation with the Other in this sense is not merely utopian, it is unthinkable and inconsistent. Even the abolition of antagonistic reality could not bring about such a reconciliation, for it would only give rise to another language, which, no matter how perfect, would inevitably have its own patterns of contradiction.

On this view of dialectics, contradiction is an inherent part of reality because it is basic to language itself. This does not mean that dialectics is merely linguistic and not social or cultural or even natural. In so far as language structures society, culture and Nature, it also determines their contradictory character. As we shall show, contradictions reveal themselves in unruly social phenomenon in the course of history; like the symptoms of a disease, these can be analysed to disclose the hidden contradictory rifts underneath the phenomenal surface. Such a disclosure of contradictions threatens the destruction of the language as a symbolic system and possibly also the society itself. Dialectics understood in this sense is, thus, simultaneously a study of contradictions in language and in reality. This sense of dialectics has nothing any longer in common with Idealist philosophy.

However, Adorno's 'negative dialectics is tied to the supreme categories of identitarian philosophy as its point of departure'.[107] Negative dialectics cannot free itself from the Idealist dialectics it negates. All its notions and conceptions derive from a negation of those of Idealism: its non-identity is a negation of Identity; its anti-totality a negation of Totality; it is anti-systematic as against the System; it is non-conceptual as against the Absolute Idea; it espouses particularity not the Whole; its 'Nature' is simply the reverse of the Idealist unity of thought and reality. Even Adorno's emphasis upon the concrete is specified partly by way of the negation of Hegel's 'concreteness' as the concept or Idea fully realised. Adorno is himself aware that his philosophy defines itself as a belated reaction against Hegel's: 'the matters of true philosophical interest at this point in history are those in which Hegel, agreeing with tradition, expressed his discontent. They are non-conceptuality, individuality and particularity — things which ever since Plato used to be dismissed as transitory and insignificant, and which Hegel labelled "lazy Existenz".[108] Even for this rejection of Hegel Adorno refers himself back to Hegel, this time the young Hegel: 'not since the youthful Hegel has philosophy — unless selling out for authorized cerebration — been able to repress how very much it slipped into *material* questions of existence'.[109] Material questions of existence bring Adorno to his characteristic view of the concrete, that which he has embodied in the phrase 'concrete philosophizing'.[110]

With this phrase we arrive at the third end of philosophy. Concrete philosophising will be expanded beyond Adorno's designation to include also the recollective function of philosophy — that whereby philosophy serves the purpose of self-knowledge. It is this compound function that acts as the modern equivalent for what used to be considered practical reason in traditional philosophy. It is also a way of applying rational thought to immediate particulars and concerns of the present moment. In order to achieve this it has to engage with 'material questions of existence' and, so, 'stringently to transcend the official separation of pure philosophy and the substantive or formally scientific realm'.[111] Indeed, one of the main causes of the present plight of philosophy is this official separation, which from the side of philosophy is rationalised in terms of the need to keep philosophy pure and untainted by any 'genetical, extra-philosophical reference to society, the notorious prototypes of which are found in the sociology of knowledge and in the critique of ideology'.[112] The much vaunted rigour of pure philosophy is in most cases merely a *rigor mortis*.

To speak thus of a philosophy given to real substantive issues does not mean selling out philosophy to the sciences, or, even worse, to intellectualised journalism. On the contrary, philosophy has a function to perform that none of the sciences or anything else can carry out, and it is on this that its continuing life depends. 'Philosophy can survive only if it gives thought to the changing conditions of human existence that no other discipline is capable of accommodating. Philosophy is that thought able to register the changing state of Man as a whole.'[113] The last sentence brings out what we mean by the recollective end of philosophy, which alone can encompass the present as a whole beyond any specialities or partialities. The special sciences provide the materials for this self-recollective attempt, but they are not themselves capable of actually making it. The study that does make it is the 'legitimate heir of philosophy', no matter how little of a family-likeness it bears to what was traditionally understood by philosophy.

According to Adorno, one of the ways that philosophy may 'serve authentic concretion',[114] and actually address itself to concrete particulars, is by borrowing as a model a method developed in science, the ideal-type method of Weber which we have already invoked. This provides a way of understanding the concrete particular and individual by means of general concepts and abstractions. The abstract ideal-types are assembled in constellations and brought to bear on the specific object, which is then understood through its likenesses and differences to the whole conceptual constellation. 'Cognition of the object in its constellation is cognition of the process stored in the object',[115] and this, in most cases, is the historical process whereby the object was produced. In this way, the old antinomy between conceptual generality and the concreteness of particulars, which made it seem that concepts could never grasp individuals — *individuum est ineffabile* — can thus be overcome. Philosophy, thereby, has a way of overcoming its own abstractness and attaining to the concrete in a manner contrary to that of Hegel.

Concrete philosophising as practical rationality replaces many of the old disciplines of the practical which no longer make much sense on their own. Ethics, philosophy of religion, Existentialism, the part of politics that goes beyond its scientific side, aesthetics as dealing with the role of art in society: all these are embraced within a general philosophy of the practical as the historically specific present. Such a transition from the traditional branches of philosophy to the modern philosophical function of self-recollection has already been prepared for in the works of many modern philosophers. Kierkegaard was one of the first, after the young Hegel. Simmel followed in the same vein in his *Philosophy of Money* which broke completely with all the traditional philosophical genres. This kind of thought was passed on through Kracauer to become a decisive influence on Benjamin and Adorno. Both were also influenced by Ernst Bloch's emphasis upon particularity and non-identity and the 'traces of utopia' to be found in them, which gave their concrete thinking its mystical aura. In France, too, following Kierkegaard, there were trends in a similar direction, first among such Existentialists as Sartre, whom Heidegger puristically accused of writing not philosophy but *belles lettres*, and then among such divergent thinkers as the theologically inclined Elull who has focused on technology, the Marxist H. Lefebvre who has written a philosophy of the everyday and the neo-Structuralist Barthes who has written on the mythology of advertising.

Canetti has said, with some exaggeration but nevertheless correctly, that 'among the most sinister phenomena in intellectual history is the avoidance of the concrete'.[116] And the reason why it is so sinister for him at present is that 'the situation of mankind today, as we all know, is so serious that we have to turn to what is closest and most concrete'.[117] Canetti is talking about the problem of survival in general and he means specifically the survival of the human race. This has become the subject *par excellence* of all present day concrete philosophising. With even greater seriousness and application than Canetti, Anders has turned towards the question of the age, according to him the question of the ages, because all of history is now staked on the one throw.[118] The problem, colloquially referred to as 'the Bomb', overshadows everything; it is the single most decisive object of all our thinking — though, of course, it is not a single object but a total technological network of military hardware so multifarious, powerful and overpowering that it is capable of annihilating all human life on earth. It is this object, that has decisively altered the meaning of life and death for every individual, irrespective of whether he is aware of it and acknowledges it to be so. It is one cause of our basic anxiety and the direst expression of our modern Nihilism, which, because of this, is so very different from anything Nietzsche implied by this term. Annihilation and nothingness mean something different for us now because death has been transformed from an individual fate to the ever-present, threatening collective destiny of mankind. The individual can no longer die in the security that at least the race will endure, that even if each man is mortal, humankind is immortal. Hence, we can no longer live for the future; there might not be one.

It has long been a traditional *topos* of philosophy that death is the most fitting subject of thought and that the aim of philosophy is to teach one how to die. Montaigne asserts this on the basis of the long tradition running through Boethius, the Christian martyr of philosophy to Socrates himself, the first philosophical martyr of all. If philosophy now is to maintain this tradition, then it must direct itself to this new kind of death. And it is precisely the philosophy that abandons traditionalistic preoccupations which keeps faith with the tradition. For the sake of thought philosophy must think the 'unthinkable'.

Notes

1. T. W. Adorno, 'Actuality in Philosophy', quoted in S. Buck-Morss, *The Origin of Negative Dialectics* (Free Press, New York, 1977), p. 69.

2. Marx and Engels, *The German Ideology*, p. 48.

3. *Will to Power*, sec. 461, p. 253.

4. Ibid., p. 253.

5. *Beyond Good and Evil*, sec. 211.

6. *Will to Power*, sec. 978, p. 512.

7. Ibid., sec. 980, p. 512.

8. Wittgenstein, *Tractatus Logico-Philosophicus*, trans. Pears and McGuinness, sec. 6.53, p. 151.

9. Ibid., sec. 6.54, p. 151.

10. Quoted in S. Toulmin, *Human Understanding*, p. 146.

11. Martin Heidegger, 'The end of philosophy and the task of thinking' in *Basic Writings*, (ed.) D. A. Krell (Harper and Row, New York, 1977), p. 373.

12. Ibid., p. 374.

13. Ibid., p. 386.

14. Ibid., p. 377.

15. Ibid., pp. 378–9.

16. Ibid., p. 388.

17. Ibid., p. 387.

18. Ibid., p. 387.

19. See ibid., p. 385 for some examples.

20. Paul de Man, *Allegories of Reading: Figural Language in Rousseau, Nietzsche, Rilke and Proust* (Yale University Press, New Haven, 1979), p. 115.

21. Ibid., p. 115.

22. Ibid., p. 131.

23. Michel Foucault, *The Order of Things*, p. 34.

24. Michel Foucault, *The Archeology of Knowledge*, trans. A. M. Sheridan-Smith (Tavistock, London, 1972), p. 206.

25. Ibid., pp. 205–6.

26. Ibid., p. 21.

27. Ibid., p. 206.

28. Ibid., p. 135.

29. Michel Foucault, *History of Sexuality*, vol. I: *An Introduction*, trans. R. Hurley (Vintage Books, Random House, New York, 1980), p. 60.

30. *Order of Things*, p. 384.

31. Adorno, *Negative Dialectics*, p. 14.

32. Ibid., p. 56.

33. Ibid., p. 10.

34. Ibid., p. 150.

35. Ibid., p. 207.

36. Ibid., p. 207.

37. Ibid., p. 404.

38. Jürgen Habermas, *Communication and the Evolution of Society*, see the Introduction by T. McCarthy, p. vii.

39. Ibid., p. ix.

40. For a grand synthesis of these influences see Jürgen Habermas, *Theory of Communicative Action,* vol. I: *Reason and the Rationalisation of Society* (Beacon Press, Harper, 1984).

41. L. T. Hobhouse, *Morals in Evolution* (Chapman and Hall, London, 1951).

42. *Communication and the Evolution of Society*, p. 15.

43. Ibid. p. 17.

44. Ibid., p. 26.

45. Kuhn, quoted in Toulmin, *Human Understanding*, p. 322.

46. Paul Feyerabend, *Science in a Free Society* (NLB, London, 1978), p. 66.

47. Toulmin, *Human Understanding*, p. 26.

48. Ibid., p. 393.

49. Ibid., p. 25.

50. Ibid., p. 350.

51. Ibid., p. 340.

52. Ibid., p. 340.

53. P. Feyerabend, *Science in a Free Society*, p. 98.

54. Ibid., p. 40.

55. Ibid., p. 38.

56. S. Cavell, *The Claim of Reason: Wittgenstein, Skepticism, Morality and Tragedy* (Oxford University Press, New York and Oxford, 1979), p. 389.

57. *Must We Mean What We Say?* (Charles Scribner's Sons, New York, 1969), p. 240.

58. Ibid., p. 264.

59. *The Claim of Reason*, p. 389.

60. *Must We Mean What We Say*, p. 324.

61. J. Derrida, 'The Supplement of the Copula', in (ed.) J. V. Harari, *Textual Strategies* (Cornell University Press, New York, 1979), p. 91.

62. Ibid., p. 84.

63. Ibid., p. 83.

64. Ibid., p. 85.

65. *Allegories of Reading*, p. 110.

66. *Archeology of Knowledge*, p. 203.

67. *Science in a Free Society*, p. 156.

68. P. Winch, *The Idea of a Social Science and its Relation to Philosophy* (Routledge and Kegan Paul, London and Humanities Press, New York, 1958).

69. *Human Understanding*, p. 489.

70. Ibid., p. 498.

71. Habermas, *Communication and the Evolution of Society*, p. 120.

72. Ibid., p. 98.

73. Ibid., p. 105.

74. Ibid., p. 97.

75. Ibid., p. 125.

76. Oral presentation at Berkeley, February 1980.

77. Adorno and Horkheimer, *Dialectic of Enlightenment*, pp. xv–xvi.

78. Ibid., p. xvi.

79. Ibid., p. x.

80. Adorno, *Negative Dialectics*, p. 45.

81. Ibid., p. 45.

82. Ibid., p. 45.

83. Ibid., p. 45.

84. Ibid., p. 45.

85. Max Horkheimer, *Eclipse of Reason*, p. 177.

86. *Dialectic of Enlightenment*, p. x.

87. Something of this critical function will be carried out in *The Ends of Science: An Essay in Scientific Authority* (forthcoming).

88. G. Steiner, *After Babel* (Oxford University Press, New York and London, 1975), p. 47.

89. Ibid., p. 47.

90. Ibid., p. 198.

91. H. G. Gadamer, *Philosophical Hermeneutics*, trans. D. E. Linge (University of California Press, Berkeley, 1977), p. 19.

92. *After Babel*, p. 137.

93. *Philosophical Hermeneutics*, p. 9.

94. Roland Barthes, *S/Z*, trans. R. Miller (Hill and Wang, New York, 1974), pp. 20–1.

95. Ibid., p. 21.

96. J. P. Vernant and M. Detienne, *Cunning Intelligence in Greek Culture and Society*, trans. J. Lloyd (The Harvester Press, Sussex, 1978), Chapter I.

97. Adorno, *Negative Dialectics*, p. 145.

98. Ibid., p. 5.

99. Ibid., p. 5.

100. Ibid., p. 5.

101. Ibid., p. 10.

102. Ibid., p. 149.

103. Ibid., p. 11.

104. Ibid., p. 6.

105. Ibid., p. 6.

106. Ibid., p. 6.

107. Ibid., p. 147.

108. Ibid., p. 8.

109. Ibid., p. 8.

110. Ibid., p. xix.

111. Ibid., p. xx.

112. Ibid., p. 138.

113. Ibid., p. 385.

114. Ibid., p. xix.

115. Ibid., p. 136.

116. Elias Canetti, *The Conscience of Words*, trans. J. Neugroschel (Seabury Press, New York, 1979), p. 14.

117. Ibid., p. 14.

118. Günther Anders, *Endzeit und Zeitenende* (Beck, Munich, 1972).

6 MODELS FOR PHILOSOPHY

1. Models of Past Philosophy

We have set out in a provisional fashion the ends of philosophy, but we have not as yet inquired how these ends might be fulfilled. Given such ends, what might the proper philosophical method be? The problem of method has thus far been avoided because it seemed hardly possible to raise it. What method can there be in an approach to philosophy such as we have outlined? It might be countered that if there is method even in madness then there must be some in this as well. In some senses of method this might well be so, but not in the sense current in post-Cartesian Rationalist philosophy. Philosophical rationality, as we now understand it, cannot follow any rationalistic method; its rationality lies partly in not being bound by such method, but in proceeding in a diversity of ways that might nevertheless be considered methodical.

Hence, instead of questioning method, which is now largely futile, we need to raise the question of procedure, of how philosophy can set about the task of fulfilling its ends. We shall try to show in what follows that philosophy has a way of proceeding by means of paradigmatic exemplars or models. The idea of a model may take many forms. A model might be highly specific — perhaps an exemplary solution, or really dissolution, of a specific problem, such as Wittgenstein provides in numerous places; this is what passes for method in Linguistic philosophy. Or it might be a more general treatment of a key set of issues usually taken together as a major problem, such as Adorno has in mind when he speaks of models and defines his philosophical 'method' in terms of them:

> The call for binding statements without a system is a call for thought models, and these are not merely monadological in kind. A model covers the specific, and more than the specific, without letting it evaporate in its more general super-concept. Philosophical thinking is the same as thinking in models; negative dialectics is an ensemble of analyses of models.[1]

The two models that Adorno offers are reconceptions of the

problems of Freedom, focusing on Kant, and of History, focusing on Hegel. Adorno explicitly distinguishes his model dialectical 'solutions' from the 'dissolutions' of Linguistic philosophy, which condemn such major issues of philosophy to being mere 'pseudo-problems'.[2]

The notion of a model might be taken in a broader sense still than that of either Wittgenstein or Adorno; it might be used to exemplify a whole discursive mode on which philosophy can model itself. Such models are exemplary procedures found outside philosophy, on which philosophy can base its own approach. These are models for philosophy which might be referred to as philosophical methods.

Ever since its inception philosophy has sought such methods by modelling itself mainly on the arts or the sciences, though on occasions other modes of discourse such as the religious, judicial, political, historical and even the mythical have also acted as models. Such models determine both the form and the content of philosophic thought; the artistic models are not merely literary stylistic devices and the scientific models are not just logical techniques. A philosophy's choice of models determines its relation to the surrounding intellectual and cultural milieu.

One of the most important literary models throughout the course of the history of philosophy has been that of drama. It was the original model behind the philosophical dialogue, first utilised by Plato and the other students of Socrates; ultimately it affected the whole conception of dialectic, which remains a 'dramatic' approach in philosophy. It is ironic that precisely in that work of Plato in which he bans the theatre and banishes the poets, the model of drama plays the leading structural role. The *Republic* opens with a dramatic conflict, located according to the convention of scene in the Piraeus, the polyglot seaport of Athens where the problem of the Polis is felt most acutely, and where an intellectual *agon* is enacted between the two main protagonists, who are contending for the souls of the new generation of young Athenians; and it ends in a dramatic reconciliation whereby the political conflicts inherent in the various types of constitutions — each of which is exemplified by one of the main characters of the dialogue — is philosophically resolved in the ideal Politeia. Plato utilised the dramatic model more explicitly than any subsequent philosopher; but this model enters implicitly into every philosophy that concerns itself with political action because one of the basic models for such action is acting. In Machiavelli the Prince figures as the main actor on the stage of public illusions, and as impresario arranging and enacting political plots in which his enemies are allotted parts and ensnared.[3] In Hobbes the Sovereign is the representative actor-agent, acting on behalf of and before the multitude whom he represents; representation of whatever kind, even that of ideas, has the basic dramatic metaphor behind it. In Rousseau there is a puritanical rejection of the 'bad theatre' of social illusions, the comedy of manners of polite society, in favour of the 'good theatre' and more 'natural' drama of the state of civic virtue. In Hegel, world-history is world-drama, a dialectical play of conflicting ideas, many of which are themselves represented by characters drawn from the dramas of the world (e.g. *Antigone*); but otherwise it is a spiritual ghostly drama without names, dates and places. In Marx the play is brought down to earth and names, dates and places supplied; it is a series of tragedies punctuated by the farce of repetition — as when Napoleon the Great is mimicked by Napoleon the Little; but ultimately the tragedy of the agonies of pre-history will culminate in the human comedy of the fulfilment of history in the eschatology of the end. In Nietzsche, the eschatological drama of the Fall into metaphysics and slave-morality is followed by the tragedy of Nihilism and the culminating transfiguration of Zarathustran man. The dramatic model is by no means exhausted in modern philosophy; numerous works even now utilise it in one way or another, including *In the Beginning was the Deed*.

There have been other literary models of great importance in shaping the discourse of philosophy. The meditation or reflective confession is also very old as a model; it goes at least as far back as the Stoic emperor Marcus Aurelius; his *Meditations* serve to convey the impassive upright bearing and invulnerability of the inner self amidst the turmoils and passions of the world. Meditation is given a new content in Augustine, where apathy takes on the meaning of Christian inwardness compounded of guilt, mortality and closeness to God. Descartes reinvokes it as the form for spiritual discipline of a quasi-Jesuitic kind, thereby inventing method in the new rationalistic sense. Rousseau utilises the seemingly 'naked' confession for a sentimental outpouring of the heart, expressive of his own uniqueness as an individual. Kierkegaard ironically removes himself from sentiment into anonymity behind the mask of the pseudo-confessions of his authorial personae, such as Johannes de Silentio. Nietzsche parodies the form by an uproarious inflation of personality that is already out of control. Most modern philosophers are not up to projecting their full self into a work, so the meditation and the confession are no longer favoured forms in philosophy.

Instead, the essay or philosophical 'experiment' has until recently been more prevalent; it has only now given way completely to the pseudo-scientific 'paper'. The essay begins as a kind of reflection in Montaigne; Bacon gives it a more pithy shortened form; it becomes more discursive and rationalistic in Locke, Hume, the French *philosophes*, and finally highly argumentative in Mill and the later English thinkers. It is the main model of Enlightenment reasonableness, with its emphasis upon moderate, calm, discursive lucidity and a tentative thinking ready to subject every topic to the trial of experience, good sense and natural reason. It addresses itself to its reader as to a civilised, morally mature equal who is able and ready to evince all these qualities of the essay in himself and judge himself accordingly. The transition from the essay to the paper marks a decisive change in the self-understanding of philosophy. This change of model represents the wishful thinking of philosophers who believe that their work can be the equal of scientific research: that, as in science, individual solvable problems can be isolated, that each of these can be subject to continuous attack by whole teams of specialists contributing papers, that each separate new paper can take the discipline a step closer towards the solution and that all papers together cumulatively support each other. What in fact happens is that prestigious academics, who set the topics and tone for the journals, put forward their latest interests as the going problem for everyone, and all others are then more or less constrained to join in the ongoing debate by arguing for or against the established positions. A flurry of papers then ensues which continues unabated until a new topic is proposed. The paper as a form thus helps to perpetuate academic conventionality.

It is partly at least to escape the paper that many modern philosophers have turned to the aphorism, which is also perhaps the oldest literary model for philosophy. The aphorism is a trope that goes back to the gnomic 'sayings' of the pre-Socratics, above all to that supreme master aphorist, Herakleitus. Thereafter it was largely neglected by philosophers until the French aphorists used it as a vehicle for corrosive wit and, more seriously, Pascal for his paradoxical thoughts on being and nothingness. In the German Enlightenment, Lichtenberg became the exponent of aphorisms of elegant irony and paradox of a serious intellectual turn. Other German aphorists learned from him. Nietzsche employed aphorisms to capture single insights in a note-like notation. Wittgenstein couched his whole philosophy in the form of single sentences or short paragraphs, which like sculptural mobiles can be rearranged and juxtaposed in innumerable alternating combinations to reveal continually new facets of relationships. Adorno used the aphorism for concrete illuminations of single aspects or fragments of a broken-up reality, following Benjamin in this respect.

There is hardly a literary form that has not served as a model for philosophy. Even the lyric poem has carried philosophical import in the intellectual poems of Goethe as well as those of Nietzsche. Nietzsche is perhaps the most innovative adapter of literary models in the whole history of philosophy; there is hardly a form — from the prophetic gospel to the scholarly paper — that escapes him. Derrida has since sought to go even further by collapsing the distinction between philosophy and literature. But even in this there are older exponents, such as Carlyle.

To speak of literature as providing models for philosophy is far from saying that philosophy is literature. Neither does it mean that philosophic thought is fundamentally metaphoric, or that it depends on ground-tropes, or that its language is inherently figural. As against such views — now becoming current, above all in the so-called 'deconstructive' school — it must be stressed that literary models are not privileged or exclusive in philosophy. Any literary model utilised in a philosophic work has to mesh in with other models not derived from literature; most frequently these will have a scientific origin, and so typically they will enforce conceptual rigour as against metaphoric figuration, logical argument as against tropic turns, and systematic theory as against formal structure. At the same time it would be equally a mistake to assume that these scientific and logical elements were the real argument or essential rational core of the philosophic work, for they are themselves no more than models which work very differently in the sciences, their original home, than they do in philosophic exile. The model must not be identified with the function it serves in another context.

Scientific models for philosophy have been as influential as literary ones right from the beginning. The geometric or, as it was later to be called, the deductive model was first introduced by the Pythagoreans as a numerology; though it was endorsed by late-Plato, it was not pursued further in ancient philosophy. The Euclidean deductive system of geometry only came into its own as a model for philosophy in the new epistemology of Rationalism, when first Descartes and then Hobbes and Spinoza sought to philosophise *more geometrico*. It became the model for method. The deductive method was introduced into modern philosophy not on the model of geometry, but on that of symbolic logic. First discovered and proposed as a model for philosophy by Frege, it was extended by Russell, taken over by the young-Wittgenstein of the *Tractatus* and accepted as almost the sole model by the Logical Positivists. It is obvious that in none of these cases is the model simply an analogy, or a convenient mode of representation, for it enters into the very fabric of what is philosophical thinking. Philosophies may be so dominated by their model that they are in danger of completely identifying themselves with it, and this leads to assertions such as that philosophy is really geometry, or logic, or methodology. Because of an all too recent spate of such assertions, mainly coming from the Logical Positivists, the deductive model is now in disrepute. When and in what new guise it might resurface is, of course, impossible to predict.

The organic, more properly called the teleological, model has been just as influential as the geometric one. First introduced into philosophy by Aristotle, it determined much of the conceptual structure of metaphysics. In Aristotle's metaphysics all the key concepts have their biological exemplars: the four causes are derived from the aspects of a growing plant, potentiality and actuality are exemplified by the seed and its realised development, the entelechy is like the flower or fruit. It might be thought on the basis of this insight that biology acts as a ground-metaphor for metaphysics and, hence, that the model is really a literary one, but as against this it can be asserted that since the organic concepts are not metaphors in biology there is no reason to take them as metaphors in metaphysics either. Of course, they are not the same concepts in both cases: they stand in a modelling relationship to each other. The organic model with its teleological emphasis never disappears but is more subtly evident in later metaphysics. Both the Stoics and neo-Platonists revive it in their conception of the world as an organism. Bruno introduces a more materialist version; and some of his ideas — living monads, for example and entelechies — are taken over by Leibniz. During the eighteenth century the developmental aspect of the model began to displace the teleological one as philosophy moved towards a cultural and historical organicism.

This move prepared the way for Historicism, which introduced its conception of time as another model for philosophy. The Historicist model was inaugurated by Vico and fully developed by Goethe and his circle. It became the dominant model during the subsequent century; there were many versions of it: Idealist as in Hegel, Materialist as in Marx, Evolutionist as in Comte and Spencer, Hermeneutic as in Dilthey. Its main rival for influence during most of this period was Psychologism, which took its model for philosophy from the newly developing sciences of psychology. Goethe was one of the important progenitors of this model also, writing phenomenological accounts of the development of the sensory faculties which he also applied to the history of thought. Eventually the psychological model extended from the philosophy of Herbart to that of James. Ultimately it transformed itself — taking a direction toward logic — into a model of the structure of consciousness, and so it became Phenomenology through the work of Brentano and Husserl.

However, the Phenomenological theory of intentionality took grammar as its main model, as its derivation from medieval philosophy clearly shows; in medieval logic and theology the *intentio* of a term or a statement or an act, also called its intentional object, is modelled on the grammatical accusative of a sentence. Grammar has always been the model for logic, even though logic was formalised by Aristotle before grammar and itself became the model for the later derivation of the grammatical forms largely carried out in Alexandria. This is the germ of truth in the oft repeated claim that the logical categories of Aristotle are really the grammatical forms of the Greek language. The error of this (see Appendix 1) is that it confuses the model with the function it serves, mistaking it for that for which it is the model. The categories are more than just grammatical forms, even though they are based on these forms; the categories are higher-order concepts serving an intellectual function. Grammar has continued to be a leading model for categorisation throughout the history of philosophy, as well as for attempts to set up artificial logical languages or logical calculi, from Raymond Lull through Leibniz to Russell. Grammar as formalised in linguistics, including Chomsky's Transformational Grammar, is again acting as a key model for the Structuralist and post-Structuralist thinkers; for example, it is the model for Foucault's notion of an 'episteme' behind the various discourses of an intellectual period.

Most of the artistic and scientific models for philosophy which we have briefly outlined have by now been so absorbed into philosophy and become so clichéd that their origins are no longer evident. Most modern philosophers have suppressed or forgotten the models for their procedures. It would require major studies to bring them back to awareness. However, there are a number of current models which are being quite explicitly utilised. Among these are the Linguistic, the Sociological and the Psychoanalytic.

Studies of language have provided models for philosophy ever since Vico. During the nineteenth century philology was a most important exemplar for philosophy; the work of Nietzsche attests to this perhaps better than that of any other philosopher — behind most of Nietzsche's insights there is frequently a philological point. Philology was also most important in Dilthey's formulation of hermeneutics. But perhaps the most comprehensive utilisation of models drawn from all kinds of sciences of language is to be found in Wittgenstein's philosophy, and this influenced Linguistic philosophy in general, though mostly the provenance of their linguistic models is disguised. Modern Formalist Linguistics, such as that of the Prague school and the later French Structuralists, together with the structuralist anthropology of Lévi-Strauss and the structuralist psychology of Piaget, have proved themselves extremely fruitful as models for philosophy in such diverse thinkers as Althusser, Goldmann and Habermas.

The latter have also drawn their models from Historical Materialism and from Sociology. Sociology has served as a model for philosophy at least since Comte. The great founding sociologists Durkheim, Simmel and Weber showed repeatedly how their sociological methods and discoveries could be made to tell in philosophy but rarely were these taken up by philosophers. The exceptions were Jaspers and his psychology of world-views, Mannheim and his sociology of knowledge and the Frankfurt school thinkers and their critical theory of society. Recently, through the work of Kuhn, Toulmin and Feyerabend, some sociological models have been entering into the philosophy of science. At present the leading exponent of sociological models for philosophy is Habermas; as we saw previously, he derives them from various sources ranging from Evolutionism to Weber and Systems Theory and he uses them in the process of developing a comprehensive theory of communication that is to be both sociological and philosophical. In this book itself sociological models, derived largely from Weber, have played a key role; the account of the relation between philosophy and science and the theory of rationality were both conceived under the aegis of his Sociology, as was the concept of the ideal-type as the methodological tool of language analysis.

The continuing importance of artistic and scientific models in philosophy hardly needs stressing. The invention and development of such new models is thus one of the key tasks of philosophical thinking. At present there is a paucity of new models and a lack of explicit awareness of the models actually invoked, as philosophy becomes a specialist discipline and its discourse degenerates into clichés whose origins are lost in the past. The only way for philosophy to break out of its stultifying isolation is to reach across to the arts and sciences and derive from them new ways of thinking and writing which it can then use to react back on them.

At the same time, if philosophy is aware that its models are no more than models it is less likely to fall into identifying itself with either the arts or the sciences, whose procedures it can never wholly adopt. Philosophy cannot simply appropriate to itself a method or technique or form from the outside. If it borrows something it must translate it to serve its own needs, and thereby endow it with a function and significance quite unlike that of its original designation. Any model, if it is to be worth using, must serve a philosophic purpose and subserve a philosophic end.

2.   The Model of Language-Analysis

One of the key ends of this work has been to offer new models for philosophy; pre-eminent among these has been the model of language-analysis. Language-analysis is, of course, modelled on psychoanalysis, but it is no more to be identified with it than Spinoza's *more geometrico* is with geometry or Plato's dialogues with drama. Derived also from the language philosophies of Nietzsche and Wittgenstein, who both in their different ways practised a kind of analysis of language, the model was developed further in the very process of being turned against them. As we have already seen, Nietzsche's pre-Freudian conceptions of sublimation and *ressentiment* were explicitly referred by him to language and cultural symbolic systems. Wittgenstein, after Freud, also spoke of sublimation in language and frequently toyed with psychoanalytic metaphors, such as language-analysis as the treatment of the neuroses of language, but he did not develop these insights in any systematic way. Our own extension and development of the model from both these sources has provided us with our closest possible approximation to a philosophical 'method' and has been invoked throughout the work. We began (in Chapter 2) with an account of the reduction of metaphysics carried out by the Faustian philosophers: Marx, Nietzsche, Wittgenstein and Heidegger; this we interpreted in terms of language-analysis as the exposure of the hidden and disguised workings of language. Language-analysis was also invoked in our *reductio-ad-absurdum* of the Logos and Cogito, the two key terms of the metaphysical tradition, in Chapter 4. Our own destruction of the destroyers of metaphysics, Nietzsche and Wittgenstein, was also in fact a reduction based on a reading of the language of their texts so as to elicit its unspoken assumptions, above all those concerning language itself. The model of language-analysis constituted itself in the very course of the double destructive *reductio*; the *reductio-ad-absurdum* of metaphysics, followed by that of the destroyers of metaphysics.

Models for philosophy have already been sought repeatedly in psychoanalysis. The Frankfurt school set itself explicitly to bring together social critique and Freudian theory. The outstanding achievement in this respect is the *Dialectic of Enlightenment* where, as we shall see, a modified Freudian model of mimesis figures as part of a general theory of the rational repression of Nature, and the return of repressed Nature is seen as responsible for the discontents of modern civilisation. Marcuse also developed a quasi-Freudian view of repressive de-sublimation to account for the conformism of affluent society. Habermas has invoked psychoanalytic therapy as a general model for the self-critique of ideology and for the overcoming of distorted communication in the course of attaining to self-consciousness and freedom. All these Frankfurt-school attempts to see in the psyche a model for society are modern versions of Plato's dictum that 'the state is the soul writ large'. Later efforts to display correspondences between the microcosm and macrocosm tend also to make similar assumptions. What defeated most of these was the failure to locate a common dimension that can encompass both psyche and society. Without this all such relationships are no better than correspondences.

Another approach emerges out of the re-interpretation of Freud carried out by Lacan. Because this focuses on the role of language, which has at once both a social and a psychic dimension, the new 'French Freud' offers better prospects for the use of psychoanalys for building a model for language-analysis. Some French philosophers have already taken up these suggestions, among them Althusser, Godelier, Deleuze, Derrida and Castoriadis, yet none has as yet developed a model for analysing the languages informing whole cultures. Invariably they have attempted to synthesise Freudian 'truths' with those of Marx, Nietzsche or Heidegger, so as, for example, to uncover a 'Marxian unconscious'.[4]

For Freud it is the mechanisms of defence that mainly account for the content and formation of the unconscious; among these he distinguishes suppression (*Unterdrückung*), repression (*Verdrängung*) and repudiation (*Verwerfung*), which Lacan was to call 'foreclosure' and endow with special importance. Suppression in the narrower sense, when it is not used as a generic term for all repression, refers to the process — which can be conscious — whereby something distressing or unwelcome is pushed into the preconscious, or even abolished altogether if what is suppressed is an effect. In the *Interpretation of Dreams* Freud uses this term in opposition to repression as simply a 'second censorship' between the conscious and the pre-conscious. However, it is repression that is the basic mechanism for the constitution of the unconscious. In its first phase as 'primal repression' it operates so that a 'first unconscious nucleus is formed which acts as a pole of attraction for the elements due to be repressed';[5] this nucleus consists of ideas to which the instincts are bound and which therefore act as their representatives. In secondary repression the consciousness maintains pressure against these ideas, which can however achieve substitute representation in the form of symptoms, dreams and parapraxes; this is the so-called 'return of the repressed'. The particular patterns of substitution formed in each unconscious, as representatives of repressed ideas seek to attach themselves to others that may enter consciousness, were, for Freud, patterns of meaning in which the truths of the individual psyche are locked. They are susceptible of analysis because, like the patterns of meaning in human language generally, they observe rules or laws in their formation. In short, the laws of primary process — condensation and displacement — govern the selection and combination of representations (words and images) by the unconscious, just as rules of grammar and syntax govern conscious language usage. It is on this basis that Lacan made his lapidary pronouncement: 'the unconscious is structured like a language'. If this 'lacanic' dictum were inverted — taking a little of Lacan's own poetic licence — to read 'language is structured like an unconscious', it might suggest a way of relating some of the concepts of psychoanalysis to philosophic language-analysis.

A serious invocation of the highly speculative Lacanian system is not, of course, in question. Nevertheless, its emphasis on the central place of language in Freudian theory and its concern with systems of mediation in culture makes it suggestive for our purposes. Language and the psyche are certainly related, but only through the complex mediation of the cultural system as a whole. Language understood as the symbolic system of a culture does structure the psyche in the way that has been extensively studied and explained by numerous sciences ranging from anthropology and social psychology to psychoanalysis. The process begins with the child's accession to language in the context of the family, as Lacan has expounded it. But this is only the beginning of the course of enculturation. Language must be understood here as embracing the whole gamut of symbolic representations, from natural language through to cultural symbolic systems and ideologies.

In our attempt to expound and explain language-analysis we shall mainly focus on the latter, the culturally elaborated symbolic systems, rather than on the former, the actual natural languages that are the object of the science of linguistics. There is, of course, a close connection between these two levels of language, which has been explored by Nietzsche, Whorf and others who maintain that cultural world-views derive from the grammatical forms of natural languages. We have taken issue with this idea because it leads to cultural relativism; however, there are interconnections between natural languages and cultural languages which need to be studied empirically and spelled out in each case. A given natural language is capable of supporting any one of a range of alternative cultural languages, as history has repeatedly demonstrated. In the process a mutual adaptation and adjustment takes place, which is also specific in each case. Hence, what we say about cultural languages, the higher symbolic systems, applies only very indirectly to natural languages, which otherwise we will not discuss. And even our discussion of cultural languages will only be carried out in the highest generality, as our intention is not to provide historical case studies, but to illustrate the approach — showing how a philosophical model is constructed in the process.

We begin by outlining some of the key mechanisms of exclusion, suppression and repression through which a cultural language as a symbolic system forms itself and maintains its identity even when subject to change. It is in these mechanisms of defence, and not in any similarity of content, that the main analogy between language-analysis and psychoanalysis is to be found. We begin with exclusion because this mechanism governs the relation between a language and those others outside it from which it has to differentiate itself if it is to retain its identity. Of course, some languages are more open than others to the outside, to other languages and cultures, and therefore less prone to complete self-enclosure. But, nevertheless, even such languages exercise some degree of exclusion. Judgements about the relative value of more open or more closed cultural strategies are not relevant in this context, though obviously such judgements will have to be invoked in assessments of open and closed societies.

A cultural language must constitute itself on primary principles of exclusion. For just as the psyche only absorbs a very restricted proportion of the total stimuli impinging on it, so, too, a language only realises a limited aspect of its total circumambient world. This does not mean that what a given language excludes pre-exists it in the world in some ready fashion or other — there is no thing-in-itself; insofar as that which is excluded can be said to exist, it can only be said so in the sense that some other language does or could realise it. Hence, we can only know what a language excludes by comparison with what is included in other languages. Indeed, an exclusion is usually a deliberate rejection of other languages, for every language forms and defines itself partly in direct opposition to the other languages around it. The foreign, alien, strange, barbaric, heathen, pagan, uncircumcised, uncivilised, uncultured — all these are different expressions of language-exclusion practised by different societies. What is thus excluded is known only to be unknown. It is the alien 'other' which is generally feared, dreaded, derided and despised, but which can also hold a secret fascination, even awe, and draw as a magnet of great attraction or guilty temptation. Because of these dangers, the social mechanisms for enforcing exclusion, and so marking the boundary of what is inside and what is outside the language, have to be all the more stringently exercised in every self-enclosed society, and they have to be frequently reinforced when they appear to be weakening and threatening the identity of the language. It is the differentiation of an inside from an outside which makes the metaphor of language as a body so apt for such languages, for as with a real body the danger is greatest at the orifices where it is open to the outside; symbolically, therefore, exclusion can take the form of puritanical asceticism which protects the language-body against poisons, pollution and illicit entries.[6]

By contrast, open societies tend to view their symbolic systems not as fully self-enclosed bodies but rather as semi-porous organisms like sponges, and these societies tend to seek to absorb other languages within themselves. Nevertheless, such strategies of cultural absorption also involve principles of exclusion since another language cannot be incorporated *in toto*; only certain of its features or elements are comprehended and the remainder is eliminated. That which is excluded is usually denigrated as worthless, stupid or incomprehensible, if it is recognised at all, for mostly it is simply not seen or acknowledged. Such situations of language absorption occur in cases of conquest of one society by another. Open societies tend to be imperialistic, actively seeking out others for incorporation. Athens and Rome, the two most open societies of the ancient world, were also the greatest imperialist powers of their time. At the same time, a conquered society or people has also of necessity to open up its language to that of the masters. The history of the Jews is perhaps the best known instance of such a sequence of interactions, spanning over two millenia.

The mechanisms of exclusion defining 'self' and 'other' in language take a totally different form when that 'other' is not culturally alien but is an older mode of the same language, or one of its earlier constituents, or even a closely related language which has exercised a continuing influence. The ever-present influence of the classical world on the Christian European, issuing in repeated renaissances, exemplifies the last of these. In all such cases the exclusion is not a blind and hostile rejection but a deferral, in which what is pushed aside is nevertheless embraced and internalised in a denied way, so that it secretly mirrors itself inside the language. It is the strange 'other' of the outside which at the same time enters into the language to become the 'other' on the inside. The process of formation of such an inside 'other' is conditioned by the linguistic analogues of the psychic mechanisms of defence, namely those of suppression, repression and foreclosure. In language these act as mechanisms of negation, such as denial, rejection, repulsion, which set up all kinds of overt and covert oppositions, conflicts, contraries and contradictions within the one language itself. These mechanisms are responsible for the diversity of dialectics of language, causing them to take many different forms.

The mechanism of suppression is the simplest of these negative 'defences'. Suppression is responsible for the setting up in any language of those polarities of positive and negative valuation by which every member of that society lives, or of which he is aware, for his character is likely to be formed by the way he orients himself to those standards of his society. Thus, all moral, political, class, religious and legal — that is to say, ideological — oppositions are of this kind; they establish the contraries good–evil, legitimate–illegiti-mate, noble–vulgar, sacred–secular, lawful–criminal. Suppression is the mechanism for setting up these polar opposites in the most literal sense that the negative side is what is suppressed, or banned, or at the very least segregated, whereas the positive side is enjoined, or enforced, or encouraged. This suppression may be effected by means of external coercions — political ones, for example, using violence, or economic ones utilising losses and gains — or through a legal or spiritual system of sanctions employing punishments and rewards; or the suppression may operate by internalised psychological inhibitors such as taboos, or the dread of impurity, or through status or cultural aspirations, or moral conscience, or in general through self-punishment by the super-ego. In different societies these separate polarities may coincide, or intersect, or even contradict each other so that, for example, those who are considered evil are also considered ignoble, heretical and criminal; or by contrast the virtuous may be considered lowly, and outlawed or condemned; such differences are the specific function of each ideology and social structure. Marx and Nietzsche have provided a rich field of theoretical understanding of how and why different kinds of suppressions operate and how they reflect themselves in the polarities of positive and negative valuations in different languages. Bakhtin's study of France at the time of Rabelais provides an original perspective on the fundamental polarity of the official or cultured versus the popular or vulgar that permeated the European mind from the middle-ages till late into the Industrial era.[7] In effect, all cultural, moral and political studies concerned themselves with polarities, since ideology is a network of such oppositions.[8]

Out of the ideological oppositions encountered in different social fields derive the contraries of language, those antitheses of positive and negative valuation around which conflicts, struggles and tensions polarise, and these we shall distinguish from contradictions in the full sense. Contradictions are hidden rifts within the structure of a society which would break it apart if they were exposed and brought into open conflict; whereas contraries produce the surface social conflicts which serve to maintain the unity of a society precisely through their oppositions. Societies and cultures are maintained as much by conflict as by consensus. Rivalries, competitive struggles, clashes of interest, cultural contrasts and all such super-structural oppositions form networks of conflict that are necessary to keep a society in being, as sociologists such as Simmel have been aware.[9] Shakespeare structures many of his play-worlds on such conflicts; *Troilus and Cressida* is a clear instance of a world based on local strife which persists with a terrifying tenacity of which the characters who bemoan the loss of 'order and degree' are not aware. The strife expresses itself as a clash of opposites in language — 'courtesie' versus 'conjecture' — and these are the terms in which the characters see their conflicts. In any such language of opposites, the conflicts they subserve are interminable; there is no way one extreme can win out over the other since they are mutually conditioning and mutually supporting. Thus, good can never overcome evil, or the law abolish crime, since in a certain sense good creates evil and the law compels crime. The mechanisms of suppression which establish the distinctions of the polar opposites maintain them both in being.

Suppression takes a more severe form when what is suppressed is censored and denied any public expression. Since censorship is always only relatively severe and rarely completely successful, that which is censored will always show up through one form of expression or another. Such expression, being illicit, can assume the character of secret, partial languages. Every society, no matter how liberal, has its secret societies speaking their own 'idiolects' which articulate their subversive values and view of the society. The criminal underworld, if it is sufficiently established, forms such a patois; so do political subversive groups in all societies, both free and repressive. Societies with established religions, such as medieval Christianity or the Orthodox or Catholic church, give rise to equally tenacious underground oppositions of heretics, cultists, marannos and nonconformists; at one time there were also those practising witchcraft, secret Masonic lodges, and old-believers. Frequently their covert 'languages' are based on an inversion of the values of the official language, so that what is officially good becomes evil, what is forbidden becomes allowed, and Nietzschean *ressentiment* in such cases takes a clear linguistic form. Apart from such group censorship, there are also, in every society, rules of what is forbidden speech in certain contexts for everybody, or what cannot be known, referred to or discussed. Thus every society has its dark secrets, things which are known but not admitted. These rules of censorship are much more severe than the codes of polite society, proscribing certain topics or words in public intercourse. Censorship an even come to censor its own existence, so that its rules are themselves forbidden expression; this is the case when they are completely internalised and not admitted even to oneself.

Thus by referring to such processes of censorship we can show how in every symbolic system there is a complex layered stratum of the unsaid formed through the operation of different kinds of suppression. This stratum in language is analogous to that which in the psyche is called the pre-conscious. It must be stressed against that this analogy is not meant as an exact correspondence. The topological model of the Freudian psyche is itself merely a model of the mind. It is a highly suggestive device useful in language-analysis, not a true picture of language structure. A language is ultimately not an individual psyche, and so it cannot be assumed to have the same structural form.

With these provisos, then, one can go further and on analogy with the psyche locate in language a stratum of the unconscious, the internal 'other'. As in the psyche, the language-unconscious is also formed by a mechanism of repression. Repression operates in language when hidden structures of meaning are constituted that are not merely unsaid, but are, strictly speaking, relatively unsayable. The unsayable is that which cannot be spoken in a given language whereas the unsaid could be spoken if it were allowed. Although the unsayable cannot be spoken, however, it does gain disguised expression in symptomatic language 'disorders' in culture that are analogous to neurotic symptoms; and also more importantly in those conflicts that threaten to destroy a culture. More direct expression would require another language altogether, an interpretative language such as that proposed here, namely language-analysis, just as neuroses require the interpretative language of psychoanalysis. Language-analysis may elicit the unsayable of a language by studying its structure of deep contradictions and locating its deepest ambivalences and 'silences'; the lucanae and gaps which are not visible to the speakers, but which reveal themselves when the language is examined in relation to its society and to the other languages that entered into its formation and are contained within it as its hidden 'other'. The technique that Althusser has elaborated as the symptomatic reading of the 'absences' in a text is but one such method of language-analysis.[10]

The most explicit expression of the repressed unconscious of a language is in its art and religion. They comprise extraordinary discourses which can plumb the depth of their own cultures and partially represent what is otherwise unrepresented. Language-analysis thus frequently begins by focusing on exceptional revelations found in a cultural language itself. Art and religion are often surrounded with awe and fear because of their disturbing power and potential danger in revealing that which threatens to destroy the language. For example, tragic art reveals to its audience — though always in a veiled and disguised way — what the society in question cannot possible countenance. This is why tragedy both moves and threatens its audience in a way that can never be fully understood by them. The Greek tragedians must have had this kind of effect on their Athenian audience, and Shakespeare on the Christian audience of Elizabethan London. Not even later critics such as Aristotle, or Dr Johnson, could explain the disturbing affective power of such tragedies as *Oedipus* or *Lear*. We can do so better partly because we are no longer so threatened, or so moved by them. It is likely, therefore, that one of the main purposes of tragic art for society is to act as a kind of psychic prophylactic by bringing about a return of the culturally repressed in the controlled conditions of ritual and theatre, sequestered from ordinary life and so made safe, for if this were to occur in social reality itself, it would unsettle the whole symbolic order. Perhaps tragedy is designed to serve such a cathartic function for society as a whole — not, as Aristotle thought, for individuals — by forestalling the possibility of a real return of the repressed during a tense and dangerous historical period. Invariably, when conditions stabilise the tragic arts cease.[11]

Social upheavels of sufficient magnitude to cause disruptions in the symbolic system of a society thus reveal the fundamental contradictions of that society, those symbolic negations that cannot be directly expressed as contrary values or figure in open conflicts. On analogy with psychoanalysis one might say that this unconscious stratum of the cultural language forms itself by a process of splitting, in opposition to the conscious stratum, in such a way that both are mutually conditioning. That in the language which is repressed constitutes the hidden basis for all that can be said, for its norms, categories and values. The spoken forms itself by contrast to a deeper silence. It is when that silence is broken, when the repressed returns in such a way that the unsayable is somehow spoken, that the symbolic structure of the language is threatened. This is, of course, not evident to the subjects whose symbolic order is losing its validity, but it can be retrospectively revealed by means of language-analysis. Analyzing retrospectively the collapse of an entire 'language-world' is like the spectroscopic analysis of the light from an exploded star: it enables us to see what it was made of before it broke up.

Language-analysis is not a purely passive method of neutral observation; like psychoanalysis it enters into the deconstitution of that which it analyses. It is itself basically a critical destructive process. The language-analysis that philosophy undertakes is a more radical continuation of its critical function. Thus, the analysis of the language of metaphysics is a continuation of the destruction of metaphysics. It continues the *reductio-ad-absurdum* of the metaphysical language forms which has already been accomplished in other ways, such as by destructive argument. Language-analysis goes further in the destruction of metaphysics by revealing the repressed unconscious basis on which metaphysical language is built. Thus analysis takes us back historically to the origins of metaphysics and the idea of Reason which it incarnates.

3.   The Genealogy of Reason — Once Again

Thus far the model of language-analysis has been theoretically expounded in very general terms. In what follows we shall apply it to the philosophical issues that are of prime concern in this book. In this section we shall once again consider the genealogy of Reason or the Logos, the rational form on which metaphysics is based. In the following section we shall attempt a language-analysis of Rationalisation, the rational form behind some of the anti-metaphysical philosophies which brought about an end to metaphysics. In this way we will reconsider the beginning and end of metaphysics without implying that these are linked as the opening and closing phases of an eschatological pattern, as Nietzsche postulated.

Our own previous destructive critique of Nietzsche will in fact yield its positive result in both these examples of language-analysis. Out of Nietzsche's eschatology of morals and his eschatological history of Western Reason we will extrapolate a more sociologically informed genealogy of morals and Reason. To do this will call for a language-analysis of the symbolic systems of whole cultural epochs such as the post-Homeric Greek and Judeo-Christian — here we can only undertake this in very general ideal-type terms. The intention is to show the general relevance and validity of a procedure rather than to provide an historical interpretation in its full complexity.

Nietzsche provided the first analysis of the repressions behind Reason and the language of metaphysics. He was the first to identify many of the defences or mechanisms of unconscious formation. And, unlike Freud, he ascribed them in the first place not to the individual psyche but to the psychology of cultures and societies. He saw them in terms of language and described them as modes of linguistic transformation even though he did not have a general model of language-analysis. He defined *ressentiment* and sublimation, the two principal mechanisms, in linguistic terms. *Ressentiment* acts in language as a mode of negation through inversion, and in Nietzsche this is the inversion of values. Sublimation is a mode of language substitution whereby an ideal term substitutes metaphorically for something that cannot be admitted and could not otherwise be expressed. What is formed on the basis of *ressentiment* constitutes itself as a negation in reaction against some other — that against which the *ressentiment* is directed — and this other is in consequence repressed and becomes part of the content of the unconscious. This mode of negation as reaction explains how the conscious surface of a language, that which is sayable within it, forms itself over against an unconscious 'other' which is repressed and unsayable. The return of this 'other' from repression — as it were, its saying — must disrupt that which depends on the working of the repression.

The clearest instance of this working of *ressentiment* is Nietzsche's account of the formation of slave-morality as against master-morality in *The Genealogy of Morals*. What is explained is the origin of the Judeo-Christian moral language and its associated moral conscience or consciousness, the two notions being closely linked in this language. This is a key step towards an explanation of the origin of rationality in its characteristic Western form, for, as Weber shows, ethical rationality is one of the most important aspects of Western rationality as a whole; out of it emerged eventually the Puritan ethic, which was to be the source of the rationality in the spirit of later capitalism. Such an explanation of rationality is not to be found in psychoanalysis itself, for Freud thinks of rationality largely in terms of 'rationalization', that is, as a specific mechanism of defence whereby something psychically unacceptable is rationalised away through an intellectualised pseudo-justification. But, rationalisation in this sense cannot explain rationality, since for it to take place the subject must already have at his disposal previously acquired rational forms and be rational in his conscious life. In other words, rationality must already exist as a social form in language before rationalisation can take place in the psyche.

According to Nietzsche the rationality of moral language derives from the so-called slave-morality. This is formed through the mechanism of *ressentiment* whereby in reaction against a prior master-morality a negation takes place so that what the master-morality calls 'good' is inverted and called 'evil' in the slave-morality. 'Evil' is its primary value, its 'good' is secondary and formed as an opposed contrary by inverting in turn the 'bad' of master-morality. This moral inversion, which he thinks of as a kind of Fall, leads inevitably towards the eventual devaluation of slave-morality; that is, to moral Nihilism and the full working out of the Nietzschean eschatological design of history, as we have already shown in Chapter 3.

For this and other reasons the whole theory is held to be suspect, if not totally bogus. Weber on the whole deprecates and depreciates the role of *ressentiment* in the formation of ethical rationality: he states that 'the motives that have determined the different forms of ethical rationalisation of life conduct, per se, in the main, these have had nothing whatsoever to do with ressentiment'.[12] Though later he does allow 'that ressentiment could be, and often and everywhere has been, significant as one factor, among others, in influencing the religiously determined rationalism of socially disadvantaged strata'.[13] And he concludes that although 'there can be no doubt that prophets and priests through intentional or unintentional propaganda have taken the ressentiment of the masses into their service', nevertheless, 'this essentially negative force of ressentiment, so far as is known, has never been the source of those essentially metaphysical conceptions which have lent uniqueness to every salvation religion'.[14] Though Weber is doubtless right, it is clear that he has misinterpreted *ressentiment* as ordinary conscious resentment, rather than the unconscious psychic mechanism it is supposed to be. This is perfectly clear when he states that 'ressentiment has not been required as a leverage; the rational interest in material and ideal compensation as such has been perfectly sufficient'[15] — as if one excludes the other.

Nevertheless, it is true that there is much to be faulted in Nietzsche's account. In particular, his view of the origin of 'evil' out of an inverted 'good' is totally implausible. As we have shown in Chapter 3, a fully articulated conception of evil is already present in the book of Genesis, which pre-dates the Exile and so any possibility of a *ressentiment* reaction. Hence moralities like those of ancient Judaism which take evil as their primary value are not slave-moralities reacting in *ressentiment* against some master-morality. They are simply another type of morality as compared to heroic moralities or those of the *kalo-kagathia* kind, which base themselves on some primary positive good such as achievement or excellence. Nietzsche was more accurate when he first referred to the two moralities in *Beyond Good and Evil* as simply two separate types than in his later historical surmise as to the derivation of one from the other in the *Genealogy of Morals*. But to say this is not to deny that the two types of moralities do historically react on each other, and that, consequently, 'evil' takes on a different meaning, colouration and depth when it is further conditioned by reaction against the 'good' of another morality. In other words, the 'evil' as sin of Christianity defining itself against a pagan 'good' has different meaning-dimensions from the 'evil' as transgression of ancient Judaism from which it derives.

We can account for this difference by applying language-analysis, modelled on psychoanalysis, to the moralities in question. Much of what Nietzsche has to say about the reactive nature of slave-morality against master-morality can be reinterpreted in psycho-linguistic terms provided that the genealogical and supposedly historical aspects of it are eliminated. What Nietzsche calls 'slave-morality' and 'master-morality' must be seen not as two separate moralities, but rather as two aspects of the one morality, its conscious and unconscious dimensions. Thus, Christian morality in its original form might be seen as embodying both these aspects; its conscious 'slave-morality' aspect forming itself in reaction against an unconscious 'master-morality' aspect through the mechanism of *ressentiment*. This 'master-morality' aspect within Christianity is, therefore, not to be identified, as Nietzsche does, with Greco-Roman paganism, *tout court*, though it does have an indirect relation to it. Master-morality is the internalised 'other' within Christian morality which is repressed and so made unspeakable in its moral language. This 'other' is an internalised introjection of Greco-Roman paganism which Christianity outwardly excludes and rejects. That paganism, to which Christianity is outwardly most hostile and which it treats with loathing and fear, inwardly re-echoes itself within Christianity as its repressed unconscious content.

Perhaps it might be more historically apt to refer to this 'other' not as 'master-morality' but as 'mistress-morality', since that which Christianity unconsciously retained of paganism is best symbolised in that ever-recurring image of Christian temptation: the naked, laughing, pagan Venus. This repressed image keeps on being re-evoked throughout the course of medieval art and poetry, as in the collection of Latin poems by vagabond monks referred to as the 'Carmina Burana', right up to the dawn of the Renaissance when it re-emerges openly, as in Botticelli's Venus. This kind of symptomatic return of the repressed attests to the presence within Christian morality of a submerged pagan 'other'. The primary object of this repression is the female body, exemplified by the body of Eve, of which that of Venus is the repressed aspect. Eve's body is accepted in its fallen state but only as symbolising the natural motherhood of humanity which cannot be done away with. However, in medieval Christianity and in Roman Catholicism the attempt is made to sublimate this; the Virgin Mary takes on the role of an ideal Mother who is sexless and bodiless. The female body in its various symbolic guises represents the contradictions on which the Christian moral language is structured. The struggle that Nietzsche discovers in Christian history between slave-morality and master-morality is not an open conflict between two moralities, but rather the covert working-out of these inner contradictions. Thus, the temporary return of the repressed during the Renaissance was to be followed by even more severe puritanical repression — of which an early foretaste was the burning of vanities by Savonarola, during which Botticelli himself incinerated many of his 'pagan' canvases — and eventually by the full rigours of the Reformation and the counter-Reformation. How this repression affects the female body can be read in the paintings of Rembrandt, above all in the famous Bathsheba which is a supreme evocation of the pathos of the flesh.

But it is now becoming apparent that the lifting of the repression on which Christian morality is structured has inevitably meant the undermining of that whole moral language. It is being reduced to absurdity, symbolically speaking, through an exposure of its repressed 'other', leading to a collapse of its inner structure of contradictions. The naturalisation of the body and of all bodily instincts and desires is one of the main ways in which this is being brought about. This is the new naturalistic 'paganism' of modernity. That which had long been unsayable in the language of Christian morality finally returned to be spoken in the new languages of moral enlightenment. There took place what the early French Positivists called a 'resurrection of the flesh'. Bourgeois morality was only a temporary holding expedient which could not last against the ever-increasing inroads of moral destructiveness, of which the present permissive age is one culmination. Just as Nietzsche had foreseen, the main attack came against the Christian idea of 'evil', the basic value of the morality; 'evil' as sin, guilt, and temptation was declared non-existent, only 'good' in one form or another was considered real. Thus, liberal individualism, utilitarianism, socialism, psychological hedonism, the 'American dream', the life of affluence — all promoted a 'good' with no necessarily contrasting evil. But once the constitutive contradiction in post-Christian moralities had been eroded away, once 'evil' is gone, then the 'good', too, eventually begins to lose its reality. According to Nietzsche, as the value-differential is equalised and the value-distinction deflated, so both polarities are reduced to nothing and, inevitably, moral Nihilism ensues. The matter is by no means settled, and the question still remains whether this is indeed the form of destruction that has ensued on the return of the repressed in the Western moral tradition. Is it a sheer annihilation that does not presage a new morality of the future, or is it a destruction that clears the way to a future moral formation?

Language-analysis on its own is incapable of providing any answer to a question of this kind; it is best able to study retrospectively destructive events which have already occurred; its application to present breakdowns is highly circumscribed since the language to be analysed is our own. We can never make our own language fully conscious to ourselves. This is why language-analysis, unlike psychoanalysis, cannot act as a therapeutic agent of culture. The psychoanalytic technique of cure and self-liberation from neuroses does not provide a model for social or cultural liberation because the self-understanding of the language of a culture is limited by self-reference in the way that a patient's self-understanding with the help of a psychiatrist and the psychoanalytic language, is not.

So far we have analysed only the sources of ethical rationality, not its complementary component in the Reason of the West, intellectual rationality. The latter originates in the transition from mythos to Logos in Greek antiquity; principally, that is, from Homeric epic to the languages of philosophy and science, and later also to those of jurisprudence and theology during the subsequent course of Greco-

Roman classicism. Once again we take our point of departure from
Nietzsche and identify symbolically these classical forms of rational
language with what he calls the Apollonian. The Dionysian then
becomes its repressed contradictory 'other'. This contradiction is
not the simple contrary opposition of the rational to the irrational,
since both these polarities define each other and co-exist on the one
level of consciousness, like good and evil. Apollo, had his irrational
side as much as Dionysus, for he was the patron god of prophetic
madness, as contrasted with the telestic or ritual madness of
Dionysus. The difference was that whereas '. . . the Apolline
mediumship aims at knowledge, whether of the future or the hidden
present, the Dionysiac experience is pursued either for its own sake
or as a means of mental healing . . . Mediumship is the rare gift of
chosen individuals; Dionysiac experience is essentially collective or
congregational . . .'.[16] Nevertheless, we are justified in taking these
symbols as also expressive of a deeper contradiction in the way
Nietzsche suggests because the Greek dramatists themselves began
to do so. This is most clearly to be seen in Euripides, above all in his
Bacchae, which dramatises a literal return of the Dionysian
repressed. Dodds remarks:

> what chiefly preoccupied Euripides in his later work was not so
> much the impotence of reason in man as the wider doubt whether
> any rational purpose could be seen in the ordering of human life
> and the governance of the world. That trend culminated in the
> *Bacchae*, whose religious content is, as a recent critic has said, the
> recognition of a 'Beyond' which is outside our moral categories
> and inaccessible to our reason.[17]

This 'Beyond' — which is seen by this critic as simply Nietzsche's
'beyond good and evil' — is however, not so much a 'beyond' as a
'within' — it is the repressed. This is very much how Euripides sees
it; the Dionysian power is within human beings and works collectively through them, as in the frenzy of the maenads. That this is the
relationship between the conscious and the unconscious is clearly
portrayed in the figure of Pentheus who has both a masculine,
rational, authoritative self and a repressed feminine, irrational and
weak anti-self. In *Medea* the feminine irrational is openly revealed
as the foreign, strange and dangerously repulsive which the Polis
culture seeks both to repress and exclude. Euripides' dramas thus

evoke in symbolic form the repressions on which the Polis — in which philosophic Reason arose — was based.

In terms of language-analysis, Reason came into being through the other psychic mechanism, that which Nietzsche called sublimation. The language of Reason is language sublimated, disguising its own nature as language and substituting instead a sublime sense of itself as Logos, Idea, category, universal, etc. This sublimation of language produces philosophy as metaphysics, a discourse whose prime purpose it is to express this denial of itself as mere language, and to present itself as referring to a more sublime reality, the world of ideas or essences. Sublimation is, thus, an unconscious mechanism which cannot be aware of itself. The only way sublimation can be revealed is through a process of de-sublimation which lifts the repressions operative in sublimation and reveals what it is that has been sublimated. We have seen that this is actually what has eventuated in modern thought, when for the first time the reality of Reason as mere language has been exposed. This is partly what Wittgenstein means when he speaks of bringing words back from their sublimated to their everyday usage (see Chapter 4). The effect of de-sublimating language has been to destroy Reason and the whole of metaphysics based on it. For, once this repressed 'other' of Reason is exposed, it can no longer sustain itself as the ultimate truth but is revealed as merely conditional on the workings of language. Whether language in a de-sublimated form — as it were brought down to earth from the transcendental heavens — can sustain a continuing sense of philosophical rationality is the definitive problem of our modern intellectual predicament. Language-analysis, though it can diagnose this predicament, cannot provide any answers to the problem. What the full result of the destruction of Reason and metaphysics will amount to is not something we can be completely aware of because we are still caught up in it. Whether a de-sublimated language can sustain philosophy and the rational discourses, above all the humanities, is still an open question. Of course, all our effort and work is directed to answering it in the affirmative, but we cannot be certain of the outcome. It is possible that the de-sublimation of language will lead to its total reduction to nothing, that it will become mere 'sound and fury, Signifying nothing'. It is also possible that language will discover a significance in its own reduction, and beginning with this signification of Nothing it will build up again a whole body of significances.

The present de-sublimation of language enables us to understand better the original process of sublimation out of which Reason arose. The actual historical causes of the emergence of an impulse towards rational sublimation in post-Homeric Greece are even less known to us than the causes of an impulse to moral *ressentiment* among Hellenistic Jews. We know in general terms that it must have had much to do with the general transformation from the archaic to the Polis civilisation; the new economy of trade and money; the colonisation of the Mediterranean and Black seas; the religious incursions, above all of the Dionysian and Orphic cults, and the humanisation of the arts, and all the other elements of the city civilisation — not least among them the new class relations and political-military dispositions; all these played an indispensable role. What we are certain of is that in the course of a few centuries at most the Homeric language of the myth-makers and poets gave rise to the new, hitherto unprecedented language of the philosopher-scientists. This was not a total transformation, however, since the Homeric mythical language enshrined in the Olympian cults continued to exist side-by-side with the new philosophies throughout the course of classical antiquity. Even at the very end the pagan philosopher Symnachus pleads with the Christians for a restoration of the statue of Victory in the Senate. This is one of the great puzzles of the 'uneven development' of classical civilisation — as the Marxists would say — to which there are many aspects.

We have thus far no proper historical explanation for the sources of the repressions in the Greek culture of the archaic age that were capable of producing the specific sublimation of Apollonian rationality on the basis of a Dionysian unconscious 'other'. It is possible that this was at least partly due to external influences to which Greece was always extremely susceptible. Some scholars surmise that Homeric language itself was closely linked to the Near East, to Phoenicia, Egypt, perhaps even the Hebrews and probably also to Hittite literature; one scholar claims that the same 'epics and sagas underlie Homer and the early parts of the Bible'.[18] Many of the cults came from outside, such as that of Dionysus from Thrace, and these might have acted as a stimulus for a differentiation of Reason from the irrational. The rational enlightenment itself began among the foreign-influenced Ionians and it took the form of an attack on Homeric religion; thus Hecateus 'found Greek mythology "funny" and set to work to make it less funny by inventing rationalist explanations, while his contemporary Xenophanes attacked Homeric and Hesiodic myths from the moral angle'.[19]

It seems, however, doubtful that external influences, though operative, can by themselves account for very much. Internal changes must be sought in Greek culture itself to explain the transition from myth to Reason. We can trace how these changes took place even if we cannot adequately explain why they did so. Most crucial were changes in attitude to and representation of the body, always a key focus for all other symbolisation since language is often conceived of as a body. A transition can be traced in literature, art and thought from what might be referred to as the archaic Homeric body to the classical Apollonian body.

Relying on the researches of literary scholars, Feyerabend maintains that 'Homeric man is put together from limbs, surfaces, connections which are isolated by comparing them with inanimate objects of precisely defined shape',[20] and that the Homeric 'body is an aggregate of limbs, trunk, motion . . .',[21] so that 'all we get is a puppet put together from more or less articulated parts'.[22] This literary analysis, according to Feyerabend, is backed up by the independent analysis of the archaic style of the so-called Geometric art where, in the depiction of the body, 'parts are shown in profile and they are strung together like the limbs of a puppet or a rag doll; they are not "integrated" to form an organic whole'.[23] Once again the style is aggregative or additive. These features are in turn backed up by the archaic attitude to knowledge which is also that of a summation and compilation of particular details with no attempt at an overall unity or essential grasp. We can follow Feyerabend's account without being driven to the conclusion he strives for — namely that a totally altered perception of the world takes place in the classical world-view, making it incommensurable with the archaic; to accept this is to embrace extreme cultural relativism.

The main symbolic bearer of classical civilisation is the Apollonian body, the body depicted in all the classical plastic arts and enshrined in the classical symbolic conception of man. It is a whole body, all of rounded surfaces with no interiors, perfect in the harmony and balance of its limbs and motion. It represents pure form in action. Whether it be the actual body of a god or a man, it is changeless and immortal. For Spengler this body is the symbolic vehicle for the 'soul' of classical culture.[24] We have argued that it is the sublimated form of actual changes carried out in the body by the Polis regimen of training and education. It was a very strict gymnastic discipline, directed to the athletic-military arts, to which the young male body was subjected. In addition, the male body was segregated from women and encouraged to desire itself in the mirror image of another male who is both a lover and a potential rival with whom to strive in public action and speech. *Paedeia* is the educational continuation of this total bodily discipline carried out in a quasi-erotic relationship between a young man and his elderly tutor. All this is the bodily foundation for the Greek cultivation of Reason. Through what psychic repressions was such a body further sublimated to produce the pure abstract form of intelligence, *Nous* or pure mind? This is the key psychoanalytic question about classical civilisation. We know that it had much to do with 'the liberation of the individual from clan and family, one of the major achievements of Greek rationalism, and one for which the credit must go to Athenian democracy';[25] so perhaps if cause and effect can be reversed, Greek rationalism might be considered the achievement, resulting from the emergence of a separate, self-contained and self-responsible individual being from the cultivation and cult of the body.

An even more puzzling question is: how did the Homeric original body become this Apollonian one? To answer this question we must first consider how the prior symbolic system or language became the subsequent one. Feyerabend sees the transition as one from an archaic 'cosmology', or really world-view, to a rational one. The latter distinguishes between much knowing and true knowledge, 'and it warns against trusting custom born of manifold experience'.[26] It sets up a true-world over against the world of appearances of everyday life, and true knowledge is only to be had of the true-world. The true-world is subject to strict rational conceptualisation and simplified into a few abstract entities having a rational structure. Its objects have an 'essence' and its people have the individual identity of a coherent Ego. Though he does not explicitly mention it, Feyerabend follows Nietzsche in this account, but unlike Nietzsche he provides no proper explanation for why the transition took place. He mentions casually 'a sizeable increase of self-consciousness'[27] as responsible for some features of the new cosmology, but this seems a reversal of cause and effect since self-consciousness is always an effect of outside changes — except for those who adopt a Hegelian point of view. Otherwise, he simply speaks of the 'irrationality of the transition period',[28] and describes the transitional poets and thinkers as 'raving maniacs', who 'speak strangely indeed',[29] engaged on the 'determined production of nonsense'.[30] In keeping with his anarchic approach to knowledge, he believes that 'madness turns into sanity provided it is sufficiently rich and sufficiently regular to function as a basis of a new world view'.[31] But why this particular madness of post-archaic Greece should become the sanity of the Reason of classical civilisation, rather than anything else — for this there is no explanation provided.

Nietzsche's explanation works in analogous terms to his previous account of the rise of ethical rationality from the inverse relation of a slave-morality to a master-morality, except that it is sublimation and not *ressentiment* that is at work. He presents the original Homeric language as structured on a contradiction of this-world and the other-world. This-world is the living present of actions of the body set in a continuously unfolding time, like a frieze with no shadows of past or future, for even the remembered past is itself another present;[32] the other-world is, by contrast, on the one hand, the radiant upper world of the gods on Olympus where men cannot reach, and, on the other, it is the lower world of Hades where men go in death, an underworld of unreal, gibbering shades. Dead Achilles would rather be the meanest slave alive than king of the underworld: the valuation of these respective worlds is unquestioned. According to Nietzsche, the philosophers who, like priests, were intent on denying life, time, change, the body and mortality set about inverting these valuations through an act of sublimation. The this-world of Homeric reality is inverted and negated by philosophy into a false-world of appearances, eventually to become the unreal underworld of Plato's cave. Set against it is a sublime form of the other-world become a true-world, the world of immortality into which one is liberated by death, where no change or corruption can take place, a world of pure being. It is this true-world which becomes the locus and source of rationality, that is, of the Logos, Idea, category and logic.

Nietzsche's account is marred by his failure to grasp that such a sublimation is purely a symbolic transformation from one language or symbolic system to another. It is not an actual acceptance or rejection of any real this-world for the sake of a fantastic other-world. Homeric man no more accepts the world as it is than philosophic man rejects it. It is simply a matter of the transition from one language to another, neither of which is ultimately truer of the world as it is, though both have their respective relative truths. The philosopher cannot be accused of simply rejecting life, time, the body and mortality for there are no such things in themselves — these, too, are symbolic realities; all he can be accused of doing is inventing a new language in which to speak of them, one of rational concepts and ideal forms. This language might, as Feyerabend insists, be poorer and simpler than the Homeric language, but without it there could have been no higher civilisation. It is the language which, though abstract and removed from the concrete particulars of the lived world, can nevertheless intellectually under-stand and encompass the world as a whole. How is it possible that one language should in this sense better grasp the world than another?

In the *Dialectic of Enlightenment* Adorno and Horkheimer set themselves to answer this question and in the course of doing so provide also an answer to the problem of the origin of Reason.[33] According to their theory rationality is successful in grasping the world because its *telos* is domination or mastery of Nature, a kind of will-to-power. The *Dialectic of Enlightenment* provides a modified psychoanalytic account of rationality in which it is seen as arising out of a repression of the natural impulses in man, primarily the mimetic impulse, leading to a controlling repression of Nature in general. The anarchic mimetic impulse, which receives direct expression in myth under the sway of the primitive terror of natural forces, is repressed both ontogenetically in the child as it is socialised, and also phylogenetically in the historical transition from primitive to civilised society. Myth, as the mimesis of the cyclic rounds of Nature, is displaced by the rational norms of enlightenment — such as self-identity, subjectivity and equivalence in exchange — devised by the proto-bourgeoisie of the economically advanced early cities. Odysseus is seen as the first exponent of the self-denying sacrifice of natural desires required to produce the Self of the rational bourgeois individual:

> The pattern of Odyssean cunning is the mastery of nature through such adaptation. Renunciation, the principle of bourgeois disillu-sionment, the outward schema for the intensification of sacrifice, is already present in nuce in that estimation of the ratio of forces which anticipates survival as so to speak dependent on the concession of one's own defeat . . .[34]

In the episode with the Cyclops in which Odysseus names himself 'Nobody', the *Dialectic of Enlightenment* sees the early expression of 'what is called formalism in fully-developed bourgeois society', and from this 'there emerges nominalism — the prototype of bourgeois thinking' which 'contains the schema of modern mathematics'.[35] It all sounds somewhat far-fetched historically, given what M. I. Finley has since informed us of the primitive socioeconomic character of Odyssean civilisation.[36]

But apart from such purely scholarly difficulties, there are theoretical problems with this account of the origin of Reason. It suffers from a neo-Hegelian propensity to read myth and primitive religion as if they were the direct expression or imitation of Nature, as 'natural languages', a view that derives from Vico. Lévi-Strauss's anthropologically informed account of the complex symbolic structure of myths reveals that in respect of closeness to Nature they are no different from the rational language of science; the one might be more concrete than the other, but not more natural.[37] Hence, it cannot be Nature itself that is either expressed in primitive languages or repressed in rational ones; repression always operates symbolically and not directly on basic drives, or mimetic impulses, as in the *Dialectic of Enlightenment*. The same difficulty that we have already located in Adorno's later identification of the Other with Nature is already present in his early work.

A much better sense of the symbolic repressions necessary to give rise to Reason is to be found in the work of Vernant and Detienne. They focus on the concept of *metis*, or Odyssean cunning and show it to be the repressed precursor of a later philosophical rationality. On this account *metis* is not to be identified with Reason, and certainly not with bourgeois instrumental, subjective reason; on the contrary, it is to be opposed to these later forms of rationality. *Metis* is a prior form of what we have called Traditional rationality, so it is already a development away from Primitive rationality; Odyssean cunning wins out over mythical thinking; in this respect the *Dialectic of Enlightenment* is correct (see Appendix 1). *Metis* is a matter of 'sleights of hand, resourceful ploys and stratagems';[38] it is a polymorphous form of rationality devised to grapple with the slippery, changing reality of myth, in the way that Menelaus seizes hold of Proteus:

It turns into their contraries objects that are not yet defined as stable, circumscribed, mutually exclusive concepts but which appear as Powers in a situation of confrontation and which, depending on the outcome of the combat in which they are engaged, find themselves now in one position, as victors, and now in the opposite one, as vanquished . . . Thus, when the individual who is endowed with *metis*, be he god or man, is confronted with a multiple changing reality whose limitless polymorphic powers render it almost impossible to seize, he can only dominate it — that is to say enclose it within the limits of a single, unchangeable form within his control — if he proves himself to be even more multiple, more mobile, more polyvalent than his adversary.[39]

It is precisely this power of *metis* and the reality it dominates that is repressed in later philosophical Reason and its altered view of reality. Philosophical Reason forms itself on this repression. *Metis* itself is elided in later Greek philosophical writing; it 'must be tracked down elsewhere, in areas which the philosopher usually passes over in silence or mentions only with irony or with hostility so that, by contrast, he can display to its fullest advantage the way of reasoning and understanding which is required in his own profession'.[40] There is no place for *metis* within the philosophical framework of thought and its conception of reality:

In the intellectual world of the Greek philosopher, in contrast to that of the thinkers of China and India, there is a radical dichotomy between being and becoming, between the intelligible and the sensible. It is not simply that a series of oppositions between antithetical terms is set up. These contrasting concepts which are grouped into couples together form a complete system of antinomies defining two mutually exclusive spheres of reality. On the one hand, there is the sphere of being, of the one, the unchanging, of the limited, of true and definite knowledge; on the other, the sphere of becoming, of the multiple, the unstable and the unlimited, of oblique and changeable opinion. Within this framework of thought there can be no place for *metis*.[41]

This is once more a restatement of Nietzsche's characterisation of philosophy as involving the opposition of a true-world and an apparent-world, but it reveals much better how this set of contraries is derived from a deeper contradiction; a repressed multifarious polymorphous reality governed by *metis*, the reality of Homeric language. The contraries of philosophy are based on a repressed contradiction which sets up an unconscious symbolic 'other' within the language of Greek rationality. This 'other' keeps on resurfacing within Greek philosophy, for it cannot be completely denied; thus, Aristotle's 'practical intelligence at least retains in its aims and in the way it operates many features of metis' and even 'Plato, too, brings into operation a kind of selection where metis is concerned'.[42] This account, thus, offers a much better beginning to a study of the origins of Reason as based on symbolic repression than that found in the *Dialectic of Enlightenment*.

Difficulties of this sort also vitiate the *Dialectic of Enlightenment* view of the so-called return of the repressed in our modern period of rationalisation coupled with rebarbarisation. According to this dialectic, the repressed that returns in the manifestation of the neuroses of modern civilisation are the very same impulses of Nature which were originally repressed when myth was expelled by proto-bourgeois reason. Nature revenges itself on modern man for the original domination by Reason by returning in a distorted form to plague him as second nature. Mimesis reappears as the cycle of repetitions of the man-made systems of production, as the fated reproduction of the status quo, as the system of tautologies of modern scientific Positivism, as the perverted mimetic impulse to transform the subject into an object, as the absolute conformity of Fascism and the culture industry, and in all the other ways in which the modern world has become rebarbarised. The dialectical cycle is complete; Reason which arises out of myth must revert back into myth. There is an analogous overall schema in Marcuse's notion of the 'logos of techne' which becomes in the end 'one-dimensional society'. Once again we encounter the familiar eschatological patterns which relate directly beginning and end and take the one as the working-out of the other.

The *Dialectic of Enlightenment* treats rationality as the one homogeneous principle; it has little sense of the multiplicity of the forms of rationality, nor of the multiple and diverse origins even of Western rationality. There is no direct continuity between Greek Reason and modern Rationalisation, anymore than there is between the Polis citizen and the modern bourgeois, or between ancient and modern capitalism, and there is certainly no unbroken identity of these. Weber's work should have disabused anyone of such simplistic ideas. It is not possible to jump directly from the Odyssean 'enlightment' to the modern Enlightenment and employ concepts derived from the latter to describe the former. Nor is it, therefore, possible to assume that what was repressed by the original Reason can possibly return in the later Rationalisation. Nature cannot act as a constant persisting throughout, such that its original repression entails its eventual return. The repressions of Rationalisation must be specific to it alone and cannot be the same as those of Reason.

4. The Destiny of Rationalisation

Rationalisation is the dominant form of rationality in the late twentieth century. To interrogate it through the critical procedures of language-analysis is to attempt to expose the structures of repression of our own symbolic systems. This is a self-reflexive undertaking which in principle cannot fully succeed, for we cannot study our own culture in its finished form as we can the cultures of the past. Nevertheless, language-analysis can afford us some partial self-understanding.

As we have shown in Chapter 1, Rationalisation in its ultimate form is based on the principle of exact repetition. The extreme forms of Rationalisation which are gradually assuming predominance in our time, seek to control everything through calculation and exact replicability. Practically speaking, for anything to be rationalised in this sense means that it can be exactly replicated as a computer model. And such a model is basically a programme made up of a very long sequence of repetitive calculations, which in most cases break down into binary digital series. The principle of calculation itself, even when not strictly formalised and mechanically executed, is that of arriving at a result through a recursive series of repetitions. And to calculate something means to control it intellectually through a surveyable operation.

The process of Rationalisation as calculative surveillance and control begins in earlier stages of science. Eventually, Rationalisation leads to the production of things that are outcomes of calculation and so are technically controlled *ab initio*; this is the advanced technological stage in which we find ourselves now. Technocracy, or domination by technology, seeks to rationalise the world by remaking everything or reducing it to a series of repetitive operations. In the scientific phase of Rationalisation it was enough to control things by directing them on the basis of a calculated knowledge of their motion, reaction or behaviour. But in the technocratic phase Rationalisation means total control through exact replication, and this entails that things must be reproducible to standard specifications. Only that which is made and can be remade is totally controllable.

Machine-produced objects and machines themselves satisfy this requirement. They can in turn be controlled by other machines that can automatically control themselves. The whole technical apparatus embracing all the productive capacities of the world might eventually be joined together as one gigantic mega-machine cybernetically self-guided. More and more parts of this system are even now being joined together and left to the guidance of computers. Only at the key nodes are human decisions any longer necessary. A world-wide grid now exists in many industries and technological systems, and total automation in individual units is also already available. The automation of the whole is not unforeseeable.[43]

As if in preparation for such a final outcome, the principle of repetition as standardisation has embraced almost the whole of production. Objects that do not fit standard requirements are merely raw material prior to the productive process; or they have the special status of art. This mode of production largely explains the homogeneity and uniformity of the modern world. For people unwittingly come to model themselves on products, and to reproduce themselves to standard specifications. They try to fit the exact requirements of the social machine; frequently they are indoctrinated and trained to do so and are discarded when their role is obsolete, to be replaced by improved versions of themselves. Hence, the working lives of the masses take on the pattern of mechanical repetition: work is repetitive, rest is repetitive, play is repetitive, relations are repetitive. Their lives become as fixed as the days and seasons. It is little wonder that they are always on the look out for a chance accident to break the monotony of routine repetition: a fleeting affair, a celebration, a death, a strike, perhaps a war. They resort to contrived chance to give themselves the illusion of the unexpected and the free; gambling and sport provide pure chance, but other varieties of luck and hazard are also much sought after.

This dialectical interaction of exact repetition and pure chance reveals itself very clearly in modern art, which both in its form and content reflects the nature of society as a whole. The rationalisation of art has meant its subjection to technological processes of 'mechanical reproduction', to use an expression first coined by Benjamin.[44] Mechanical reproductive processes are the basis of new arts such as cinema and photography, but they have also entered into electronic music, architecture, design, many styles of painting and even concrete poetry. The content of many arts, from totally serialised music to super-realist painting, is also based on the principle of exact repetition and replication. Within such repeatable and mechanical processes the artist allows himself the freedom of the entry of pure chance, emanating from his own subjective volition or from random procedures. Automatic writing, action painting, composition by stochastic processes — all these are justified as the intrusion of some degree of spontaneity and imagination, but actually they are the celebration of chance itself.

Rationalisation has advanced furthest, not in the production for life, but in the production for death. The whole system of war-machines is gradually being taken out of human control. The communications network of surveillance is largely automated; little can stir on land or sea, in inner or outer space without being automatically tracked, recorded and identified. The machines of maximum annihilation find their own way to their pre-plotted targets. Soon the decision to fire will be largely left to computers. The war-making potential of each of the two superpowers is becoming an integrated system. Each system is automatically attuned to the other and responds to its pre-calculated behaviour. A chance accident could set off an uncontrollable chain of repetitions to bring this repetitive world to an end.

The ultimate outcome and meaning of Rationalisation is death. But the illusory promise it has long held out is unending life. The ideal, sublimated language of Rationalisation is the ideology of Progress, and this offers the prospect of unceasing amelioration of life in all respects: culminating all these advances is the secret hope of overcoming death. Progress will gradually free Man from his human condition and enable him to transform himself by his own labours to god-like proportions. This is the unspoken wish-fulfilment dream of Progress. In a more consciously explicit way it merely preaches the continual overcoming of human shortcomings and calamities through ever greater Rationalisation. All human needs will be supplied, suffering will be abolished, the evils of power will be gradually dispersed through enlightenment, men's imperfections will be removed and their creative capacities extended, and, finally, language will be clarified and systematised and made incapable of confusion. In the long term, we are supposed to believe, Progress may even overcome the fragility of the human body, extend the fleeting lease of human life and, thus, gradually defeat death, our only mortal enemy.

The death to be overcome was death as it had long been feared and dreaded in the Western Christian tradition. The promise of Progress was directed at answering the fears of death of a specific cultural tradition. Death in itself is not something that can be confronted, just as Nature in itself cannot be repressed; it is only death as a symbolic reality and meaningful entity that can be denied or overcome. It is the meaning of death as given in the languages of our Western tradition that Progress set itself secretly to overcome. For it is in this tradition that death takes on the repulsion and loathing of a corrupt charnel body, and that it becomes an active enemy cutting short man's life-time. And analogously, all the other evils of the human condition that Progress sets itself to undo are evils as defined within the languages of the West. Suffering now assumes the negative prominence it does because of the positive valuation ascribed to it by Christianity. Guilt and sin are for similar reasons rejected in favour of innocence. Present needs are specified in terms of what has long been found lacking and wanted. The wrongs that Progress sets itself to right, such as injustice, disorder, irrationality, imperfection and falsehood, are all defined in terms of the classical languages of Reason and Rationalism. The philosophies of Progress seek to solve the very problems that metaphysics presents as in need of solution. All in all, the language of Progress forms itself in response to all the earlier languages of the Western tradition.

We have, therefore, an answer to our question of how the language of Rationalisation is constituted and what it is that it represses. For just as the language of Christian morality formed itself on the basis of a represses paganism — which we previously referred to as the 'mistress-morality' — so that within the Christian conscience there lurks an unconscious pagan 'other'; so, in turn, the language of the new paganism of Progress forms itself around its own inner, unconscious 'other'. This 'other' is made up of the repressed earlier languages of the Western tradition, both Christian and neo-classical. Progress represses within itself all those negativities of our tradition that it secretly hints it can overcome. The key among these, to which all the others refer, is the Christian sense of death. Everything that is subject to death and corruption in the Christian and neo-classical dispensation becomes part of the content of the unconscious 'other' of Progress. The body is the chief among these, for it is traditionally blamed for the impermanence and imperfection of human life and all its endeavours; this is why Progress strives to deny and repress this mortal body and seeks to substitute for it a machine-body which can be controlled and repaired and kept functioning indefinitely like any other mechanical contrivance. Time was similarly traditionally despaired of because of its mutability, lack of endurance, its waste and loss and sterility; so Progress once again represses this negative aspect of time and presents only a positive temporality that is all accumulation, growth, development, and which retains everything and loses nothing — in short, progressive time. Language that is traditionally deceiving, ambiguous, ambivalent, fictive and fallacious is displaced in favour of a new fully rationalised universal medium of communication made up of clear concepts, logic, perfect calculi, exact science. And so the repressions continue through all the traditional negatives of evil, need, suffering and power; each one is denied and replaced by a new positive of Progress.

What is repressed is bound to return, but not in its original form. The repressed that returns at present is not that of the original traditional negatives. It is not the old Christian *timor mortis* that we now need to cope with. The death that returns from repression in the mute horrors of our time is death as it has become transformed by Rationalisation. This is a new kind of death never encountered before on this scale: the death in the repetition compulsion. Repetition as the basic principle of Rationalisation reveals itself to be a principle of death. This repetition compulsion is beyond the point of mere individual neurosis, for it embraces the whole system of production. Standardised repetition and exact replication, which ensure rationalised control, by the very same token bring about unchanging fixity, rigidity and uniformity, and so transform the living into the unliving. People in the thrall of Rationalisation transform themselves into products of their own production; they become gripped, fixed, unyielding bodies controlled to the point of catatonic monumentality. They learn to act like calculating instruments. It is still possible for the individual to escape this kind of psychic death, but it is hard to avoid restriction on the freedom to shape one's life, for the cycles of repetition determine most possibilities of acting and being. The term 'social-machine' is no mere metaphor; it has become a kind of second nature. A technocracy is the prime agent reducing everything it can to a function in this total treadmill system. This reduction is in effect an annihilation. If Rationalisation were allowed to work out its logic to its final conclusion, it would end up in the sheer physical annihilation of everything.

Thus, the return of the repressed of Rationalisation is evident in all those negative phenomena that collectively make up modern Nihilism. These have been extensively studied by many thinkers, beginning with Kierkegaard, Marx and Nietzsche, and the names coined for them are already familiar terms: estrangement, alienation, subjectlessness, destruction, devastation. Nihilism is made up of all those disguised 'nothings' that are the negatives of our Western civilisation transformed by Rationalisation into the 'problems' plaguing us just when they were supposed to have been overcome by Progress. The needs that were to have been satisfied have returned as new lacks; the sufferings overcome have come back as psychic torments; the body strengthened and healed has incurred new incurable infirmities; the time saved has been lost; the language clarified is incapable of further expression; all in all, the evils to which we momentarily felt superior are back, transformed into crises from which there seems no escape.

Nihilism is, thus, the manifest symptom of repressions carried out by Rationalisation whose meaning is largely unconscious; just as Progress is the conscious idealised sublimation of Rationalisation which denies those very meanings. Progress and Nihilism are the key contradictions on which the language of Rationalisation is structured. Both are aspects of Rationalisation and not mere outcomes of it. Hence, both are in the last resort identical, their identity being based on their unity within Rationalisation. The one cannot be without the other, so that as long as Rationalisation persists as the dominant rationality of our world, so long will it be subject to both Progress and Nihilism. The one can never defeat the other, and at present we are incapable of overcoming either.[45]

Thought cannot achieve much on its own, but one of its present aims must be to understand Rationalisation. We have taken some tentative steps in this direction by showing that Rationalisation is not synonymous with rationality, but merely one of a number of other rational forms. Philosophy has much to contribute to the development of alternative modes of rationality through a language-analysis of Rationalisation that will critically undermine and so weaken the hold of this useful but dangerous form of rationality. This might open the way to a revision and recovery of some of the other forms now so neglected. Since some of the greatest achievements of Rationalisation are to be found in the sciences, this will involve a philosophical critique of science. To fulfil this function philosophy must once again seriously concern itself with scientific knowledge.

Philosophy is not independent of the sciences. The future course of the sciences will, therefore, be telling for philosophy as well. If the sciences proceed further in the direction of Rationalisation — towards Big Science and techno-science with its routines of industrialised research, and towards mechanised repetition and reductive procedures — then philosophy will have a merely marginal status. However, if alternative sciences emerge and succeed in introducing other approaches, philosophy might find a *new* role for itself in the context of such developments.

At present in some sciences there are moves towards what might be called integrative approaches.[46] Scientists in such fields have begun to realise that the reductive procedures on which they have so far relied are not of much use in dealing with very complex objects and systems — the actual concrete situations confronting science in the real world, rather than the restricted abstractions of the laboratory. Thus, for example, the triumphs of molecular biology in theoretically reducing all life to the molecular structure of DNA, impressive as they are, cannot account for such complex biological processes as embryo formation, growth and organic regeneration.[47] For this a new kind of integrative genetics is required. There are similar problems of complexity in many fields of science which call for analogous integrative solutions. The ecological sciences are pioneering such new methods because they have to deal with complex natural systems.

Such moves toward integrative science, now as yet in their infancy, open the way for a new role for philosophy. In dealing with complex objects and systems many sciences have to come together and interact, for such objects cannot be restricted to the few parameters within which one specialised science normally works. As scientific research of necessity has to become more multidisciplinary, this opens up properly philosophical problems in the integration of the sciences. Philosophy can no longer deal with them by propounding a generalised meta-physics whose categories applied to all sciences. Recent attempts to provide something analogous to this for modern science, such as General System Theory, seem to have failed. Philosophy will have to find other ways of relating the sciences. If it can do this room might also be found for the philosopher in the scientific institutions of the future, as envisaged by Wiener and others, where integrative research is practised.

Philosophy that uses the model of language-analysis has also much to offer the sciences, especially social and cultural sciences

concerned with providing an understanding of the concrete developments of our contemporary world. It works closely with the results
of all the available sciences, and seeks to unify them in a
comprehensive synthesis that no science can achieve on its own. A
philosophic approach that avoids the pitfalls of 'pure' philosophy,
a recollective mode of thought, might fulfil the functions of
philosophy outlined in this work: it might be a concrete mode of
understanding through translation and dialectical mediation given
to the most self-searching destructive critique. As a mode of
conceptual thought it would employ all the rational means of
argument, definition and critique. But at the same time it would be
able to avail itself of models drawn from the arts, and, thus, be able
like the arts to approach close to lived reality. No subject of artistic
expression would be closed off from philosophic reflection and
recollection. As in the past, all the serious topics of though might
once again be opened to philosophy.

But we must beware of issuing empty promissory notes to be
redeemed in the future. Philosophy might be bankrupt, for there is
no guarantee that anything of substance and worth will be achieved
in this way if the sociological and socio-logical tendencies are against
it. Nevertheless, if the conditions are favourable this attempt to turn
the end of philosophy to the ends of philosophy might not be
altogether without consequence.

Notes

1. T. W. Adorno, *Negative Dialectics*, p. 29.
2. Ibid., p. 211.
3. N. Jacobson, *Pride and Solace* (University of California Press, Berkeley, 1978), Chapter 2.
4. For an exposition of the concept of a 'Marxist unconscious' in the context of an attempted synthesis of Freud and Marx see Richard Lichtman, *The Production of Desire* (Free Press, New York, 1982), Chapter 7.
5. J. Laplanche and J. B. Pontalis, *The Language of Psycho-analysis*, trans. D. Nicholson-Smith (Norton, New York, 1973), p. 393.
6. Mary Douglas, *Natural Symbols*, Introduction.
7. See M. Bakhtin, *Rabelais and His World*, trans. Helene Iswolsky (MIT Press, Cambridge, Mass., 1968).
8. One study that closely parallels that undertaken here has just come to my attention as this book goes to press. It is Michael Thompson's *Rubbish Theory* (Oxford University Press, Oxford, 1979). Thompson provides an anthropological-economic study of the processes of devaluation and revaluation whereby cultural objects are consumed by being degraded to rubbish and sometimes retrieved to become valued antiques. Those which we consign to the rubbish category are

rendered invisible by the symbolic system, sometimes literally so. His study of the relation of the visible and invisible thus parallels our own of the spoken, unspoken and unspeakable. Thompson also refers his approach to whole symbolic systems or what he calls world views. He, too, allows for repression, which he calls 'monster exclusion', the monsters in question being those objects which are anomalous, paradoxical or contradictory. The theoretical highlight of his approach is his account of the cyclical relation between world view and action, that is, social practice, which is governed by a repressive mechanism he calls the 'monitor'. In effect, this is a theory of creativity and destruction: '. . . an inevitable concomitant of this type of creativity is its negative aspect — something which was once visible and not rubbish becoming invisible and rubbish should it intrude in any way'. This is what Thompson calls the destruction of value or 'destructivity' (p. 149).

Once again we have an instance of work by a social theorist which is of considerable philosophical importance. It remains to be seen whether philosophers will take note of it.

9. See G. Simmel, *Conflict and the Web of Group-Affiliations*, trans. K. Wolff and R. Bendix (Free Press, New York, 1966), pp. 17–20.

10. L. Althusser, *Reading Capital*, trans. B. Brewster (NLB, London, 1972), p. 143.

11. See Girard's thesis on the periods of 'sacrificial crisis'. René Girard, *Violence and the Sacred*, trans. P. Gregory (The Johns Hopkins University Press, Baltimore, 1972), Chapter 2.

12. Max Weber, 'The Social Psychology of World Religions' in *From Max Weber*, (eds.) H. Gerth and C. W. Mills, pp. 270–1.

13. Ibid., p. 276.

14. Ibid., p. 277.

15. Ibid., p. 277.

16. E. R. Dodds, *The Greeks and the Irrational* (University of California Press, Berkeley, 1951), p. 69.

17. Ibid., p. 187.

18. C. H. Gordon, *The Ancient Near West* (Norton, New York, 1965), p. 102.

19. Dodds, *The Greeks and the Irrational*, p. 180.

20. P. Feyerabend, *Against Method* (NLB, London, 1975), p. 242.

21. Ibid., p. 243.

22. Ibid., p. 243.

23. Ibid., p. 233.

24. This is Spengler's fundamental insight into classical civilisation. See *The Decline of the West*, trans. C. F. Atkinson (Allen and Unwin, London, 1932).

25. Dodds, *The Greeks and the Irrational*, p. 34.

26. Feyerabend, *Against Method*, p. 261.

27. Ibid., p. 265.

28. Ibid., p. 270.

29. Ibid., p. 268.

30. Ibid., p. 270.

31. Ibid., p. 270.

32. Erich Auerbach, *Mimesis* (Doubleday Anchor, New York, 1957), Chapter 1.

33. T. W. Adorno and M. Horkheimer, *Dialectic of Enlightenment*.

34. Ibid., p. 57.

35. Ibid., p. 60.

36. M. I. Finley, *The Ancient Economy* (Chatto and Windus, London, 1973); and *The World of Odysseus* (Penguin, 1962).

37. Lévi-Strauss, *The Savage Mind* (Weidenfeld and Nicolson, London, 1972), Chapter 1.

38. *Cunning Intelligence in Greek Culture and Society*, p. 4.

39. Ibid., p. 5.

40. Ibid., p. 4.

41. Ibid., p. 5.

42. Ibid., p. 4.

43. It has been foreseen by Ellul. See J. Ellul, 'La Technique Considérée en tant que Système', *Etudes Philosophiques*, 2 (1976), pp. 154–7. Ellul, however, believes this trend to be fated and inevitable, which is not the view maintained in this work.

44. See W. Benjamin, 'The Work of Art in the Age of Mechanical Reproduction', in *Illuminations*, trans. H. Zohn, (ed.) H. Arendt (Collins/Fontana, London, 1973), pp. 219–54.

45. For a further exposition see *In the Beginning was the Deed*.

46. In a forthcoming book provisionally entitled *The Ends of Science: An Essay in Scientific Authority*, integrative approaches in the sciences will be discussed at length.

47. H. F. Judson, *The Eighth Day of Creation* (Simon and Schuster, New York, 1979). See in particular the conversation with Francis Crick and Sydney Brenner on pp. 202–21.

APPENDIX 1: A MODEL OF RATIONALITY

I

The following discussion of rationality is simply intended to bring together the separate strands of debate carried on throughout the book on this matter, mainly with reference to Weber, Nietzsche and Wittgenstein. What emerges out of it is not rigorous enough to be called a theory of rationality, but it might be referred to as a kind of 'composite picture' or, really, a philosophical model of rationality. Its starting point is Weber's sociological method of ideal-type concept construction. The comprehensive model of rationality is a constellation of such ideal-typical forms of rationality; each one is itself of such generality that it can in turn be divided into a further constituent constellation. None of these ideal-type forms is in any way a normative standard of rationality; each is merely a sociological concept useful for describing actual standards of rationality to be encountered in discourse and action throughout history. This is why these ideal-types cannot be taken for strict definitions as these have traditionally been understood in philosophy. Nevertheless, the model of rationality does descriptively define and delimit what has been meant by this term in the history of discourses, and thereby it establishes the bounds of rationality in history. In this way it may also serve as an exemplar of the philosophical method of working with models in place of normative or stipulative definitions.

The basic ideal-type forms of rationality to be found in history may be loosely designated as Primitive, Traditional and Rational rationality or, to avoid pleonasm, Western rationality — though historically this last form is by no means confined to the West. To avoid excessive elaboration, Primitive and Traditional rationality will not be further subdivided, but Western rationality will be differentiated into Reason, Rationalism and Rationalisation. These forms are in no sense intended to be construed along an evolutionary line of rational Progress. It is true that in Western history the predominance of one form often follows that of another, but this must not be taken to mean that the later ones are in some absolute sense more rational. For it is always a question of relative predominance; none of the forms is ever completely absent, nor is any one of them more original than another. For example, Rationalisation, the form dominant at present, is by no means the last evolved; early instances of it can be found even prior to the Reason of Greek metaphysics, as in Sumerian mathematics and astronomy, Egyptian bureaucracy and Greek formalised geometry. Nor can it be judged the most rational, for in many respects it can lead to irrationalities by comparison with the other forms, as is apparent to all critics of modern Rationalisation.

The main forms of Western rationality can themselves be further analysed either into separate subdivisions or into their differing constituent aspects. In principle such analysis is interminable, for there is no end to the distinctions that can be drawn. Within Rationalisation, for instance, one can distinguish modern from pre-modern modes, formal from substantive aspects, formalisation from practical rationalisation, and so on. Since all these distinctions define different variants of the one general form, it follows that the meaning of rationality shifts somewhat from type to type as there is no essential core common to all cases. The concept of rationality is like a game-concept in Wittgenstein's sense, and that is the same as saying that it is a shifting constellation of forms. Thus, even within the one clearly delimited general sub-form of Rationalism, such as that of scientific objective rationality, there is a slight change of meaning of the word 'rational' not only from one branch of the sciences to another, say from physics to economics, but also more subtly within any one science with each major theoretical revolution; for example, the move from Newton's to Einstein's physics is also a change in the meaning of scientific rationality because it brings with it a differing scientific method with somewhat different criteria of valid theorisation. But this must not be taken to mean that the two standards are utterly incommensurable, as Feyerabend insists, but only that comparison between them does not take place on the basis of some superordinating scientific methodology or absolute standard of rationality. Accepting a theoretical advance in the sciences entails being prepared to accept an altered standard of rationality, but not a totally new one, and the alteration must be in keeping with what had gone before.

And this point, which holds good for the most complex and most historically advanced forms of rationality, also applies in a modified way to the simplest and most historically primitive ones. Among these, too, there are many variants and variations, but this must not be taken to mean that the standard of Primitive rationality changes from tribe to tribe, or that each primitive language has its own rationality. Differing systems of classification, beliefs, practices and social structures can pertain to the same one general type of rationality, provided that the basic structures are homologous.

By Primitive rationality, in the first place we simply mean that which is inherent in the cultural languages of historically considered primitive people, without losing sight of the fact that such a mode of rationality can also be partially reproduced in a much more historically developed language. But this is not to say that it is the basic rationality of all languages; all languages possess proto-rational foundations, such as grammar, syntactical structure, pragmatic conventions of usage, and so on; these we shall later distinguish from Primitive rationality, properly so called. Attention was first focused on this form of rationality by the work of Lévi-Strauss. Prior to that, the very idea of such a thing ran counter to the Logocentric and Eurocentric anthropological tradition which deemed Western rationality the only possible one and considered all primitive language-forms irrational. From Frazer and Lévi-Bruhl onwards primitive thought was considered illogical, operating purely by analogy or some simple mental mechanism such as association; Lévi-Strauss was the first to argue persuasively that primitive thought (*pensée sauvage*) had to be considered rational even though its standards differed markedly from those of our own modern scientific thought. His work thus extended the bounds of what we consider rational, and it had the effect of redrawing what Wittgenstein called 'the boundary of the natural limits corresponding to the body of what can be called the role of thinking and inferring in our life'.[1] But in so doing Lévi-Strauss implicitly demonstrates that there are no given natural limits of what is considered rational, but rather demarcations subject to changing interpretation, which is not a matter of 'arbitrary definition' but of anthropologically informed philosophical investigation of actual languages, not merely of possible language-games.

According to Lévi-Strauss, Primitive rationality is basically a complex system of classification utilising concrete particulars, such as the different natural species, for this purpose. Classifying in itself, 'as opposed to not classifying, has a value of its own, whatever form the classification may take',[2] for 'any classification is superior to chaos and even a classification at the level of sensible properties is a step towards rational ordering'.[3] The rational ordering of primitive thought 'meets intellectual requirements' and not merely practical needs, just as our own science does. Seen from our own scientifically

rationalised point of view, Primitive rationality is frequently ineffi-
cient and ineffectual and cannot accomplish what are supposedly its
ends; for example, shamanistic medicine based on totemic relations
of sympathetic magic rarely cures the organic ailments it treats, and
this makes it seem merely irrational from our point of view — though
even in this instance it is not fully apparent to us what psychic utility
such 'curing' has for its practitioners. However, as Lévi-Strauss
points out, such Primitive rationality can be extremely efficacious
even by our standards. During the neolithic period the so-called
'sciences of the concrete' based on this form of rationality succeeded
in inventing and perfecting the basic arts and crafts of social life:
'agriculture, animal husbandry, pottery, weaving, conservation and
preparing of food, etc'.[4] These achievements involved 'methods of
observation and reflection which were (and no doubt still are)
perfectly adapted to discoveries of a certain type: those which nature
authorized from the starting point of a speculative organization and
exploitation of the sensible world in sensible terms'.[5] Hence, Lévi-
Strauss affirms that although 'this science of the concrete was necessarily restricted by its essence to results other than those destined to
be achieved by the exact natural sciences', nonetheless 'it was no less
scientific and its results no less genuine'.[6]

Lévi-Strauss explores at some length the distinction between this
science of the concrete and modern science, or in our terms between
Primitive rationality and modern Rationalisation. The difference
between them is not that between mythological fantasy or dream
subjectivity and objective reality; both 'sciences' refer themselves to
the same world for similar purposes, but they do so in different ways:
'one is supremely concrete, the other supremely abstract; one
proceeds from the angle of sensible qualities the other from that of
formal properties'.[7] Unfortunately, Lévi-Strauss does not account
very clearly for this difference for he keeps changing his terms; at
one point he speaks of 'savage thought as a system of concepts
embedded in images',[8] but earlier he had specified that 'the
elements of mythical thought similarly lie half-way between
percepts (images) and concepts',[9] namely, that they are signs, and
signs he defines in a Saussurian manner 'as a link between images
and concepts'. He seems to speak as if there were three separable
entities involved: images (percepts), signs and concepts, and as if
signs stood between images and concepts. It is hard to get a clear
sense of these relationships, of how they can account for the
difference between myth and science. It might have been better to

have treated the sign as an element of language, thus common to both, and then to have gone on to distinguish signs acting as symbols from signs acting as abstract concepts. Symbolic thinking could then have been further specified as concrete thinking in contrast to abstract thought, in much the way that the activities of the *'bricolleur'* are distinguished from those of the engineer, and the artist's from the scientist's.

These examples are of further importance in that Lévi-Strauss correctly insists that primitive thinking is still current and valid in activities such as *'bricollage'* and art, those which scientific rationalisation has not yet totally expropriated; hence, that Primitive rationality is not a superseded historical stage surviving as a mere fossil till this day, but that it is a *sui generis* form of rationality. It follows from this that 'concrete science' and rationalised science are not the primitive and developed stages of the one progress of rationality, but rather complementary rational modes, one of which is very old and the other quite recent, and these exist side by side and continue to perform their different functions. Generalising this insight to rationality as a whole, we can say that different forms of rationality are not mutually exclusive; rather they complement each other, and that rational 'progress' does not make the earlier forms superfluous. Rational development ought to mean the accretion of newer forms to join the older ones rather than a displacement of the earlier by the later. Unfortunately, modern Rationalisation with its ideology of Progress has tended to eliminate all forms of rationality in favour of itself, but this is no more to be countenanced than any of the other depredations of progressivism.

The illusion of rational Progress has also been furthered by ignorance of the rational capacities of primitive languages and societies; many rational features which sociologists, Weber among them, considered the hallmarks of modern industrial societies have been shown by anthropologists to be quite common among primitive people. Thus, disenchantment and secularisation have been taken since Weber as the distinctive features of modernisation and as measuring the distance reached by a society along the road to rational enlightenment, yet, as Mary Douglas informs us, 'there are secular tribal cultures':[10] 'Secularization is often treated as a modern trend, attributable to the growth of cities or to the prestige of science, or just to the breakdown of social forms. But we shall see that it is an age-old cosmological type, a product of definable social experience, which need have nothing to do with urban life or modern science'.[11]

We see in this instance, and the examples Mary Douglas provides to back it up, that many of the rational forms we think of as exclusive to modern Rationalisation are in fact constituents of Primitive rationality: 'The truth is that all the varieties of scepticism, materialism and spiritual fervour are to be found in the range of tribal societies.'[12] We know from other sources that all the features of democratic political rule and rational decision-making are also to be found among primitive people: assembly, debate, orators, moderators, president figures, consensus, majority, and so on.[13] Realism in art is not a new discovery either, nor the outcome of a rational perfecting of technique, as some art historians, including Gombrich, still believe; highly realistic pictures are to be found in pre-historic cave paintings and among the most primitive bushmen.[14] One could continue this count almost indefinitely for there is little that is the exclusive product of modern science and rationality, apart from the most obvious technological achievements.

Even Weber, who had no concept of primitive rationality, was not altogether unaware of the capacities of savage thought; the savage, Weber allows, knows his natural environment in some respects better than the average modern man: 'The savage knows incomparably more about his tools',[15] and his knowledge is adequate for his needs — though otherwise Weber adopted the conventional judgement that magic and myth are irrational and that the course of rationalisation entails their elimination, that it is a process of disenchantment. The anthropology of his time could hardly have disabused him of this idea.

In a similar relatively uncritical, fashion Weber opposes rationality to tradition and treats the latter as non-rational, as when he contrasts rational-legal to traditional authority, which he saw as based on the 'eternal-yesterday'. The overall world-historical picture that Weber presents is that no civilisation could break out of the cycles of traditional self-repetition except the West, with its twin Greco-Roman and Judeo-Christian roots. Nevertheless, Weber does explicitly refer to a form of rationality that is found predominantly in traditional societies. Having already stated that 'rationality may mean different things',[16] Weber goes on to distinguish a number of types of rationality, the last of which is distinctly that which we are calling traditional:

'Rational' may also mean a 'systematic arrangement'. In this sense, the following methods are rational: methods of mortificatory or of magical asceticism, of contemplation in its most consistent form — for instance, in yoga — or in the manipulation of the prayer machines of later Buddhism. In general, all kinds of practical ethics that are systematically and unambiguously oriented to fixed goals of salvation are 'rational', partly in the sense that they distinguish between 'valid' norms and what is empirically given.

As Weber defines it, Traditional rationality is characterised by systematic arrangement and methodical procedure, and is typified by rules and techniques for doing things, such as algorithms. Weber is in fact referring to Traditional rationality whenever he specifies a set ordering of procedures. His studies of ancient bureaucracy (Egypt and Byzantium), of traditional or ancient capitalism ('all over the world for several millenia the characteristic forms of the capitalist employment of wealth have been state-provisioning, tax-farming, the financing of colonies, the establishment of great plantations, trade and money-lending'),[18] of the rationalisation of sacred law and the codifications of patrimonialism, are among the many cases in which he implicitly invokes a notion of Traditional rationality.[19]

From these studies we can derive the following characteristics of Traditional rationality. Unlike Western rationality, it is not logical or conceptual in a strict sense; rather it tends to be rule-bound, prescriptive and formulaic. But unlike Primitive rationality it is given to explicit codification and systematisation, so that it has norms of consistency and methods of interpretation with which to overcome the more evident impossibilities. Thus, it is able to codify myths into epic cycles and holy scriptures and set up a pantheon on the principle of the division of labour among the gods ruling the universe. On the same rational basis there can be a codification of laws, practices and those techniques which establish the sciences in their traditional forms, and these can be extremely accurate in their results, sometimes unmatched by modern science until relatively recently; for example, the calendrical calculations of the Mayas were as accurate as eighteenth-century astronomy and the lobotomies practised by the Incas have been surpassed only in our time. The hermeneutic methods of traditional textual interpretation are as sophisticated as any practised now, allowing, of course, for the absolute presuppositions on which they are based and which are usually unacceptable to us. Because they are handed on as sacred revelations, such texts can be interpreted but not changed, except through charismatic or other such authoritative enactment. Traditional rationality is, thus, capable of change and self-modification but not through a principle of transformation inherent in itself, as is the case with Western rationality.

However, Weber's view of Tradition tends to be too static; he frequently identifies it with mere habituation, and he does not allow for its continuing relevance even in a modern context. Traditional rationality cannot be completely eliminated, for wherever knowledge cannot be fully rationalised, that is, transformed into scientific knowledge, there it has to rely on traditional modes of knowing, on practical experience, personal judgement, rules and prescriptions learned 'on the job' or inherited. And such knowledge needs continually to be invoked since there are always limits to what can be rationalised; the fields in which it is still utilised are innumerable: political and social decision-making, assessment of character, personality or suitability of people, psychoanalytic interpretation, the judgement of literary texts, grading of papers, and so on. The field of the law is particularly subject to traditional norms, and the mode of rationality utilised in judicial judgement is still far closer to the wisdom of Solomon than it is to the rationalism of Newton. And wherever commonsense is invoked it is usually a synonym for Traditional rationality.

The culture of England, with its common-law traditions and its belief in commonsense and the 'reasonable man', still upholds a version of Traditional rationality as against forms of metaphysical Reason and scientific Rationalisation more prevalent on the continent. In the English conservative tradition from Burke to Oakeshott there is a continuing effort to sustain and preserve a sense of Traditional rationality in politics and society as against all continental attempts at Rationalism; even for a modern thinker such as Oakeshott political knowledge is still a matter of traditional recipes and prescriptions, of knowing how to go about doing something, rather than of rationalised planning and theoretical constituting. Modern English commonsense linguistic philosophy is a highly sophisticated attempt to maintain a kind of Traditional rationality against the whole Western history of metaphysical Reason; the arguments invoked by Moore and the Oxford philosophers against metaphysics are basically no different to the derisive jibes and stage ploys directed against Socrates and all philosophers by traditionalist Athenians such as Aristophanes.[20] Even the sciences in England have until quite recently tended to take a distinct traditionally rational turn; in Weber's time 'the differences between English Physics and Continental Physics has been traced back to such a type difference within the comprehension of reality';[21] and, certainly, if one has in mind the almost craft-like hydro-dynamic electrical models of Faraday or even the practical atomic models of Rutherford one has some sense of what this difference in physics must have been like, though of late such distinctions have almost completely disappeared due to the triumph of relativity theory and quantum mechanics.

It is likely that in the near future there will be a resurgence of Traditional rationality. Rationalisation in the form of technology, science and organisation will continue to fail in crucial respects and to show itself to have in-built limitations; and as non-Western people assume a larger role in world affairs and come to realise that Western rationality has served them ill, it is likely that they will seek to draw sustenance from their own traditional ways of doing things and make some of these available to the world. This is already happening in fields such as medicine where Chinese acupuncture, Indian yoga techniques of relaxation and many other traditional body lores have proved themselves in some respects superior to Western mechanistic medicine. There also seems to be a return to traditional knowledge in law and decision-making procedures, where excessive rationalisation and misapplication of scientific methodology has proved itself counter-productive. Thus, for example, in policy making some recent theorists, such as Lindblom and Cohen, are arguing for a greater reliance on what they call 'ordinary knowledge' as against professional 'social inquiry' or rationalised knowledge.[22] And others — such as Ivan Illich in his arguments against modern schooling, medicine, transportation and the social-service professions — are, in effect, also making a plea for a return to traditional knowledge. The ideologies of Rationalisation are now rapidly becoming so discredited that the usual cries of obscurantism against such revisionists are no longer much heeded.

Until very recently it seemed as if Rationalisation would totally dominate and render both Primitive and Traditional rationality extinct, just as Western man has virtually eliminated both traditional and primitive man. This was certainly the end towards which Rationalisation was striving under the name of Progress. It saw itself as the rational culmination of history, having already succeeded the earlier Western rational forms of metaphysical Reason and Enlightenment Rationalism. Only in the West has rationality assumed these self-transforming forms, and this is what distinguishes Western rationality from all others. However, as we have seen, even in the West there are no clearly delimited progressive stages of rationality; though some forms predominate during certain epochs, none is ever completely lost or made redundant. The sequence of predominant forms of rationality from Reason through Rationalism to Rationalisation produces the sense of time as history progressing onwards in sequential epochs or stages that thinkers have enshrined in philosophies of history. But the illusory nature of such thought is now becoming apparent with the progressive crisis of Rationalisation on all fronts, extending from the evident dangers of the annihilating technology in the hands of the State to the now visible falterings of the sciences.

In its final crisis-laden culmination, Rationalisation has become that mode of Formal rationality which operates by strict procedures of exact calculation, quantification, formalisation and organisation. Basic to it as a mode of rationality is the principle of exact replicability or repetition; namely, that anything can be exactly reproduced at will: either it can be deductively arrived at through recursive computations, or it can be produced to standard specifications so that all its operations can be precisely predicted. If something cannot be itself physically reproduced, then at least a mathematical model of it can be devised which is a replica of all its operational properties, and this model can then be studied to provide information about its original. Computer models are the ultimate in replication, so in a sense they are the highest stage of Rationalisation.

This degree of Formal Rationalisation is an extreme limit case; most of the other forms of Rationalisation do not require exact reproducibility or repeatability, that is to say, total surveyability and exact understanding. Some form or other of Rationalisation is evinced in such contemporary phenomena as Big Science and technology, industrial capitalism, bureaucracy, positivist rational-legal legitimacy, egoist individualism and the aesthetic formalism of avant-garde art. When these historical phenomena first arose they were invariably seen as progressive tendencies of rational development, but by Weber's time they were already perceived as part of the 'iron cage' of modern society and the ground of modern Nihilism. In their early stages most of these tendencies were also furthered by

Rationalism, or Enlightenment reason, which is nevertheless a somewhat different form of rationality, relying on analytic thought rather than formalisation and exact intuition rather than computation.

Weber has little to say directly about Rationalism, which he does not explicitly distinguish as a distinct form of rationality, apart from the occasional reference to the *naturalis ratio* or *lumen naturale*, to *raison* or *éclarté* of the so-called 'Age of Reason' and to the revolutionary potential of rationalist natural law. For example, Weber comments as follows on the French Civil Code:

> As a product of rational legislation, the Code Civil has become the third of the world's great systems of law . . . The attainment of this position can be explained by its formal qualities; for the code possesses, or at least gives the impression of possessing, an extraordinary measure of lucidity as well as precise intelligibility in its provisions . . . To this clarity and simplicity much has been sacrificed in formal juristic qualities and in the depth and thoroughness of substantive consideration. Thus, both as a result of the abstract total structure of the legal system and the axiomatic nature of many provisions, legal thinking has not been stimulated to a truly constructive elaboration of legal institutions and their pragmatic interrelations . . . But these characteristics are the expressions of a particular kind of *rationalism*, namely the sovereign conviction that here for the first time was being created a purely rational law, in accordance with Bentham's ideals, free from all historical 'prejudices' and deriving its substantive content exclusively from sublimated common sense in association with the particular *raison d'état* of the great nation that owes its power to genius rather than legitimacy.[23]

In his assessment of the Code, one of the great achievements of Rationalism, Weber also implicitly provides a definition and partial critique of Rationalism in general, and reveals its strengths and weaknesses as a form of rationality. One can only wish that he could have done so explicitly for all forms of Rationalism for it is an extremely important form of rationality.

It was the dominant mode of rationality during the early period of modern science, when it took the twin guise of philosophical Rationalism and Empiricism, or analytic reason and this eventually became critical reason. Its roots go back, however, to the ancients, at least as far back as the Ionian rationalists, the Sophists, the Atomists and the Sceptics. And in many ways Rationalism still continues whenever critical reason is invoked in an effort at clarification or enlightenment, as it is often in the philosophies of Nietzsche, Wittgenstein and the Frankfurt school. Even our own attempt to specify a mode of critique as destructive reason is still linked to enlightenment critical reason, from which it ultimately derives.

Rationalism is to be distinguished from the main tradition of Western metaphysical Reason largely in terms of its critical spirit. Reason is relatively uncritical, tending rather towards speculation, system building and even dogmatism. Its main achievements are metaphysical philosophy, monotheistic theology and abstract science and law. These achievements were carried through in Greco-Roman civilisation and Judeo-Christian religion largely by philosophers and prophets respectively. Weber has subjected to sociological analysis the prophetic drive to ethical consistency and Nietzsche has sought to explain psychologically the philosophic will to Truth. Together they provide a genealogy of Reason, as we have already shown.

Rationalisation is in most respects the contrary form of rationality to Reason. The progressive inroads of Rationalisation into ever newer spheres of the modern world have succeeded in almost completely eliminating Reason. This as we have shown, has produced one crisis of rationality after another and could lead to the collapse of our world-civilisation. Rationalisation is not a self-sustaining form of rationality; it implicitly depends on other social forms to maintain it. Hence not everything can be rationalised; if the attempt is made to do so, then inevitably it will be self-defeating. Rationalisation itself however, is not the one, uniform mode of rationality. It has inner tensions and oppositions within itself. Even maintaining these, and not allowing the most extreme forms of normal calculating 'rationalization to prevail, is already a way of preventing the worst from ensuing'.

For Weber the future hope of rationality lies in the continuing tension between the two aspects of Rationalisation that can be analytically separated: the Formal and the Substantive: 'No matter what the standards of value by which they are measured, the requirements of formal and substantive rationality are always in principle in conflict, no matter how numerous the individual cases in which they may coincide empirically.'[24] In the economic context of this statement the difference is that between 'the extent of quantitative calculation or accounting which is technically possible and which is actually applied . . .' and 'the degree in which a given group of persons, no matter how it is delimited, is or could be adequately provided with goods by means of an economically oriented course of action'.[25] In a modern rationalised economy the difference is that between Capitalism and Socialism, and the conflict between these two systems of rational economy is Weber's most current example of the incompatibility between Formal and Substantive rationality: 'When a planned economy is radically carried out, it must accept the inevitable reduction in formal ration-ality of calculation which would result from the elimination of money and capital accounting. This is merely an example of the fact that substantive and formal rationality are inevitably largely opposed.'[26] The modern opposition of Capitalism and Socialism involves much more than mere economics; it touches on most other aspects of social life and thought, and goes back to earlier forms of the clash between Formal and Substantive rationality. To Weber it offers hope for the continuing conflict and struggle that is freedom in history. The recent trends for the convergence of both systems toward a common State-regulated bureaucratic order, or what Weber referred to as State Capitalism, would have struck him as confirming his 'iron cage' fears for the future course of Rationalisa-tion.

The Frankfurt school thinkers, following both Marx and Weber, have pursued this final premise to its furthest conclusion. They see in the continuing inroads of Rationalisation, or what they call instru-mental reason, the possibility of an end to freedom and history itself. Adorno and Horkheimer argue that the rationalisation of the partial aspects of social life into formally separate spheres of specialisation produces an overall irrationality, exemplified in the incidence of modern rebarbarisation; and Marcuse maintains that the logic of technical domination produces the repressive tolerance of one-dimensional society. As against this dead-end of Rationalisation they sought to oppose another mode of rationality, which they called critical theory or negative reason. This is a direct continuation of the critical reason of Kant and the Enlightenment and so it represents a contemporary form of Rationalism.

We must also seek to develop forms of critical reason capable of coping with the realities of Rationalisation and the modes of thought that sustain and further these in the realm of ideas. We must be particularly concerned with the crisis of rationalisation in the sciences which has started to make itself manifest since World War II. The confusion in existing theory and a failure to develop new theoretical understanding points to a breakdown of the scientific methodology of which even Weber was quite confident. The gradual displacement of theoretical or pure science by technically directed research produces a crisis of scientific rationality in itself and not merely in relation to its further consequences on society, such as those the Frankfurt school had diagnosed. The continued inroads of technology and organisation into science, if they remain unchecked, could lead to the collapse of science as a way of understanding and coping with the world.

II

The model we have sketched out by way of a sociological definition of Rationality can be applied like any such definition to cope with the conceptual problems arising in philosophy on this subject. However, our aim is less to provide answers to such problems than to indicate how they might be 'dissolved' in Wittgenstein's sense, using a model deliberately devised for this purpose, without in any way appealing to common language or linguistic usage. The most general problems that arise can be focused in the following questions: Which of the forms is ultimately more rational? Can they be ranked in terms of a common rationality, or are they fundamentally incommensurable, each with its own validity?

The different forms of rationality are indeed different forms of rationality: neither completely alike and differing only in degree because they are different *forms*, nor utterly unlike and incomparable because they are all forms of *rationality*. In the very process of giving an account of each of them we have in effect been comparing and contrasting them, showing how they are alike and how they differ. But that does not mean that we placed them in terms of the one standard as varying degrees of the one scale and judged them accordingly. There is no superordinating universal measuring rod of rationality. Nor did we locate them along a line of ever-increasing rational progress as ever greater realisations of an Idea of Reason. Indeed, though some of the forms of rationality can be said to be historically more primitive or older than others that developed subsequently, this is not to say that each newer form makes the previous ones obsolete or that any is ever to be completely discarded — though the nature of modern society makes more difficult or dangerous the full utilisation of some of the earlier forms of rationality. Deciding what kind of rationality to apply in a given case to a given task always requires an evaluative, critical judgement, the results of which can never be taken for granted. In the process of making such a judgement one necessarily has to compare the different rational approaches in terms of the advantages and disadvantages of each in relation to the matter at hand.

The 'more rational' is not necessarily the better if 'more rational' simply means technically more complex or historically more sophisticated. To decide which is better, or more rational in an evaluative sense, it is incumbent on one to carry through a critical argument that will determine what mode of thought is more appropriate for a given problem. For this is what is at stake in questions of alternative forms of rationality. Such an argument inevitably brings one to the level of philosophy, though it is rare for a professional philosopher to apply himself to such issues with any seriousness. Any one who has done so will be aware that it is never possible to pre-judge the issue in favour of the latest technique of rationalisation as against even Primitive rationality. It is true that one would not decide to use the mythical and magical methods of Primitive rationality for the task of building skyscrapers, but neither would one use instrumental-rational techniques for the construction of novels and poems — emotional engineering is a scientistic misnomer. A mythical framework for a novel, with its attendant metaphoric structure of relationships akin to sympathetic magic, might be the only way of arriving at and conveying a complex human truth, as Joyce's *Ulysses* and Mann's *Doktor Faustus* well exemplify. It is also perfectly rational to apply a mythical model to the inner drama of the human psyche, as the notion of the Oedipus complex in psychoanalysis demonstrates. That the psychoanalytic method of treatment has much in common with Shamanism, as Lévi-Strauss shows, does not argue against its rationality; it only qualifies the kind of rationality it is, and helps one in determining in what sense it is a science. Its method of interpreting symptoms and dreams has also much in common with the hermeneutics of reading texts, which is a form of traditional rationality, but again this does not mean that it is irrational by some higher canons of scientific methodology.

However, despite these evident virtues in earlier forms of rationality, it remains the case that in a modern society their re-application can only be appropriate for certain well specified uses; we cannot return to them and invoke them wholly, as and when we please. The dangers of rebarbarisation or of reactionary regression are all too evident. Thus, for example, a complete return to metaphysical Reason is now impossible no matter how much we might bewail the loss of its cohesive function in the sciences — though it might become possible again in ways unimaginable to us at some future time. The destruction of the Logos and Cogito as principles of reason at the hands of modern critical philosophy has made unavailable to us large dimensions of Reason and Rationalism. When the basic concepts of metaphysics and classical epistemology were dissolved, the rational methods deriving from them were rendered irrelevant.

In the context of the modern world it is undeniable that Rationalisation has numerous advantages over every other form of rationality. It is usually 'technically' superior to every other and enables the most 'efficient' modes of purposive-rational action to be accomplished and universal communicability to be achieved. It is this mode of action that can best carry out what modern society so requires: the control of men and domination of Nature. Our society is one organised for maximum production and this calls for the continuous extraction of matter and energy from natural sources. In this project modern Rationalisation offers the most success; within these goals it can accomplish much more than any other form of rationality. And apart from its productive goals, the rationalisation of any specific mode of activity usually results in improvement — considered in isolation. But when all these partial rationalised activities are added together the whole rarely manifests the rationality of its parts. The modern world is thus faced with the paradox of continual improvement and progress in all its parts together with mounting crisis leading to the threat of collapse overall. Rationalisation is in this respect the direct antithesis of Primitive rationality: this displays a relative inability to order rationally its partial actions, to improve them or to make them efficient, being incapable of rationally arranging means and ends or distinguishing cause from effect, but it does succeed in producing an overall well-balanced order, a structure that can integrate everything within its cosmos, producing the stability that primitive people have enjoyed for so long. Which are we to say is in the long run more rational? The question is certainly worth asking for it has no ready answer.

The world-wide success of Rationalisation is largely due to its power of universal communicability, its communicative rationality. Men who can rely on the languages of Rationalisation can communicate with each other despite all the differences of culture, creed, mentality and race; and so they can organise themselves and act to achieve their common goals. Those who communicate in the languages of the modern sciences can achieve an impersonal understanding and can co-ordinate their actions as in no other way. This is what makes science the perfect instrument of modern world-wide universal civilisation. Scientists who subscribe totally and unthinkingly to this form of rationality fondly imagine that this universality bespeaks the language of all intelligence in the universe; they have a delusion that they might communicate with creatures on other worlds in coded mathematical theorems or basic laws of physics. Little do they realise how restricted this language is even on earth, and how within the sciences themselves contradictions abound and incoherence can so easily supervene at every major step. It is true, of course, that a surprising measure of agreement and comprehension prevails among those who are initiated into the languages of the sciences. They generally agree in the results their methods produce, but they do not always concur about which methods to use: logicians agree about what constitutes the validity of their conclusions (provided they can accept the given system of logic), mathematicians recognise the soundness of a proof (provided they accept the given mode of proving), engineers abide by their calculations (provided they know what laws to apply), physicists also go by their calculations (provided they know which system of mathematics to employ) — everywhere in science there is agreement, with the ever-present potential for disagreement. It is on the measure of agreement won at any given point in the development of science that the communicability and ultimately the rationality of science depends. There is, of course, no guarantee that the agreement so far won in science will continue; it could break down and science as a human enterprise cease or take a quite different turn.

Modern Rationalisation has thus far compelled agreement to a far greater degree than any prior mode of rationality. This is why it is capable of achieving such universality. In this respect it has built on the prior universalising achievements of metaphysical Reason, which had in its time made possible the cosmopolitanism of the ancient world, being a superior medium of communication for large empires as compared with the diversity of Traditional rationality. The philosopher is the earliest of universal types. The arguments of

Reason compel to the limited extent that even though metaphysicians need not accept each others conclusions, they are required to consider each others reasoning and are bound by a common vocabulary of concepts, categories, hypotheses and principles. This is the mode of argument by dialectics, one of the earliest modes of rational communication in the West. Yet dialectics acknowledges by its very nature the separation of philosophers into rival schools — namely, that philosophers cannot communicate with near unanimity as do scientists.

However, the universal communicability of modern Rationalisation is beset with its own shortcomings. Those who employ highly rationalised languages of science can speak to each other with less and less chance of misunderstanding but only at the cost of having less and less of anything substantive to say. Perfect Formal rationality is only won at the expense of Substantive rationality. Universality and impersonality themselves require us to disregard all the special differences that give men their unique identity. Languages that have become totally rationalised — such as formalised systems and the so-called computer languages — are indeed perfectly communicable without the slightest practical chance of misunderstanding, but in such languages calculations can be performed yet nothing said. As soon as one wishes to say anything of substance and import, one must necessarily abandon perfect communicability and embark on a course open to the misunderstanding and incomprehension inherent in every living language in which the possibility of ambiguity, vagueness and therefore richness of meaning, has not been artificially suppressed through systematic formalisation. The total and permanent elimination of the very possibility of confusion is in principle impossible, as Wittgenstein has shown, for no matter how many strict rules there may be governing how something is to be taken, it will always be possible to mistake their intention — and also the rules governing those rules, and so on.

Languages that are over-rationalised also tend to lose one of the distinctive properties of Reason and Rationalism: their inherent self-reflexivity, and, hence, their capacity to enable self-consciousness and self-criticism. Reason provides self-reflexive categories such as that of Thought (*Nous*), and Rationalism provides the categories of the Subject (Mind, Ego, Spirit); both therefore permit the kind of self-understanding that is impossible with the non-reflexive categories of Rationalisation. Rationalisation entails fixing the domain of applicability of concepts so as to eliminate self-reference, with its possibilities for paradox and contradiction; in logic this is achieved through restrictive devices such as Russell's theory of types. Reflexivity can only be achieved through specially devised metalanguages, and these in turn require meta-metalanguages, for it is not possible for such a language to refer directly to itself. By contrast, the languages of Reason and Rationalism are always self-referring or directed to themselves as well as to that outside themselves; hence, they are more immediately self-critical. Due to this they have an inherent capacity for self-alteration and change which is not present in logical calculi, mathematical systems or technological and organisational orders; these must be changed from the outside, as it were, by being replaced with an alternative. The self-knowledge and clarification provided by self-generated philosophical development has been one of the driving forces for change both for the individual and society.

All such considerations belong to an overall comparative study of the different forms of rationality. Such a study would elucidate the unique features of each and the advantages or disadvantages of each in relation to given criteria, as well as its potential uses and abuses. This kind of study must not be confused with a pragmatic-utilitarian theory of rationality, such as was espoused by the Pragmatists and on occasions by Nietzsche, according to which rationality is to be assessed in terms of use for practical purposes. As practical advantage often means no more than purposive activity directed at mastering Nature, it is invariably argued by those following this approach that Formal Rationalisation is the most rational form. This pragmatist-utilitarian consideration often leads Nietzsche to espouse crude scientism and the view that any kind of fabrication that works is rational. By contrast, on our view the question of rationality invokes standards of truth and it is decided by whether a certain form of rationality elicits the relevant truth in a given case. However, the standards of relevant truth can vary: truth may be that which is pragmatically efficient, or realistic, or best able to explain reality, or that which is most significant, or able to elucidate meaning, or that which permits the most coherence or consistency, and so on. However, invoking a standard of truth as the criterion of rationality is not resorting implicitly to some particular super-rational absolute norm; truth is not an absolute standard, it is merely the best standard in any given context. Hence, in different contexts, it is judged in different ways; for example, logical, aesthetic, empirical and ethical truths are arrived at quite differently. There is no one Truth that is applicable to everything indifferently. Truth itself is not judged independently of the form of rationality necessary for its discovery. This makes the whole argument outlined here circular, but circularity is unavoidable where two notions are inextricably bound up with each other: rationality and truth depend on each other and one can not be determined without the other — they are mutually supporting. They both stand in complex logical relations to criteria of power, utility, communicability, value, and all other considerations that are relevant to, but are not identical with, either rationality or truth. We shall see something of how these relations obtain in the examples that follow.

However, it is clear from the discussion so far that forms of rationality are commensurable and that a critical philosophical comparison of them can be made, for it is possible to assess the kind of truth they afford in relation to a given problem-situation. This does not mean that such a comparison is easy or always conclusive; sometimes, indeed, it will be impossible to decide which is the relevant norm of truth or which form of rationality unambiguously relates to it. For example, to take an issue with some contemporary relevance, if one of the problems confronting the world at the moment is that of the rationality of different methods of agricultural production, then in most cases the 'laws' of modern economics provide us with the standards for assessing the economic efficiency and performance, and, hence, the rationality of methods of agriculture. These laws are true by the accepted canons of scientific validity. By such standards the primitive methods of cultivation will be found to be economically most irrational. However, if the issue is not merely one of economic rationality in this sense — that of one facet of activity abstracted from a total life context and called production — but the rationality of how men relate to their environment, then the verdict might indeed be very different. If the issue is one of how the harmony and balance of Man and Nature is maintained, then the modern economic laws of production are not the correct standards of rationality. One might, indeed, argue that Traditional or Primitive standards of rationality are far more relevant, and one's verdict might well be that a primitive form of agriculture is the most rational one, whereas a technically advanced, cash-crop mode of production is irrational since in the long run it threatens irrevocably to upset the ecological balance, to poison the earth, pollute the biosphere and eventually even to starve humanity. Even in specific respects one might argue that primitive agriculture is highly rational ecologically because it preserves the genetic purity of numerous strains of the one crop species,[27] whereas modern agriculture is irrational because it relies on a few selective hybrids of high yield with all the attendant dangers if these should fail. This, of course, does not settle the issue, for clearly from both a horticultural and philosophical point of view one is not likely to accept a one-sided verdict for the one or the other, but to see both as the opposed theses of a dialectical debate, indeed, the very debate that is even now going on both in speech and action between modernising economistic progressivists and ecological conversationists.[28] The conclusion of such a debate cannot be delivered as a simple verdict, for clearly what is ultimately at stake is to what extent the economic rationality of modern industrial production, of which mechanised agriculture has become part, is to be tempered by considerations based on older forms of rationality and their rival claims to utility and truth.[29]

Another example of an equally difficult, and perhaps in the last resort irresolvable, problem of rationality is that of deciding which psychological approach provides us with the most salient truths concerning mental phenomena, such as the nature and meaning of dreams. Does the most up to date formally rationalised and rigorously scientific experimental psychology with its technological apparatus and calculations give us the real, objective truth of dreams, as Crick insists?[30] Or perhaps a quasi-hermeneutic procedure of reading dream-texts in relation to a specific personal history, such as Freud favoured, which is in principle no different from traditional textual interpretation, is after all the better method of arriving at the essential truth of dreams? Or, perhaps a hieroglyphic deciphering of archetypal dream symbols by referring them to universal myths and to the racial unconscious, such as Jung advocated, which is very like primitive oneiroscopy, is ultimately the truest and best account of dreams? Which of these is more rational? It would be futile to look for a single over-arching scientific methodology able to answer this question. And yet one does not give up totally baffled, but proceeds on the extremely difficult comparative examination able to do justice to all these approaches and to assess their measure of truth and rationality.

In the social sciences, too, one is continually confronted with opposed approaches whose rationality and truth it is extremely difficult to assess with any confidence. For example, in politics the newest methods of political science are by no means always preferable to the very oldest, such as those basing themselves on Aristotle's *episteme politike*.

Does all this, therefore, mean that rationality is purely relative? This brings up the old philosophical conundrum as to whether rationality is universal or relative, which relates closely to the issue of whether it is 'objective' or 'subjective'. A few comments on this will have to suffice.

The classical view is that rationality is the one universal principle, without contradiction, which alone is capable of acting as the correct standard of truth. On this view, as Hegel put it, the rational is the real. What is correct about this classical view is that every form of rationality is indeed universally applicable; what is false about it is its assumption that there is but the one universal form. The universal applicability of every form of rationality is proven by the possibility of judging every society, no matter how different from our own, by the standards of the very latest norms of scientific rationality. The laws of economics, politics or psychology are applicable to all historical periods. The value of doing so and the measure of truth elicited depends, of course, on the nature and purpose of the study. This is a point which Weber firmly established in the course of the so-called *Methodenstreit* in economics at the turn of the century between neo-classical economists such as Menger and historicist economic historians such as Roscher.[31] What was at issue was whether the 'laws' of economics hold universally in the way that scientific laws, say in physics, do, or whether each historical epoch has its own 'laws' and economic formations. Weber asserted that the so-called 'laws' of economics, such as Gresham's law, are in effect rational ideal-types, which can be employed universally to gauge the extent to which 'the typically observed course of action can be understood in terms of the purely rational pursuit of an end, or where, for reasons of methodological convenience such a theoretical type can be heuristically employed'.[32]

> The ideal types of social action which for instance are used in economic theory are thus 'unrealistic' or abstract in that they always ask what course of action would take place if it were purely rational and oriented to economic ends alone. But this construction can be used to aid in the understanding of action not purely economically determined but which involve deviations arising from traditional restraints, affects, errors, and intrusions of other than economic purposes or considerations.[33]

It will, thus, often be the case that rational economic 'laws' can not be heuristically employed with any fittingness or propriety, but that other economic principles or formations, such as the '*oikos*' or 'city' or 'handicraft' economy, will be far more appropriate in a given case; and these will be deemed irrational from a modern economic point of view. Nevertheless, the rational laws are universally applicable. The point holds in general for all forms of rationality, which are all universally applicable with greater or lesser appropriateness.

The relativistic or historicist standpoint on rationality is also partly correct and partly mistaken. It is mistaken in maintaining that each historical period or each separate language has its own unique norms of rationality valid for itself alone. If this were so, it would make scientific historical study impossible, for all rational standards would only be applicable to their own period and there would be no way of comparing those of different periods, or even of understanding those which were very different from our own. Historical relativism ultimately entails historical solipsism. In fact, comparative historical study is possible, and this presupposes the universal applicability of standards of rationality, for, as Weber showed, it is essential to apply our modern standards of rationality, for purposes of analysis, comparison and causal attribution, to peoples and epochs who had quite different rational norms and to whom ours were utterly unfamiliar. And as we saw, comparisons between different kinds of rationalities are possible at every stage, and this, too, presupposes the comprehensibility of other rationalities. Nevertheless, the relativistic position is correct in so far as it insists that there are different forms of rationality and that the rational does not always mean the same thing, but changes its meaning relative to its context.

However, the variation in the meaning of rationality does not change drastically with every separate language, epoch, culture or civilisation. It is not relative to that degree. There are relatively few basic general forms of rationality, and the divergence within these might only be slight. Not every primitive tribe has its own distinctive form of rationality, for even though its language of myths and totemic classifications might be unique to itself, the overall structural form of these might be the same as that of many other tribes. This is the lesson that structural anthropology has taught us. Chinese rationality, even though it is distinctive of a whole civilisation, is not completely *sui-generis*, but displays traits that link it to the general type of Traditional rationality. And it is certainly not incommensurable with other forms of rationality, such as our sciences; if it were, Needham could not have written his history of Chinese science. In our own tradition of Western rationality the various stages and epochs are also comparable to each other. Aristotelian physics is comparable to Galilean and Ptolemaic astronomy to Copernican, though the comparison must not be carried out with a progressivist bias, implying that the latter is always in all respects the more rational and better; this is one point in favour of Feyerabend's incommensurability thesis, which is otherwise so much beside the point.[34] Much had to be given up when science switched from Aristotelian to Galilean physics; the metaphysical coherence of a general theory of action at once physical, biological and human in which motion, growth, change and activity could be subsumed under the same general concepts was replaced by a separation of secondary from primary qualities, of subjective will from objective motion, and a completely mechanistic treatment of all instances of the latter. The undoubted scientific gain in the rationalisation of physics had its correlative philosophic loss in the disruption of the rational unity of the world. To say this, however, is not to advocate a return to Aristotle, for a metaphysics once destroyed cannot be reconstituted nor can one choose at will what one will believe.

Earlier rational forms and forms of rationality are always potentially recoverable, but actual recovery is difficult and involves an indirect dialectical process of historical mediation, or, simply put, learning from the past. The lesson of the past is not an easy one to learn. A too precipitate attempt at the revival of mythic thought has led to some of the horrors of mythological irrationality in our century. But anthropologists and others have shown us the importance of a proper study of myth for a better understanding of modernity: Lévi-Strauss in his structural approach to comparative mythology and comparative studies of what he calls 'hot' and 'cold' societies, Mary Douglas and Victor Turner on the omnipresence of phenomena such as rites of passage and pilgrimages, and Canetti on the universal relevance of mythic insights. Traditional rationality, too, is beginning to be better appreciated even in the sciences, as Michael Polanyi's emphasis on 'tacit knowledge' implicitly reveals.[35] Reason and Rationalism have, of course, always been with us, since the attempts by rationalisers completely to do away with them never succeeded. The continuing influence of metaphysical Reason in political thought is attested by the recent writings of Strauss, Voegelin and Arendt. There are, indeed, serious difficulties with all such efforts, but this does not mean they are not worth making.

III

There remains one major philosophical issue that still requires clarification, and that is the relation between rationality and language. We have applied indifferently the term 'form of rationality' both to forms of language and to non-linguistic social forms. Indeed, in Weber the basic forms of rationality are types of action and not modes of speech; *'wertrational'* and *'zweckrational'* are referred to as 'forms of behaviour',[36] though Weber does think of them as applying also to beliefs, propositions and arguments. However, this is less of an inconsistency than might appear, for both speech and action are dependent on language. Wittgenstein's metaphor of the language-game reveals the mutual interrelationship of speech and action. To paraphrase Kant's celebrated dictum: speech without action is blind, and action without speech is dumb. Speech that is totally internalised and divorced from action is a private language, which as we have seen is a conceptual monster; and action in no way mediated by speech is mere behaviour without human meaning, like that of a dumb beast. Hence, rational forms of speech and action are intimately bound up with one another: a rational action is accountable in terms of reasons capable of being given in the form of a justification, if not always as a fully thought-out practical syllogism in Aristotle's sense; on the other hand, a verbalised intention, decision or argument can be acted out in deeds. Action takes its significance from language, and language becomes instantiated in action.

The difficult problem in determining the relation between language and rationality is to decide which has priority: is language founded on a rational basis, or is rationality grounded in language? Is language *per se* rational, or is it merely the pre-rational matrix of rationality? Does rationality inform language, or is it itself a form of language? Are linguistic structures rational? What is the relation between grammar, syntax, semantics and rationality? All these questions receive a clear answer in the metaphysical tradition, which is premised on the principle that 'in the beginning was the Logos' and for which language as opposed to thought is of secondary significance. In the modern Faustian tradition, whose basic principle is 'in the beginning was the Deed', and for which words and deeds are inseparable, they receive a very different answer.

In modern Faustian philosophy the ground of rationality is necessarily language. In a way this was already recognised in the original designation of reason as Logos, which in the first place means speech and assertion, but this original meaning was subsequently obfuscated — though never completely forgotten, at least by the Greeks — as the meaning of Logos began to shift away from speech and towards the more numerical Latin *ratio*. It has taken the modern recall in philosophy to bring rationality back to its original meaning, as Heidegger might put it. We might put it a little differently, since the modern discovery of Language is very different from the original Greek conception of *legein* or saying. Nevertheless, for us every rational form is in the first place a form of language. But this, as we shall see, must not be taken crudely to mean that rational forms are merely linguistic formulae and even less so figures of speech in the rhetorical sense. Logic must still be kept separate from Rhetoric and concepts from metaphors.

The conceptual destruction of the Logos and the Cogito has had a decisive effect on our whole conception of the relationship between language and rationality. It has meant no less than the simultaneous destruction of the metaphysical conception of 'objective' Reason and the epistemological conception of 'subjective' Rationalism, both of which entailed a hypostatisation of rationality as prior to language. Thus, on the modern conception language is neither extrinsically determined by any transcendent order or universal or Form, nor is it intrinsically governed by any inner ratiocinative thought or idea or categorial schemata. The consequences of this destruction are no less decisive for many modern philosophies that seek to base language on a rationality extrinsic to itself, such as those Positivist schools that bind language to logic. That language is not formed by logic, but logic by language is the inversion of the main doctrine of the *Tractatus*, which Wittgenstein carried out in the *Investigations*. As we saw earlier, according to his later philosophy logic is not a 'sublime', unshakeable order that underlies language; there are no simple logical forms behind the confusing multiplicity of discursive forms of ordinary language; it does not provide 'super-concepts' against which the ordinary meanings of words can be systematised and judged.

Wittgenstein's notion of logical-grammar also seems to establish correctly the relationship between logic and grammar. The whole metaphysical tradition from Aristotle up to and including Hegel maintained that logic underlies grammar. Modern logicians still insist on this relationship; Russell took it that the ordinary grammar of sentences is misleading regarding the 'true logic' of propositions. On the other hand, modern philosophers and philologists, such as Nietzsche, who tried to teach philosophy its philological lesson, argued that logic and all the categorial and rational forms are nothing but versions of the ordinary grammatical structures. Cassirer and Benveniste, among many others, have independently tried to show that Aristotle's categories are merely the grammatical forms of the Greek language. Wittgenstein seems to have understood better the relevance of grammar for logic; he realized that grammar becomes logic only when it is 'idealized', systematically rationalised towards a certain ideal extreme, and that logic is, therefore, an extrapolation from grammar; but from this it must not be concluded that its origins determine its subsequent role or meaning. The grammar of the Greek language may well have furnished models for the Aristotelian categories and for logic, but a model does not determine nor is it identical to the function it serves. Wittgenstein's error was to suppose that the logical-grammar of language was inherent in language and so something 'given' to be surveyed; he did not fully grasp to what extent it is a matter of philosophic interpretation, even to a larger extent than with ordinary grammar, which is more a matter of objective categorisation.

As we saw, Wittgenstein's arguments against the Logos and Cogito established two basic essential features of language: that it is arbitrary and that it is common in a special philosophic sense. These essential features carry over to those forms of language we call rational, hence they are also features of rationality. But what might it mean to say that rationality is arbitrary and common?

To speak of rationality as common means that it is governed by the requirement of intelligibility that holds for language in general, namely, the requirement of interpersonal agreement. There can be no purely private reason. Anyone who is proceeding rationally, such as counting, inferring or arguing, just as anyone who is proceeding in an orderly or systematic way, such as continuing the series 2, 4, 6, 8 etc, can only be said to be doing so provided others are agreed he is proceeding in the appropriate manner, that is, one that is recognisable to them as satisfying the established norms. However, the conditions of agreement do not hold universally, for as we have seen, different forms of rationality call for a different kind of agreement and what is considered correct for the one need not be so for the other. But some form of agreement there must always be; otherwise there can be no notion of correctness and, hence, none of rationality. Rationality is arbitrary only in the sense that it does not impose inexorably one set way of proceeding, as it is not a universally binding constraint on all language. Rationality is arbitrary in that it is a 'free' invention of language forms. It is a form of formal creation, and not the result of the discovery of a pre-established order or structure in things themselves.

These points are raised in Wittgenstein's dialogue on the imaginary case of someone continuing the series 2, 4, 6, 8 in a way that is totally at odds with our 'natural' sense of continuation, which is in turn an analogue of someone who seems to be inferring or reasoning in what is to us a totally irrational fashion (see Chapter 4, section 2):

> That is someone may reply like a rational person and yet not be playing our game.
> Then according to you everyone could continue the series as he likes, and so infer anyhow!
> In that case we shan't call it 'continuing the series' and also presumably not 'inference'. And thinking and inferring (like counting) is, of course, bounded for us, not by an arbitrary definition, but by the natural limits corresponding to the body of what can be called the role of thinking and inferring in our life.[37]

Yet, if it is not a more 'arbitrary definition' that dictates what is to be considered rational, then what are those 'natural limits corresponding to the body of what can be called the role of thinking and inferring in our life . . .'? For what can be 'natural' about any such limits? Further along in the same dialogue Wittgenstein is in fact saying the opposite: 'if you draw different conclusions you do indeed get into conflict e.g. with society and also with other practical consequences'.[38] So it seems that the limits of what is considered rational are not 'natural', that is determined by the nature of things, but instead social and practical, and that means in the last resort 'arbitrary' in the sense given it earlier.

Indeed, as we saw, different societies have quite different ways of relating means to ends, cause to effect, of judging equivalences, identities and sameness of categories, and even of inferring, measuring and counting — rational practices do differ. Does this mean, therefore, that there are no limits whatever 'corresponding to the body of what can be called the role of thinking and inferring' in human life as a whole in its historical multiplicity? Are there, then, no limits to what can be considered rational? It is possible, of course, unilaterally to prescribe such limits by insisting that it is 'the body of what can be called thinking or inferring in *our* life', meaning in our modern society, which is to count as setting limits to what can be called rational. But so to impose our standards as the only possible mode of being rational is to foster the progressivist delusion, the wilful refusal ever to acknowledge that modern Rationalisation can be less rational than earlier forms. But on the other hand, it cannot be merely a matter of arbitrary definition as to what is considered rational and so within the 'limits corresponding to the body of what can be called the role of thinking and inferring in our life'. Such limits cannot be as narrow as the rationality of modern society, but neither can they be so wide that the procedures and practices of all societies must all be considered equally rational. Rationality can neither be universal in the sense of always invoking the one fixed standard, nor can it be relative in the sense of each society having its own standard. In the former eventuality every earlier or non-Western society would have to be judged adversely, in the latter there could be no way of judging any society; nor could comparisons be made between the rationality of one society and another. We are faced here once again with the old problem of universality and relativity in a new guise. Our previous solution to this problem was to insist on the limited variety of known general forms of rationality, so that any putative candidate for rationality which was too unlike these general types would be outside the limits of rationality, that is to say, unrecognisable to us as a possible form of rationality. Within these limits a large variety of forms was possible since there could be a continuous range of differences between one type and another. This answer is in a general way in keeping with Wittgenstein's verdict as to what is to count as inferring, counting or even continuing a series, etc. when he insists that something too unlike 'our' practice and its role in life must be excluded, where 'our' refers to the full range of historical possibilities.

It follows from this view of rationality that speaking a language need not in itself be considered rational, since something recognisable as a language might yet fall outside the limits of acceptable rational forms. Indeed, basic language capacities are not in themselves rational, such as using words correctly, knowing how to go on according to given rules, continuing series and counting etc. Even being able to employ grammatical syntactical rules is in itself not fully rational. Nevertheless, all of these are the necessary preparations for rational speech, that is to say preconditions for thinking rationally. In this sense they might be considered proto-rational. Grammar develops into rationality when it becomes a 'logic of discourse' and is not merely syntax. This 'logic' need not be explicitly articulated nor need it be syllogistic in the Aristotelian manner. But it needs to evince some principles of consequence and incongruity, even such as play a part in riddles, jokes and humour of the Lewis Carroll type. All primitive people have a clear sense of such logical principles. The Odyssean word play on 'Nobody' in the Cyclops episode is one such example; though it is made too much of in the *Dialectic of Enlightenment*, where it is taken as an exemplification of nascent bourgeois reason; analogues to it exist in many myths of primitive people.

However, the presence of such rational elements in jokes and myths must not be represented as the rationality of figurative language in general. Figures of speech in the rhetorical sense are not rational forms; metaphors, metonymies, symbols and other literary tropes are usually non-rational, even sometimes indeed illogical and thus irrational. The forms of language that figure in poetry and rhetoric are different from those which form logic and science because the latter have standards of truth and validity whereas the former do not, being more a matter of aptness, or imaginativeness, or persuasiveness. This difference was not given explicit definition till Aristotle, but it was nevertheless registered in speech at all times in less explicit ways. However, Aristotle's definitions of logic, rhetoric and poetics are not still to be accepted unmodified, for they are themselves part of our metaphysical heritage. They did not even remain unchallenged in their own time; the rhetorical tradition extending from the Sophists has always fought against too sharp a segregation of poetry and science. This tradition was revived strongly during the Renaissance; only to be pushed back again with the rise of Rationalism and the new sciences when figurative speech was banned from scientific reporting and rational canons were rigidly applied by the new scientific academies. The dispute has continued and the claims for rhetoric have been upheld by thinkers, such as Vico, early-Nietzsche, Jaspers, Heidegger, Ricoeur and Derrida, who put forward one version or another of the view that language is fundamentally figural and so metaphoric. At its extreme this is interpreted as meaning that rationality, too, as a form of speech, is really metaphoric. As against this we have tried to argue that though concepts and metaphors or logic and poetry are forms of language, they function differently and so cannot be identified.

Notes

1. Wittgenstein, *Remarks on the Foundations of Mathematics*, p. 2.
2. C. Lévi-Strauss, *The Savage Mind*, p. 9.
3. Ibid., p. 15.
4. Ibid., p. 264.
5. Ibid., p. 16.
6. Ibid., p. 16.
7. Ibid., p. 269.
8. Ibid., p. 264.
9. Ibid., p. 18.
10. Mary Douglas, *Natural Symbols*, p. x.
11. Ibid., p. ix.
12. Ibid., p. x.
13. There are numerous tribes who have some of these political forms, and even one or two, among them a tribe in the Southern Sudan, who have all.
14. E. H. Gombrich, *Art and Illusion* (Pantheon Books, New York, 1960), Chapter IV.
15. Max Weber, 'Science as Vocation' in *From Max Weber*, p. 139.
16. Weber, 'Religious Rejections of the World and their Directions' in *From Max Weber*, p. 293.
17. Ibid., pp. 293–4.
18. Weber, 'The Sociology of Religion' in *Economy and Society*, vol. 1, (eds.) G. Roth and C. Wittich (University of California Press, Berkeley, 1978), see XV, p. 614.
19. Weber, 'The Sociology of Law', *Economy and Society*, vol. II, sec. V and VI.
20. Commonsense philosophy has always been traditionalist. Linguistic philosophy is frequently only commonsense philosophy in modern dress. In fact, the derivation of the thought of G. E. Moore from the commonsense philosophy of the Scottish Enlightenment, especially from that of Thomas Reid, is well-documented. Henning Jensen claims that through the influence of Moore the Scottish common-sense philosophy also influenced Wittgenstein and the Oxford School. See 'Reid and Wittgenstein in Philosophy and Language' in *Language, Logic and Philosophy*, Proceedings of the 4th International Wittgenstein Symposium, September, 1979, (eds.) R. Haller and W. Grassl (Hölder-Pichler-Temsky, Vienna, 1980), pp. 192–4.
21. Weber, *From Max Weber*, p. 293.
22. C. E. Lindblom and D. Cohen, *Usable Knowledge* (Yale University Press, New Haven, 1979), Chapter 2.
23. Weber, 'Sociology of Law', in *Economy and Society*, vol. II, pp. 865–6.
24. Weber, *The Theory of Social and Economic Organization*, (ed.) T. Parsons, p. 212.
25. Ibid., pp. 184–5.
26. Ibid., pp. 214–5.
27. See Lévi-Strauss's account of the length to which savages go to maintain plant purity and diversity: *The Savage Mind*, p. 73.

28. See Suzanne Peters, 'Organic Farmers Celebrate Organic Research: A Sociology of Popular Science' in *Counter-Movements in the Sciences*, (eds.) H. Novotny and H. Rowe, Sociology of the Sciences Yearbook 1979 (D. Reidel, Dordrecht, Holland, 1979), p. 251.

29. See M. Godelier, *Rationality and Irrationality in Economics* (NLB, London, 1972). Godelier provides an extensive discussion of this issue from a very different point of view to that advocated here; his is a progressivist Marxist approach; but it brings out well the relative rationality of primitive economy.

30. See the recent theory of dreams put forward by Francis Crick and G. Mitchison, 'The Function of Dream Sleep', *Nature*, July, 1983, vol. 304, pp. 111–14.

31. Weber. 'Objectivity in Social Science' in *Methodology of the Social Sciences*, pp. 94–110.

32. Weber, *The Theory of Social and Economic Organization*, p. 108.

33. Ibid., p. 111.

34. Feyerabend, *Against Method*. However, Feyerabend qualifies his earlier view considerably in *Science in a Free Society*, pp. 65–70.

35. See M. Polanyi, *Personal Knowledge* (Routledge & Kegan Paul, London, 1969), Part II.

36. Weber, *The Theory of Social and Economic Organization*, p. 115.

37. Wittgenstein, *Remarks on the Foundations of Mathematics*, pp. 33–4.

38. Ibid., p. 34.

APPENDIX 2: REDUCTION AND REDUCTIVISM

Modern science is inherently reductive, but not necessarily reductivistic. Failure to distinguish the two concepts has led to serious misconceptions and sometimes even to unfounded criticisms of science which are actually only criticisms of reductivistic interpretations of reduction. Hence, no account of reduction can fail to come to terms with the challenge of reductivism; otherwise it risks unknowingly falling into it or being wrongly identified with it. As reductivism is a positivistic interpretation of reduction, so it is in the context of, typically, a Logical Positivist philosophy that reductivism must be understood for only there does it have philosophic meaning. A rejection of such Positivist interpretations leads to a rejection of reductivism, that is, to a denial of its meaningfulness and to alternative attempts to interpret reduction in a non-reductivist sense.

A clear instance of confusion of reduction with reductivism is to be found in a piece by Hilary and Steven Rose.[1] To begin with they assert that 'the most powerful paradigm in Western science [is] that of reductionism'. This they call the ideology of science and identify with Positivism:

> The ideology of science . . . claims that the methodology of the natural sciences, generally understood to mean a reductionist methodology of the type discussed below, has universalistic importance . . . The ideology of science is thus positivistic. The clearest exponent of this viewpoint has been the molecular biologist and archetypal reductionist Jacques Monod; he has argued this case extensively in his recently published book *Le Hasard et la necessite* (1970).[2]

Rose and Rose thus identify Positivist reductivism with the quite ordinary reductions and reductive methods of molecular biology. This is expressly put in the following statement:

> Reductionist tools are those which, either by simplifying the system under study (as for example by choosing a worm or sea slug, both favoured laboratory animals), or by limiting the aspects chosen for examination (as for example by considering

only certain forms of 'emitted' behaviour) make the experimental problem more approachable and subsumable with the general methods and theories of science developed for less complex systems, living or non-living.[3]

The 'reductionist tools' here referred to are simply the ordinary reductive methods of science; they do not of themselves warrant reductivist interpretation. That molecular biology is reductive is hardly worth disputing; it is an inherent part of the research programme of this science. As Yoxen states, speaking of one of the founding originators of this programme: 'Muller thus reduced the question of "life" to the problem of gene structure . . . What is particularly interesting about this highly reductive idea is that it places a specific problem in a fundamental position in biology.'[4] But this or any other example of the reduction of the complex (life) to the simple (gene) does not in itself justify a reductivist interpretation. In so far as science abstracts a few generalities from the rich and multifarious particularity of real objects and explains them by imposing an abstract, intellectualised and simplified model or schema, it is necessarily exercising a reductive function. Abstracting from objects to a few parameters, which are sometimes best exemplified by the simplest of real objects, is an inherently reductive method that most sciences cannot do without; it is the basic procedure of those sciences — physics, for example — which Pantin calls 'restricted'.[5] Ravetz has argued that most scientific explanations consist of the solution of problems on intellectually constructed models which are not themselves the real objects of our everyday perception and knowledge; and such models or scientific 'objects' are in an original and fundamental sense reductions.[6]

Roszak, too, has emphasised the inescapably reductive aspect of modern science without being able to distinguish it from reductivism. He uses the same word for both, so that when he correctly states that 'reductionism . . . has been there since Galileo boldly read the human observer out of nature by concluding that the primary qualities of reality are its objective measurables', he really means 'reduction' not 'reductionism'.[7] This is the case when he states, again correctly, that 'reductionism is quite simply inseparable from single vision. It is born from the act of objectification . . .'[8] But unfortunately, to Roszak reduction and reductionism or reductivism are all the one feature of science, and he sadly regrets that 'the scientific community is incapable of eradicating the vice'.[9] Though he is prepared to grant that 'undeniably there are aspects of reductionism that merit appreciation',[10] he only really appreciates this 'in science which is free of any reductionist intention'.[11] In an extensive appendix entitled 'the Reductionist Assault' he indiscriminately lists as instances such diverse research activities as Artificial Intelligence programing, drug and behavioural therapy and molecular biology.[12] He quotes approvingly the statement of Leon R. Kass of the National Academy of Sciences that 'there is nothing novel about reductionism, hedonism and relativism; these are doctrines with which Socrates contended'.[13] Thus reduction assumes something of the character of an original sin of science.

Rose and Rose also use reduction and reductionism interchangeably; sometimes switching from one to the other meaning in the course of the same sentence, as when they say:

> The apotheosis of biological reductionism is to be found among the molecular biologists such as Monod and Crick who argue essentially that in the long run all biology is to be derived from a study of the properties of macromolecules of which the cell is composed (such as DNA) and their interactions, and may be best understood by studying the chemistry and organization of a particular bacterium present in the human intestine (Escherichia coli) or — even more reduced — a virus which preys upon bacteria.[14]

The second part of the sentence invokes the ordinary procedures of scientific reduction when it refers to simple organisms being studied in order to understand complex ones. The first part of the sentence, however, imputes to Monod and Crick a reductivist interpretation of their work when it ascribes to them the view that 'all biology is to be derived from a study of the properties of macromolecules'. The key word here is 'derived from', for if 'derived from' means the same as 'deduced from' then the phrase reads: 'all biology is to be deduced from a study of the properties of macromolecules', and this is an assertion that can only be made within a Positivistic reductivist interpretation of biology.

Biology can be reduced to a study of macromolecules in the quite ordinary sense that cells and organisms do not have any other properties apart from those determined by macromolecules, that is, they are made up of such molecules and do not have any higher 'emergent properties', as vitalism or organicism would require. In this sense all life can be said to be simply a function of molecules. However, from this it does not follow, as the reductivists would have it, that all life and its properties can be deduced from the properties and laws of macromolecules, that is, that biology can be deduced from chemistry and chemistry from physics. If X can be reduced to Y, it does not always follow that X can be deduced from Y. Reduction and deduction can only be assumed to be mutually interchangeable within a Positivistically interpreted reductivist methodology, not otherwise. It is not in fact possible to deduce biological laws and concepts from those of physics and chemistry, even though physical and chemical laws and concepts subsume and explain those of biology. This is what Norbert Elias asserts when he states that:

> The actual terms used in different sciences concerned with the exploration of composite units whose properties depend — more or less — on the configuration of the component parts are often very different: conformation, shape, form, organization, integration, figuration are some of them.[15]

Thus, in biology there is no way of deducing the cell as an organisational configuration from chemistry and physics, even though every process that goes on within the cell is reducible to the macromolecules of chemistry and physics.[16]

And the same point may also be made in reverse. The laws we can deduce from chemistry and physics will not serve to explain the complex configurations or complex systems or organisms in the so-called 'unrestricted' sciences of geology, meteorology, or biology. This point is made by Pantin:

> . . . [though] it has become abundantly clear that these same laws of matter and energy hold for living organisms and indeed for our own bodies. This does not mean that the laws deduced from the study of inanimate systems will necessarily serve to explain the special features which distinguish living matter, or the behaviour of an amoeba or of a mammal, or the expressions of the human faculty. So far, we only say that the manifestations of none of these special attributes require the contravention of those physical laws, whatever additional ones may be required for their description.[17]

This is the fundamental reason why the unrestricted sciences cannot be deduced from the restricted ones, and why they must seek to explain their complex objects with methods, theories and concepts that are quite different. The Logical Positivist project for a Unified Science is a logical utopia that is in principle and practice unrealisable. The rationale for it is to be found in Logical Positivist reductivism, which seeks to deduce all sciences from the laws of physics.

It is only in the Positivistic methodology of science that reduction and deduction are taken as mutually interchangeable. In a recent study of the philosophy of science Suppe establishes this as the cardinal point of the Positivist approach. Speaking of theory reduction from a secondary to a primary science, he states:

> Nagel characterizes such reduction, thusly [sic], 'the laws of the secondary science employ no descriptive terms that are not used with approximately the same meanings in the primary science. Reductions of this type can be taken as establishing *deductive* relations between two sets of statements that employ a homogeneous vocabulary'.[18]

In characterising the extremely influential deductive-nomological or 'covering law' model of explanation put forward by Hempel, Suppe notes that the key to it is 'the requirement that explanations must be arguments which yield, deductively or with high probability, the explanandum E';[19] for 'according to Hempel, an explanation of some event (whose description is known as the explanandum) consists of a suitable *argument* wherein the explanandum "correctly follows" from the premises (known as the explanans) of the argument'.[20] It is clear why Logical Positivism seeks not merely a reductive, but also a deductive interpretation of science: its ultimate aim is to transform science into a deductive system. The construction of such a system has long preoccupied the Logical Positivists in their programme for a Unified Science. And its failure marks what Suppe and others have called 'the swan song of Positivism'.[21]

Reductivism derives its annihilating propensity precisely from this deductive requirement: for if X, which is reducible to Y, can also be deduced from Y, then X is nothing but Y. The formula 'X is nothing but Y' has been rightly shunned as the archetypical expression of reductivism. In terms of Positivist reductivism, biology is 'nothing but' chemistry, psychology is 'nothing but' biology, mind is 'nothing but' brain, and society is 'nothing but' the behaviour of human organisms.

Scientific reduction, *per se*, does not demand such 'nothing but' conclusions. Science is reductive, but it also permits a principle of conceptual complementarity that is the very opposite of reductivist, and for which the appropriate verbal formula is 'both-and' rather than 'nothing but'. Thus, biology is both the chemistry of molecules and a science of living forms not deducible from chemistry; psychology is both the biology of behaviour and a science of mind, which in turn is both brain physiology and conscious life. There is at once a complementarity of qualities, of sciences and of concepts.

Conceptual complementarity occurs whenever it is possible to affirm that two sets of concepts inherent in conceptually distinct modes of description or explanation are both applicable to the same thing, situation, or reference point, in such a way that it may be characterised as being both X and Y, where X and Y are conceptually diverse qualities. The thing, situation or reference point can also be said to be the one object and also two separate 'objects', as, for example, both organism and mind. For conceptual complementarity to occur in the sciences, the two set of concepts — deriving from two sciences — must be in a relation that makes the one reducible or explicable in terms of the other, but not deducible from it. The complementarity is conceptual because it involves, not two separately identifiable items or phenomena, but only two separate concepts or conceptual 'entities'; and these give rise to different 'objects' in the sense in which one speaks of the 'object' of a concept or a mode of explanation. Most sciences, and especially so the more complex ones, deal with different 'objects' in something like this sense because, as Whitley puts it, '. . . distinct explanatory approaches require distinct means of ordering and describing phenomena, emphasizing different properties and relations so that the "same" object can be understood and described in a number of different ways',[22] or, in other words, there are different 'objects' involved in the technical sense of 'object'.

The most debated example of conceptual complementarity is that which obtains between the concepts 'mind' and 'brain' in the two complementary sciences of psychology and neurology. Thus the mind, as an 'object' of the system of concepts and descriptions invoked in psychology, is a conceptually different 'object' from the brain, the 'object' of neurology. But otherwise mind and brain are not distinct things in any other sense. The two objects 'mind' and 'brain' are conceptually related to each other in the way that the two sciences they subtend are related: neurology explains psychology, and so in that sense psychology can be reduced to neurology but not deduced from it. Analogously it can be said that 'mind' can be reduced to 'brain', but from this it does not follow that mind is nothing but brain.

The conceptual differences separating the sciences of psychology and neurology are rooted in and have their basis in the 'bodily' and 'mentalistic' forms of speech of ordinary language. However, this does not mean, as the Linguistic Positivists believe, that ordinary language contains the real 'truth' of these concepts. Language that is naive because it is theoretically unsophisticated is governed by other prejudices which can be even more misleading than the theoretical assumptions of philosophy and science. Indeed, the theories of philosophy and science are themselves 'applied' in ordinary language through the course of history and they transform it accordingly. This is an historical and social process whereby theories are adopted as common prejudices and embedded in ordinary forms of speech. Thus ordinary language is no ultimate grounding of concepts nor repository of their 'truth'.

However, the diversity of languages does serve as a model for understanding the relationships between complementary concepts; these are like different languages which can be translated into each other up to a point but not completely. Such partial translatability provides a good analogue for the relations between the concepts of mind and those of the brain.

Some assertions concerning the mind can be 'translated', that is, correlated with, some concerning the brain, but for most others we do not have as yet any such correspondences — it being the continuing aim of the sciences to establish more of these. This is a scientific empirical quest allowing of no *a priori* assumptions. Hence in this respect the relation between the mind and brain is also empirical and to be developed through further research, which would proceed like the search for new rules of translation. And as this research develops so the concepts 'mind' and 'brain' have to be modified and theoretically altered to accommodate new empirical findings. It is for such reasons that what we now mean by 'mind' and 'brain' is very different from what Descartes meant. Thus, the conceptual relation between 'mind' and 'brain' is a continually changing one which depends upon the empirical and conceptual changes in the relation between the two sciences of neurology and psychology. It is possible to argue that in principle there will never be a final conclusive result, that is, a complete 'translation', and that both sciences will continue to exist side by side since the possible 'translations' or correlations between them are in principle inexhaustible. If that is so, then there is no such thing as establishing once and for all the definitive relation between mind and brain. It is likely that an analogous conclusion holds for most other examples of conceptual complementarity, which are in principle not susceptible to a final deductive, 'nothing but', exhaustive dissolution.

Conceptual complementarity bears a close relation to scientific complementarity as propounded by Bohr for the Quantum physics of wave and particle. Bohr himself supposed that Quantum-theory complementarity was merely one instance of the general complementary character of the whole of reality. In an essay on this issue entitled 'Continuity versus Discontinuity in Science', Norman Jacobson quotes Bohr as saying that complementary modes of description are 'essential for our account of the behaviour of living organisms', are necessary to 'conciliate the apparent contrasting viewpoints of physiology and psychology' — precisely the mind to brain relation discussed previously — are required to understand 'the individual within his community', and 'different nations and even different families within a nation', and finally are involved in the relationship between 'science and art'. Some of these cases are examples of conceptual complementarity; others clearly are not. There are different modes of complementarity involved which Bohr failed to distinguish: the complementarity of individualistic as against holistic descriptions of society is very different from the complementarity of wave mechanics as against matrix mechanics in Quantum physics; and neither of these properly qualify as conceptual complementarity like that of neurology and psychology or brain and mind, which are two discrete conceptual realms. The character of the complementarity in question depends on the nature of the opposition between the complementary alternatives. Complementarity arises where there are two exclusive but unavoidable alternatives which are mutually negating but not dialectically contradictory; both can be true of something at once. Complementarity is thus different from dialectics, where the thesis and antithesis are two distinct moments. Dialectics arises where there are meaningful contradictions involved, as typically in the humanities; complementarity arises where there are only alternatives involved, as between different descriptions deriving from two sciences. Thus dialectics is more characteristic of History and complementarity of Nature, but in neither case exclusively so. Putting it paradoxically, it might be said that complementarity is a non-contradictory form of dialectics.

Complementarity in the conceptual sense can be invoked as a test to separate mere reduction from reductivism. Only reductivism insists that if X is reducible to Y then X is 'nothing but' Y. On a complementarist interpretation of reduction, it is possible to assert that where X is reducible to Y, X is both Y and alternatively not Y. This is why reductivism is intellectually annihilatory, for to assert that X is 'nothing but' Y is to annihilate X as anything distinct from Y. On the other hand, complementarist reduction can be destructive but not annihilatory, for to assert that X can be reduced to Y is to destroy X as an inherently autonomous entity; however, it is also to deny that X is totally identical to Y. Thus on a complementarist interpretation it can be granted that in a scientific sense the mind can be reduced to the brain without affirming that mind is 'nothing but' brain, insisting instead that mind is not identical to brain, but is conceptually distinct and complementary.

The problem of reductivism might appear to be merely an intellectual issue in the interpretation of science, but in the present stage of techno-science it is also fraught with grave practical implications. Its challenge is even more daunting after the 'swan song of Positivism', in Suppe's phrase. Positivism might now be nearly dead, but the reductivist modes of thought which it spawned have almost become part of the self-understanding of science; it is prevalent among scientists such as, for example, Monod and Crick, whom Rose and Rose castigate for their interpretation of molecular biology. As reduction becomes more than just an intellectual theoretical possibility and is increasingly realised through practical techniques, so it tends to confirm a reductivist interpretation for those minds that already hold it. Thus, with the onset of genetic engineering it has come to seem to those who are reductivistically disposed that life is nothing but a complex molecule, for now they can control life processes technologically by manipulating their molecular constituents. Analogously, the new technologies of brain manipulation have also made it seem probable, for those already inclined to think that way, that the brain is all there is to the mind. As long as genetics was largely a theoretical science and neurology relatively ineffective on the level of detailed brain functioning, it was still possible for anti-reductivists to insist that not everything was reducible. So, for example, the older neurologist Eccles has stoutly maintained, with Popper's support, a dualist position of an old-fashioned interactionist kind not significantly different from that of Descartes. But such views have come to seem increasingly anachronistic as practical technologies of reduction have been developed. Techno-science has tended to confirm reductivism even without the benefit of a Positivist philosophy. This makes it seem as if all that is left for the philosopher to do is to bow in silent adoration before the technical triumphs of science, a posture in fact adopted by the Antipodean philosophical school of reductivist Physicalists.

This new technological challenge of reduction can only be met intellectually by a better grasp of the complementary nature of the languages of science. For this task an intellectual investigation will be called for that can only bear the nearly antiquated name of philosophy. This is one function that philosophy can still sustain even when so many of its others have deteriorated. However, it must not be assumed as self-evident that philosophy will be allowed to fulfil even this function in the age of techno-science.

Notes

1. 'Do not adjust your mind, there is a fault in reality' in *Social Process of Scientific Development*, (ed.) R. Whitley (Routledge and Kegan Paul, London, 1974), p. 155.
2. Ibid., pp. 153–4.
3. Ibid., p. 155.
4. Edward Yoxen, 'Giving Life a New Meaning' in *Scientific Establishments and Hierarchies*, (eds) N. Elias, H. Martins and R. Whitley, Sociology of the Sciences Yearbook 1982 (Reidel, Dordrecht, Holland, 1982), p. 131.
5. See C. F. A. Pantin, *The Relations Between the Sciences* (Cambridge University Press, Cambridge, 1968), Chapter I.
6. See J. Ravetz, *Scientific Knowledge and its Social Problems* (Clarendon Press, Oxford, 1971), Part II, Chapter 5.
7. Theodore Roszak, *Where the Wasteland Ends* (Faber and Faber, London, 1974), p. 249.
8. Ibid., p. 253.
9. Ibid., p. 253.
10. Ibid., p. 248.
11. Ibid., p. 252.
12. Ibid., pp. 264–374.
13. Ibid., p. 274.
14. 'Do not adjust your mind, there is a fault in reality', p. 155.
15. 'The Sciences: Towards a Theory' in (ed.) R. Whitley, *The Social Process of Scientific Development*, p. 26.
16. Even the molecular biologists have become aware of these problems of levels and configurations, and that what takes place at a more complex level cannot be

simply deduced from simpler level phenomena. Thus Sidney Brenner has declared: 'and here there is a grave problem of levels: it may be wrong to believe that all the logic is at the molecular level. We may need to get beyond the clock mechanisms'. Crick himself has now also realised that the reductive programme in biology might be nearing completion and that biology needs to return to the complex problems that it had 'left behind unsolved. How does a wounded organism regenerate to exactly the same structure it had before? How does the egg form the organism?' Quoted in H. F. Judson, *The Eighth Day of Creation*, pp. 220 and 209.

17. *The Relations Between the Sciences*. p. 129.

18. *The Structure of Scientific Theories*, (ed.) Frederick Suppe, Second Edition (University of Chicago Press, Chicago, 1979), p. 54.

19. Ibid., p. 622.

20. Ibid., p. 620.

21. Ibid., p. 619.

22. 'Changes in the Social and Intellectual Organization of the Sciences' in *Social Science Yearbook 1977* (eds.) E. Mendelsohn, P. Weingart, R. Whitley (Reidel, Dordrecht, Holland, 1977), p. 152.

INDEX